**French Provincial Police and the Fall
of the Second Republic**

French Provincial Police and the Fall of the Second Republic

Social Fear and Counterrevolution

By Thomas R. Forstenzer

Princeton University Press
Princeton, New Jersey

Publication of this book has been aided by the
Whitney Darrow Publication Reserve Fund of Princeton University Press

This book has been composed in Linotron Palatino

Clothbound editions of Princeton University Press books
are printed on acid-free paper, and binding materials are
chosen for strength and durability

Printed in the United States of America by Princeton
University Press, Princeton, New Jersey

To my mother and the memory of my father

Contents

Preface   ix

Introduction   xi

1 An Anatomy of a Permanent Counterrevolution   3
2 The Contending Social Factions ca. 1840-1848   24
3 Career Patterns of the Prefects and *Procureurs-Généraux*   55
4 Reports from the Provinces   103
5 The Limits of Repressive Techniques before the Coup   149
6 From Frustration to a Totalitarian Revolution   226

Appendixes

1 The Prefects and Their Departments   249
    Map   249
    Personal and Career Data for Prefects
    in the Sample Departments   250
    Sociopolitical Sketches of the Sample Departments   260
2 The Standard Interpretation: Social Fear
    after 1849 as a Hoax   278

Notes   283

Sources and Bibliography   319

Index   331

Preface

This book is the product of more than fifteen years of research projects and papers—even my senior thesis at Reed College—all of which have focused on the ideology and dynamics of the right. In the hope of elaborating a more general and inclusive theory of counterrevolution, I shall be turning my attention to the cultural roots of Italian fascism and ultimately to the politics of post-World-War-II Western Europe as other cases of right-wing revitalization and radicalism in the face of threats (real or perceived) from the left.

This particular book, and the more general project of which it forms a crucial part, would never have been undertaken or completed without the advice, encouragement, and, most important, the friendship of Gordon Wright.

I am also indebted to Philip Dawson, who gave me valuable criticism and guidance in preparing an earlier version as my doctoral dissertation. Peter N. Stearns, Traian Stoianovich, and Warren Susman were generous in providing advice, encouragement, and—when necessary—invaluable research and writing time. At various stages in researching and preparing this work, I benefited enormously from conversations with Louis Chevalier, Maurice Agulhon, and Romano Mastromattei. Arno Mayer, Gordon Craig, John O. Lenaghan, Harold Poor, and Rudolph Bell read the entire manuscript (at different stages of its existence) and provided needed perspective, criticism, and advice.

I owe a special debt of gratitude to certain scholars whose specialties are somewhat removed from my own, but who broadened, directed, and sustained my interests by their teaching, example, and friendship. F. Smith Fussner, Richard H. Jones, the late Howard D. Jolly, and Gail Kelly of Reed College first introduced me to the rigors and joys of history and the social sciences. Barton J. Bernstein and Paul Seaver showed me that profound ethical commitments, activism, and scholarship could be combined successfully. Barrington Moore Jr., challenged me to account for the *absence* of revolution in the development of British Chartism, forcing me to make my assumptions explicit and then to evaluate them. Donald Weinstein has always been an example of scholarly commitment, teaching excellence, and personal courage to me. He taught me to teach, and his warm encouragement helped this book to completion and publication.

I wish to thank the Foreign Area Fellowship's Western European Studies Committee for the training and research grants that supported this study. The Rutgers Research Council provided a grant that made possible the statistical analysis in chapter 6.

Consultancies with UNESCO provided this historian with needed exposure to present-day problems and the "fringe benefit" of time and lodgings to carry on archival research. I particularly wish to thank Pierluigi Vagliani, Ehsan Naraghi, Ruth Lazarus, Helen and Daniel Chenut, Arthur Gillette, and Thierry Lemaresquier for their friendship and support.

John Reynolds was both a brilliant and patient guide through the computer world. Charles Quinn, Deborah Kasner, and Frederick (Bud) Burckhard were able, intelligent research assistants.

Finally, Ida Forstenzer, Bernard E. Riley, Phyllis Riley, and Billy, Joanne, Kathi, Regina, and Donna provided safe harbor for a scholar who needed some peace, if not quiet. Jeanne Marie Riley Forstenzer, acute critic and most warm and delightful wife, is owed more than can be expressed. Nicole Elizabeth Forstenzer came along when most needed.

Winter 1980

Introduction

In its narrowest political sense, revolution is a struggle between established authority and outlaws who menace the very existence of the state. Insurrection, an extralegal appeal to force by subordinate groups against entrenched elites, is a criminal activity unless and until the rebels prevail. By the same token, counterrevolution, the defense of the status quo against the threat of revolution, is an attempt at law enforcement, a police activity. The clash between insurgents and a government is therefore a complex and comprehensive interplay of "cops" and "robbers," but one in which the social definition—the identity—of the "cop" and "robber" is itself at issue. For both sides, force is generally the final arbiter.

The antagonists in such a clash are usually described by scholars in quite different terms. The words used to portray a revolution are more highly charged with the imagery of lawlessness and chaos than those used to describe a counterrevolution. Insurrection is generally described as an upsurge, an upheaval instigated by a rabble, a mob, or, more recently and more respectfully, a crowd. When an establishment defends itself against a revolutionary threat, historians' descriptive terms are far less emotive and violent—quell, quiet, suppress—perhaps because the counterrevolution is carried out through institutions, by officials. A remarkable semantic bias seems to treat the two sides of the same conflict as separate and almost unrelated events—one frenzied and intense, the other mechanical and coldly rational. Yet it seems reasonable to expect that considerable emotion and intense stress would be experienced on both sides of the barricades in a revolutionary situation. The stakes involved are very high indeed. The rebel is a felon until he has actually seized power; the defender of the status quo acts legally and legitimately only so long as he retains control.

Revolution and counterrevolution represent considerably more than the two faces of a political phenomenon. Also at issue are the economic interests, psychological resentments, and cultural justifications of social classes, or at least those sections of social classes that mobilize either to overthrow or defend a given social and political system. "Normal" political give and take, usually contained within a rarefied and closed social stratum, becomes obsolete when the bases of the established system are indicted and assaulted by "outsiders." In such an open conflict for mastery, political and economic haves and have-nots are pitted against each other; but neither ballots nor barricades nor bayonets are as important to our understanding of the struggle as the social visions that justify their use. World views and political strategies of both revolutionaries and counterrevolutionaries are fused into a single, turbulent social dynamic.

France has had an especially turbulent history of revolution and repression. Since 1789, each regime, regardless of its particular form of organization or its specific claim to legitimacy, has tried to survive against forbidding odds. Governments have continually been threatened with death by revolution or coup d'état, and a centralized police system has been passed down from regime to regime because it has seemed the best instrument for keeping a government literally on top of things.

The words used to describe this police apparatus are themselves evidence of a fundamental struggle for survival. *Police et l'ordre publique* have come to mean something quite different than the same terms in English translation. The French system of police (largely, though not entirely, supervised by the prefects and attorneys general) has taken on a tremendous breadth of activity in a society subject to sudden changes in political organization at the top. The evolution of a stalemate society has led to the development of a police system that reflects the chronic instability of French governments and the division of French society into warring strata of the *satisfaits* and the economic and political have-nots.

The word *police*, in the United States and Britain, means the police force: the police respond to a threatened or an actual breach of the law. And the law itself, by statute or precedent, defines violation of the civil peace in terms of specific actions against persons or property. In France, however, and in those countries that share the French legal system, the term *police power* suggests much more than the apprehension of malefactors and the prevention of particular crimes:

it means the general good order of society. This has far-reaching consequences. Responsibility for the maintenance of public order goes well beyond the prevention of crime or of disorder in public places; it covers the regulation of an extremely wide range of matters in the economic and social field as well. The power to regulate society in this way is called the police power.[1]

Thus *police* and *administration* (the regulation of society) have overlapping meanings in France. It is difficult to imagine anything beyond the sphere of the purely private and personal that cannot become the subject of *police* regulation in this broad sense. The general task of maintaining a civic atmosphere hostile to crime and disorder has extended the particular functions of the police into areas like price control, licensing, and education, as well as into such operations as press censorship and political repression. To make a police agency responsible for preempting all forms of turbulence is quite distant from the usual Anglo-American practice of not placing "prior restraints" on many forms of economic, social, and political behavior. Practically everything a prefect does in his department would, therefore, be defined as *police* activity. The French government's ability to legislate and enforce what it defines as public order is, by the same regulatory reasoning, almost limitless.

Certainly the most important role of the police power in France since 1789 has been the attempt to create political security for each regime. Alexandre-François Vivien, the great legal theorist of the mid-nineteenth century (and a key figure in the Conseil d'état and the assemblies of the Second Republic) argued that the essence of police and administration in France was the vigilance of the state vis-à-vis those who menaced the existing government and social system with revolutionary change.[2] The maintenance of the status quo, according to Vivien and other conservatives, requires the continued existence of an administrative system (the prefectoral corps) that gives the state "unity of command" from its ministers in Paris down to the mayor of the tiniest commune.[3]

Another salient feature of the French notion of political police is the "arsenal of preventive measures, constantly perfected" that has been legislated since the Great Revolution.[4] Governments have armed themselves with an extremely comprehensive corpus of statutes that outlaw specific forms of political action defined as threats to public order. Excellent examples of these preemptive limitations on civil liberties are the laws restricting association and muzzling the press passed in 1834 and 1835 by the Chamber of

Deputies. Indeed, many political police measures dating back to the mid-nineteenth century remain on the books today. Each successive French regime has been understandably hesitant to divest itself of the legal weapons developed by its predecessors. Each one has embraced the philosophy expressed by a twentieth-century prefect of police: "Better to prevent than to heal."[5]

Certainly this was the case for the regime that gained power in the aftermath of the French revolution of 1848. The brief existence of the Second Republic was marked first by a revolutionary surge to the left, which immediately conquered universal manhood suffrage. Soon thereafter, the French elites mobilized to defend themselves against the persistent demands of a growing movement for radical economic and social reform. Conservatives gained control of the new republic. They began an energetic campaign of repression against democrats and democratic socialists. Finally, the Second Republic was itself dismantled by its president, Prince Louis Napoleon Bonaparte, and replaced by a plebiscitary dictatorship pledged to the defense of "society."

Throughout the crisis years from 24 February 1848 until the coup of 2 December 1851, both counterrevolutionaries and revolutionaries based their actions on their perceptions of the motives, potential strengths, and possible initiatives of their antagonists. Economic, social, and political interests clashed in an atmosphere of impending civil war. Social worlds, with their conflicting values of good and evil, justice and tyranny, and order and disorder, came into collision. Compromise was impossible. Either the incumbent elites of mid-nineteenth-century France would continue to dominate society, or they would be replaced by groups that had embraced a new and very different notion of the proper distribution of wealth and power in a "good society."

Perhaps it is natural that the dramatic early months and the final death throes of the Second Republic have drawn attention away from the continuous struggle between radicalism and conservatism that so strikingly characterizes the history of this regime. Although historians have paid careful attention to the overthrow of the July Monarchy and to the development of radicalism during the period leading up to the explosion of June 1848, they have done little research on the equally important repression of potential revolutionaries after 1848, repression that continued for three years and preceded Louis Napoleon's seizure of power. Bonaparte, his coterie, and the "technique of the coup d'état" have been studied.

There has been speculation on the Parisian political context of the coup and on the possible reasons for the failure of conservatives to resist effectively the authoritarian pretensions of this outsider, a professional conspirator with no political links to the traditional ruling groups.[6] But little research has been devoted to the national political and social backdrop of the coup. And this absence of curiosity has persisted despite the puzzling fact that the successfully defended elites lost possession of direct political power. They remained at the top of the economic and social hierarchy; but on 2 December 1851 these groups found themselves partially subordinated to a new political class—a small group of conspirators headed by Bonaparte himself and the bureaucrats who had actively or passively supported the pretensions of the prince-president.

If it can be documented that the coup took place in an atmosphere charged with the fear that society was menaced by radical revolution, then it may be possible to approach a new understanding of social conflict and counterrevolution during the supposedly quiet years of the Second Republic, which followed Louis Napoleon's election as president in December 1848 and the left's debacle of June 1849. Although it was driven underground, the radical movement remained largely intact and won impressive electoral victories in 1850. Whether or not social revolution was "objectively" possible during the three years leading up to the coup is a purely theoretical and unresolvable problem; but whether key groups within the political elite believed such an upheaval to be a possibility during those years, or feared it as a future probability in 1852 (the year in which the republic's constitution required almost simultaneous presidential and legislative elections and barred Louis Napoleon from seeking reelection), are problems of fact that can be solved by research.

Research Strategy

This study will examine the way in which a particularly important group within the French ruling classes experienced and responded to the social crisis of the Second Republic: the men who staffed those branches of the bureaucracy responsible for public order. The parts of the administration with which this study is primarily concerned are the political police agencies in provincial France: the prefects and the attorneys general (*procureurs-généraux*).

The prefect and the *procureur-général* were (and are) jointly responsible for law enforcement in France. In the department to which he is assigned, the prefect is the principal administrative officer. He is in charge of routine police activities such as investigation and protection of public order. The attorney general's territorial jurisdiction consists of a group of contiguous departments forming the *ressort* of a court of appeals. Like an American attorney general, he prepares and argues the government's side in civil and criminal cases. Although the prefect and the *procureur-général* function within separate state bureaucracies, the former in the Interior Ministry and the latter in the Justice Ministry, these two civil servants must work closely together to ensure the maintenance of public order in any particular department. They do not have permanent tenure in office. Their loyalty to the incumbent political leadership is in principle and usually in fact assured by their removability. They are subject to appointment, promotion, and dismissal by simple ministerial decree.

During the troubled years between the revolutionary birth of the Second Republic and its death by coup d'état, these were the governmental figures who most directly confronted the new political situation of universal manhood suffrage and intensified class conflict. As we shall see, once Louis Napoleon assumed the presidency and appointed a cabinet drawn exclusively from factions within the Party of Order, the short-lived control of the Second Republic by genuine republicans came to an abrupt end. The bureaucratic systems, which had been in disarray since the February revolution, were placed on a regular footing and turned against the democrats and democratic socialists who had established the republic. Men drawn from the traditional social and economic elites were appointed (or reappointed, many of them having served the July Monarchy) to manage the state's police apparatus.

The prefects and *procureurs-généraux* became the battlefield commanders in a class war. Their periodic reports to their respective Parisian headquarters were accounts of the skirmishes and protracted campaigns fought by opposing social forces and ideologies. These law-enforcement bureaucrats represented the antidemocratic and antisocialist position of the elites in their clash with the radical social vision of the newly organized, articulate, and forceful opposition of the left. The advancement of a prefect or a *procureur-général* depended on his energetic defense of the status quo and his loyalty to the government of the prince-president and the Party of Order. On the one hand, the role of the prefect or prosecutor was that of an intelligence gatherer, the eyes and ears of the establishment in its struggle with radicalism. On the other, these bureaucrats were given the power and encouragement to act as the elites' mailed fist, which was to strike any enemies of the existing social order once such antagonists had been "sighted."

Their perceptions and actions were recorded in regular reports, which they were required to file with their ministerial superiors. In an age in which private communication over any distance was slow and expensive, the prefects and *procureurs-généraux* were provided by the government with a technologically advanced and costly system of telegraphs, heliographs, semaphores, and daily dispatch coaches to ensure a rapid and steady flow of information from the provinces to Paris and of orders from the capital to the departments. The ministers and the supervisory personnel of the Justice and Interior ministries in Paris were almost completely dependent upon the observations of the prefects and *procureurs-généraux* for their understanding of national political and social developments and of trends in public opinion. The reports were secret—strictly for the use of ministers and bureaucrats.

If the left represented a serious cause for concern among the French elites in the years 1849, 1850, and 1851, then such a threat would surely have been evident to those directly responsible for public order during this period. The repressive drive of the Party of Order—successful as early as 1849, according to Karl Marx, Alexis de Tocqueville, and most historians of the period—was the primary mission of the prefects and *procureurs-généraux*. The reports submitted by these civil servants chronicle their efforts to suppress the radical movement and prevent dissemination of "subversive" propaganda in their localities. These regular dispatches also contain the bureaucrats' evaluation of the success or failure of their repressive campaigns and their estimates of radical strength in their departments. In short, the internal communications of the Justice and Interior ministries can be expected to reveal whether the men actually responsible for defending the status quo sensed a slackening of tension or a continuing danger of revolution until Louis Napoleon's coup d'état.

A secondary theme of this book is the role of the prefects and *procureurs-généraux* in the destruction of the Second Republic. If the government's most important domestic civil servants turned against the Legislative Assembly—against the Orleanist leadership of the Party of Order—and supported the partisan maneuvers of

Louis Napoleon, then an important characteristic of the counter-revolution may have been a temporary breakdown of bureaucratic discipline under the stress of social fear. Discipline is the sine qua non of bureaucracy as defined by its leading sociological analyst, Max Weber.[7] A functionary is subjected to rules, procedures, and a system of appointment and promotion, all designed to guarantee his submission to hierarchical superiors.

Michael Crozier has noted, however, that those who seemingly perform subordinate functions in a bureaucracy (his example was the repair crew in a French tobacco factory) can enjoy surprising prestige and power over the enterprise when they are specialists in handling sudden breakdowns in the system. Their task of "crisis intervention" places them in so strategically important a niche in the chain of command that they can deal with upper management almost as equals.[8] Prefects and attorneys general were (and remain) prestigious figures in the French civil service, but, in their role as crisis managers, their power may have temporarily rivaled that of their ministerial superiors. Louis Napoleon, as president, had the constitutional power to appoint, promote, or dismiss these officials if his orders were countersigned by the minister concerned. On occasion, Louis Napoleon succeeded in appointing cabinets more loyal to his personal power than to the majority in the Legislative Assembly. The police bureaucrats were in the enviable, if risky, position to choose the branch of government, and thus the faction, that commanded them. Arno J. Mayer considers this political mobilization of the bureaucracy to be an essential feature of counterrevolutionary crises.

> In normal times, the personnel of these institutions is relatively undivided; it also claims that its functions, which are directed to the maintenance of order and system, are politically neutral, are "above" politics. Crisis conditions undermine this harmony and dispute this pretense. At all levels, but most consequentially at the higher echelons, government functionaries, both civil and military . . . become politicized; they are reminded of their social station as well as of their class and family ties, and they begin to make partisan choices.[9]

The French prefectoral corps and centralized system of state's attorneys are agencies specifically charged with the defense of the established political system and social structure. Under stress, some of these officials may have acted as independent power brokers and private members of the threatened French notability rather than as disciplined servants of an established parliamentary system.

The relatively complete Justice Ministry correspondence for the years of Louis Napoleon's presidency, preserved at the Archives Nationales, and the small but useful collections of prefectoral reports found in departmental archives will be used to analyze the perceptions and actions of law-enforcement bureaucrats in a sample of seven departments. (Practically all the reports on political police matters sent by the prefects to the Interior Ministry in Paris during the republic were destroyed either during the empire or in the flames of the Paris Commune.)

The prefects and *procureurs-généraux* appointed during Louis Napoleon's presidency were uniformly committed to defending the social hierarchy and were ordered to carry out precisely the same antidemocratic and antisocialist policies throughout France; the sample was chosen in such a way as to "place" these police officials in the widest possible range of social and political settings—from the most untroubled and conservative departments to those beset by intense social and political struggles (see Appendix 1 for detailed descriptions of each department).

The selection of departments was based on the results of the election to the Legislative Assembly held in May 1849. This election was the first one that clearly showed political differences among the departments. Two elections had already been held under the republic's novel system of universal manhood suffrage, but neither yielded results sufficiently clear for our purposes. The first, the election of the Constituent Assembly, occurred in an atmosphere in which all candidates, monarchists and socialists alike, campaigned as republicans. And the balloting took place in April 1848—before the electorate had been given an adequate opportunity to evaluate the political programs of those running for office. The second, the presidential election of 10 December 1848, was an overwhelming victory for Louis Napoleon Bonaparte. But he had presented himself in such ambiguous terms that his landslide had been more a plebiscite for a charismatic name than for a man running on a particular platform.

In the middle of 1849, however, after six months of rule by Louis Napoleon and a conservative cabinet, the voters were finally presented with their first clear-cut electoral choice in determining the future development of the republic. According to many French historians, it was the first democratic *and* ideological election in modern French history.[10] Two political coalitions had emerged by May 1849, and they presented opposing slates of candidates in almost every department of France: the Party of Order, representing the political faiths of the entrenched elites; and the Mountain, a fusion of "advanced" republicans (who had embraced democratic socialism) with the moderate republicans (who stood only for political democracy).

In any one department, the list of candidates presented by the Party of Order usually reflected the established local prevalence of one of the major conservative factions: legitimists, Orleanists, or, in a very few departments, Bonapartists. Regardless of which faction was the strongest, however, an effort was usually made to "balance the ticket" by including the leaders of other local conservative groups or by other compromises designed to keep local intraelite squabbles from destroying the electoral unity of the right wing. The Party of Order's campaign in 1849 was directed and sometimes financed from Paris by the caucus of conservative deputies in the out-going Constituent Assembly—the so-called Comité de la rue de Poitiers. François Goguel has described this coordinated national effort as the first example of the modern political party in French history.[11]

The Mountain did not become a fully unified coalition of moderate republicans and democratic socialists until after the events of June 1849. During the elections in May, however, the two branches of the democratic faith had already joined forces in many departments to promote a single electoral list of candidates for the left. The moderate republicans found themselves caught in a fatal crossfire from both extremes of the political spectrum. They reeled under the government's energetic assault on all democratic factions, and they also suffered attacks from the democratic socialists for failing to support social reforms and for supporting General Cavaignac's suppression of the Parisian rising of June 1848. Although an important force in the Constituent Assembly, the moderates had lost their dominant position in the republican camp to the democratic socialists by the time of the elections to the Legislative Assembly. Only twenty moderates were elected, and most of these because they ran on preponderantly radical slates.[12] The Mountain's strong showing in these elections was a victory for the radical wing of the republican movement, one that was won despite the government's enforcement of press and association laws designed to cripple the democratic forces. Almost two hundred Montagnards were elected to the new assembly (out of 750 seats), and Alexandre Auguste Ledru-Rollin, their leader, led the list of winners in four departments. According to Jacques Bouillon, a new political phenomenon came into being in May 1849: "In the 1849 elections, a red France emerged which worried the authorities and terrified conservatives."[13] Whole regions of France gave important support to the Mountain: the western and northern areas of the Massif Central, Alsace, and the region dominated by the city of Lyon. Radicalism won few victories in Provence and the Midi, because legitimism was unified and strong in these regions; but it demonstrated considerable power in the southeast. Peasants were turning in great numbers to the "red" lists in all these regions and became the main source of the Mountain's strength.

The departments to be studied in the succeeding chapters were selected because, as a group, they represent different levels of conservative and radical strength in the elections of May 1849. Departments that were electorally controlled by the antirepublican coalition were chosen because each of them reflects the clear dominance, within the Party of Order, of one of its three component factions: legitimists (Vendée), Orleanists (Gironde), or Bonapartists (Charente-Inférieure). The departments in which the republican opposition was strong (Rhône, Gard, Allier, and Jura) were chosen because they offer examples of different levels of support enjoyed by the most radical group within the democratic camp: the democratic socialists. These choices were made in order to vary the levels of political and social stress experienced by the law-enforcement bureaucrats assigned to particular departments: the greater the power of the extreme left in a given department, the more difficult the job of the prefect and *procureur-général* responsible for public order. Most of the departments chosen were rural, but two partly urban departments, one radical (Rhône) and the other conservative (Gironde), have been included in order to provide a more complete picture of the social and political problems faced by the law-enforcement bureaucrats under the Second Republic.

French Provincial Police and the Fall
of the Second Republic

1 An Anatomy of a Permanent Counterrevolution

Much is known about the revolutionary process and the radical movement under the Second Republic, but we have been handicapped by our comparative ignorance of the forces that ultimately defeated the radicals. This historiographical blind spot is present not only in the writings on this particular era; it is part of a general imbalance in the way virtually all violent social conflicts have been studied by historians and social scientists. In his recent attempt to elaborate a model for the study of counterrevolutions, Arno J. Mayer points out that

> ever since 1789 the study of revolution has been pursued far more intensively and systematically than the study of counterrevolution. Eventually specialists in the sociology, politics and psychology of knowledge will want to explain the motives and causes for this disproportion in scholarly and intellectual concern. Meanwhile it is indisputable that there exists a much more significant fund of empirical and conceptual knowlege about revolutions than about counterrevolutions.[1]

Mayer illustrates his argument by comparing the quality and volume of the scholarly attention "lavished" over the past century on the French Revolution of 1789 with the very recent appearance of a few serious studies on the counterrevolutionary aspects of the period from 1789 to 1815. These works include Jacques Godechot's survey of royalism during these years and Charles Tilly's pioneering sociological investigation of the Vendée uprising.[2] "Even so," according to Mayer, "the counterrevolutionary 'side' of the French Revolution still awaits its Labrousse, Mathiez, Cobban and Soboul."[3]

The historiography of other major counterrevolutions is similar, in this respect, to the French.

It is not really surprising that Crane Brinton's *Anatomy of Revolution* was not matched or followed by an "anatomy of counterrevolution." When he set out to hypothesize recurring patterns in the English, American, French and Russian revolutions, Brinton enjoyed a number of enviable advantages. To begin with, he himself was a seasoned specialist in the well plowed history of the French Revolution. In addition, he was able to draw on a considerable accumulation of assimilated data about the other three revolutions; he was attuned to social scientists who were formulating heuristic concepts of revolution; he was challenged by the raging Russian Revolution, which continued to shake the world about him. Would-be students of comparative counterrevolution enjoyed none of these advantages. Until very recently they faced a relative empirical and conceptual wasteland.[4]

A result of this "wasteland" has been a concentration on right-wing uprisings against revolutionary regimes to the detriment of studies of a more common counterrevolutionary phenomenon: the preemptive and often chronic mobilization of elites and governments to ward off budding revolutionary threats. Revolution need not be successful or even likely for counterrevolution to begin.

In fact, more research has been done on the counterrevolutionary aspects of the Great French Revolution than on the official resistance to the radical movement during the Second Republic, and this imbalance between the study of revolution and counterrevolution remains a serious problem in the general writing of nineteenth- and twentieth-century French history. Even after the centennial year of the Paris Commune we still lack a systematic study of the winning side in that struggle: the Versailles government. And despite the considerable outpouring of works on the French social and political crisis of the 1930s, no analysis has yet been made of this period (and especially the fall of the Popular Front government) as a counterrevolutionary mobilization of French elites against basic social reforms. Indeed, the most important survey of the French right from the Restoration to the Fifth Republic, René Rémond's *The Right Wing in France*, describes the varieties of the conservative, reactionary, and radical right more as intellectual traditions than as dynamic movements for the defense of vested social and economic interests.[5]

Students of contemporary French national character, political scientists like François Goguel and Stanley Hoffmann, are much more sensitive to the problem of France's dual tradition of insurrection and authoritarianism than historians have been. Neither

Goguel nor Hoffmann treats counterrevolution as a particularly dynamic process, but they both at least recognize the antirevolutionary side of French political life as an effective deterrent to a real threat of insurrection in modern France. In *La Politique des partis sous la IIIe république*, Goguel uses the rather rough distinctions of "movement" and "resistance," or defense of the "established order," to reduce the multiparty constellation of the Third Republic to two fundamental and opposed political tendencies.[6] This dualism, vaguely characterized as a clash of "temperaments," is seen by Goguel as the outstanding national characteristic of French political life at least since 1871. The side of movement, representing the Jacobin (egalitarian and democratic) and socialist traditions, is the political force for social change and the potential source of violent revolution in France. On the side of order, traditionalist (or large landowning) interests and liberal (commercial and industrial) elites coalesce, according to Goguel, to block the reforming or revolutionary dynamic that challenges their hegemony. Goguel concludes that these opposing sides canceled one another and paralyzed the nation under the Third Republic and had a similar impact on France after World War II.

Stanley Hoffmann agrees with Goguel's view of France as a nation divided by an unresolved conflict over the social question. But Hoffmann does not limit his argument to the Third and Fourth republics. He attempts to define the polarization of French political culture on the basis of behavior patterns and established institutions that date back at least to 1789 and form an unbroken, self-feeding cycle of conflicting extremisms in French political life. Hoffmann argues that France suffers from social, economic, and political stalemate precisely because it has had a history of revolutionary upheavals.

In the last decade of the eighteenth century, a propertied class of commoners, the bourgeoisie, won its status as a ruling class by a violent assault on monarchical absolutism and aristocratic privilege. But, according to Hoffmann, its victory was a fragile one; it had to be defended from enemies to the left and right.[7] During the nineteenth and twentieth centuries, Hoffmann sees the bourgeoisie joining forces with the other property-holding class of commoners in France, the peasantry, in order to defend its delicately balanced "middlingness" against the unpropertied urban working classes and against the anticapitalist and unmodern nobility. This "consensus group" of bourgeoisie and peasantry could ally with the aristrocracy in defense of property and society. But it could never compromise with the proletariat. Even under regimes of universal suffrage, the French working classes were closed off from effective participation in national politics. In addition, they were deprived of the means to achieve social mobility, because France experienced neither the increased productivity and lower prices nor the rising wage levels of an industrial revolution, as did Great Britain and Germany. Consequently, the urban working classes have effectively been read out of French society and confined in what Hoffmann calls a "social ghetto" separated from the consensus group by a "poisoned" gulf of "severe tensions."[8] The pariah classes had a single hope for collective self-help in so rigid a political system. And it was a means already used and hallowed by the bourgeoisie itself in its struggle with the aristocracy: revolution.

The social question in France, from Hoffmann's point of view, is intimately tied to the collective legacy of the Great Revolution, the revolutions of 1830 and 1848, and the Paris Commune: Is the revolution complete when civic equality is established among economically and socially unequal citizens, or must it continue until egalitarianism takes on a social meaning? On one side, the proponents of thorough social change constitute a force for "potential insurrection." The explosiveness of this revolutionary menace to France's "stalemate society" is all the greater because the social question not only divides the elite consensus group from the proletariat, but also creates important schisms within the elite itself. The political history of France

> is largely the history of political divisions in the bourgeoisie—
> an overall division between the counterrevolutionaries who re-
> fused to accept government by consent and those people who
> wanted it, and a division among the latter, split into conserva-
> tives afraid of too much democracy, democrats closer to Rous-
> seau than to Locke, and socialists dissatisifed by the stalemate
> society.[9]

Despite internal divisions, however, the consensus group has a traditional political response to potential explosions in French society: "limited authoritarianism." In the interest of social defense, the elites have repeatedly adopted illiberal forms of government. The dictatorial regimes—those of Napoleon I, Napoleon III, and Philippe Pétain—have brooked little legal or political opposition to their power to suppress radical activity. According to Hoffmann, these governments gave the French civil service a relatively free rein to administer the nation's internal affairs. He argues, however, that they were "limited": the police-state regimes made no attempts to meddle in the existing economic system or to disrupt the established social hierarchy.[10]

"Limited authoritarianism," however, has been more than a mere response to revolutionary outbursts; it has played a permanent and institutionalized role in French society. Hoffmann maintains that the Great French Revolution was an attempt by the bourgeoisie to throw off the legal and administrative "straitjacket" of the Old Regime. But the bourgeoisie found it necessary to defend its victory from the aristocracy and the proletariat by preserving and strengthening the centralized system of administration that it inherited from the absolute monarchy. Since the era of the Revolution, all local and intergroup conflicts in French society have been settled "from the top" by a bureaucratic hierarchy commanded by the central government in Paris. The centripetal pull of Paris has drawn all real decision-making power to the bureaucracies in the capital itself, regardless of whether the regime has been democratic or dictatorial. Hoffmann credits this process of centralization with giving an aura of illegitimacy to all private, face-to-face efforts by individuals or groups (including political parties) to solve the problems of French society and politics. He thus argues that the potential for revolutionary violence in France has prevented the development of truly democratic authority patterns, even under such liberal and popularly elected regimes as the Third and Fourth republics.

Hoffmann sees this centralized civil service as the main prop of both dictatorship and democracy in France. His own discussion of its "chilling effect" on free and private forms of social and political interaction suggests, however, that Hoffmann's definition of a bureaucratic "limited authoritarianism" is in itself too limited and too static. He describes France as a nation in which civil liberties are tightly circumscribed despite the constitutional guarantees of the republican regimes. Moreover, Hoffmann emphasizes that these more liberal regimes have periodically been jettisoned in order to free the civil service to exceed legal restraints in the defense of the social order. Hoffmann contradicts himself. On the one hand, he claims that France has been shaped by the struggle between two equal forces: revolutionary violence and authoritarian resistance. Yet his own analysis demonstrates that these forces were not equal at all: the bureaucracy has dominated public political and social behavior without itself being subjected to any clear democratic and legal direction. The authoritarian trait in French political culture is limited in Hoffmann's definition only because the civil service has not intervened in the economic activities of the elites from which it is recruited and which it is appointed to protect.

In his consideration of the French bureaucracy, Hoffmann does not fully discuss an outstanding feature of the authority relationship that has been established between French citizens and the state over more than a century and a half: the police powers of the civil service. Both republican and dictatorial governments have often claimed that the need to maintain order, as defined by the consensus group, is more important than the protection of the civil liberties and legal rights of "dangerous" citizens. The liberal "freedoms from,"which limit censorship, arrest, and imprisonment, are subordinated to the sweeping emergency power of the state and its police bureaucrats. This power has existed in France almost without interruption from the time of Louis XIV down to the present Fifth Republic. Although the jury system and the delicate independence of the judiciary have sometimes acted as brakes to this absolutist tradition, French governments have always been able to deploy a police state in defense of a threatened social and political order.[11]

The French elites defeated the violent social upheavals of the nineteenth century by elaborating an administrative system that has prevented a renewed insurrectionary surge under the Third, Fourth, and Fifth republics. Hoffmann and Goguel consider this as the natural and inevitable result of a society permanently fraught with revolutionary dangers. They consider counterrevolution as a mere corollary to revolution—as a historical process without a logic, mystique, and program of its own. They ignore the possibility that in contemporary France, although a revolutionary tradition persists, it may well be a permanent counterrevolution that has been the major force in molding the nation's internal authority patterns, administrative structure, and socioeconomic institutions.[12]

In their dualistic conception of French history and in their minimization of the dynamic quality of counterrevolution, Hoffmann and Goguel owe a heavy intellectual debt to Alexis de Tocqueville and Karl Marx. Tocqueville's *Recollections* of the period 1848-1850, his *Old Regime and the French Revolution* (which contains thinly veiled observations on French national character at mid-nineteenth century), and Marx's *Class Struggles in France* and *The Eighteenth Brumaire of Louis Bonaparte* are, in themselves, documents of critical importance in the history of the social sciences.[13] The conclusions reached by the liberal aristocrat and the communist intellectual often converge or complement one another, and they have formed the conceptual underpinnings of our modern analysis of social and political conflicts. The centralized bureaucracy and its impact on French political behavior were first analyzed rigorously by Tocqueville; Hoffmann's model for the "stalemate society" is a more precise sociological application of Tocqueville's elegantly phrased musings on the coming of the 1789 Revolution and on the fall of the Second Republic. In addition, Gougel's discussion of the "Party of Resistance" and Hoffmann's consideration of the "consensus group" reflect Marx's dissection of the Second Republic's Party of Order into its constituent social classes. Indeed, Marx's emphasis on the peasantry, petty bourgeoisie, and bureaucracy as crucial to the rise of Louis Napoleon became a methodological template for studies of settings and periods far removed from the France of the Second Republic.[14]

Without unduly denigrating the importance of scholars and their works, it may safely be assumed that Marx's greatest impact (whether or not his writings were correctly understood or appropriately applied) has been on the thought and action of socialists and communists. For both Marx and Tocqueville, an interpretation of the Second Republic's collapse became a central element of a comprehensive social theory, but in Marx's case the theory has influenced the practice of key national and international movements at critical points in their histories. The tumultuous history of the Second Republic, then, interpreted and disseminated by these most gifted witnesses, has become considerably more than prologue to the present. On the related levels of modern social theory and modern political practice, the vitality of Tocqueville and Marx has ensured the application of their theories to current events.

Yet the brilliance and durability of the theories may have had the unintended effect of obscuring the actual events and forces that brought on the fall of the Second Republic. After all, Tocqueville and Marx wrote while the republic and the coup of 2 December had all the immediacy and intensity of *choses vécues*. Each theorist had a personal stake in the outcome of France's mid-nineteenth-century crisis. To expect complete accuracy under the circumstances would be as absurd as to suppose that the theories themselves close the case on the period or on counterrevolution. Many social scientists and historians continue, however, to apply the theories without a critical perspective on the context in which they were formulated.

The works of Tocqueville and Marx are understandably flawed, both factually and methodologically. Both men recognized that between February and June 1848 the revolution developed from a political struggle to an overt social conflict. But neither focused his attention on the continued impact of this social question after 1848—from 1849 to 1851. Instead, they viewed the republic's collapse as the result of an intraelite power struggle, which took place only after the revolutionary "fever" had run its course. Marx and Tocqueville thus concur in severing Louis Napoleon's coup d'état and his establishment of a dictatorship from the revolutionary aspects of the Second Republic's history. Therefore, in order to discover how the counterrevolutionary side of events from 1848 to 1851 has been relegated to the position of a minor theoretical problem, we must consider the assumptions and general interpretations that got started with these two writers.

It is understandable that Tocqueville was blind to the dynamism of the Party of Order's repressive drive: he was a leading figure in this alliance of legitimists, Orleanists, and Bonapartists. Foreign minister when much repressive legislation was passed with his support, Tocqueville was also a leading proponent and defender of the French expeditionary force sent to crush the Roman Republic. Tocqueville's personal narrative trails off at a time when he felt confident that the Party of Order had completely destroyed the new radical threat to the social system. In rapidly moving from a political revolution to one which demanded fundamental social reform, the radicals had simply overestimated the potential for change in France. According to Tocqueville, they had provoked the formation of the powerful conservative alliance that crushed the revolution on the barricades of June 1848 and then arrested or dispersed the radical leaders during the demonstrations against the Roman expedition, which took place in June 1849. Having analyzed the revolution with a keen scientific eye, as a dynamic process that moved steadily to the left until it overextended itself and was defeated, Tocqueville then becomes a moral philosopher. He attributes the weakness of the now conservative republic to the sinfulness of man, to the petty factionalism of the component groups within the Party of Order.

> We had won, but, as I expected, our real difficulties were now to appear. I had, moreover, always held to the maxim that it is after some great success that the most dangerous threats of ruin usually emerge; while the danger lasts, one has only one's adversaries against one, . . . but after victory one begins to have trouble with oneself, one's slackness, one's pride and the rash security born of success; and one succumbs.[15]

In *The Old Regime and the French Revolution*, which he wrote after the coup, Tocqueville continues to stress the theme of hubris and corruption as the reason for France's inability to evolve a liberal-parliamentary political system. But in his later work, Tocqueville expresses his moral judgment of the French in institutional and social terms. With his characteristic mixture of aristocratic hauteur and liberal idealism, Tocqueville views his countrymen as a people corrupted by the materialism of the new bourgeois ruling class and by the centralizing drive of the government. This centripetal pull, given new strength under the Bourbon monarchs and made still stronger and more efficient by the victorious middle class, drew all power to Paris. Designed first to subject the French to a monarch's pride and then to the selfishness of a social class, this administrative system also made possible the magnification of Parisian riots into French revolutions. Centralization, as Tocqueville saw it, sapped the civic virtue of the citizenry. To him, the results were equality without freedom and democracy without a sense of community responsibility and solidarity.

Tocqueville prefaced his study of France in the eighteenth century with an attack on the dictatorship that supplanted the Second Republic.

> Love of gain, a fondness for business careers, the desire to get rich at all costs, a craving for material comfort and easy living quickly become the ruling passions under a despotic government. . . . It is in the nature of despotism that it should foster such desires and propagate their havoc. Lowering as they do the national morale, they are despotism's safeguard, since they divert men's attention from public affairs and make them shudder at the mere thought of revolution[16]

Here, Tocqueville allusively describes Louis Napoleon's coup d'état against a background of the elite's fear of revolution. But he argues that revolution was a "mere thought" used by the tyrant to seize and hold absolute power; despotism itself was the natural result of France's political and institutional heritage, rather than an outgrowth of the specific circumstances of the Second Republic's social crisis. Tocqueville's "Letter to the London *Times*," published a few days after the coup, was written to denounce Louis Napoleon as a "revolutionary" who had struck down the legal government of the Legislative Assembly on the cynical pretext that France was again threatened by radical ferment.[17] In sum, Tocqueville saw the coup as another French revolution made possible by bureaucratic centralization, one in which Louis Napoleon merely manipulated the elite's fear of social upheaval in order to subject the freedom-fearing French to a new and comfortable (because politically egalitarian) absolutism.

Marx's first attempts to apply his theories of historical change to an immediate situation are more probing and systematic than Tocqueville's writings on the Second Republic. Indeed, Marx found the French events so challenging that it took him two "tries" to explain them, at least to his own satisfaction: *Class Struggles in France* (1850) and *The Eighteenth Brumaire of Louis Bonaparte* (1852). Taken together, the two pamphlets confront the rise of Louis Napoleon and the coup's climacteric to the republic as events requiring social and economic, as well as political, analysis. Refining and reifying ideas formulated in earlier essays, Marx exposes each political party and program as a disguised ideological weapon in an underlying confrontation between distinct social classes, a clash that is obscured by the posturing of political spokesmen. In both essays, Marx attempts to prove a key contention in his break with Hegel and the Left Hegelians: the state, religion, ideology and ideas, far from causing historical change, are only results of social conditions. If viewed from an exclusively ideological and political perspective, things are not as they seem.

Nor are all things possible, even in the apparent turmoil of a revolutionary situation. The limits, pace, and direction of change are determined by existing economic and social relations and not by the vagaries of ideas or "accidental" personalities. Particularly in the *Eighteenth Brumaire*, which covers the full chronology of events, Marx's aim is to show that the same analysis that permitted him to foresee an eventual proletarian victory in *The Communist*

Manifesto also allows him to account for the short-term defeat of socialism during 1848-1851. Too many ghosts and dying social classes cluttered the historical stage for the final battle between the "modern" antagonists (bourgeoisie and industrial proletariat) to be enacted. Vestigial classes—the aristocracy and small-holding peasantry—managed to subsist within the developing capitalist society; and a doomed class, the petite bourgeoisie, still avoided the extinction that awaited it when France embarked on full-scale industrialization.

Simultaneously "farce" and "tragedy" to Marx, the defeat of the French left and the fall of the Second Republic were the necessary steps toward the economic and social changes that would ensure an ultimate proletarian triumph. He begins the *Eighteenth Brumaire*, his autopsy of the republic, on a note of optimism.

> Easy come, easy go. . . . During the years 1848 to 1851 French society has made up, and that by an abbreviated because revolutionary method, for the studies and experiences which, in a regular, so to speak, textbook course of development would have had to precede the February Revolution, if it was to be more than a ruffling of the surface. Society now seems to have fallen back behind its point of departure; it has in truth first to create for itself the revolutionary point of departure, the situation, the relations, the conditions under which alone modern revolution becomes serious.[18]

Like Tocqueville, Marx concludes that socialism was simply not on the agenda of the French revolution of 1848. He similarly relegates counterrevolution to the dependent role of a reflex, the inevitable rectification of a political problem by the dominant classes of mid-nineteenth-century France. Marx viewed the conservative, counterrevolutionary side of events as a mechanical, unself-conscious, and curiously passive process. Even the ferocious repression of the June Days is presented more as a natural catastrophe than as a mobilization of energies, resources, and emotions fully as complex and dynamic as the dawning of proletarian consciousness on the other side of the barricades. Writing as both social clinician and socialist politician, Marx is not averse to "blaming the victims." He reserves some of his sharpest barbs for those closest to his own position, portraying leaders of the French left as, at best, well-meaning bunglers who repeatedly drew the workers into a premature, suicidal struggle.

What is most striking in Marx's two essays, however, is not only the drumroll of explanatory insights, which build on each other almost sentence by sentence, but the tantalizing—and confusing— ambiguity with which he leaves the reader who turns directly from *Class Struggles in France* to *The Eighteenth Brumaire of Louis Bonaparte*. Marx sees social revolution as an immediate possibility in chapter 3 of the first pamphlet (written more than eighteen months before the coup); but such a result is treated as a chimera, at any point in the republic's existence, throughout the later work. Friedrich Engels, in his 1895 preface to *Class Struggles*, tries to explain this contradiction by pointing out that Marx had not seen "that the industrial prosperity which had been returning gradually since the middle of 1848, and which attained full force in 1849 and 1850, was the revivifying force of the newly strengthened European reaction."[19] Yet Marx, in the *Eighteenth Brumaire*, makes no such appeal to economic changes to explain his earlier predictive error. The organization and content of the second pamphlet constitute an admission that he had neglected something of far greater significance to his theories than a recovery of international trade. The centralized bureaucracy and Louis Bonaparte himself, mere mirrors of social forces in the first essay, suddenly leap into prominence in Marx's final attempt to explain the death of the republic. And they are presented as determining historical agents.

> But under the absolute monarchy, during the first Revolution, under Napoleon, bureaucracy was only the means of preparing the class rule of the bourgeoisie. Under the Restoration, under Louis Philippe, under the parliamentary republic, it was the instrument of the ruling class, however much it strove for power of its own.
>
> Only under the second Bonaparte does the state seem to have made itself completely independent. As against civil society, the state machinery has consolidated its position so thoroughly that the chief of the Society of December 10 [Louis Napoleon] suffices for its head, an adventurer blown in from abroad, raised on the shield of a drunken soldiery.[20]

In 1850, Marx had seen the constitutional republic as "the only possible form" for the united rule of the economic elites.[21] In December 1851 the republic and the political power of these ruling classes had been conjured away by a cardsharper's trick, and Marx was confronted by precisely that phenomenon which he had dismissed from Hegel's dialectics: the state.[22] Freed from its moorings in concrete social and economic reality, the "superstructure" had apparently assaulted and conquered the "structure." In the *Eighteenth Brumaire*, Marx's convergence with Tocqueville's vision of a France dominated by its political institutions seems complete. But Marx struggles against such a seeming blow to his developing materialist philosophy and hedges his theoretical bet. First, he insists that Louis Napoleon's rule would be a brief interregnum between bourgeois republics and thus between working-class assaults on the bourgeoisie: "But when the imperial mantle falls on the shoulders of Louis Bonaparte, the bronze statue of Napoleon will crash from the top of the Vendôme Column."[23] It would take twenty years before both statue and column would come down, almost a generation before overt class struggle again broke out in France. Next, Marx attempts to provide the Bonapartist regime with roots at least in fragments of social classes. And here he resorts to some tortuous and contradictory dialectics to reintroduce "structure" as the foundation of his political analysis. With reference to the bourgeoisie itself, he seems to violate his own strictures on the subordination of political parties to the social classes they represent:

> the *extra-parliamentary mass of the bourgeoisie* . . . by its servility towards the President, by its vilification of parliament, by its brutal maltreatment of its own press, invited Bonaparte to suppress and annihilate its speaking and writing section, its politicians and its *literati* . . . in order that it might then be able to pursue its private affairs with full confidence in the protection of a strong and unrestricted government.[24]

Marx thus argues that Bonaparte enjoyed the covert support of the business class, which was frightened by the specter of red revolution. Yet earlier in his essay he had insisted that the bourgeoisie knew that it was in no danger of social upheaval after the Mountain's defeat in June 1849.[25]

When Marx actually associates Louis Napoleon with particular social groups, however, he avoids making a direct connection between the prince-president and the bourgeoisie. He seems to flounder about, first calling Bonaparte the chief of the lumpenproletariat, then the political voice of the army and civil service, and finally the representative of the peasantry.[26] Essentially, Marx invents these three social groups as the class basis for Bonapartism. The lumpenproletariat is particularly difficult to identify in the context of mid-nineteenth-century France. Marx simply asserts that Louis Napoleon's Society of 10 December was made up of criminal elements, the dregs of society. Yet at this time the proletariat itself was called the "dangerous class" by the elites because of the high incidence of crime, alcoholism, and prostitution in the working-class slums of the great cities.[27] In Marx's scheme it appears that a criminal who supported socialism was proletarian, while one who supported Louis Napoleon was lumpen.

In discussing the other two groups in his Bonapartist constituency, Marx glosses over important radical movements among the lower ranks of the army and civil service and among the peasantry. First, he maintains that humble soldiers and such state functionaries as schoolteachers provided decisive electoral and organizational support for the left during 1849 and 1850.[28] He then concludes his essay by sweepingly insisting that simple soldiers and bureaucrats of all grades were essential props to the dictatorship.[29] But the contradictions in Marx's argument are most dramatically evident in the way he supports another concluding assertion: "Bonaparte represents a class, and the most numerous class in French society at that, the *small holding peasants*."[30] He immediately qualifies his definition of the peasantry as a social class, adding that

> in so far as millions of families live under economic conditions of existence which separate them from those of other classes, and put them in hostile opposition to the latter, they form a class. In so far as there is merely a local interconnection among these small holding peasants, and the identity of their interests begets no community, no national bond and no political organization among them, they do not form a class.[31]

Marx then attempts to deal with the obvious objection that important segments of the rural population supported the left and that serious peasant uprisings broke out in several *départements* on the day after the coup. He "refines" his characterization of the small farmers by insisting that only Bonapartist "troglodytes" belong in the peasantry considered as a social class:

> The Bonaparte dynasty represents not the revolutionary but the conservative peasant, not the peasant that strikes out beyond the condition of his social existence, the small holding, but rather

the peasant who wants to consolidate his holding, not the country folk who, linked up with the towns, want to overthrow the old order through their energies, but on the contrary those who, in stupefied seclusion within this old order, want to see themselves and their small holdings saved and favored by the ghost of the Empire.[32]

Economic classes are the driving force of political conflict, but political positions are used to define the members of the classes. The circle is complete.

The analytic frameworks developed by Marx and Tocqueville seem to break down as each tries to account for the coup d'état. In the attempt to make sense of this event, which was so crucial to the political and social development of France, Marx contorts his definitional categories, and Tocqueville lapses into ethical criticism. Each concludes that profound economic and social change was impossible at this point in French history. Their discussions of the Mountain's defeat in June 1849 and the continued existence of a conservative republic are, therefore, mechanical narratives of a predetermined process. They treat the subsequent—and sudden—transformation of a parliamentary democracy into a dictatorship on 2 December 1851 as an afterthought—a political quirk, which took place after the French elites were again secure in their social position and in their control over the republic.

Marx and Tocqueville (and scholars who continue to rely largely on their models for the study of the Second Republic or of other crisis-fraught regimes) have overlooked an important aspect of social conflict: the attitudes and perceptions of the participants. People, as individuals and members of social groups, make and experience events. Theoretical conceptions and even a wealth of evidence about the "underlying" economic and social structures of a particular historical period are not necessarily sufficient for a satisfactory interpretation of why certain events took place. The beliefs and perceptions that they shared about the world they inhabited caused them to act or react in specific ways. It is the historical actors' definition of their situation—and not our modern, detached, and "scientific" one—that is at issue in any analysis of their behavior.

Marx and Tocqueville assume that everyone seeks power and profit and shares similar economic interests and social experiences. Both theorists, and those who follow them, assume that historical actors use a coldly rational "felicific calculus," an unwavering social compass that works in all situations. But this is to ignore the psychological dimension of social conflict. Political elites cannot be expected to pursue "business as usual" under circumstances that take them by surprise and confront them with unforeseen challenges to their economic and political dominance. Suddenly faced with a novel and dangerous situation, individuals may experience the perfectly appropriate, though "irrational," emotion of fear. They may overreact to menaces that seem enormous to them but that observers, with the clarity and detachment of hindsight, have later evaluated as hollow threats or momentary nuisances.

In fact, most historians of the Second Republic have considered the notables' fear of revolution to be illusory (see Appendix 2). It is therefore important to remember that the Second Republic existed during an era of intense social crisis. In 1848, the narrow oligarchy that had governed France since the Restoration was suddenly subjected to a new constitution, which extended the right to vote, and thus genuine civil rights, to all adult males—to peasants, artisans, and industrial workers. Not content with winning political equality, important groups within these lower classes (together with their allies within the bourgeoisie) carried the assault on the world of the notables to the more fundamental issue of the distribution of wealth and property in France: the social question. For the first time in French history, the elites were challenged by an organized mass movement that threatened to seize power and reform society either through its force of numbers at the polls or its force of arms at the barricades. The inchoate and ad hoc "revolutionary crowd," as it has been described by George Rudé and E. J. Hobsbawm, had matured by the time of the Second Republic. The "primitive rebel" was now a member of a developing national movement that extended beyond the great cities and into the villages of rural France. An explicit demand for progressive taxation, free public education, social (or cooperative) workshops, nationalized railroads, and cheap rural credit replaced the vaguer sentiments of the past. This new political force of the previously mute and disfranchised struck at the most basic interests shared by the French elites. And the threat it represented may not simply have disappeared after 1849 as Marx, Tocqueville, and many historians have argued (see Appendix 2).

On the other side of the barricades was an equally vigorous social group, established rather than insurgent. Rooted in an economic elite that has maintained its primacy, Orleanism exemplifies Hoffmann's general "constant" in the French equation of stalemate: limited authoritarianism. It is a reflection of the concrete economic and social hegemony of the French bourgeoisie. It is also an example of what Robert Michels called the Iron Law of Oligarchy.

Writing in 1911 and sharing with his contemporary, Gaetano Mosca, a fascination with the durability of oligarchic practices and attitudes into the democratic (and even social-democratic) twentieth century, Michels sought the roots of elitism in psychology and in the structure of complex organizations: "It is organization which gives birth to the domination of the elected over the electors, of the mandataries over the mandators, of the delegates over the delegators. Who says organization says oligarchy."[33] Michels is also writing within the Marxist tradition. He acknowledges the importance of socioeconomic stratification (ownership of land and commercial and industrial capital by elites) as a crucial cause of political inequality, but goes on to emphasize the more abstract components of elitist ideologies as equally important for explaining how oligarchies survive even though revolutions depose one dominant class or another. Pitting a subordinate class against its "betters," a revolution requires political leadership. The catch, according to Michels, is that the revolutionary leaders learn a great deal, perhaps too much, from their entrenched adversaries. The aristocracy was the "fencing master" of the bourgeoisie just as the middle class remains the political "instructor" of socialist movements.[34] Thus aristocratic aptitudes and attitudes remain with bourgeois and proletarian leaders.

Leisure, education, and access to "high culture," all products of privilege, give the bourgeois or proletarian leaders the skills essential to their tasks. To command and organize their constituencies, revolutionary elites must have the abilities to reflect and theorize, to write and speak persuasively, and to administer large and complex institutions. Access to such tools will necessarily be limited to those "rebels" whose upbringing, education, and experience are closest to that of the oligarchy they hope to overthrow. Indeed, the leadership of subordinate social classes may be composed of "traitors" to the dominant caste, as Michels demonstrates in his study of the German and Italian socialist parties.[35] Most important, the new elite's skills justify *to itself* its minority control over the political system, even in the name of universal human rights and democracy: "The victorious bourgeoisie of the *Droits de l'Homme* did, indeed, realize the republic, but not the democracy. The words *Liberté, Egalité, Fraternité* may be read to this day over the portals of all French prisons."[36]

Oligarchs rule because they believe they have earned the right to do so. They identify public virtue with personal characteristics of wealth, cultivation, intelligence, objectivity, or just plain efficiency. Michels sees these "ethical embellishments," or the self-justifying ideology of the oligarchs, as a mask for an "instinctual" desire to pass along political dominance from one generation to the next. Power becomes private property and therefore subject to inheritance: "The hereditary transmission of political power has always been the most efficacious means of maintaining class rule."[37]

The relevance of Michels' observations to the Orleanist oligarchy is strikingly illustrated in the memoirs of Charles de Rémusat, member of the July Monarchy's last parliament and the minister of the interior some years before the 1848 revolution. Acknowledging the collapse of Orleanism and the advent of democracy, he called his children together on the first morning of the Second Republic:

> Now even if their social condition would not be changed, in place of sharing almost without effort in the benefits provided by the State, in political life; they would have prejudices to defeat, hatreds to face: They would need more work, courage, persistence, merit to succeed and, in the case of a more radical democratic change, even to subsist. Toilsome professions could become their only recourse.[38]

The shock of sudden loss evoked in Rémusat a resolve to defend his beliefs: the "ethical embellishments" of his claim to privilege for himself and his children. Speaking of himself in the third person, Rémusat expressed his conservative liberalism as a concern for the survival of civilization and order:

> And now would this man, so quick to take umbrage at offenses to the least interest of liberty, so prompt to battle against abuses or minor faults, set down his arms and shut himself at home when liberty could be threatened violently and, with it, order, humanity, justice? Tyranny, in anarchist form, could be at our gates. . . .[39]

Certainly consciousness (or ideology) does not float about in thin air, cut off from the economic, social, or political institutions. But, as we have seen, social thinkers since Marx and Tocqueville have been forced to consider the distance that often separates attitudes and perceptions from "objective" social reality. From the time of Michels, Weber, and Freud to our present era of Neumann, Adorno, and Marcuse, theorists have tried to "freeze" and disentangle the complex interactions between the ideas and predispositions of people and the "hard evidence" of the social structures within which they act. Sharing their intellectual roots in Enlightenment rationalism, both liberal and Marxist theorists have repeatedly been challenged by situations that suddenly derail or switch tracks on the locomotive of progress. Antonio Gramsci and Georg Lukács are perhaps the best-known early Communist writers who found it necessary to revise Marx (or "Official Marxism") on the impact of culture, the state, and class consciousness (both bourgeois and proletarian) on the pace, if not the direction, of social change in periods of counterrevolution.[40]

Influenced more directly by Max Weber than by Marx and his followers, American social scientists have recently proposed a number of models for the analysis of crises, stress, violence, and sudden eruptions of "irrational" behavior. Neil J. Smelser, a sociologist with a remarkably informed interest in historical problems, has put forward a general model that has direct bearing on our concern with the role of social fear in destroying the Second Republic. In his *Theory of Collective Behavior*, Smelser argues that the most explosive kind of threat, one capable of producing the most extreme and violent response, is a menace directed against fundamental values of good and evil. When these values are attacked, established conceptions concerning "nature, man's place in it, man's relation to man and the desirable and non-desirable" are no longer secure.[41] According to Smelser, a group believing its world view to be threatened will change or jettison established procedures and institutions (norms) in order to preserve more fundamental notions of right and wrong (values). Smelser illustrates his argument by pointing out that groups have sometimes turned to charismatic dictators to defend and revitalize their values when an existing social and political system seemed incapable of "handling" (co-opting or repressing) a threat to such established beliefs.[42]

Smelser does not further refine his notion of "collective behavior" to distinguish threatened social elites, but his theory is readily applicable to the crisis of the Second Republic. If key members of the French political elite viewed the republic—even the conservative republic of the Party of Order—as incapable of suppressing the radical threat to their interests and values, and if they believed that very little time remained in which to deal the left a crippling blow before the anticipated revolutionary outbreak of 1852, then they may have compromised their commitment to constitutional law and embraced a dictatorship to defend their vision of the "good society." Since the establishment of the Second Republic, radicals had been hammering away at the social hierarchy and its government, which was still dominated by a ruling class of wealth and social pedigree. Against the background of a recent revolution, the elites under the Second Republic may have seen the continued existence of the left as an intolerable menace. Having witnessed that, after decades of oligarchy, a single day of street fighting was sufficient to establish political equality among all Frenchmen, a notable might have viewed a similar birth of social equality as a frightening possibility. A perception of the left as strong enough to launch a revolution, win a victory at the polls, or even continue to gain adherents among the lower classes constituted a sufficient threat to traditional values to provoke desperate social fear among the elites.

If the aim of the radicals was seen as the total transformation of the social universe, then the goal of the counterrevolutionaries was nothing less than a total prophylaxis of French society—a preemptive attack on the left to regain control over a world gone out of joint. The coup (and the mass arrests that followed it), far from being the aftermath of the left's "defeat" in 1849, may well have been the elites' response to a chronic sense of danger.

All of our present-day models and theoretical paraphernalia, when stripped of their jargon and equations, take us back to Marx and Tocqueville. But, in considering the problem of social fear, we must also acknowledge the acuity of a social scientist of another kind, one who was also an eyewitness to the Second Republic: Gustave Flaubert. Whereas the *Recollections*, *Class Struggles in France*, and *The Eighteenth Brumaire of Louis Bonaparte* are concerned with what people thought and calculated, Flaubert's *Sentimental Education* tells us what they felt as public turmoil invaded their private lives. Here, the outrage and violence of a threatened elite are suggested in a few striking sentences. Writing about the aftermath of the June Days of 1848, Flaubert describes the lynch-mob psychology of the bourgeoisie and aristocracy (or what Smelser defines as collective behavior).

> Despite their victory, equality—as if to punish its defenders and ridicule its enemies—asserted itself triumphantly: an equality of brute beasts, a common level of bloody atrocities; for the fanaticism of the rich counterbalanced the frenzy of the poor, the aristocracy shared the fury of the rabble, and the cotton nightcap was just as savage as the red bonnet. . . . Intelligent men lost their sanity for the rest of their lives.[43]

To Flaubert, the fury of June 1848 had not dissipated by the morning of the coup, 2 December 1851.

> "What! Isn't there going to be any fighting?" Frederic asked a workman.
> The man in the smock answered:
> "We're not such fools as to get ourselves killed for the rich! They can settle their own affairs!"
> And a gentleman, darting a sidelong glance at the workmen, muttered:
> "Filthy Socialists! If only they could be wiped out this time!"[44]

2 The Contending Social Factions ca. 1840-1848

The groups that contended so violently for mastery of the Second Republic were spawned considerably earlier than 24 February 1848. They had been produced, yet contained, by the slow-moving social evolution of nineteenth-century France. The most explosive among them were the lower-middle- and lower-class political organizations with radical social demands. These groups had been placed under particular pressure by the institutions and practices of the July Monarchy, and they reacted violently in 1848. The intensity of the crisis atmosphere surrounding the republic's brief existence contrasts rather dramatically with the apparent placidity and orderly optimism of the preceding period—the *juste milieu*. The 1848 revolution was defeated, but the revolutionary threat remained. In addition, social structures, political institutions, and, most important, the people and their mental outlooks, which had developed within and adapted to the framework of the July Monarchy, were unexpectedly thrown out, with the establishment of the republic, into the uncertainty of mass participation in politics. Formal political oligarchy, the hallmark of Louis Philippe's regime, was suddenly replaced by formal democracy, at least for men.

The Orleanist Oligarchy under Attack

The leading political and bureaucratic figures of the Second Republic, at least after Louis Napoleon's election as president in December 1848, had occupied much the same positions under the previous regime.[1] Connected by common ties of family, class, and political caste (membership in the censitary elite of the July Monarchy), these men quite naturally clung to the social and political vision of their immediate past. A recent student of *juste milieu* political thought places their outlook in the category of self-delusion, even when considered independently of the regime's eventual collapse: "a dream fantasy of what is *not* social realty . . . a kind of unwitting self-deception which either refuses to face or egregiously miscalculates the historical reality of the present."[2] How much more ill-adapted their attitudes must have seemed after 1848, within a democratic framework! Yet the elites neither discarded the core of their beliefs nor completely lost the struggle for the maintenance of oligarchy, however masked or informal, in French political life after 1848. René Rémond demonstrates convincingly that Orleanist ideology, understood as the elitist liberalism of the haute bourgeoisie, has long survived the regime from which it took its name.[3] This conservative liberalism "implied the necessary superiority of the social elites."[4] The hardiness of the elites is reflected in the longevity of their ideology: the liberal or Orleanist empire of the late 1860s; the republic of dukes early in the Third Republic; the power of Pierre Etienne Flandin and Paul Reynaud between the wars; and finally the role of the Orleanist independent republicans after World War II. *Juste milieu* political theory has been realistic enough to adapt to changing political and social circumstances while remaining steadfast in its conservatism.

Members of the July Monarchy's exclusive political club could not know in 1848, however, or in 1851, that their privileged status could survive democracy. For them, oligarchic elitism, the ideology of an established and satisfied elite, would seem to be the basic value threatened by the democratic and socialist forces under the Second Republic. Lacking the hindsight we now enjoy, they viewed their enemies through a perceptual lens adapted to the France they had dominated for eighteen years prior to the February revolution. They, too, had achieved power in the wake of an insurrection, and their social fear (their "red scare" under the new republic) was aroused by the unexpected attacks on a world they had constructed to satisfy their material needs and ideological sensibilities. The loss of self-assurance and the resultant social fear of the French upper classes after 1848 are best exemplified by the fact that they found safe harbor from the crisis not in an Orleanist constitutional government, but within the garrison state of a renascent Bonapartism. To understand the particular form of the stress experienced by this elite, we must briefly examine the unique oligarchy they fashioned under the July Monarchy. Only then can we understand the oppositions they aroused and the sense of loss and threat they experienced after 1848.

The July Monarchy's existence was bracketed by two revolutions, and its search for stability was haunted by still another: the Great

Revolution of 1789. The conflicting forces of that earlier struggle had driven France first to radicalism and finally to Caesarism. Consequently, the victors of 1830 sought a constitutional system that avoided both personal rule and what they saw as mob rule: they established an oligarchy of conservative liberals. Men of middling status in relation to the aristocracy above them and the rural and urban masses below, they tried to construct a bridge to the future that could guarantee both order and orderly progress. Ultimately their political system proved too brittle to survive even the relatively slow economic and social changes in France during the first half of the nineteenth century. Although an alternative conception of a liberal *and* democratic society had been voiced among them before the July Days and during the Orleanist regime, once they gained power the wealthy commoners of the period overwhelmingly chose conservatism over any political experimentation.

The bourgeoisie, the beneficiary of Louis Philippe's regime, was itself a class in transition. It was not yet secure in its peculiar identity or its special economic "mission."

> The Orleanist leadership was recruited from the upper bourgeoisie then, but we must not be misled by words, the permanence of which, when applied to changing realities, is often deceiving. We do not refer to large scale industrial capitalism. . . . Above all, land remained the principal wealth. . . . This bourgeois society still remained by its customs, tastes and ideas, very close to the world of the soil.[5]

Indeed, the conservative consensus included groups outside the haute bourgeoisie: the military and administrative aristocracy of the empire, and the liberal faction of the Ancien Regime's nobility. As a political class, it accepted and even promoted to office those impecunious intellectuals who expressed its vision of the past, present, and future. One of these, François Guizot, came to dominate the cabinets of the regime's last eight years. Within this governing group existed a remarkable consensus on the meaning of classic liberalism. Most of them shared an agreement so total on the nature of society and government that contemporary observers and latter-day historians are struck by the absence of any fundamental disagreements in the proceedings of the regime's parliaments.[6]

This political class immediately began to write its outlook into law. Although the militant striking force of the July revolution was the republican crowd, its political arm remained the officials elected under the narrow enfranchising laws of the Restoration. Thus political initiative, after July, swiftly passed from the insurrectionary crowd at the Hôtel de Ville to the liberals in the Chamber of Deputies. Louis Philippe was sworn in as king by this chamber; he promised to respect the rights of parliament and to abide by the provisions of the charter as revised by the chamber. These revisions reflected the constitutional concerns of the deputies. They did not eliminate the possibility of more fundamental changes in the political system: they were limited to a settling of accounts between crown and parliament and between State and Church. Catholicism lost its special status, the king's right to rule by decree was withdrawn, and he was specifically barred from suspending laws passed by parliament or from refusing to execute such laws.

Within a year of the July revolution, other basic enabling laws were passed. The most important was the electoral law, which entrusted only the very rich with the vote. The amount of direct taxation (most of it levied on landed property) that qualified a citizen to vote was lowered in 1831 from 300 to 200 francs. This increased the voting list from 90,000 to 166,000, or one-half of one percent of the population.[7]

The same laws also lowered the required *cens* for men who could actually stand for election to the Chamber of Deputies. At most this group, which had to pay an annual rate of 500 francs or more, numbered only 57,000. Studies of the actual representation sent to parliament, however, indicate that most deputies paid well over the required figure on their properties. A careful study of the actual governing class of the July Monarchy has fixed the figure of 1,000 francs a year in direct taxation as the best measure of whether a man was a "grand notable."[8]

These early limits on political participation could have served as acceptable starting points for the increasing democratization demanded by the street fighters of 1830, but the two forms of liberalism—one classic and oligarchic, the other democratic—could not coexist.

Political liberalism and social conservatism, these were the two pillars of the program, the two sides of Orleanism as inseparable as the opposite slopes of a mountain. . . . The alliance was signed on the day when Orleanism identified itself with the program of *resistance*. . . . Orleanism, originating on the Right, was to remain there, although it pretended to be in the Center.[9]

The limitations on active participation in government were never relaxed or reformed, for any dilution of the ruling class would have required a decision by that group itself. Down to the final, fatal crisis of the Orleanist oligarchy, the notables felt confident in their monopoly of power and justified in their exclusiveness.

The July Monarchy frequently has been called a regime of the grande bourgeoisie.[10] Wealthy commoners clearly dominated politics throughout the reign of Louis Philippe, but they can be called "bourgeois" only in the strict sense: most of them inhabited large towns or cities. Their fortunes may have been made through commerce, industry, or finance, but the social and political status of the Orleanist notable came from owning land.[11] Far from rejecting the values of the traditional rural nobility, the French bourgeoisie learned much from its "fencing master" and embraced many aristocratic notions of respectability.[12] To achieve social prominence, to become an accepted member of the elite, the parvenu became a landlord. The cens itself, that key to the tightly circumscribed ruling class, was levied almost exclusively on real estate. Although direct taxes were paid also on certain licenses (patentes) to run factories or mines, the assessments rarely were high enough, or the enterprises themselves large enough, to reach the enfranchising figure of 200 francs. The cens taxes were never reformed to assess very many industrial or commercial entrepreneurs who owned no land. Such entrepreneurs made a great deal of money during the July Monarchy, but a social stigma was apparently attached to the bourgeois "ideal type" who insisted on reinvesting his gains in his business. Instead he was expected, indeed required by law if he wished to become a notable, to emulate the landowning aristocracy. Under such a system, of course, professionals who amassed considerable fortunes as doctors or lawyers also were barred from the elite unless they diverted a substantial amount of their income into land purchases. Several times during the July Monarchy, measures were introduced to include so-called professional "capacities" as qualifications for the suffrage. Each such amendment was rejected.[13]

Orleanism was, therefore, the political creed of those who had risen under the regimes of the Great Revolution, the empire, and the Restoration. This group of great landholders included commoners, members of the old aristocracy who accepted and participated in "bourgeois" enterprise and land speculation (like Louis Philippe himself), and the Napoleonic aristocracy that had benefited from the emperor's land grants to his loyal officers. No real disagreement divided these elites. They simply had achieved wealth by different routes and under different forms of government. Under the bourgeois monarchy they constructed a political system to defend and extend the gains they had made in the turmoil of the years after 1789.

Within only five years of the July Days the forces of resistance had swept aside the revolution's promise of civil equality for all. The Orleanist elite, while professing a concern for individual freedom, proceeded to construct a police state as its bulwark against the enemies to the right and left of the *juste milieu*. By establishing a ruling class of notables, the revised Charter of 1830 necessarily created a disfranchised class of plebians.

Left out of the government entirely, the republicans began to reorganize. After 1832 they proclaimed a new credo, one that combined a genuine humanitarianism with the tactical necessity of seeking a power base among the poorer urban elements of the disfranchised 99 percent of Frenchmen: "It is the duty of society to provide a living for all its members, either by procuring them work, or by assuring the means of subsistence to those who are unfit to work."[14]

The men committed to resistance responded fiercely to the stubborn growth of republicanism and to its new and frightening link with the "vile multitude." In 1833 the government unsuccessfully prosecuted twenty-seven leaders of the Société des droits de l'homme et du citoyen. A few months later the minister of interior, Adolphe Thiers, proposed a far-reaching prohibition on all forms of association. Passed in 1834, the law was aimed against both the clubs of the political opposition and the workers' mutual aid societies, which were becoming increasingly republican. This legislation has been termed "reactionary even in comparison with the Napoleonic Code."[15] No group, no matter how small, was allowed to assemble without prior authorization. Violation of the law meant that leaders and members alike were subject to stiff prison sentences and heavy fines.

The Orleanist edifice of repression was completed in 1835. The so-called September laws, promulgated after Fieschi's attempt to blow up the king with an "infernal machine," had the "avowed object . . . to withdraw the rights of the Charter from political groups which did not accept the form of government established in 1830, and to silence legitimist and republican newspapers."[16]

The revised charter had abolished direct government censorship of the press. Only five years later, however, the Chamber of Deputies felt compelled to fall back on a legal device that, without directly contradicting the charter, would still muzzle the opposition. It banned any personal criticism of the king or of the form of government by defining such dissent as criminal libel. References to alternative forms of government were forbidden: republicans could not call themselves republicans, nor could supporters of the older branch of the Bourbons refer to themselves as legitimists. Fines for press offenses were raised dramatically, and the deposit (a form of surety bond) required of national newspapers was increased to 100,000 francs, a huge sum, four times greater than that required under Charles X. A form of self-censorship was thus imposed on the press.[17]

Criminal procedures for the enforcement of these laws were now slanted in the prosecution's favor. Only a simple majority of jurors was henceforth necessary for a conviction, and the jury was shielded from public pressure (which favored the accused in many large cities) by a requirement that deliberations take place in secret and that individual votes not be recorded.[18]

Since juries, which were drawn from a much larger segment of the population than the electorate, still balked at handing down convictions in political cases, the Ministry of Justice in 1835 directed its prosecutors to charge the opposition with offenses petty enough to fall within the jurisdiction of the single-judge, nonjury Correctional Tribunals.[19] Fines and sentences imposed by these minor police courts were relatively small, but they bled a newspaper summoned time after time. La Tribune expired in 1835 after 111 trials with only 20 convictions.[20] It was one of thirty republican newspapers to fold in the wake of the September laws.[21]

Still another September law circumvented jury trials for such matters of especial gravity as "provocation to attack the person of the King or to overthrow the form of government, and affronts intended to provoke hatred or contempt of the King."[22] These cases were to be tried before the most stalwart supporters of the July Monarchy, the members of the Chamber of Peers, who were appointed for life by the king and convened as the nation's high court of justice.

The July Monarchy's repressive machinery has been called "a sad commentary on the 'liberalism' of the French bourgeoisie."[23] It interests us here as an index of the self-certainty and ruthlessness with which the Orleanist oligarchy maintained its claim to power. From their bristling legal battlements, the beneficiaries of the July Monarchy proclaimed a political and social "science" that justified their domination.

Their liberalism was expounded as a defense of the haute bourgeoisie and of constitutional, parliamentary government. The enemies were extremists to their left and right: aristocratic legitimists who desired a return to the Ancien Regime, and republicans who sought a continuation of the Great Revolution's Jacobin legacy. It was a conservative, a defensive, and ultimately a contradictory ideology—the ideology of a dominant class in a society slowly changing from aristocratic and rural to urban and industrial.

Enunciated early in the Restoration by Pierre-Claude Daunou and Benjamin Constant, elaborated by a younger generation of liberals (Pierre-Paul Royer-Collard, François Guizot, and Prosper de Barante) later in the same period, the political and social science of the notables vested civic virtue in the wealthiest commoners, who stood between the nobility and the masses: "Above is a certain desire to dominate, against which it is necessary to guard; below, ignorance . . . complete incapacity."[24]

Constant and the Doctrinaires saw wealth, and thus economic independence, as the essential characteristic of those politicians who could best guarantee everyone's freedom. Parliament would be an assembly of economically substantial men immune to the blandishments of both throne and "mob." Basic rights essential for the defense of the individual against arbitrary authority were to be enjoyed by all citizens and guaranteed by the constitution: security in the ownership of property, equality before the law, and freedoms of speech, press, assembly, and religion.[25] Limiting political participation to the very rich, however, insured that private property was safe from governmental depredation. If the poor, or even the modestly comfortable, were permitted to vote or sit in the Chamber of Deputies, they would use their force of numbers to expropriate their social and economic betters.[26]

Wealth was considerably more than a guarantee of respect for property. Landed wealth in particular offered the rewards of leisure, reflection, and intellectual refinement. Stated economically, a proprietary ruling class could be expected to devote its time to a disinterested, dispassionate—in sum, to a rational—consideration of the world. The very rich would protect society from the meanness and envy that warped the judgment of the less fortunate, and they could thus be expected to rule wisely in the best interests of all.[27] Guizot maintained that the political monopoly of the wealthiest commoner was beneficial for the citizen excluded from direct political participation: "He [the notable] does not exclude him, he represents him, he protects him, he covers him, he experiences and defines the same interests."[28]

These theorists of classic liberalism articulated the interests and attitudes of the oligarchs, who in turn shaped the July Monarchy's consensus. Their political doctrine was essentially negative and fundamentally conservative: they knew precisely what they wanted to avoid. Once in power, therefore, they compromised their faith in basic civil liberties. The police state and a vision of a harsh, but strangely vulnerable, yet nevertheless natural social hierarchy formed the Orleanist heritage, which the elite brought to the troubled years following the 1848 revolution.

In the Orleanist world, productive efficiency and profits became the means of mobility into the social elite. *"Enrichissez-vous"* was Guizot's rejoinder to those who wanted the censitary voting requirement lowered or abolished, and the voting rolls of the July Monarchy did increase from 166,000 in 1831 to almost 250,000 in 1847, as new commercial and industrial wealth was accumulated.[29] The merchant, speculator, or factory master bought real estate, became a landlord, and gained respectability.

Thus, to Guizot and the other classic liberals, society became increasingly democratic as more and more enterprising men "got rich." Given the almost purely monetary index of elite status during the July Monarchy, it was only natural that economics became the science that explained society to the notables. Social status, or rather the right to make political decisions for society, resulted from a pre-Darwinian notion of natural economic selection. If man was perfectible, superiority had to be proven in each individual case by personal success. The social world view of the notables combined a justification of their status (a position they felt they had earned) with a corollary explanation of why extreme poverty not only persisted, but actually seemed to increase with industrialization.

Around 1840, a new word entered the French language: *paupérisme*. It came into existence as the result of a rash of statistical studies of lower-class life in industrial cities. Two ministerial surveys, in 1834 and 1840, and a number of local studies carried out by chambers of commerce and departmental *conseils généraux*, were motivated largely by the increasing problem of indigence in the great urban industrial centers and by the rising need of the poor for assistance from private charity and local agencies.[30] Between 1827 and 1836, small towns became cities as industry grew. Saint-Etienne grew during these years from 16,000 to 54,000 inhabitants, and the population of factory centers like Roubaix and Mulhouse increased a similar amount.[31] In the period 1840-1848, French towns of 3,000 or more grew by 2,000,000, with most of the immigrants inhabiting dark and dense "rookeries of the poor."[32]

Although a debate has raged over the impact of the factory system on the standard of living in Britain, scholars agree that salaries and the standard of living of unskilled factory operatives tended to decline as France industrialized.[33] The pioneering statistical work of Dr. Louis René Villermé, Antoine-Eugène Buret, and Count de Villeneuve-Bargemont, which appeared around 1840, portrayed a world of unrelieved misery in the industrial cities. Their calculations demonstrated that workers in most industries could not possibly earn enough to sustain the housing, diet, clothing, and heating necessary for health. Buret showed that the annual cost of these necessities to a family of three in Lille was 1,051 francs, while a man, woman, and child who were fully employed in a factory could together earn no more than 864 francs a year.[34]

The profound Christian morality of Buret and Villeneuve-Bargemont and the humanitarian outrage of the physician Villermé, all of whom called for state intervention to guarantee the well-being of the lower classes, were rejected by almost the entire censitary elite. The classic liberals linked the discovery of working-class suffering—material, social, and psychological—with another result of rapid urbanization: crime. The phrase *classes laborieuses, classes dangereuses* entered common upper-class parlance at the same time as the word *paupérisme*.[35] Villermé's own study had shown the widespread practice of factory women seeking their *cinquième quart de la journée* in the streets as prostitutes.[36] Tocqueville reported that in the years between 1827 and 1841 the number of criminals increased in relation to the population at large by the proportion of three to seventeen, which is more than a quintupling of the crime rate.[37]

To the notables, the social question became a moral issue. Louis Chevalier and A. J. Tudesq have shown, in brilliant studies of elite perceptions of the lower classes, that urban workers were portrayed in scholarly works and in literature as physically and morally deformed—as a different and subhuman species.[38] Some members of the upper classes, notably legitimists like Villermé, blamed pauperism on the new Orleanist oligarchy. Men slightly to the left of the dominant consensus, like Tocqueville's friend Rémusat, called for government action because poverty threatened society with revolution. But those who spoke for the majority of the notables viewed poverty as the result of preordained inequalities among men, differences that amounted to the boundary between civilization and primitive societies.

This attitude, which has much in common with the European view of subjected populations in Asia and Africa, was an odd mixture of complacency and fear. The elite feared the ferocious violence of the lower classes portrayed so graphically by Eugène Sue in his *Mystères de Paris* (a great best seller of the forties), but at the same time the official theorists of the ruling class explained the very fact of lower-class status as the result of vice, sexual license, and drunkenness. For Charles Dunoyer—prefect, *conseiller d'état*, and "spokesman for bourgeois economics under Louis Philippe"[39]—misery was an essential component of progress: "it is good that society has inferior places where families that behave badly are liable to fall and from which they cannot rise except by means of good conduct: extreme poverty is this formidable hell."[40]

The Opposition to Orleanism

Republicanism after 1840

Paris, of course, remained the headquarters of the republican movement. Here existed, side by side, an intelligentsia of largely unenfranchised middle class professionals and a dissatisfied mass of artisans. The differences in emphasis, outlook, and tactics among republicans reflected this social diversity in the capital.

The editorial offices of its major newspapers became the movement's focal points after the republican societies were repressed. With its circulation of four thousand, *Le National* was, since the time of Armand Carrel, the most important republican daily. Always distinguished by the moderation of its tone (until Carrel's death in a duel in 1836), the newspaper avoided any consideration of the workers' sufferings and interests. *Le National* confined itself to cautiously worded criticisms of the *"escamotage"* (swindle) of July 1830 and of the regime's timid foreign policy. Carrel is said to have crossed out the word "proletarian" whenever one of his reporters tried to slip some social commentary past the watchful editor.[41]

Although in the forties, *Le National* did depart from Carrel's policy and addressed the problems posed by pauperism, the newspaper's central concern remained the winning of political equality. Its new editor, Armand Marrast, had been a partisan of violent revolution until his exile in England, but he returned much impressed by the lawful and orderly example of Chartism. He adopted the strategy of alliance with the dynastic opposition in urging a modest expansion of the electorate, for he "sought to disarm the aversion of the middle classes to republicans."[42] *Le National*'s social program was mild, calling for the workers' right to organize and for reduction of taxes on consumer necessities.[43] Social amelioration, for Marrast and his associates (the Garnier-Pagès brothers, Alexandre Marie, and Eugène Bethmont), did not involve any qualification of property rights or the transformation of the social order.

The moderation of their social outlook was reflected in their unhurried approach to political change. In 1842 the younger and surviving Garnier-Pagès argued that revolution was justified only against despotism and that the July Monarchy could be reformed peacefully: "In those countries where one enjoys liberty without however possessing equality of rights, one must not resort to insurrection except at the last extremity and one must not conspire."[44]

Other republicans disagreed. Godefroy Cavaignac returned from exile in 1840 astonished "to see the republicans pacified and soft."[45] In 1841 Alexandre Auguste Ledru-Rollin shocked many moderate republicans of Le Mans by calling on the members of that unique electoral college to support an immediate democratization of the suffrage and vigorous government action to meet the needs of the poor.[46] Brought to trial for this radical *profession de foi*, undoubtedly because he won the election, Ledru-Rollin gave the courtroom a taste of oratory that differed markedly from the measured pronouncements of *Le National*:

And you, attorney-general, who gives you your investiture? The ministry. Myself, elector, I throw out ministers. In the name of whom do you speak? In the king's name. Myself, elector, history is there to show it, I make and I unmake kings. Attorney-general, on your knees, on your knees before my sovereignty.[47]

In 1843 he joined Godefroy Cavaignac, Etienne Arago, and Ferdinand Flocon in floating *La Réforme*, a republican newspaper strongly critical of *Le National*. They attacked Marrast's flirtation with the dynastic opposition and opened their pages to such overt socialists as Louis Blanc and Pierre Leroux. The revived radical wing of republicanism tried to carry on the policy first adopted in the thirties by the short-lived Société des droits de l'homme: the fusion of political democracy with working-class demands for profound social change.

Whereas workers derisively referred to *Le National* as the "gentlemen's journal," *La Réforme*, despite its subscription list of only one thousand, penetrated the slums of Paris and Lyon to be read aloud at popular cafes.[48] *La Réforme* was cautious in its espousal of socialist principles, but its very discussion of them and its actual endorsement of Louis Blanc's plan for "social" workshops meant that the association of individualism with republicanism was giving way to a more radical linkage of socialism with democracy.[49] If Ledru-Rollin and Flocon, who became editor after Cavaignac's death, were not socialists, they were certainly *socialisants*. The social question thus split republicanism into two factions. *Le National* embraced Lamartine and his conversion to the faith of the Girondins; *La Réforme* helped revive the social republicanism of the Terror and of Gracchus Babeuf.

Socialism

If Ledru-Rollin and his coterie were social reformers because they were first and foremost republicans, others came to republicanism because they saw political democracy as the means to socialism. A humanitarian concern for the plight of the poor was perhaps the most striking feature of the 1848 revolution, one which sets it off from the major movements of the Great Revolution and from the July Days of 1830.[50] These earlier political upheavals occurred in an atmosphere still saturated with the belief that poverty was natural and unavoidable. In 1789 and 1830, and even in 1792, "They [the rebels] were preoccupied with ensuring that individuals had equal . . . opportunities more than with leveling their material conditions of life and they fulminated against oppression more than against misery."[51]

As we have seen, it was under the classic liberalism of the July Monarchy that the social question moved to center stage in French thought. Socialism, really multiple answers to the social question, was scarcely less important in the intellectual life of the forties. While Dunoyer, Baron de Gerando, and others prepared the Orleanist brief for social inequality, their opponents produced what Jules Michelet called "a volcano of books, an eruption of utopias" that propounded a rather different social vision.[52] Socialist writings circulated freely and widely among the middle classes and the increasingly literate workers of the large cities. Growing from the eccentric seedbeds of Saint-Simon and Fourier, the quasi-religious, utopian socialism of the thirties and forties was indulged by the government. Society could be poked, probed, dissected, and even damned as long as the form of government was spared.[53]

In a single year—1840—Louis Blanc's *Organization of Labor* appeared in book form (it would go through five editions before the revolution); Proudhon's *What is Property?* was issued; and Etienne Cabet published his now forgotten but immensely influential *Travels in Icaria*. Earlier, Lamennais had broken definitively with the Church and written three works that stigmatized the economic competition and social inequality of the July Monarchy as violations of Christian morality: *The Words of a Believer* (1834), *The Book of the People* (1837), and *Modern Slavery* (1839). While not himself a system builder, the defrocked abbé had an enormous influence on all concerned about the social question. The socialist-inspired novels of George Sand (a close friend of Ledru-Rollin, Godefroy Cavaignac, and Pierre Leroux) and Eugène Sue were often serialized in newspapers with circulations considerably larger than those of the republican press.[54]

To Considérant, Cabet, Proudhon, Lamennais, and others, socialism had little or nothing to do with politics. Government was often irrelevant to their visions of moralized societies in which people naturally associated in cooperatives or communes to share in the products of their labor. The strongly ethical tone of these apolitical socialists explains the appeal of their writings among the poor and the privileged alike. In different ways they succeeded in touching a primitively Christian core of beliefs in an increasingly urbanized and impersonal society. They eschewed politics because they expected a moral social order to evolve out of an abhorrent state of disharmony and suffering. The poor and oppressed could change their way of life by adopting alternative modes of production and consumption without reference to the existing system of private property. Socialism would grow from the bottom up, beyond the reach of the rich who dominated government and industry.

The socialism of the working-class quarters of Paris, Lyon, Saint-Etienne, Lille, and other centers of industry was extremely eclectic.[55] It was more a mood than a rigid doctrine. The multiple routes to a new society and the many "shapes of things to come" appear contradictory, but to the individual worker they all expressed the same vague, desperate hopes. The socialist pantheon could encompass and unify men whom historians categorize as utopians or terrorists, hard-headed reformers or visionaries, idealistic Catholics or opportunistic politicians.

Louis Blanc and Pierre Leroux followed different paths to republican socialism. Blanc began as a republican and became a socialist, while Leroux adapted his mystical "religion of humanity" to republican political activism. Together they argued against the apolitical trend in socialism and insisted that the road to social change led first to the achievement of political democracy. Like other socialists, they based their optimism on the fact that the vast majority of Frenchmen suffered under the existing system and that, by sheer force of numbers, the masses had the power to take destiny into their own hands. Unlike the anarchists or the utopians, however, Leroux and Blanc believed that political power was the most efficient guarantee of the swift and comprehensive establishment of the workers' control over factories and workshops. Armed with the ballot, the masses could redefine the role of government and make it serve the material interests of the majority. In their writings and political activities during the forties, the proponent of social workshops and the Saint-Simonian visionary joined in urging socialists to unite with the republicans of *La Réforme* in the fight for democracy.[56]

Another fusion of socialism and republicanism remains to be considered: the conspiratorial faith of Louis Auguste Blanqui, Armand Barbès, and François-Vincent Raspail, which was embodied in their secret society, Les Saisons. These men differed from the utopians and the men of *La Réforme*, socialists and republicans alike, in their pessimistic evaluation of the role that the masses could play in overthrowing the existing system. Great changes, to Blanqui and Barbès in particular, did not involve great numbers. They held that revolution could come about only by the disciplined action of a well-trained band that struck at the strategic moment in the interests of the apathetic or hesitant majority. The right to vote was less important than the right to take up the gun, and the legitimacy of the barricade derived from the deep-running general will of the masses, not from their active assent.[57] Although the membership of Les Saisons and its allied branches, concentrated almost exclusively in Paris and Lyon, remained relatively small, the popularity of Blanqui was such that on his release from prison in 1848 the club he formed numbered three thousand Parisian workers.[58]

For all its confusion, romanticism, and vagueness, the radical republicanism of the July Monarchy stands in stark contrast to the dominant social "science" of the oligarchs. For many members of the lower and middle classes, the purely political equality that the July Monarchy denied them was already insufficient. Indeed, the new élan of republicanism and the romantic cult of the people, which developed during the forties, created an intellectual atmosphere in which it was possible to rehabilitate the memory of the radical phase of the Great Revolution. What we would call "revisionist" histories of that radical period, written by Lamartine, Michelet, Blanc, and Alphonse Esquiros, appeared during the two years prior to the 1848 revolution:

> it had not been a brief and shameful parenthesis in the history of the Revolution, but a new revolution, that of 1792 which was just as exalting and generous as that of 1789. . . . The republican party had no need for these writers to declare themselves for it explicitly; voluntarily or not they served it as moral guarantees.[59]

Legitimism

Led by the great landowning aristocracy and by the Catholic clergy, those who rejected Louis Philippe's claim to the throne formed a permanent subversive movement within the ranks of the censitary elite. In the west, from Brittany to Bordeaux, and in the Midi, the nobility and clergy commanded the deference of their peasant tenants and frequently of town-dwelling artisans.[60]

By the mid-thirties, when it was apparent that the July Monarchy had achieved a considerable measure of stability, tactical debates divided the legitimists. Many insisted on total abstention from the Orleanist government; their internal emigration became a familiar literary theme of the period.[61] They believed that Louis Philippe's misbegotten monarchy would eventually collapse and that the time of Henry V would come. Others, like the Vicomte de Falloux, the Comte Benoît d'Azy, and the great jurist (and commoner) Pierre-Antoine Berryer, held that legitimists should participate in local and national government in defense of their interests and those of the Catholic church.[62] Their particular target was the Guizot reform that placed all education, from primary schools to the universities, under government direction. They insisted, with only limited success, on freedom of instruction: the freedom of the Church to exercise its historic mission of teaching the traditional religious values, which of course ran counter to the rationalist individualism of the Orleanist elite.[63]

The Abbé de Genoude, editor of the major legitimist newspaper, *La Gazette de France*, went even further than these deputies. He preached that democracy would serve the cause of a new Bourbon restoration by extending the franchise to peasants and townspeople who looked to the chateau and the parish church for political guidance. The abbé argued for short-term alliances with the republicans to oppose Guizot's officially supported candidates. Partisans of the *juste milieu*, especially in the Midi, found themselves confronted by a coalition of contradictory nostalgias and symbols: the red flag of the Mountain and the white standard of the Bourbons.

The legitimist social vision was based on a hierarchy of orders headed by a hereditary nobility and king. By birth and breeding, aristocracy and royalty were the natural leaders of France's ancient provinces (legitimists never accepted the division of France into departments) and of the nation as a whole.

> Against the individual emancipated by the Revolution, against the individualism that they criticized vehemently, they asserted the rights of groups. Holding this point of view, they ultimately came to ally with other critics of individualism—the first socialists, for example—and they would join with them for the entire century in censuring a certain liberal individualism descended from the tradition of '89 and the Civil Code.[64]

Eclipsed under the July Monarchy, legitimism would emerge as a major force in the democratically elected assemblies of the Second Republic. Genoude's program of embracing universal suffrage proved to be only partially successful after 1848. The tragedy of legitimism under the Second Republic was that democracy made it strong enough to defend the existing social order and to reassert the clergy's right to control education, but never sufficiently powerful to erase the bourgeois legacy of the Great Revolution.

Bonapartism

The cult of the Little Corporal was an ecumenical church indeed; it was freely invoked by all political groups under the July Monarchy. Legitimists and republicans joined in contrasting the dynamism and bravery of public figures under the empire with the smugness and material greed of the Orleanist notables. The July Monarchy, its peers and its ministers, used the memory of the Grand Army as a way to win support from all classes of the population and to make up for a lackluster foreign policy.[65] Most French families boasted a veteran of the Napoleonic wars.[66] By a not uncommon quirk of cultural memory, the horrors and sufferings of twenty years of war were eclipsed by the shared recollection of glory among rich and poor, marshal and obscure *grognard* alike.

Yet at the height of this imperial nostalgia, when Napoleon's remains were returned to France and interred in the Invalides, the Bonapartist heir-presumptive was serving a life sentence in the fortress of Ham for his second attempt to rouse a garrison against the July Monarchy. For this act of treason Louis Napoleon was tried, convicted, and sentenced by the Chamber of Peers, made up in large part of marshals and generals ennobled by his uncle.

If any specifically political doctrine can be called "Bonapartist" during the reign of Louis Philippe, it is embodied in the writings and actions of Louis Napoleon himself. Whether or not he actually turned out to be "Saint-Simon on horseback" as Napoleon III, his pamphlets published between 1839 and his comic-opera escape from prison in 1846 are certainly the *professions de foi* of a man influenced by the teachings of utopian socialism. In *The Extinction of Pauperism* (1844), he treated the liberal ideal of "laissez-faire" as a disorder that only government intervention could correct. He singled out industry not for its contributions to human progress, but for its effect on workers. Louis Napoleon's criticisms show the impact of his reading at the "university" of Ham, reading which included the works of Louis Blanc and Robert Owen:

Breaking men as well as material in its gears, [industry] depopulates the countryside, masses populations in spaces without air, weakens both the spirit and the body and finally—when it can think of nothing more to do with them—throws in the gutter those who have sacrificed their strength, their youth, their existence to enrich it.[67]

Yet he never clearly propounded the form of government that a Bonapartist restoration would bring to France. Either by conviction or design, the pretender faithfully reflected the ambiguities of the Napoleonic legend. By turns a quasisocialist who defended law, order, and property, or a believer in competition who was an ardent protectionist, the philosophizing prince seems to have considered his most important literary effort of the prison years to be the still-respected *Studies on the Past and Future of Artillery* (1846), which established his intellectual heredity as the nephew not only of an emperor, but of the Great Artillerist.[68]

When Louis Napoleon was an exile or a prisoner and certainly when he was president of the Second Republic, constitutionally limited to only one term, it is probably fair to say that his most absorbing intellectual discipline was the pursuit of the main chance. Thus the stockholder in *Le National* and the would-be friend of Etienne Cabet would soon align himself with the notables in resisting the forces for social change unleashed by the revolution of 1848.[69]

The Dynastic Opposition and the Guizot Ministries

The moderate opposition within Orleanism itself was far more politically significant before 1848 than the republicans, legitimists, or Louis Napoleon and his tiny group of friends and hangers-on. Members of the dynastic opposition formed the second largest group in the chamber and shared the classic liberal outlook of their colleagues in Guizot's majority. They were led by Odilon Barrot. Practical reformers rather than theorists, the conservative opponents had no quarrel with the Orleans dynasty or with the terms of the revised charter, but only with the actual practices—they called them abuses—of the king and his ministers.

The dynastic opposition charged that Guizot's long-term dominance was a subversion of constitutional government. Guizot argued that the July revolution was fought to establish the primacy of parliament and its ministers; yet the dynastic opposition attacked Guizot and the conservative majority for permitting Louis Philippe to retain the initiative in government.[70] Tocqueville, in his *Recollections*, blamed the king himself rather than Guizot for the monarch's fall.[71] He wrote that Louis Philippe, an able politician in his own right, used Guizot to create a political machine that made the "constitutional" monarch the real master of parliament.

> Posterity, which sees only striking crimes and generally fails to notice smaller vices, will perhaps never know how far the government of that time toward the end took on the features of a trading company whose every operation is directed to the benefit that its members may derive therefrom. These vices were linked to the natural instincts of the dominant class, to its absolute power, and to the enervation and corruption of the age. King Louis-Philippe did much to make them grow. He was the accident that made the illness fatal.[72]

Historians have confirmed the judgment that the regime degenerated into a "parody of its intentions."[73] Perhaps the most obvious examples of official vice involved the partisan use of the civil service by the king and his ministers. The reformers (and republicans and legitimists as well) charged that elections to the Chamber of Deputies were often "rigged" by the centralized administration and that Guizot's majority was largely composed of salaried bureaucrats who were rewarded for their pliancy by bribes in the form of jobs, promotions, and decorations. In all, eighteen attempts were made to pass a bill banning the simultaneous holding of appointive and elective office. It was resoundingly defeated every time.[74] After all, more than 20 percent of the deputies sitting in judgment on such a bill would have been barred from the chamber had it passed.[75] On the theory that men who paid a *cens* of 500 francs could afford to be independent of the Treasury, deputies were not salaried. Yet even the very rich were greedy for government pay and honors. The dynastic opposition, joined by the republicans, demanded adequate pay for deputies in order to make the legislature immune to ministerial bribes.

Perhaps the most serious assault on the charter's liberal principles (and Guizot's most blatant repudiation of his belief in the rights of political parties) was the civil service's rigging of the restricted electorate to assure victory for those who supported the cabinet. The prefects and subprefects, those specifically responsible for local law enforcement, stretched and frequently broke electoral laws to please their superiors, keep their posts, and earn promotion. Qualified voters were barred from their electoral colleges; polling places were located as far as possible from centers of opposition strength. Balloting was scheduled for times when opponents would find voting most inconvenient, and the ballots themselves were often forged or invalidated. Opposition electoral tracts were impounded though no press laws were violated. Attorneys general and their subordinates, of course, refrained from investigating and prosecuting their fellow functionaries. In short, the centralized administration acted with alacrity and impunity to keep Guizot's majority intact.[76] Within an electorate composed of the richest one-half of one percent of the population, power was monopolized by an even more restrictive clique around Guizot and the king.

The key demand of the reformers was the lowering of the electoral requirement to a *cens* of 100 francs and the admission of professional men to eligibility with no tax requirement at all—the so-called vote by *capacités*.[77] This would have doubled the electorate and swelled the ranks of the dynastic opposition with grateful members of the middle class.

Neither democrats nor social reformers, partisans of the dynastic opposition disdained and feared the lower classes as much as did Thiers (their sometime ally in the chamber) and Guizot. Their aim was to expand the oligarchy, not to overthrow it. Yet in the wake of their resounding defeat by Guizot in the carefully "managed" election of 1846, these mild reformists unleashed the fatal political crisis of the oligarchy—the Banquet Campaign of 1847-1848. They emulated their British counterparts and took their case to the country, to those who could not vote. And they did so at a time when France was racked by disastrous harvests and a paralysis of credit and commerce.

Robert Michels and Gaetano Mosca both argue that an oligarchy faces its most severe test when a closed clique of rulers resists the ambitions of other members of the elite. The losers are often tempted to seek support among the plebians in order to achieve power among the oligarchs. It is a desperate and dangerous tactic.[78]

Recognizing the perils of such a gambit, Thiers, Tocqueville, Charles de Rémusat, and Jules Dufaure counseled against the Banquet Campaign and took no part in it. Barrot, Léon Faucher, and such newcomers as Jules Baroche opened their attack by appealing to the existing electorate.[79] By November 1847, however, Ledru-Rollin had overshadowed Barrot as the crowd pleaser at many banquets, and those who could afford a subscription were far outnumbered by humble onlookers. Reformist toasts "To political conscience" gave way to such radical ones as "To universal suffrage" and "To the unity of the French Revolution, to the indivisibility of the Constituent, the Legislative and the Convention."[80]

A month before the revolution, Tocqueville had half-skeptically predicted the whirlwind that the dynastic opposition was calling down upon both the regime and its own social class:

> Do you not see that opinions and ideas are gradually spreading . . . that tend not simply to the overthrow of such-and-such laws, such-and-such a minister, or even such-and-such a government but rather to the overthrow of society, breaking down the bases on which it rests? . . . And do you not realize that when such opinions take root and spread, sinking deeply into the masses, they must sooner or later . . . bring in their train the most terrifying of revolutions?[81]

Barrot, Baroche, Faucher, and Dufaure became the ministers responsible for law enforcement during the conservative phase of the Second Republic. Confronted by the social question they had unwittingly enflamed, these moderate reformers of the July Monarchy became leaders of a new conservative coalition, the Party of Order, after they were overtaken by the 1848 revolution.

The Crystallization of Social Fear

The focus of the following chapters is neither Paris nor the explosive early months of the Second Republic. Events in the capital have been made familiar by the work of many scholars. My concern is to portray, without a detailed day-by-day narrative, how Parisian events provided the notables with a common touchstone for the social fear they would experience until the republic was dead. The June Days, the invasion of the Constituent Assembly on 15 May, and the February revolution itself would be fused in their memories into a single panoply of chaos.[82]

Tocqueville was disconsolate: "I had conceived the idea of a regulated and orderly freedom, controlled by religious beliefs, mores and laws . . . and now I clearly saw that I must give it up forever."[83] His friends reported that both Thiers and Barrot had gone "half mad" when the dynasty fled and the chamber was dissolved.[84]

It soon became evident that the notables who remained in Paris (many fled the city in fear for their lives) ran no risk of arrest or physical danger, but their concern and that of the conservative press soon turned to the survival of their social system. Doctor Véron, owner of *Le Constitutionnel*, wrote: "The day after the February revolution, the Parisian bourgeois trembled for his head and, when he was nearly certain of keeping it, he trembled for his purse."[85] Prosper Mérimée, in a letter to Madame de Montijo (Eugénie's mother), wrote that "Now a single resource remains, it is to try to maintain order in maintaining that which exists."[86]

Excepting a few demonstrations set off by the news of the revolution in scattered towns and in such large cities as Lyon, Lille, and Rouen, the provinces remained quiet. Despite the effervescence of Lyon through June 1848, Justin Godart rejects "the legend of terrorism which historians have attached to the activity of the Voraces [the most militant of the radical clubs in the city's working-class suburbs]" and shows that "The truth is that, more than anyone, the Voraces were . . . passionate defenders of order."[87] Like notables elsewhere, those of Lyon looked to Paris and Parisian events for clues about the future.[88] Reports from the capital, in the form of private correspondence or the daily arrival of a Parisian newspaper, provided the notables (and the local conservative press) with the vocabulary of social fear that would become the elite's political lexicon.

Beginning in March and April, only weeks after the revolution, the Orleanist and legitimist newspapers of the capital emerged from a wait-and-see stance to attack the political and social "excesses" of the Provisional Government. On 12 March *Le Constitutionnel* described the regime's shortening of the working day as an assault on the natural, immutable laws of economics.[89] On 15 March *L'Assemblée Nationale* stigmatized the work of Louis Blanc and the Luxembourg Commission for Workers as "the disorganization of labor."[90] Early in April *Le Constitutionnel* argued that Blanc's proposed cooperative workshops were "utopias" that could never work "because they take no account of our own nature nor of the social milieu in which we live."[91] Conservative newspapers warned the Provisional Government that continued discussion of these innovations and any postponement of elections for a Constituent Assembly (a demand of the radical Paris clubs) would spell economic disaster for France. Indeed, the notables plunged the nation into a depression even more severe than that of 1846 by hoarding currency and withholding credit. Shares in the Bank of France fell to half their value during the republic's first two months, as did the price of the 6 and 3 percent *rentes* (government bonds).[92] The economy was paralyzed; thousands of urban workers found themselves jobless in the wake of the revolution. And the provincial press written and read by the notables followed the great Parisian dailies in blaming the new republic for the disaster.[93]

Underlying the notables' fear for the present and future was a horror of a particular past: the Terror. Reviewing France's history since 1789, Tocqueville felt that "here was the French Revolution starting over again, for it was always the same one."[94] His sense of a return to an age of popular excess led him to berate his best friend and fellow member of the Academy, Ampère:

> I tell you that this people whom you so naively admire has just proved that it is incapable and unworthy of living in freedom.
> . . . What new virtues has it discovered, and what old vices has it discarded? No, I tell you, it is always the same; just as impatient, careless and contemptuous of the law as ever; just as easily led and as rash in the face of dangers as its fathers before it.[95]

Le Courrier de la Gironde, on 14 March, was still not reassured by the Provisional Government's abolition of the death penalty for political offenses, a measure taken precisely to calm those who trembled at the thought of a renascent Robespierre. It told its readers that the new regime had merely prevented a new Terror from going as far as the scaffold.[96]

The election in April of an overwhelmingly moderate Constituent Assembly did not calm the notables' fear of the Paris crowd or of a renewed drive for profound social change.[97] *La Réforme*, the radical republican organ, recognized defeat, at least for the moment. "The hour is solemn. . . . We hide nothing: the elections were made against the men who prepared and proclaimed the republic."[98] Tocqueville, who recognized that the majority of the assembly was made up of members of the former dynastic opposition, celebrates their victory (and his own election) but immediately goes on to the most bloodthirsty and cynical passage in the *Recollections*:

I had always thought that there was no hope of gradually and peacefully controlling the impetus of the February Revolution and that it could only be stopped suddenly by a great battle taking place in Paris. I had said that immediately after the 24th February, and what I now saw persuaded me that the battle was not only inevitable but imminent, and that it would be desirable to seize the first opportunity to start it.[99]

What he saw were the Parisian radical clubs spreading their influence over the mass of workers enrolled in the National Workshops. What he expressed was a common desire among conservatives, newly vested with control over the republic, to have done, however violently, with the danger.

The coming struggle was signaled by the uprising of 15 May. On that day the Paris crowd, including several thousand workers from the National Workshops, invaded the assembly to dramatize two demands: the creation of a Ministry of Progress to guarantee the right to work and the dispatch of a French army to support the Polish revolution. In the midst of the hubbub, Aloysius Huber, chief of the coordinating Club des Clubs, proclaimed the dissolution of the assembly and, with other prominent club leaders, led the demonstrators to the Hôtel de Ville to create a new (and radical) government. (It remains a subject of considerable debate among historians whether Huber was a paid police provocateur or simply crazy.)[100] The result was a disastrous blow to the club movement and a new cause for alarm among the notables. The assembly's Executive Commission, composed of moderate republicans (with the single exception of Ledru-Rollin) had no choice but to put down this rebellion against the representatives of universal manhood suffrage. The *rappel* was sounded; the National Guard and army cleared the Hôtel de Ville, arrested the leaders for high treason, and shut the meeting halls of the three largest clubs. Ledru-Rollin and Lamartine led the forces of order. On 7 June a new law, proposed unanimously by the Executive Commission, required demonstrators to disperse at the first request of the police. All members of a crowd in which any individual was found to be armed were liable to ten years of imprisonment. This first counterrevolutionary legislation of the Second Republic was the response of the republicans of *Le National* and *La Réforme* to the violent pretensions of the conspiratorial left and to the demands of the assembly's conservative majority for its suppression. The law was "more severe than anything on the statute books."[101]

Yet the notables were not reassured. They were pleased, of course, by the failure of the riot, but they chided the Executive Commission for softness toward the radicals and even for complicity with them. Rémusat wrote: "The inaction of the Parisian populace, . . . the good conduct of the armed forces and the excellent attitude of the Assembly turned the day to the profit of order, but not of the executive authority. The government knew nothing, prevented nothing, did nothing."[102] The *Journal des Débats* maintained, on 18 May, that the country, not the government, had defended order.[103] The legitimist *Gazette de France* told its readers that "democracy always has communism as its outcome."[104] The Orleanist *Courrier de la Gironde* saw the members of the Executive Commission as "profligates, traitors and . . . thieves." [105]

Though Barbès, Blanqui, and Raspail were jailed, and the clubs virtually dissolved, the National Workshops remained. For Odilon Barrot, the events of 15 May did not solve the major question of the period: "It had to do very simply with whether French society would or would not be: it was a question of life and death."[106] Enrollment in the workshops had grown from 14,000 in March to 110,000 in June.[107] The assembly's majority, led in this matter by the legitimist Falloux, moved abruptly to close them and to send the unemployed away from Paris. Rémusat argued that the National Workshops were "asylums opened to paid idleness and recruitment to rebellion."[108] Doctor Trélat, a moderate republican of long standing and minister of labor, told the workshops' director, Emile Thomas, "it is a permanent center of insurrection, they must be closed."[109] Even Ledru-Rollin held that the workshops were a chronic menace to the Constituent Assembly, though he differed from his colleagues in demanding that new workshops be established in the provinces in order to absorb the unemployed who were encamped in the capital.[110] Tocqueville was genuinely surprised when George Sand warned him at a dinner party: "Try to persuade your friends, sir, not to drive the people into the streets by rousing or offending them, just as on my side I want to instill patience into our people; for if it comes to a fight, believe me, you will all perish."[111] He did not believe her prophecy.

It did come to a fight, but those who perished were mostly at the opposite end of the social spectrum from Tocqueville. The Executive Commission took the first step to close the workshops on 21 June. All bachelors under the age of twenty-five were barred from the workshops and ordered to enlist in the army. Within forty-eight hours Paris was the scene of that insurrection . . . which was the greatest and strangest that had ever taken place in our history, or perhaps in that of any nation: the greatest because for four days more than a hundred thousand men took part in it, and there were five generals killed; the strangest, because the insurgents were fighting without a battlecry, leaders, or flag.[112]

Now the Terror's shades had become flesh. The trauma, no longer confined to the past, erupted into the present. Yet the bare truth, however bloody, needed embellishment. The notables needed a new imagery of fear. Insurrectionists' banners, never produced, were said to carry the mottoes "Pillage and Rape" or "To the Victors, Plunder; to the Vanquished, Fire." Poisoned cigars and brandy laced with vitriol were reported to be the wares of traitorous shopkeepers. A guardsman was reported sawn in two by the woman who had captured him, though she was later acquitted unanimously. Twenty-two thousand ex-convicts were said to be behind the barricades, though *La Gazette des Tribunaux* reported later that only twenty-two such individuals were among the eleven thousand punished for the June Days.[113] Lord Normanby, the British ambassador, drew on newspapers ranging from the sensational *Constitutionnel* to the stodgy *Gazette des Tribunaux* to *Le Moniteur Officiel* (all of which repeated the same rumors) in describing the insurgents' "poisoned bullets" and the atrocities suffered by wounded or captured guardsmen.[114] The fearsome images of the "dangerous classes" of the forties fused with those of the September Massacres and the Terror. *La Réforme*, whose editors had joined Ledru-Rollin in opposing the insurrection, called this chorus of horror "The Conspiracy of Calumny." Its editorial of 1 July pointed out that not a single tale had been verified and that "these hideous stories" were invented by the "reactionary" press "for the benefit of its ideas and its statesmen, entombed in the barricades of February."[115]

Early in July, it became clear how well-founded was *La Réforme*'s concern to save the republic from the hysteria surrounding the June Days. While notables both in Paris and the provinces could rejoice in the defeat of "anarchy," they still saw democracy as a new threat to their interests and social standing. On 1 July, *Le Courrier de la Gironde* made clear its commitment to reverse the revolutionary verdict of 24 February: "We have never believed in the possibility of the Republic in a country as large and populous as our own."[116] Although the defeat of the June insurrection in

Paris was quickly followed by the disarming of the Lyon clubs, *Le Courrier de Lyon* saw safety only in some form of dictatorship: "Who is the savior, who will come to deliver us from agitation in the streets and civil war?"[117]

For a time General Eugène Cavaignac, surviving brother of the republican leader, seemed to fit the bill. He replaced the Executive Commission during the June fighting and was made prime minister by the assembly. Acting in concert with the monarchist groups in the assembly, which had already united to form the Comité de la rue de Poitiers, Cavaignac and his cabinet of moderate republicans took the path of outright reaction. A committee was appointed to investigate the events of 15 May and 23 June. Significantly, it was made up entirely of monarchists and its chairman was Odilon Barrot. Charges were trumped up against Louis Blanc and Marc Caussidière, a radical republican who had served as prefect of police since 24 February; and, although neither man had taken part in the insurrections, the mood of the assembly was so ominous that these two deputies fled to England. Ledru-Rollin himself was charged with complicity with the insurgents, but the "proofs" were so absurd and the accused radical so eloquent in his own defense that the matter was dropped. Even so, Cavaignac and Marrast seem to have hesitated in coming to his defense.[118]

Counterrevolution, which would now continue unabated until the coup d'état, was begun in earnest by three other actions of the cabinet and the assembly. The rue de Poitiers faction demanded that Hippolyte Carnot, a man of *Le National*, be replaced as minister of education. His ministry had just published a primer for the children of the new republic that, though it attacked socialist ideas, still taught that a democratic government had a responsibility to the old, the sick, and the unemployed. This son of the "Organizer of Victory" and a living reminder of the Committee of Public Safety was sacrificed by Cavaignac. Education had been clearly marked out by the nascent Party of Order as a weapon for the defense of social privilege.

The coalition formed by the Cavaignac republicans and the monarchists, cemented by Carnot's dismissal, now went on to limit substantially the right of association and freedom of the press. In a law passed by a vote of 629 to 100, *all* public and private meetings were subjected to government authorization and control. Non-political meetings required the consent of the mayor. Political organizations—the clubs—were barred from corresponding with each other and from acting together on a regional or national scale.

All meetings had to be held in public and the responsible officer of each group had to submit a written report of the proceedings to the police. Police agents could attend any political meeting and were not required to identify themselves. Secret societies were prohibited.[119]

This law on clubs also circumscribed freedom of speech. Discussion of "any proposal contrary to public order and morality"—a broad definition for a crime punishable by fine and imprisonment—was forbidden.[120] And, doubtless because of the important role that women have always played in the revolutionary crowd since 1789, they were expressly denied entry to political meetings. Certain of these regulations would be suspended during election campaigns: national electoral committees would be allowed to function temporarily, although meetings would still be open to police observation and speeches would still be subject to prosecution. Private political banquets, which were not supposed to take place with any regularity, were also exempted from certain regulations. The delicate treatment of banquets and electoral associations was only an expedient, however. When the Party of Order gained control of the cabinet, the moderate republicans found themselves hampered by their own repressive laws. As Seignobos observes, "The moderate republicans had forged this weapon to destroy socialism in Paris; the Party of Order would soon use it to fight republicanism in all of France."[121] This would occur immediately upon the election of Louis Napoleon as president and his appointment of the Barrot-Faucher-Falloux ministry.

The Cavaignac cabinet, through its spokesman Sénard, the minister of interior, went on to propose a new press law to replace the July Monarchy's system of controls, which had been swept away by the revolution. Until June, the absence of the old requirement of a deposit and of the stringent libel laws of the *juste milieu* had made possible the birth of a press free and cheap without precedent, not only in Paris, but in the departments as well. In the capital alone, more than 450 newspapers were started, though most of them survived only a few weeks.[122] Anything went. It is easy to imagine the shudder of pride and awakened possibility experienced by the Parisian workman, and the one of pure terror felt by the proper bourgeois, to see newspapers named *Le Père Duchesne* and *La Lanterne* hawked freely in the streets. It was certainly too much for the moderate republicans. During the June Days, Cavaignac had used his dictatorial powers to shut down eleven newspapers and to imprison their editors without trial.[123]

In the laws of 9 and 11 August 1848, the Second Republic reestablished the publishing controls that had existed under the Restoration and the July Monarchy. Money deposited as bond was required of all newspapers that dealt with political topics. Although the measure was presented as a liberalization of the 1835 press law (it did considerably lower the bond required), Parisian dailies were still forced to raise the large sum of 24,000 francs in order to publish. Provincial newspapers paid 6,000 francs. Numerous publications simply could not raise the money and ceased to appear once the law was passed. The most famous of these was Lamennais' *Le Peuple Constituant*, which closed with the famous headline: "*Silence au Pauvre.*"[124]

Two days later the assembly passed a revised seditious libel bill that simply changed the wording of the July Monarchy's law. It severely punished "offenses and attacks" on the republic, the assembly, the principle of private property, and the "rights of the family."[125]

Now that the republic had its press laws, the old machinery of administrative surveillance and enforcement was reinstated. Each newspaper had to name a director who was personally liable for all offenses charged against his publication. To ensure the enforcement of the libel laws, the director was required to deposit a personally signed copy of his newspaper at the nearest *parquet* and prefecture. The prefects and prosecutors, if they moved quickly enough, could impound an entire issue before it was sent out for sale or to subscribers. The director would be out of pocket for the printing costs whether or not he was subsequently convicted of an actual offense.[126] The cops-and-robbers game of the July Monarchy, played between the administration and the press, had been restored by the new republic. Editors, writers, and directors of republican newspapers (in the provinces they were often one and the same person) had to be prepared to be fined into personal bankruptcy and to spend months in jail.

Reflecting the social fear of the notables, Cavaignac and other men of *Le National* had thus turned republican legality against radicalism. It was in the same period—immediately following the June Days—that the government reestablished the prefectoral corps and demanded renewed zeal from its attorneys general.

Until 1848 only one group in France, the notables, possessed the power to pursue its interests and enact its beliefs about the "best" organization of state and society. With the fall of Louis Philippe other interests and ideologies challenged this monopoly: those of urban workers, the lower-middle class, and the peasantry of certain regions. These groups would unite in a struggle for their democratic and socialist ideals. They had developed their own radical world views during the July Monarchy, and after the February revolution—even after the June Days—they believed that they could win.

Against them stood the institutions and legal tradition that have embodied authoritarianism in France since Napoleon. The instruments of his political counterrevolution, the prefectoral system and the *procureurs-généraux*, would soon serve the social needs of the notables and the political ambitions of his nephew.

3 Career Patterns of the Prefects and *Procureurs-Généraux*

The Law-Enforcement Bureaucracies

Two ministries and their respective bureaucracies have usually been responsible for public order in France from the time of the Directory to the present: the Ministry of the Interior and the Ministry of Justice. Their hierarchies of authority and status, which extend from the offices of the ministry in Paris into the smallest commune, are the only police powers tolerated in the state: agents of the national government carry out law enforcement, and local authorities are formally subordinate to them. When the mayor of a commune or a justice of the peace issues an arrest warrant, he does so as the lowest official in a national bureaucracy. He is ultimately responsible to the two most important police agents in provincial France: the prefect who heads the administration of a department and the attorney general who represents the government in proceedings before a court of appeals and who supervises the state's attorneys in the lesser tribunals in half a dozen departments.

The basic territorial unit for the administration of law and order is, therefore, the department. The division of France into its eighty-three departments was decreed on 4 August 1789 and was defined in detail in the decree of 26 February 1790. The decree of 4 August was passed in order to establish the equality of French citizens regardless of their diverse regional affiliations. Originally, the department was meant to be the cornerstone of a decentralized political system. Each was to be administered by a locally elected council. Centralization, however, was reimposed under the Terror and institutionalized under the Directory and the Consulate. Thus the centripetal contraction of French governments, beginning with the earliest Capetian monarchs, continued during the era of the Great Revolution.[1]

The Constituent Assembly did not abolish France's ancient provinces (despite Taine's charge that the Revolution cut out departments with "geometric scissors").[2] The boundaries of the traditional regions were largely respected, but the provinces *were* subdivided into departments of roughly equal size—no boundary was to be more than a day's ride from the *chef-lieu*, the seat of the administration. Itself centralized, with authority concentrated in the *chef-lieu*, the department rules its constituent parts, the communes (and after the year VIII, the *arrondissement*), just as Paris came to regulate directly the affairs of the departments.

The Prefectoral System

Although the Constituent Assembly's legislation of a new map of France ("that great experiment in voluntary geography," according to a recent commentator) did much to subordinate regions and localities to the national government, it remained for the Directory and the Consulate to place the department at the base of an administrative pyramid with its apex at Paris.[3]

Originally, according to the law of 22 December 1789, the departments were to be governed by an elective council that met once a year and by a smaller "directory" chosen by this council to carry out daily business.[4] Under the Terror, this elective control was qualified by the appointment of *représentants en mission* armed with full emergency powers to suspend local administrations and run the department as agents of the central government.[5] Later, in the midst of the "federalist crisis" of 1793, the convention appointed permanent commissioners with the authority to override any departmental assembly.[6]

It remained for the Consulate to obliterate the principle of elective departmental administration and turn France into what Gabriel Hanotaux called *"métropolarchie."* The law of 17 February 1800 established the prefectoral corps and placed the affairs of each department in the hands of an appointee of the Interior Ministry. The terms of the law itself and a series of circulars to the first prefects clearly established that henceforth the department was subject to the central government's initiative. In introducing the law, Pierre-Louis Roederer sweepingly defined the prefect as the holder of all active power in his department.[7] Administration, to the drafters of the law, was an "art" that included "direction, impetus, surveillance, rectification."[8] In other words, the law would give "all power to the prefect" as long as he remained a faithful agent of the central government. According to a circular of 1800, only Paris could interpet laws and executive decrees. The prefect was denied this discretionary freedom: "The basic ideas must come from the center; it is from there that a uniform and common impetus must come."[9]

Bonaparte, the first consul, invested the prefect with the sovereignty of the national government and granted him a salary and status commensurate with such responsibility. The prefect was not, however, supposed to function as a proconsul or "small-scale emperor"; he was to be strictly an instrument of the executive power. Every major prefectoral function was carefully anticipated and outlined by an ever-growing body of laws, decrees, and circular instructions from Paris. The prefect was required to report regularly on conditions in his department and immediately inform the government of any new, unforeseen developments. Concerned primarily with the maintenance of law and order, he was also responsible for all state services in his department: from raising and inspecting the annual "class" of conscripts to ensuring the quality of roads and bridges to maintaining such social services as hospitals, orphanages, and schools. The prefect was appointed by the Interior Ministry and carried on most of his correspondence with its various bureaus; he was also the agent of any other ministry that called upon him to provide or oversee local services under its jurisdiction. The prefect was not to leave his department without the express approval of the government; furthermore, each year he was expected to make a tour of the entire department and submit a detailed survey of prevailing economic, social, and political conditions.[10]

From 1800 to the present, prefects have had no assured tenure in office. Not until 1945 were any conditions set forth in law, other than a minimum age of twenty-five, for entry into the prefectoral corps. Thus the government has had an entirely free hand in the selection of its agents. Similarly, promotion in the prefectoral corps has been irregular. The first actual classification of prefectoral ranks (based on the importance of individual departments) did not occur until after the coup of 1851.[11] Until then, salary was related to the cost of living in a particular *chef-lieu*.[12] Prefects have rarely been natives of the department they administer.

Ultimate responsibility for carrying out government policy in his department was the prefect's alone, until very recently. An elected departmental council has existed since 1830, but its influence was strictly advisory until 1946.[13] The prefect has carried out his duties with the aid of his direct subordinates: the councilors and secretaries in the prefecture, and the subprefects who administer *arrondissements* other than the one where the *chef-lieu* is located. French mayors have also been subordinated to the administrative hierarchy. They must carry out prefectoral decrees and instructions and can be suspended or revoked by the prefect.

The prefectoral system has survived virtually unchanged to the present day because it has served as the pliable and efficient instrument of every French regime. Regimented by a strict bureaucratic discipline, limited in their discretion by a whole system of instructions and orders emanating from Paris,

> The prefects thus became, since the empire, faithful delegates, acting with promptness along lines of orientation decided by the political teams in place in Paris; for this reason, the institution was easily passed around among regimes based on the most opposing principles.[14]

Police power, in the active and regulatory French definition of the term, is largely the province of the prefect. But in carrying out his comprehensive duties, the prefect must work closely with other agents of order: the men who prosecute lawbreakers once they have been brought into court.

The Attorneys General

The present system of courts and state's attorneys in France dates from the same year as the foundation of the prefectoral corps: the year VIII, or 1800. In a sweeping change, the first consul and his advisers simply made every magistrate in France a civil servant appointed by the executive branch of the government. In a small way, the Directory anticipated Napoleon by setting up a system of departmental tribunals and by appointing a considerable number of judges, but Bonaparte's reforms established the judiciary as an appointive arm of the state on a much broader scale and with much more permanent results.[15]

Under the Ancien Régime, judicial posts had the same legal status as real estate: they were personal property. A position in the magistracy could be purchased, leased, passed on to one's heirs, or sold. Such offices, which were taxed just as land was, often carried with them the guarantee that the incumbent would be ennobled after twenty years and that the title (as well as the office) would then pass into his family. This prerevolutionary system of property-in-office was justified as a guarantee of the magistrate's independence of the crown. Bonaparte continued this principle of independence, but he put it on a very different foundation. From the constitution of the year VIII until the present time, judges, at least in principle, have become independent of the government upon their appointment to the bench. Despite certain wholesale purges that followed changes of regime, judges have enjoyed permanent tenure in office. Sovereign in his court, the French judge has generally been left free from the instructions and orders of the ministries. Of course, since each step in the judicial hierarchy from the humble court of first instance to the Cour de cassation is reached by ministerial appointment, an ambitious magistrate remains dependent upon the good graces of the minister in power.

The prosecutor, however, is required to act as an agent of the minister of justice and can be removed from his post at any time. As the government's representative in court, the prosecutor is part of the law-enforcement (police) apparatus of the state. Like the prefect, the *procureur-général* is a bureaucrat subject to the direct control of the central government.

In fact, in apprehending lawbreakers the prosecutor and the prefect share an overlapping jurisdiction, which requires that they work together closely. Napoleon's *Code d'instruction criminelle* (1808) made them both officers of the *police judiciaire* charged with the investigation of crimes and the issuance of arrest warrants.[16] As the practice had evolved by the mid-nineteenth century, criminal investigations generally were carried out jointly by a police officer responsible to the prefect and by a *juge d'instruction* appointed by the prosecutor. It was the task of a *juge d'instruction*, usually a young magistrate at the beginning of his judicial career, to act both as a detective and as a one-man grand jury in deciding whether a case in fact exists against an individual. After preparing a preliminary indictment, he handed the case over to a prosecutor for presentation in court.

The prosecutors formed a hierarchy capped by the *procureur-général* attached to each court of appeals. At the time of the Second Republic twenty-seven such appellate tribunals existed in France, including one in Algiers.[17] The attorney general who headed the appellate *parquet* (a kind of district attorney's office) at each of these courts was responsible for every criminal investigation and prosecution before every court in a group of departments. Like the prefect, the *procureur-général* took his orders directly from his minister in Paris and reported regularly to the Justice Ministry on conditions relative to public order in his circumscription. He carried out his responsibilities through a hierarchy of subordinates, some of whom, like his chief assistant (the first advocate general) and his own staff of *substituts*, worked under the attorney general's personal supervision at the court of appeals itself. Other subordinates, attached to tribunals at the level of the *arrondissement* or department, acted on his written instructions and reported to the appellate *parquet* on local developments requiring the attention of the attorney general.[18]

The prefect was legally responsible for the broad range of administrative activity bearing on the "general good order of society." The attorney general, however, was limited to acting after an actual breakdown of public order. But these two highest provincial bureaucrats of the Interior and Justice ministries dealt with each other as equals. Through their respective ministers, prefects and *procureurs-généraux* commented on each other's performance. Each could seriously affect the career of the other by criticism or commendation, which was automatically passed to the ministry concerned. Both independently conveyed to Paris a wide array of social, political, and economic information. Together they would be the frontline soldiers of the sociopolitical elite of mid-nineteenth-century France when it came under attack after the revolution of 1848.

The Prefectoral Corps Under the Second Republic

One of the first acts of the Provisional Government in February and early March of 1848 was the abolition of the prefectoral system. The moderate and radical republicans who suddenly found themselves in charge of France not only took the obvious step of dismissing Guizot's administrators, but also dismantled the system in which these men had made their careers. On 8 March 1848 a decree abolished the prefectoral corps as it had existed since 1800.[19]

The same measure also envisioned the establishment of a national school of administration, a new *grande école* on the order of the Ecole Polytechnique.[20] A month later the school was founded by another decree and, at first, attached to the *Collége de France*. More than two hundred students began the three-year curriculum of history, economics, statistics, accounting, and law.[21] Competitive

examinations, scholarships, and a uniform curriculum were to replace the old system of administrative recruitment based on personal influence, family connections, and membership in the notability of the *juste milieu*. Important positions in the bureaucracy
would now be accessible to enterprising sons of the middle and
lower-middle classes. Unfortunately for the future of republicanism
in the Second Republic, the Ecole d'administration was suppressed
by the Legislative Assembly in November 1849. The conservatives
who dominated this legislature were merely concluding the restoration of the notables to the prefectoral corps. France would have
to wait almost a century to get its Ecole nationale d'administration,
founded in 1945.

The Provisional Government did not, however, even temporarily
do away with administrative centralization. The republicans of
February were well aware that France had accepted the new revolutionary judgment of Paris only in its negative sense: the overthrow of the July Monarchy. Republicanism, universal suffrage,
and social reform remained beyond the ken of most Frenchmen.
Except for the familiar left-wing enclaves of Paris, Lyon, and certain other cities in the north and east, the republican faith had to
be taught to a peasantry that traditionally deferred, in all political
matters, to local notables. The new government faced the difficult
problem of establishing and staffing a temporary administration
that could spread republicanism to the countryside before the April
1848 elections for a Constituent Assembly.

The Provisional Government was free, for a short time, to replace
the prefects with commissioners (one or often two or three to each
department). They were to prepare and administer the first French
elections ever held on the basis of universal manhood suffrage.
The list of commissioners was published on 10 March, two days
after the first decree calling for a national school of administration.[22]

The near simultaneity of these two decrees indicates the serious
personnel problem that faced the apparently victorious leaders of
the Second Republic. There simply were not enough republicans
in France with the requisite political and administrative experience
to do the challenging and difficult job assigned to the new commissioners. Although the majority of the commissioners appointed
in March were republicans of the "day before," a significant number were members of the dynastic opposition and had rallied to
the Provisional Government only after the revolution had been
victorious in Paris:

All the appointees, with the single exception of Emmanuel Arago . . . were natives of the district to which they were sent. . . . Of the eighty on whom information can be found, 110 were actually appointed, . . . fourteen belonged to the Dynastic Left, twenty-two were moderates like Lamartine, twenty-two belonged to the *National* group, and only twenty-two followed the banner of the *Réforme*.[23]

Soon after these temporary administrators had been appointed, Ledru-Rollin, who was acting as minister of interior, dispatched two circulars outlining their mission. Both documents were sent out just as most of the commissioners learned of their designations. One, dated 8 March 1848, ordered them to appoint only veteran republicans, *"hommes de la veille, pas du lendemain"* (men of the day before the revolution, not those of the day after) to posts in the civil service.[24] The circular of 12 March went even further in the direction of an all-out effort to republicanize the country. Ledru-Rollin answered the queries of the fainthearted, republican and liberal alike:

What are your powers? THEY ARE UNLIMITED. Agents of a revolutionary authority you are also revolutionary. The victory of the people has imposed on you the duty of proclaiming, of consolidating its work. . . . The education of the country is not completed. It is for you to guide it. . . . Support only those candidates who appear to present the best guarantee of republican opinion. . . . Let election day be a triumph for the revolution.[25]

Yet these exhortations did not steel the commissioners to their task. The men of the dynastic left, and even some of the moderate republicans, proved too timid or simply lacked the experience, temperament, or conviction to master their local opponents. Within a week of their appointment, Ledru-Rollin named a new group of commissioners to aid the original group in some departments and also sent out a team of commissioners general to oversee the spread of republicanism in whole groups of departments. Drawn largely from the radical republican circle of *La Réforme*, these were old friends who could be trusted to carry out the policies proclaimed in the March circulars.[26]

The strongly partisan orders issued from Paris coupled with the appointment of left-wing, even socialist, "proconsuls" stirred up a hornet's nest of protest from frightened provincial notables. The local elites, made up of legitimists and Orleanists, could not help but be reminded of the Terror's *représentants en mission*. Hostile rather than intimidated, they often united to resist the newly arrived radical commissioners and commissioners general. The historian of Bordeaux under the Second Republic describes the local result of Ledru-Rollin's attempt to stiffen the republicanism of the temporary administrators. The first commissioner had attempted to curry favor with the city's Orleanist commercial bourgeoisie.[27] Commissioner General Latrade was dispatched to remedy this softness. A man of *La Réforme*, he was seen by the Bordelais elite as a firebreather and was literally run out of town by a crowd of well-dressed young men that invaded the prefecture on 20 March 1848.[28]

The commissioners and commissioners general of Ledru-Rollin had a very short time to carry out the orders in the March circulars. Many of them successfully presented themselves for election to the assembly, but the republicans of the "day before" still failed to win a majority.[29] The hope that France would elect only proven republicans within a few weeks of the fall of the July Monarchy was shown to be a romantic dream.

When the Constituent Assembly convened on 4 May 1848, the administrative revolution of 1848 had run its course. Within a few days Ledru-Rollin was removed from the Interior Ministry and replaced by a republican of a more moderate temper. (He remained, however, a member of the Executive Commission at the insistence of Lamartine.) Between 20 May and 8 June—only five days after the *clubiste* invasion of the assembly and the abortive proclamation of a new revolutionary government by Huber—the prefectoral system was reestablished and new prefects sent to every department.[30] The renaissance of the prefect never seems to have been discussed on the floor of the Constituent Assembly or in the Executive Commission itself.[31] It was the only administrative system that had a regular basis in law, and the controversial nature of the commissioners and commissioners general made their retention in many departments impossible, even as a temporary measure. These apostles of republicanism had failed to carry out an impossible task. The commissarial experiment was a casualty of both the elections and the bizarre uprising of 15 May.

The conservative, nonrepublican majority of the Constituent Assembly was not yet confident or unified enough to assume executive control. Surrounded by revolutionary Paris, it contented itself with supporting a government of moderate republicans. Men of *Le National*, like the new interior minister, Antoine Sénard, were honest democrats, but they believed that the revolution had been completed with the establishment of universal manhood suffrage. The socialist demands of the Parisian clubs and the social re-formism of Louis Blanc and Ledru-Rollin were too radical for these purely political democrats. The conservative majority of the as-sembly could safely assume that republicans of this stamp could be counted upon to protect the social system against the radicals.

Sénard, and his short-term predecessor Adrien Récurt, did at-tempt an innovation in the selection of prefectoral personnel. The new corps of administrators was a half-and-half mixture of inex-perienced republicans, largely professional men who had been connected with *Le National*, and veteran subprefects, *conseillers*, and secretaries general of the Orleanist regime who had become *"républicains du lendemain."*[32] Only one of the new appointees had been a prefect at the time of the revolution.[33] This change in the administrative elite lasted only six months. By January of 1849 only thirty members (fewer than ⅜) of the first prefectoral corps of the Second Republic still would be in service.[34] From that time forward the prefects reflected the paradoxical character of the Second Re-public: a republic without republicans.

During the presidency of Louis Napoleon, there were two whole-sale purges of prefects. Within a year of his inauguration, the new men appointed in 1848 were replaced by career bureaucrats who had made a profession of administration under the July Monarchy and, in some cases, the Restoration. In the months just before the coup of 1851 this group was itself purified of those who could not be trusted to support the president against the Legislative Assem-bly.

Prefectoral Careers in the Sample Departments

From Louis Napoleon's inauguration as president to the night of the coup d'état, the seven departments in our sample were the responsibility, at different times, of twenty-two prefects. I have been unable to find the dossier of only one of these men: Cazavan, prefect (apparently in title only) of Vendée for the few weeks from just before the presidential election until his dismissal on 2 January 1849.[35] The departments themselves represent a broad range of social and political conditions and of status within the hierarchy of prefectoral assignments (see Appendix 1 for details). The twenty careers open to discussion (one prefect in the sample administered first Jura, then Rhône) are quite sufficient for an analysis of the major trends in the recruitment, promotion, or dismissal of prefects for the three-year period with which this study is concerned (see the table of personal and career data in Appendix 1).

Following the inauguration of Louis Napoleon, the first prefectoral purge resulted in the dismissal of three moderate republicans: Armand-Alexis Coquet in Allier, Paul-Emile Wissocq in Charente-Inférieure, and Colonel Ambert in Rhône. Coquet and Wissocq fell in November of 1849.[36] Even the intervention of the powerful conservative deputy Drouyn de Lhuys could not save Wissocq. In a letter to the minister, written a few months before the dismissal, Drouyn de Lhuys praised Wissocq's moderation and commitment to order.[37] But Charente-Inférieure was too important a Bonapartist stronghold to be left in the hands of any republican, however mild he may have been. Ambert was relieved of his duties at Lyon even earlier—only three weeks after the inauguration.

All three owed their positions as prefects to the coterie of *Le National*. Coquet had been the private secretary (*chef de cabinet*) of two public works ministers under the Provisional Government and the Executive Commission.[38] The most influential of the two, Alexandre Marie, recommended Coquet for a "small prefecture," and two days later his former assistant was sent out to Allier.[39] Wissocq, in a letter asking for a prefectoral assignment, emphasized his long-standing membership in republican secret societies.[40] He had been a friend of both the Cavaignac brothers and of Garnier-Pagès the elder since the early days of Aide-toi le ciel t'aidera.[41] In the first two years of the July Monarchy, Wissocq was active in La Société des droits de l'homme. At that time, he worked with Armand Marrast, later editor of *Le National* and the mayor of Paris under the Provisional Government.[42] Ambert, the republic's first prefect of the important department of Rhône, had been a very close friend of a previous editor of *Le National*, Armand Carrel. His otherwise skimpy dossier bears the notation that Ambert had been Carrel's second in his fatal duel with Emile de Girardin, founder of *La Presse*.[43]

Coquet, Wissocq, and Ambert had pursued professional careers in Paris. Both Coquet and Ambert were members of the Paris bar.[44] Wissocq, a *polytechnicien*, had worked for fourteen years as an engineer at the Naval Ministry before retiring to his properties in the Pas-de-Calais.[45] Of the three, it is safe to assume that only Wissocq paid enough of the right kind of taxes to have had the right to vote under the July Monarchy. He is the only one who described himself as a landed proprietor, and his income was probably sufficient to meet the censitary requirement for the ballot.[46]

In comparison with the prefects who succeeded them, these republicans of the "day before" were men of modest means. Coquet reported a yearly income of 2,000 francs; Wissocq disclosed an annual revenue of 3,000 francs; Ambert's dossier describes him as "sans fortune."[47] The average private income of the bureaucrats who were kept on or appointed as administrators of our group of seven departments after 1848, but before the coup, was 18,500 francs per year.[48] This figure is more than six times greater than the income of Wissocq, the richest republican who was dismissed.

Of those first prefects of the republic in our sample whose careers survived the purge of 1849, only one had been a republican before the revolution: François-Victor-Adolphe de Chanal, the first prefect of Gard. A graduate of the Ecole Polytechnique, Chanal participated in the street fighting of July 1830 and was imprisoned for a few months for his role in the abortive republican insurrection of 1833.[49] He then spent fifteen years as an artillery officer in the French army.[50] In 1848 Ledru-Rollin sent him as commissioner to Hautes-Alpes, and he was one of these temporary officials of the Provisional Government to be named a prefect in the summer of 1848.[51] After less than a year in Gard, he was sent to the prefecture of Bas-Rhin at a time when a revolution had broken out across the border in Baden.[52]

His career as a favored prefect ended temporarily when he was removed from his post at Strasbourg in May 1850. The reasons for his dismissal were quite grave. According to a memorandum of the Ministry of Interior, Chanal had supported the republican list of candidates in a by-election for deputies to the Legislative Assembly.[53] Several members of the deputation of Bas-Rhin had been convicted of treason for their role in the quasi insurrection of 13 June 1849. The new list included such important radical leaders as Flocon and Martin (de Strasbourg), men who had voted for the impeachment of Louis Napoleon because of the Roman expedition of 1849. The republicans won the election, something probably beyond the control of any prefect in then-radical Bas-Rhin. Instead of remaining a republican casualty of the ministry's vigilant hunt for subversives, Chanal was appointed prefect of Ain ten months later.[54]

The explanation for Chanal's charmed life is that although he was a sincere republican, his family and his friendships lay in the camp of Louis Napoleon Bonaparte. When he was born in 1811, the three witnesses to his certificate were his father, a senior official in the administration of the emperor's household; his maternal granduncle, a division chief at the Naval Ministry; and his uncle, an inspector in the imperial household.[55] The notation of Chanal's temporary dismissal from the prefectoral corps in 1850 referred to his reputation for "profound loyalty" to the prince-president until the election of the red list in his department.[56] Later, when Chanal protested the coup d'état, he was not punished. A letter from Prince Napoleon (the emperor's cousin) to the minister of interior, dated 17 January 1870, shows that Napoleon III reinstated this maverick as a colonel in the army, placed him in command of the artillery school at La Rochelle, and sent him on a personal mission to the United States during the Civil War.[57] According to Prince Napoleon, the emperor knew Chanal personally and was "benevolently inclined" toward him.[58]

Chanal differed from the other republican prefects in the sample in one other important respect. His annual income amounted to 6,000 francs, double that of Wissocq and triple Coquet's.[59] He was almost certainly a member of the electoral elite of the July Monarchy.

Thus the only prefect who was a "republican of the day before" and survived the purification of the corps that took place in 1849 owed his position to friendships with the Bonaparte family. Chanal was reappointed as a prefect at the time in 1851 when even conservatives of doubtful loyalty to Louis Napoleon were dismissed. The men of the Elysée must have understood that Chanal's attachment to the Bonapartes and his demonstrated commitment to the maintenance of public order would prevent him from taking any overt action against the president once the coup had been announced.

Two other prefects appointed in 1848 for whom we have personal dossiers also kept their jobs after 1849: Baron Neveux (Gironde) and Bonaventure Pagès (Jura). Far from being republicans of the "day before," these men had long been members of the prefectoral corps under the previous regime. Their careers under the July Monarchy, however, were not models of success. The son of a small-town postmaster, Neveux was a parvenu who entered the political class by marriage rather than by birth. It took him seven years to win powerful enough support to be placed at the lowest echelon of the prefectoral corps: secretary general. His first letter of application was sent to Casimir Périer in 1831, but Neveux's lack of wealth and connections kept him waiting until 1838.[60] He was successful only after he had married into a family with a modicum of social standing and political influence. His father-in-law, who had been a colonel in the Imperial Guard, was not himself powerful enough to place Neveux in the Ministry of Interior. But in 1837 this ex-artillerist began "a veritable rolling barrage of solicitation and recommendations" that mobilized his old superior officers and won Neveux a job in 1838.[61] In the end it took the recommendations of a lieutenant general, a marshal of France, and two deputies to win him an extremely modest post.[62]

Neveux spent ten years, first as a secretary general and later as a subprefect, without much hope of an appointment as prefect in his own right. As soon as the news of the February revolution reached his subprefecture at Vitry, Neveux offered his services to the new republic.[63] According to Neveux's biographer, he placed himself at the disposal of Ledru-Rollin out of pure opportunism.[64] Neveux saw the revolution as a means to win the advancement denied him under the old regime. The subprefect who in 1843 had begged the minister of justice to permit him to bear the title of his deceased father-in-law, the Napoleonic Baron Greiner, wrote to Ledru-Rollin five years later: "Citizen minister, I have the honor of declaring to you that I support the Provisional Government which presides over the destinies of France."[65] In May 1848 he was made a subcommissioner, and in July, with the support of the conservative deputies from Gironde, Neveux was named to the important prefecture at Bordeaux. His timing had been impeccable. A move to the left in May and back to the right after the election of the Constituent Assembly had earned Neveux not only a long-coveted prefectoral assignment, but one at a major city.

Unlike Neveux, Pagès was most certainly one of the most important notables of his native department, Pyrénées-Orientales, for he was a proprietor with revenues of 25,000 francs per year. Although a year younger than Neveux, his rise in the prefectoral corps was rapid. Pagès was recommended to Casimir Périer in 1830 by the new prefect of his home department and by all of its deputies to the chamber.[66] After entering the administration in 1831, the same year he submitted his letter of application, Pagès served eight years as a subprefect.

In 1839, at the age of thirty-three, he was appointed prefect of

Haute-Loire, but on 12 June 1840 *La Presse* criticized his appointment as arrant nepotism. His brother was a *maître des requêtes* at the time, and his brother-in-law was a deputy.[67] Finally, in 1841, he moved to the prefecture of Lozère, and there his promising career under the July Monarchy ended abruptly. Pagès refused to support a budgetary maneuver made by one of the deputies from Lozère that amounted to a payoff to certain "influential electors."[68] In 1843 he was dismissed and never reassigned to another post until Louis Philippe was overthrown.

Secure in his own future, Pagès waited until the reaction that came in the wake of the June Days before applying for reinstatement as a prefect. His letter of 20 October 1848 made no pretense of republicanism. Pagès merely outlined the reasons for his dismissal and presented himself as an honest man who had been victimized by the corrupt regime of Louis Philippe.[69] Recommended in a letter signed by several deputies from various departments (all of them conservatives), Pagès was named prefect of Jura within a month of his application. In 1849 he was transferred to Côte d'Or, and in 1851 he was sent to Ille-et-Vilaine.[70]

Like the moderate republicans who owed their brief administrative careers to the men around *Le National* and like Chanal, who survived professionally because his republicanism was offset by the friendship of the Bonapartes, Neveux and Pagès were also high-status civil servants by virtue of their personal connections. But the power group with which these latter two were linked was fundamentally different from the relatively new political forces represented either by the coterie of Louis Napoleon or by the circle of *Le National*. Neveux and Pagès belonged to the ruling class of the censitary regime, which the revolution of 1848 supposedly had overthrown. However unsuccessful their careers had been under the July Monarchy, they were members in good standing of the Orleanist establishment.

If Neveux and Pagès were relatively quick to serve the republic it was because the revolution gave them an opportunity to turn over a new leaf in their administrative careers. They remained loyal to the world of the notables, which, in their separate ways, both men inhabited. And each of them survived the first purge of the prefectoral corps in 1849 because each could at least be counted upon to preserve the social order.

At the time of the Executive Commission and during the government of General Cavaignac, the moderate republicans succeeded in filling about half the prefectures of France with their own people. Bonaparte, in early 1849, had no such nascent political party at his command. He possessed only the small circle of supporters who had participated in his adventures of 1836 and 1840. Louis Napoleon could not even count on the support of the nobility created by his uncle, which had been one of the main props of the July Monarchy.

His name and its legend had won Louis Napoleon the presidency. But actually to govern and eventually to monopolize power, the president needed first the support and then the acquiescence of the Party of Order, which dominated the Legislative Assembly. This coalition of conservatives was made up largely of Orleanists and legitimists, who were held together only by their fear of social change. From these groups Louis Napoleon had to recruit a collection of men (never an actual party, even by the definition of the times) and make them an instrument that guaranteed the permanence of his power.

In 1849 the administrative elite of the new republic was replaced by prefectoral veterans of the old regime. The bureaucracy charged with the maintenance of public order now reflected the counterrevolution that had become safely ensconced in the Legislative Assembly. A president who sought an imperial restoration appointed Orleanists to administer the republic. From their ranks, and from those of other state bureaucracies, including the army, he would gather his own political force.

The new prefects appointed to our sample of departments under Bonaparte's presidency were, in fact, old boys of the July Monarchy. Members of the notability, firm defenders of the social and political hierarchy of the old regime, most of these men refused to rally to the republic and had simply retired until they were again called upon to defend a conservative regime: the "republic without republicans." I have been able to study the dossiers of eleven prefects assigned to our departments between Louis Napoleon's inauguration and the reshufflings and dismissals that immediately preceded the coup. Ten of them had been prefects or subprefects before 1848 and had an average private income of 15,000 francs per year. They were clearly notables in their own right. Those who had recommended them for government service under the old regime occupied the apex of power and status within the oligarchy. Their dossiers abound with letters of recommendation from important state functionaries, deputies, generals, and peers of France. Their average age was forty-eight.

The eleventh, Gabriel-Léonce Cortois, vicomte de Charnailles, who became a prefect only in 1851, had entered the service of the Ministry of Interior for the first time (as a subprefect) in August 1848 without any republican *"profession de foi."* His uncle was the chairman of the conservative Réunion de la rue de Poitiers.[71]

Let us first look at the men who replaced the moderate republicans of 1848. Wissocq turned over the prefecture of Charente-Inférieure to Charles-Jean Brian in November 1849. Brian, who had an annual income of 20,000 francs, had entered the corps in 1837.[72] He was recommended by Vice Admiral Amauret, minister of the navy and colonies, and by the prefect of Seine-Inférieure, Baron Dupont-Delporte, peer of France.[73] Brian had been a prefect for seven years before the coming of the revolution in 1848.[74]

Coquet was replaced at the same time as Wissocq. His successor, Charlemagne-Emile de Maupas, now began a career as a strong prefect that would earn him the prefecture of police in 1851 and a central role in the plotting of the coup d'état. Maupas entered the Ministry of Interior in 1840, probably on the recommendation of his father, an important landowner in the department of Aube.[75] Maupas reported an income of 25,000 francs in 1851, but he noted on his personnel form that his revenues would triple when his wife came into her inheritance.[76] In February 1848, Maupas was the subprefect at Beaune. Like Neveux, Maupas immediately placed himself at the disposal of the Provisional Government. After proclaiming the republic in his *arrondissement*, Maupas wrote to Ledru-Rollin: "Permit me . . . to add here my own loyal and frank adherence to all the others which I have the honor to present to you and to offer you the expression of my zeal and sincere devotion to the principles which the revolution has caused to triumph."[77] Maupas' efforts to remain in the prefectoral corps failed. Ledru-Rollin dismissed him. When he finally did become a prefect, Maupas distinguished himself by the zeal with which he hunted down republicans.

He owed his return to office, first as subprefect at Boulogne in January 1849 and then as prefect of Allier in December of the same year, to the personal support of the president.[78] He had been introduced to Louis Napoleon during the presidential campaign by a mutual friend, Count Joachim Clary, younger brother of Désirée.[79] Maupas had not only become a prefect at the age of thirty-one; he had entered the Bonapartist inner circle.[80]

In January 1849 the republican Ambert handed over the prefecture of Lyon to a pillar of the old regime: Denis-Victor Tourangin.

Like Ambert, Tourangin had also been a journalist and lawyer, until a revolution catapulted him into the prefectoral corps. But Tourangin, a friend of Guizot and Count de Gasparin, was a man of 1830 and a man of resistance. Guizot appointed him prefect of Sarthe directly after the July Revolution and Gasparin, perhaps Guizot's closest friend and political associate, recommended Tourangin's promotion to the important assignment of Doubs (Besançon) in 1833.[81] Prefect of Doubs until the 1848 revolution forced his resignation, Tourangin was recalled to Lyon by Léon Faucher in 1849 "to lend the government the support of your name, your experience and your enlightenment."[82] The new prefect of Rhône was sixty-one years old and going blind, but Faucher and his successor at the Ministry of Interior, Jules Dufaure, begged him to stay on and assure order in Lyon through the legislative elections of 1849 and the formation of a new ministry.[83] Tourangin retired just before the outbreak of the June 1849 troubles in Lyon and was later rewarded by being made a senator of the empire.[84]

The importance of Rhône and particularly of the city of Lyon to the public peace of France meant that those sent to administer it during the presidency of Louis Napoleon were uniformly men of very high stature in the prefectoral corps. Tourangin's replacement was Hugues-Iéna Darcy, a man whose administrative career also began in 1830. Promoted to prefect in 1839, he had been in charge of the difficult department of Gard for five years, until he was ousted during the revolution of 1848.[85] In January 1849 Darcy was reinstated in the prefectoral corps and assigned to the important department of Moselle. He was transferred to Lyon in June. A notation in his dossier written just before his appointment to this troubled jurisdiction describes Darcy as one of the "two or three prefects of the greatest ability."[86] In December 1849 Darcy left Lyon to become undersecretary of state at the Interior Ministry under Ferdinand Barrot and succeeding ministers. His income is listed in his dossier as varying between 12,000 and 15,000 francs yearly.[87]

Darcy's successor, and the man who would oversee the department of Rhône for the two years before the coup, enjoyed the additional status of being the government's special commissioner for the entire sixth military district. Martial law had been proclaimed for the entire region surrounding Lyon after the June 1849 insurrection. Charles-Aristide de La Coste du Vivier a peer of France under the July Monarchy, was appointed to these extra-departmental responsibilities at the same time he took up the duties of prefect of Rhône in December 1849. The government clearly counted upon La Coste's long experience and his prestige within the prefectoral corps to help him coordinate the civil and military authorities.

The son of a Napoleonic cavalry general, La Coste entered the prefectoral corps for the first time in 1816. After six years, in which he had risen from secretary general to subprefect, he was removed from the service in 1822, just when the ultraroyalists were reasserting their control over the government of Louis XVIII.[88] Despite the pleas of Thouvenel, deputy for Meurthe, La Coste was not reinstated until after the glorious days of July 1830.[89] Since no specific reasons for his dismissal are given in his file, it seems that La Coste's imperial pedigree kept him unemployed until the ultras and their absolutist king were overthrown.

La Coste became a prefect a month after the July Revolution. He was prefect of Bouches-du-Rhône (Marseille), a peer of France, and a *conseiller d'état* in February 1848.[90] Almost two years later he was brought out of enforced retirement and, by the particular recommendation of the council of ministers, appointed to Rhône, a position perhaps even more important, due to its regional powers, than that of the prefect of police in Paris.[91] This dean of the prefectoral corps was the Orleanist functionary par excellence. With a personal revenue of 25,000 francs, La Coste was not only a notable by virtue of his considerable wealth, but a well-rewarded member of the active political class of the old regime.[92] His appointment as the civilian counterpart of General de Castellane, a soldier who had made his career under the July Monarchy and the commander of the sixth military district (Lyon), amounted to an administrative restoration of Orleanism in one of the most republican regions of France.

The Vendée was a different kind of trouble spot, one which required a specialist in local affairs to assure harmony between the legitimist and Orleanist factions of the Party of Order. Casimir Bonnin, who replaced the very short-term republican prefect Cazavan on 2 January 1849, had been subprefect of the department's *arrondissement* of Fontenay for fourteen years. Bonnin was one of only ten subprefects of the July Monarchy to remain in office after the February 1848 revolution.[93] This involved no sudden access of republican fervor in a veteran Orleanist bureaucrat, but rather a continuation of the department's administration, at the insistence of local notables, to insure public order and to provide "honest brokerage" between the conservative factions. The city council, mayor, and National Guard officers of Fontenay wrote Ledru-Rollin on 8 March requesting that Bonnin be kept at his post. Local legitimists pointed out that their subprefect had never lent himself to Guizot's electoral maneuvers and had "always protected the complete freedom of voting."[94] Both Orleanists and legitimists lauded Bonnin's commitment to order as evidenced by his firmness in putting down local grain disturbances in 1847 and by his arrest of twenty-two peasants after the February revolution for invading private property and claiming it as common pasture.[95]

Vendée was clearly seen as a special department, certainly as one in which republicanism was not at issue, given that Bonnin's immediate superior since 1845, Prosper Gauja, remained as administrator of Vendée throughout March 1848 and returned as Cavaignac's prefect from June through November of the same year. Gauja was thus the only prefect of the July Monarchy to be named a commissioner of the Provisional Government.[96]

After the election of Louis Napoleon, Bonnin, like Gauja, benefited from his role as an "area specialist." When Gauja, with his fourteen years prefectoral experience in the legitimist west, was promoted to the important prefecture of Loire-Inférieure (Nantes), Bonnin's years as subprefect made him Faucher's obvious choice for the prefecture at Napoléon-Vendée.[97] By far the least wealthy of the prefects in our sample appointed after January 1849, Bonnin had a yearly income of 3,500 francs and "only one domestic servant."[98] He was nonetheless connected by friends and family to the July Monarchy's elite. Under the Restoration, Bonnin had been private secretary to Viscount de Beaumont, a major figure in the opposition to Charles X and, after the 1830 revolution, an important member of both the prefectoral corps and the Chamber of Deputies. Beaumont took his secretary with him to the prefecture of Basses-Pyrénées in 1830 and, four yars later, saw that Bonnin was promoted to subprefect in the Vendée.[99] In January 1849 Bonnin enjoyed not only the support of the entire parliamentary delegation from Vendée, but also that of his brother, a wealthy notary and conservative deputy from Vienne.[100] He would remain prefect of Vendée until September 1851.

The promotion of Pagès from Jura to the more important prefecture of Côte d'Or (Dijon) opened the way for the return of another July Monarchy prefect to active service: Charles-Jean Besson. Prefect of Ain from 1846 until the February revolution, Besson was a man of July 1830 in every way. His father had been a veteran bureaucrat of the empire, rising from paymaster to the Grand Army during the Russian campaign to a series of positions in the Administration of Conquered Territories. Kept on for a while as a subprefect during the Restoration, Besson's father paid for his background when the resurgent ultras fired him in 1822. His revenge came in the wake of the 1830 revolution. Guizot appointed the senior Besson as prefect of Charente a few days after the revolution.[101] His father's services and honors certainly helped the younger Besson's administrative career, which advanced from relatively modest posts during the thirties to the important position of secretary general of Rhône in 1840 to his own prefecture in 1846.[102]

Charles-Jean Besson won his own spurs by joining his fellow students of the Ecole Polytechnique on the barricades of the 1830 revolution and winning the July medal for his bravery.[103] He entered the Interior Ministry with the additional, and powerful, support of General Fabvier, minister without portfolio in the first cabinet of the July Monarchy and head of the Commission de Récompenses nationales for the heroes of the revolution. In 1846 he was supported for a prefecture by Hippolyte-Paul Jayr, prefect of Rhône and by Adrien-Marie Devienne, presiding judge of the civil tribunal of Lyon and a key member of Rhône's delegation to the Chamber of Deputies.[104] Devienne is also a member of our sample of bureaucrats; he would serve as attorney general at Bordeaux during the Second Republic.

Besson's rise in the prefectoral crops accelerated under the presidency of Louis Napoleon. He left Jura in the fall of 1849 for a series of increasingly important assignments: Maine-et-Loire (Angers) in 1849, Haute-Garonne (Toulouse) in 1850, and Nord (Lille) in 1851.[105] His replacement as prefect of Jura, Baron Louis-Charles de Vincent, was also the son of an imperial functionary: a brigadier general ennobled by the emperor.[106] The younger Vincent had himself fought in the Grand Army, rising through the campaigns of Russia, Germany, France, and Waterloo to the rank of cavalry captain at the age of twenty-two.[107] And there his career was blocked by the Restoration. He remained at the same rank for the next fifteen years and only received new honors and a chance at a new career after 1830. A participant in the July Days, Vincent was rewarded by promotion to officer of the Legion of Honor in 1831 and, four years later, he was appointed subprefect at Toul, site of an important military camp in eastern France.[108] He was recommended for this post by three of the most imposing figures of the regime: Thiers, General de Baudrand (peer of France), and General Jacqueminot, leader of the conservative majority in the Chamber of Deputies and chief of the General Staff.[109] Yet despite their continuing support for promotion to a prefecture and the additional endorsement of this request by the crown prince himself, Vincent remained at the same post for thirteen years.[110] His immediate superior, the prefect of Meurthe, reported that Vincent "administers with zeal but a bit superficially."[111]

Like Neveux, Vincent found a way out of his blocked career by a series of opportunistic maneuvers under the new republic. Dismissed by the Provisional Government, Vincent waited until the election of the Constituent Assembly before rallying to a more moderate republic. He wrote to the Interior Ministry in May 1848 emphasizing his military background and patriotism, pointing out that his father was a colonel in the army of the "old republic" (neglecting to mention that the same old soldier was a baron and general of the empire) and expressing his devotion to the republic.[112] The Cavaignac government named him to the important subprefectoral post of Le Havre in July.[113]

Louis Napoleon's election gave Vincent an opportunity to play on a different set of credentials. In February 1849 his brother-in-law, Count de La Morlière, wrote the president a personal note asking that Vincent be appointed to a prefecture. The count reminded Louis Napoleon of their old friendship and of his Bonapartist credentials: student at the Lycée Napoléon and officer in the Imperial Guard. He went on to point out that Vincent was a Napoleonic baron, graduate of the Imperial Cavalry School, and veteran of the campaigns of 1813 through 1815. Vincent, argued the count, had only accepted a subprefectoral post under Cavaignac because "a moderate and energetic man" was needed at Le Havre in the aftermath of the June Days.[114] Writing as an "old soldier," La Morlière asked Louis Napoleon to "concede that administrative ability joined with the services of an old 'brave' of the Grand Army make it imperative that a veteran be chosen ahead of the conscripts."[115] Little over a month after his brother-in-law sent the letter, Vincent was appointed prefect of Lot. He was promoted to the prefecture of Jura in September 1849. By the summer of 1850, Vincent had entertained Louis Napoleon at Lons-le-Saunier, winning his friendship and a promotion by presidential decree to the grade of commander of the Legion of Honor.[116] In 1851 Vincent moved first from Jura to Seine-et-Marne and finally to the prefecture of Rhône. The forgotten subprefect of Toul had risen to one of the two most powerful and prestigious positions in the prefectoral corps in less than four years. At the same time that Vincent took up his wide-ranging duties at Lyon in November 1851, Maupas became prefect of police, the other post at the top of the prefectoral hierarchy.

Charles Becquey, Vincent's successor in Jura, and Eugène Lagarde, Chanal's replacement at Nîmes, had each served the regime of Louis Philippe. Like Vincent, both had been subprefects at the time of the revolution. Indeed, Becquey had made a career of being a subprefect, having risen since 1827, when he received his first assignment, to become the administrator of the important *arrondissement* of Le Havre from 1837 to 1848.[117] Lagarde, a much younger man, had been a subprefect from 1841 to 1848.[118] Though neither of them attained the stature of Darcy, Tourangin, or La Coste, each was a notable in his own right and owed his administrative position to personal connections with major figures of the July Monarchy.

Becquey entered the prefectoral corps under the Restoration. His marriage had brought him an annual income of 20,000 francs and the redoubtable support of his wife's uncle: Valory, director general of Ponts et Chaussées under Louis XVIII and *receveur général* (chief tax assessor) at Mâcon through much of the Orleanist regime.[119] Valory and his equally important friend, Jean Calmon (the most powerful deputy from Lot and, simultaneously, director general of the Bureau of Land Registration) saw to it that Becquey eventually rose to the subprefecture of Le Havre, a coveted assignment with responsibilities equal to those of a prefect in a backward, rural department. In 1840 Calmon, on the "insistence of M. de Valory," recommended Becquey for a prefecture, but Becquey remained at Le Havre until the February revolution.[120] Becquey became subprefect at Saint-Etienne in 1850 and was finally appointed a prefect in 1851 with the support of Valory and Drouyn de Lhuys, another important figure in the Party of Order.[121]

Eugène Lagarde began the July Monarchy as the personal assistant to no less a figure than Casimir Périer. He was recommended to the interior minister in 1841 by Périer's surviving brother Joseph, by the seemingly ubiquitous Calmon (deputy from Lagarde's home department), and by the peer of France, Count de Mosbourg.[122] Forced out of office by the February revolution, Lagarde was appointed prefect of Gard a few months after Louis Napoleon won the presidency.

Becquey and Lagarde were in their fifties in 1851. In that year two much younger men were appointed to prefectures in our sample of departments: vicomte de Charnailles and Alphonse-Charles Boby de la Chapelle. With Maupas, who was only thirty when he became prefect of Allier, these two men were the only prefects appointed to the sample departments after Louis Napoleon's election to the presidency, but before plans for the coup were made final, who were under forty years of age. Like Maupas, Charnailles and Boby de la Chapelle showed their willigness to serve the republic before the election of Louis Napoleon. And again, like Maupas, both would serve as prefects after the coup and into the Second Empire.

Gabriel-Léonce Cortois, vicomte de Charnailles, was described as a "proprietor in easy circumstances" before his entrance into the prefectoral corps.[123] He resembled the moderate republicans described near the beginning of this chapter only in his inexperience.

His Orleanist credentials were impeccable. Charnailles' wife was the daughter of Countess de Danremont and the niece of General Baraguey d'Hilliers.[124] The general had commanded one of Louis Philippe's expeditions in Algeria. After the revolution of 1848 he was elected a deputy for Doubs, one of his former military posts, and soon became the president of the Réunion de la rue de Poitiers, the caucus of all the conservative deputies to the Constituent Assembly, and, in effect, the central committee of the Party of Order.[125] Baraguey d'Hilliers was one of the principals in the negotiations that led to the rue de Poitiers' endorsement of Louis Napoleon for the presidency.

His nephew entered the service of the Ministry of Interior in August 1848 as a subprefect, undoubtedly because Cavaignac was wooing Baraguey d'Hilliers, his old commanding officer in Algeria, for political support. The viscount's fortunes rose, however, with those of Louis Napoleon. In 1849 he succeeded Maupas as subprefect of the port city of Boulogne. Two years later Charnailles again followed Maupas, replacing him as prefect of the difficult department of Allier.[126] This occurred in March 1851, just at the time when the president and the Legislative Assembly were at loggerheads over the question of revising the constitution to permit

Bonaparte to run for reelection. Since January of the same year, when Louis Napoleon had dismissed General Changarnier as the military commander of Paris, rumors of a possible coup d'état by the Elysée had been widespread. Changarnier, who was also a Party of Order deputy, had been the assembly's shield against any possible military participation in a coup. Indeed, Changarnier had announced that he would use his troops to arrest Louis Napoleon in such a contingency.[127] Bonaparte dismissed him despite the protests of the assembly and began in earnest the process of extricating himself from political dependence upon a coalition of legitimists and Orleanists.

Charnailles owed his sudden promotion to this conflict. His uncle, General Baraguey d'Hilliers, had gravitated away from his old colleagues of the rue de Poitiers and had become a man of the Elysée. In 1849, Bonaparte gave the general command of the Roman expedition and named him minister plenipotentiary to the Holy See.[128] When Baraguey d'Hilliers returned to his seat in the Legislative Assembly, it was as a defender of the president against Changarnier, who apparently coveted the presidency for himself, and against other members of the Party of Order who were loyal either to the legitimist pretender or to Louis Philippe's son.[129] When Changarnier was deprived of his command over the capital's garrison, his replacement was General Baraguey d'Hilliers.[130]

Alphonse-Charles Boby de la Chapelle, who became prefect of Vendée in September 1851, was somewhat older and considerably more experienced than Charnailles. Assistant to a prefect at the age of twenty-six, subprefect at twenty-nine, Boby de la Chapelle was well launched in his career when the 1848 revolution overtook him at his subprefecture at Saumur.[131] He owed his early start and steady rise in the prefectoral corps under the July Monarchy both to his own father and his father-in-law. Boby de la Chapelle senior had married well. His wife, Julie Aurélie Simon, was a member of the wealthiest family in their home department (Seine-et-Marne) and was, in fact, the daughter of one of the ten most heavily taxed individuals in all of France.[132] Her brother was Emperor Napoleon's subprefect at Provins, the seat of the Simon family's landholdings and power.[133] Her husband rose from a minor post in the departmental administration to become mayor of Provins and, under the July Monarchy, prefect of Lot-et-Garonne.[134]

Their son, Alphonse-Charles, also married well. His father-in-law was the eldest son of a Napoleonic baron and had himself served the emperor as a subprefect. The Orleanist regime eventually appointed Baron Boullé (who inherited the title) prefect of Finistère, a post he held from 1836 to 1848.[135] Boby de la Chapelle entered the administration as his father-in-law's assistant and, three years later, became a subprefect in Finistère—that is, under Baron Boullé's personal supervision.

Despite the honors and positions that he and his family owed to Louis Philippe, Boby de la Chapelle wasted no time in attempting to win favor with the Provisional Government. On 28 February 1848 he wrote Ledru-Rollin: "The first measures of the Provisional Government inspire my total confidence; I place myself at your disposition without any mental reservation."[136] Ledru-Rollin dismissed him. Cavaignac, at the request of the Saumur City Council, reinstated Boby de la Chapelle in his old subprefecture only a month before the presidential elections.[137] But it was under Louis Napoleon that Boby de la Chapelle was promoted to a prefecture. And he would remain prefect of Vendée until 1862.

The President's Men

The notables and Louis Napoleon agreed on the desirability of stabilizing a social world that had been out of joint since February 1848, but to reestablish an empire the Bonapartist pretender had to go it alone. He had only the presidency, not a party of his own. He therefore detached ambitious and enterprising members from the political groupings of notables and used them as destroyers of the "republic without republicans" and of the direct political power that the censitary elite had monopolized under the July Monarchy. From the Party of Order, the president had won a few men to his banner. He had made Ferdinand Barrot, Eugène Rouher, Jules Baroche, and others ministers whenever he could, even though they did not represent the two major factions of the conservative coalition.

Because the Legislative Assembly was jealous of its constitutional powers, Louis Napoleon had to fall back on cabinets made up of Orleanists and legitimists whenever he needed parliamentary support. He especially needed support for increasing the funds allocated to his debt-ridden official household and, most important, for revising Article 45 of the constitution. (This was the provision that barred the president from seeking reelection.) Thus, Léon Faucher, a staunch defender of the assembly's prerogatives, but a supporter of the move to withdraw Article 45, was called in as prime minister and minister of interior from April to October 1851. Throughout the latter months of his ministry, when it had become apparent that leftist and legitimist votes in the assembly would block revision, the Elysée's plans for the coup were secretly completed. Politicians like Rouher and Baroche were not privy to the plan, for the president, with the prudence of a veteran conspirator, relied only on men who had no power independent of his own.[138] The execution of the coup was entrusted to his half brother, Morny, his old friend Persigny, and to bureaucrats and soldiers who owed their rapid rise to the president himself.[139]

Speculative history is always a risky business, but so is any conspiracy to seize control of a government. Louis Napoleon, Morny, and Persigny undoubtedly asked themselves a number of "if" questions in planning their move. Had anything gone even slightly wrong, if the assembly supported by the Parisian crowd had held off the attack of the Elysée for any length of time, the prefects would have been free to choose sides. They could have followed the legal orders of a duly constituted cabinet against the criminal "attack on the national representation" attempted by the president. The prefects could have refused to transmit the proclamations of a president who was in violation of the constitution. Even worse, they could have called out the National Guard to march on Paris and defend the assembly. The prefects had done this when the Parisian artisans and workers had risen against the Constituent Assembly in June 1848.

Orleanist civil servants had been reliable defenders of the social order against the radicals. They owed their careers, however, to the traditional political and social elite of the July Monarchy. They were members in good standing of this ruling class that was embodied in the Party of Order. With its majority in the assembly, the conservative coalition was institutionalized as the legislative branch of the government. To carry out the coup and to establish his dictatorship, Bonaparte could not fully trust men who for years had been loyal members of the Orleanist elite. Under the Second Republic, they still exercised the plenitude of police powers that belonged to the prefectoral corps. Once again, the president purged and reshuffled the administrative bureaucracy.

We have discussed fifteen prefects who were either retained in office or appointed to our sample of departments during the presidency of Louis Napoleon. In all, eight of them were removed from the prefectoral corps in the months immediately preceding and following the coup.

Of course, only seven prefects administered our group of departments at any one time. By 27 November 1851 (five days before the coup) the majority of these incumbent prefects was out of office: Bonnin, prefect of Vendé; La Coste, prefect of Rhône and special commissioner for the sixth military district; Neveux, prefect of Gironde; and Becquey, prefect of Jura.

Bonnin was the first to fall. His replacement by Boby de la Chapelle in September 1851 marked the end of this prefectoral career. He was a casualty of Louis Napoleon's struggle with those legitimists who consistently voted against revision of Article 45 in the hope that a Bourbon restoration would replace the republic. Vendée was a center of such irreducible "white" opposition to the Elysée, and Bonnin was considered too close to the local elite to be kept in office: "his old and numerous friendships in the area hindered the independence of his action and particularly did not permit him to struggle successfully against the maneuvers of the legitimist party."[140] Bonnin, however, was not himself a legitimist. Twelve years after his dismissal, the empire denied him the title of "honorary prefect" because he remained too loyal an Orleanist.[141] Bonnin, the "area specialist," was fired because he continued to act as a pacifier and intermediary among the local elites—his role in the Vendée since 1834.[142]

Rhône and surrounding departments had been under martial law since 1849, and by all accounts La Coste had done an excellent job coordinating the services of the prefecture with those of the *parquet* and the military command. In October 1851, however, he suddenly submitted a letter of resignation claiming exhaustion.[143] Perhaps at the age of fifty-seven his responsibilities, now equal to those of the prefect of police in Paris, were too great a drain. It is far more likely that La Coste, the Orleanist peer of France, wished to avoid occupying so important a post when the president moved against the prefect's old friends in the Party of Order. During the previous summer his military opposite number and friend, General de Castellane, had been sounded out by the Elysée for the command of the Paris region and therefore a direct role in any possible coup.[144] Castellane refused, and a few months later, amidst resurgent rumors of an impending coup, La Coste asked to be replaced.

As soon as the Faucher ministry had fallen, La Coste's resignation was accepted. Baron de Vincent (who had been prefect of Jura in 1850) was sent to Lyon in November.[145] Weeks before the coup, Vincent issued the following partisan proclamation to his new administrative charges throughout the region under martial law: "Let everyone unite around the flag of order, raised by the entire country on 10 December; this banner which Louis Napoleon . . . has known how to hold so high and so firmly for three years and which, you can be sure of it, he will never lower in the face of anarchy."[146]

Having survived the first prefectoral purge under Louis Napoleon's presidency, Neveux was dismissed as prefect of Gironde on 27 November 1851.[147] He had successfully held onto his post at Bordeaux for more than three years with the support of the Orleanist elite that controlled Gironde. Neveux then made a miscalculation that doomed his career: he remained too closely tied to such local Orleanist leaders as the Gautier brothers and former mayor Duffour-Dubergier. The newspaper that spoke for the Orleanists of Bordeaux was *Le Courrier de la Gironde*. After the dismissal of Changarnier in January 1851, *Le Courrier* began a campaign of criticism directed against Louis Napoleon.[148] Neveux was informed that the president considered *Le Courrier* to be the journal of the prefecture.[149] Throughout 1851, the prefect tried manfully to show the Elysée that he was devoted to the Bonapartist cause, but Neveux had shifted his loyalties too often and now too late. He returned to obscurity while his former subordinate, Georges Haussmann, arrived in Bordeaux just after the coup and began his rise to the highest honors of the empire.

Becquey, prefect of Jura, fell on the same day as Neveux. Apparently he lost his post for similar reasons. In a letter dated 17 December 1851, De Royer, the *procureur-général* at Paris, interceded for Becquey with the new interior minister, Morny. The attorney general argued that Becquey's loyalty to Louis Napoleon had been wrongly doubted and that the prefect had energetically repressed the revolt of 3-4 December 1851 in Jura even though he was no longer officially responsible for the department.[150] Morny rejected this plea. It seems that Becquey's defense of order after the coup was not an acceptable token of a personal conversion to Bonapartism.

Three other prefects we have discussed kept their jobs for a brief interval after the coup d'état before they too were dismissed: Pagès, Darcy, and Lagarde. Pagès, who had been prefect of Jura in 1849 and now administered Ille-et-Vilaine, was fired within days of the president's seizure of power. An unsigned memorandum in his dossier described Pagès as an "Orleanist" who was "hostile to the president."[151]

A month after the coup Darcy, La Coste's predecessor at Lyon, lost his post as undersecretary of state at the Interior Ministry and was excluded from the prefectoral corps.[152] His dossier provides no direct explanation for Darcy's abrupt dismissal after a distinguished career under both the July Monarchy and the Second Republic. Only two years before the coup Ferdinand Barrot, a friend of the Elysée, had promoted Darcy from prefect of Rhône to an important managerial position in the ministry itself. But Darcy had gone on to serve under Léon Faucher, a defender of the rights of the assembly and an Orleanist, who remained an obstacle to any dictatorial solution as long as he remained interior minister. Morny and Persigny, not to mention Maupas, were certainly unprepared to countenance the devotion to bureaucratic duty that had led Darcy to serve their enemy. They probably suspected Darcy of Orleanism. And their suspicions were borne out by his failure to make any appeal to Louis Napoleon for reintegration into the prefectoral corps. Indeed, Darcy did not return to his post in the Interior Ministry until the early days of the Third Republic, when Marshal MacMahon reappointed him as undersecretary of state.[153]

Eugène Lagarde, prefect of Gard until his transfer to Gers shortly before the coup, fell for quite different reasons. According to his dossier, Lagarde was dismissed for "softness" in dealing with the insurrection that broke out in his department on 3 December 1851.[154] In fact, Lagarde had committed the cardinal sin of being arrested by the rebels and was dismissed for no other reason than the temporary misfortunes of civil war. Brashness in confronting the rebellion, not softness or cowardice, ended his career.[155]

Only one prefect in our sample went so far as to resign in protest of the coup: Chanal, the republican who enjoyed the benevolence of the Bonapartes. He sent a strongly worded letter of resignation as soon as news of the coup reached his prefecture of Ain. He wrote the ministry again on 5 December saying that he had taken all the necessary precautions to maintain order, but that the "outrage committed against the national representation" made it "more painful each day" to serve the government.[156]

Chanal remained true to his commitment to republican institutions and refused to serve in the prefectoral corps of the empire.

Protected by Morny and Prince Napoleon, he returned to the army and rose to the rank of colonel by 1870. In that year, he volunteered to serve the Government of National Defense as a subprefect and went on to become a center-left deputy in the parliaments of the Third Republic.[157] Chanal was one of only eight prefects in all of France who protested the Eighteenth Brumaire of Louis Bonaparte. Only one other of these protestors, Pardeilhan-Mezin, was a republican. The rest were loyal Orleanists.[158]

Unlike Chanal and La Coste (who seems to have resigned in anticipation of the coup), the prefects in our sample who were dismissed shortly before or soon after 2 December 1851 had not chosen sides. The power struggle had broken out *within* the Party of Order; their error had been to act as nonpartisan bureaucrats at a time when Louis Napoleon and his coterie expected them to choose between the assembly and the Elysée. By conviction, habit, or inappropriately prudent calculation, these veteran Orleanist civil servants had identified the cause of order with the rule of specific social elites, not with the leadership of a single man. Resolute defenders of hierarchy against the radical republican threats of political and social change, these *attentistes* found themselves paralyzed, outmaneuvered, and out of power (like most of the legitimist and Orleanist deputies to the Legislative Assembly) once the prince-president had determined to "go it alone." None of these prefects, not even the moderate republican Chanal, considered for an instant any direct opposition to the coup. Between the radical defense of the republic by the insurrectionists of December 1851 and the radical defense of order by the men of the coup d'état, they chose order. And, like the conservative politicians, they quietly withdrew from public life often hoping—even begging—to be kept on in the new order.

Those in our sample of prefects who continued to hold office after the coup had made more audacious political choices by December 1851. Brian (Charente-Inférieure), Charnailles (Allier), Vincent (Rhône), Boby de la Chapelle (Vendée), Besson (formerly of Jura, now prefect of Nord), and Maupas (by January 1852 the head of the new Ministry of Police) had stepped outside the presumably neutral role of the bureaucrat (but still within the antirepublican consensus of the Party of Order) by rallying to the president's personal standard.

Brian was designated by Louis Napoleon to head one of the few departments in France that had voted Bonapartist even in the elections to the Constituent Assembly. Such a political fief could have been entrusted only to a man who was devoted to the president. The conditions of the job required that Brian maintain good relations with the local elite, which was led by such ardently Bonapartist veterans of the Grand Army as General Regnault de Saint-Jean-d'Angély. Undoubtedly Brian kept his position at La Rochelle from 1849 until his retirement in 1856 because he rapidly changed from being a veteran bureaucrat of the July Monarchy into an active political agent of the Elysée.

The son of an imperial functionary who was dismissed under the Restoration and made a prefect under the July Monarchy, Besson was indebted to Louis Napoleon for salvaging a lackluster career. Promoted prefect only in 1846, at the age of forty-seven, Besson languished as subprefect and secretary general while La Coste and Darcy became prefects in their early thirties. Desperate—and ambitious—enough to cite his July Medal in asking Ledru-Rollin for a prefectoral assignment in 1848, his star rose rapidly under Louis Napoleon.[159] Besson was a declared partisan of the president by 1850 when, as prefect of Haute-Garonne (a major assignment), he launched an energetic attack on the legitimists who opposed the revision of Article 45 of the constitution.[160]

Baron de Vincent owed his promotion to prefect to Louis Napoleon, and at fifty-six years of age he finally launched the brilliant career denied him as a soldier under the Restoration. Still a subprefect under the July Monarchy and under Cavaignac, it is hardly surprising that Vincent, the Grand Army veteran and Napoleonic noble, had rallied with enthusiasm to the prince-president well before the coup.

Like Vincent, Boby de la Chapelle could claim an imperial pedigree through his father-in-law, Baron Boullé. Boby de la Chapelle's career had also been no model of success under the July Monarchy. And he too had served the government of General Cavaignac as subprefect. Promoted to a prefecture in September 1851, he immediately declared his support for Louis Napoleon against his legitimist and Orleanist critics. "The hour of danger," he reminded the Vendéens on taking office, "must not be that of division."[161]

Vicomte de Charnailles (who had also served the Cavaignac government as a subprefect) was already in the prince-president's camp when he was sent out to succeed Maupas at Moulins. The defection of his uncle, General Baraguey d'Hilliers, from the conservative coalition in the assembly had been an important political victory for Louis Napoleon in 1850. The thirty-five-year-old Charnailles was rewarded with a prefecture and remained in active service until his retirement in 1869.

Maupas, who had solicited the support of Ledru-Rollin with a ringing republican *profession de foi*, was elevated by Louis Napoleon from obscure subprefect to minister of police in less than three years. One of the architects of the coup, Maupas' phenomenal success at the age of thirty-three was due to his willingness to take great risks in the service of his ambition. His desire for rapid advancement made him a ruthless fighter for the president. He corresponded with Louis Napoleon, over the head of his minister, throughout his tenure as a prefect. His direct communication with the chief of state was, according to Maupas' own admission, a flagrant breach of bureaucratic discipline.[162] A prefect was to report only to the interior minister, who presumably enjoyed the support of a majority of the assembly. In his memoirs, Maupas justifies himself on the grounds that the ambiguous separation of powers established in the constitution of 1848 was working to the detriment of the defense of order.[163]

On 7 March 1851 Maupas was appointed prefect of Haute-Garonne (Toulouse). He received a personal letter from the president explaining why, after only two years as the administrator of a small rural department like Allier, he was being posted to one of the most important jurisdictions in France:

> you owe it to your constant energy, to your clearly defined and openly avowed attitude—in short to the sentiments you express in your last letter. You wish for an important populous centre. Toulouse is the principal one in the south. . . . In the event of difficulties arising, you could usefully exercise your influence on other departments.[164]

Bonaparte went on to describe his strategy in confronting the Orleanists and legitimists in the Party of Order.

> You have succeeded in understanding my policy. . . . Loyalty toward all parties, firmness against all, and should they dare to come to an open conflict, energetic resolve in opposing them— such must ever be your line of conduct. I rely upon your intelligent devotion.[165]

Shortly after his appointment, Maupas attempted to frame certain prominent toulousain republicans by planting compromising papers and weapons in their houses.[166] This was too much for the attorney general and the first president of the local appeals court. Maupas was denounced to his minister, Faucher, for attempting to compromise the independence and prestige of the judiciary by drawing these magistrates into the plot. Faucher called him to Paris in late September 1851, after Maupas had evaded answering the minister's written questions for more than a month. After an angry interview in Faucher's office, Maupas was dismissed as prefect of Haute-Garonne and not assigned to another post.[167]

In spite of his disgrace, Maupas had the approval of the president in flouting the judicial authority of the Toulouse Appeals Court and in defying Faucher. While Maupas was receiving barrages of criticism in Toulouse and from the Interior Ministry, the president sent him the following letter:

> My dear Monsieur de Maupas,
>
> I regret that you should incur reproach where you deserve nothing but praise. But the most intelligent minds are not perfect, and one must bear with their foibles. [An obvious slighting reference to Faucher's legalistic liberalism.]
>
> In any case you may rely upon me, for I appreciate at their worth your loyalty, your personal merits and your devotion.
>
> Most affectionately yours,
> Louis Napoleon[168]

Maupas' style—his lack of scruples—clashed with the legalistic sensibilities of the local conservatives and of Faucher himself. Of course, both the Party of Order in the assembly and the president were in complete agreement on the need to crush republicanism. The difference was that men like Faucher were liberals in the nineteenth-century meaning of the term: socially conservative, antidemocratic believers in parliamentary institutions and the rule of law. The president of the republic and his young protégé did not share this classic-liberal value system.

On 26 October 1851 the Faucher ministry fell, and Louis Napoleon immediately appointed Maupas to the most important administrative post in France, the prefecture of police. A few weeks after the coup, in which he played a leading role, Maupas was made minister of police with the power to oversee the entire prefectoral crops in its establishment of the new regime.

The new look of the dictator's prefectoral corps was due to its composition—older men whose ambitions had been thwarted under previous regimes, younger men seeking rapid advancement amid social and political crisis—and, for both groups, a remarkable facility for rapid shifts of loyalty. Except for Brian, all the survivors discussed above either offered to serve or did serve the Provisional Government or the Cavaignac government. Anyone who could trade on Bonapartist titles or credentials put aside his more respectable Orleanist history and habit, dusted off his imperial memorabilia, and offered the new concoctions as guarantees of loyalty to the prince-president. Those who lacked the proper past made up for it by their zeal to leave legitimism, Orleanism, or even moderate republicanism behind them to prosper under a second empire. The new, "purified" prefectoral corps of 1852—taken as a whole—bears out the changes demonstrated in our sample. It was younger, richer, and far more politicized than the more seasoned prefectoral corps of 1850.[169]

The prefects sent out to Gironde, Gard, and Jura on the eve of the coup are excellent examples of the new qualities required under the dictatorship. Georges Haussmann, called to Paris from his prefecture of Yonne and ordered to Bordeaux by Morny himself, had been an Orleanist old boy in the most literal sense. Louis Philippe's son and heir was Haussmann's school chum at lycée, and the royal household saw to it that Haussmann was appointed a subprefect at the age of twenty-three. Removed from his important subprefecture at Blaye (Gironde) in February 1848, Haussmann nevertheless remained in the prefectoral corps (as an assistant to the commissioner and then the prefect at Bordeaux) throughout the early months of the Second Republic. Morny had also been a member of the Duc d'Orléan's circle, and he recruited Haussmann to his half brother's cause even before the presidential election of 1848.[170] Haussmann was one of the first prefects appointed by Louis Napoleon upon his inauguration, and it was as a member of the prince-president's coterie that he arrived in Bordeaux to consolidate the coup.

Henri-François Pougeard du Limbert was only thirty-four years old when he was sent to the turbulent Gard hours after the coup. Louis Napoleon had promoted him to prefect two years earlier, confident that Pougeard du Limbert offered multiple guarantees of loyalty to the Elysée. The young prefect's grandfather and father had been members of Napoleon's prefectoral corps. His father, made a baron under the empire, also served as a general in the Grand Army and in April 1848 was elected as a Bonapartist deputy from Charente.[171] A supporter of the prince from the first, Pougeard du Limbert was an example of a rare breed in the early days of the Second Republic. By family ties and personal convictions, he was a sincere Bonapartist. Despite his youth, he was just the man to confront the democratic socialists and legitimists who had controlled Gard's political life under the republic.

Aldebert, vicomte de Chambrun, is the youngest and one of the richest prefects in our sample. Appointed prefect of Jura just before the coup, Chambrun was only thirty years of age, but already declared an annual income of between 80,000 and 90,000 francs from his land holdings.[172] Chambrun, on entering the prefectoral corps as a subprefect in 1850, brought with him substantial political support for the prince-president. Scion of a family that dated its title back to the Crusades, son of a soldier who had resigned his commission in protest of the 1830 revolution, Chambrun was a noteworthy defector from the legitimist camp. Chambrun's appointment and early promotion repaid an even more substantial and pressing political debt of the president's. Godart, Chambrun's father-in-law, was the director general of Baccarat Crystal and one of France's most influential industrialists. He had been an early (and timely) supporter of Louis Napoleon. Through Portalis, the attorney general at Paris and a member of the president's inner circle, Godart had let it be known that his son-in-law wanted a prefectoral assignment.[173] The viscount's career was launched immediately. It was to be a brief one.

Louis Napoleon needed the kind of endorsement that Chambrun's name, wealth, and marriage gave him at the time of the coup, when his dictatorship and his seizure of the Orleans properties caused dismay and opposition among many members of the notability. By the mid-fifties, with the regime consolidated, Napoleon III could dispense with potentially independent power brokers within his prefectoral corps. Repeatedly passed over for promotion to more important prefectures, Chambrun resigned in anger in 1854. He went on to direct Baccarat himself and later became a liberal, opposition deputy in the Corps Législatif.[174]

Chambrun's very early retirement was by no means an isolated case. Baron Dubois de Romand was appointed prefect at exactly the same time as Chambrun and without any previous experience as a subprefect. He was forty-one years old, married to an enormously wealthy Russian aristocrat, and thus the beneficiary of annual income even greater than the viscount's: 100,000 francs.[175]

Paul de la Hante, son of the founder of both the Banque de Lyon and the Paris-Orléans railway company, was made prefect of Allier in 1853 at the age of twenty-eight. His parental allowance alone amounted to 6,000 francs per year, and, like his brothers, he eventually received a 200,000-franc advance on his inheritance.[176]

These three richest members of the prefectoral corps were all out of service by 1856. Louis Napoleon and his interior ministers, Morny and Persigny, preferred more modest (and more malleable) prefects for the longer-term interests of the Second Empire. Political patronage given in return for support of the coup could be, and often was, withdrawn. Writing in the Caesarean third person, Chambrun complained to Persigny:

> He has seen the chief and master of the cause he served rise from the presidency to the Empire, he has seen his friends become ministers, senators, councilors of state. Now it is clear that there is an incongruity between his name, his fortune, his talent and the services he has rendered on the one hand and, on the other hand, his situation in Jura; it only remains for him to resign—he resigns.[177]

Independent wealth bred temerity. Louis Napoleon preferred the more modern solution of binding his prefects more closely to him by increasing their salaries. Directly after the coup, he doubled the pay of most members of the prefectoral corps, especially those with the least seniority, and increased the top of the salary scale from 30,000 francs per year to 50,000.[178]

The major trends in the recruitment and career patterns of the prefectoral corps, from its resurrection in July 1848 until its final complicity in the attack on the assembly and the constitution, reflect the decline of the republic, a decline which began almost at its revolutionary inception. In 1849 moderate republicans were replaced by experienced civil servants of the old, Orleanist regime—an administrative restoration of the notables. Having made the political institutions of the Second Republic safe from republicanism, the Party of Order then faced the task of repressing the left and its ideas of social reform. The Orleanists and legitimists could work in harmony with President Louis Napoleon to defend the social hierarchy. But as the president's term in office neared its constitutionally established end, the forces of order differed over the final goal of their counterrevolutionary enterprise. Louis Napoleon's imperial dream was, in fact, the most modern of the three antirepublican ideologies. Bonapartism was the myth of the parvenu political opportunist: the alert and pragmatic hustler who could distill personal power from public turmoil. Whereas the Orleanists and legitimists appealed to established ideologies and represented specific social classes within the elite, Louis Napoleon acted on facts alone and prevailed by force. No prefect imbued with laws and customary procedures could serve Bonapartist ends in 1851. Only political condottieri could advance the president's cause effectively. With the coup d'état, the prefectoral corps was returned to its Napoleonic source. It would again be a civil praetorian guard, deriving its status and powers from a leader who stood above the law.

The *Procureurs-Généraux* under the Second Republic

The prefect was only part of the law-enforcement team in provincial France. His administrative and police activities were complemented by the work of the *procureur-général*, who alone had the power to launch judicial investigations (*instructions*) and the responsibility of arguing the government's case in court. Unfortunately, biographical information on the attorneys general is quite meager compared with the wealth of data available on the prefects. As Tudesq found in his monumental study of the great notables, the Justice Ministry's personnel files are very difficult to find and contain practically no notations of the private wealth or background of the magistrates.[179] I have been able to locate the service folders of five of the eight *procureurs-généraux* who were responsible for our sample of departments during the presidency of Louis Napoleon. These files generally contain little more than a list of posts held. Letters of recommendation, estimates of private revenues, and evaluations of bureaucratic performance are almost entirely lacking.

Even the superficial knowledge of how long an individual *procureur-général* served in his *ressort* indicates a major difference under the Second Republic between career patterns in the *magistrature debout* (those magistrates who stand to argue the government's case in court) and those in the prefectoral corps. All of the eight attorneys general in our sample, three of whom were appointed before the election of Louis Napoleon, were still members of the magistracy by the time of the coup and continued to serve under the empire. Six of the eight were still administering the same *par-*

quets in 1852 as in February 1850.[180] The *procureurs-généraux* seem to have formed a relatively stable group during the troubled years: 1849, 1850, and 1851.

The five files I have been able to consult point to another major difference between *procureurs-généraux* and prefects. Four of the five *procureurs-généraux* were already residents of the cities to which they were assigned as *chefs de parquet*. Apparently, the bureaucratic practice of the Justice Ministry was not based on the same suspicions that the Interior Ministry has traditionally directed against its provincial agents. Prefects, of course, rarely have been posted to their home departments. The attorneys general, however, were trusted to be more responsive to the commands of the central government than to any long-standing local alliances.

The long tenure in office of the *procureurs-généraux* we have studied, and their "hometown" assignments, are even more remarkable in comparison with the professional insecurity of the prefects when we consider that both groups, after 1848, were recruited almost entirely from the civil service of the July Monarchy. Given their past service and their personal connections, the attorneys general could have been suspected by Louis Napoleon of being partisans of the Orleanist faction within the Party of Order. Yet the political evaluations and estimates of loyalty to the Elysée that abound in the files of the prefects are absent from the dossiers of the attorneys general.

The service folders available for consultation are those of the five *procureurs-généraux* assigned to the appeals courts of Bordeaux, Lyon, and Nîmes: in Bordeaux, folders are available for Troplong (March 1848–February 1850) and Adrien-Marie Devienne (February 1850 through the coup); in Lyon, for Alcock (March 1848–May 1849) and Gilardin (May 1849 through the coup); in Nîmes, for Léon Thourel (December 1848 through the coup). The three for whom no dossiers could be found were all appointed by July 1849 and served through the coup: Damay in Poitiers, De Sèze in Riom, and Loiseau in Besançon.

Since no files were available for the immediate predecessors of those *procureurs-généraux* who were appointed or kept on during the presidency of Louis Napoleon, it is impossible to provide a firsthand description of the changes that took place within the *parquets* during the months just after the revolution of 1848. According to Baroche's biographer, however, the *magistrature debout* was purged of any republicans in the first months after Louis Napoleon's election. Baroche himself replaced a moderate republican as attorney general in Paris and assisted Odilon Barrot, the prime minister and minister of justice, in directing similar changes in other *ressorts:*

> The *parquets*, especially, had been changed to a considerable degree since the Revolution, many magistrates of the monarchy having been replaced by republican lawyers. It was felt that these republicans would not be sure enough allies in the struggle undertaken by the government against the partisans of social democracy. Just as Baroche himself had succeeded Corne, he successively replaced republicans at the *parquets* with monarchists: "It was at this time," he wrote, "that I was able to bring back old friends who had been revoked on 24 February, notably . . . M. Casimir De Sèze [attorney general at Riom after July 1849].[181]

No ascendancy of the republicans over the *parquets* in 1848, however brief, occurred in the ones we have studied. Baroche's friend De Sèze took over the attorney general's office at Riom as the successor to another veteran magistrate of the July Monarchy, Letourneux, who functioned as *procureur-général* for this *ressort* for eighteen months after the February revolution. Letourneux had been an important member of the *magistrature debout* in 1840.[182] Loiseau, for whom I have found no dossier, took office as attorney general at Besançon during the government of General Cavaignac and continued to hold that position in 1852.[183]

Alcock and Troplong, for whom service folders are available, were both appointed by the Provisional Government, yet neither was a republican. Both of them continued in office well after Bonaparte's election as president. Although each of them was transferred out of his post as *procureur-général*, both continued to serve as high magistrates through the coup d'état.

When he was appointed attorney general at the Appeals Court of Bordeaux, Troplong took his first major judicial office. In selecting him, however, the Provisional Government was by no means favoring a republican. Troplong was a respected member of the notability of Bordeaux. Twice during the July Monarchy he was elected unanimously to the municipal council of this strongly Orleanist city.[184] Troplong's older brother was an important figure in the world of the *juste milieu*. By 1847 the brother was both a *conseiller* at the Cour de cassation, the highest court of appeals, and a peer of France.[185] Under the Second Republic, Troplong continued to enjoy the protection of his eminent brother, who by 1849 was first president of the Paris Appeals Court.[186] Clearly, the Provisional Government had chosen a man of the old regime as its first attorney general at Bordeaux.

Troplong's career as a *procureur-général* came to an end early in 1850. He became a presiding judge at the Nîmes Appeals Court, and he considered this new job a form of "exile" from his native city even though it involved no loss of status within the magistracy.[187] The reasons for his involuntary transfer from Bordeaux are not entirely clear. According to a notation in his dossier, the Justice Ministry felt that his effectiveness as their attorney general was severely compromised by his recent marriage to a "fallen woman" (*une femme dépourvue de réputation*).[188] Recently, Troplong had bungled the prosecution of the Bordeaux branch of Solidarité Républicaine: he lost the case on a technicality. The prefect (Neveux) and members of the local judiciary had complained about his incompetence to the justice minister.[189] Yet Troplong, with the decisive support of his brother, continued to serve as an important magistrate throughout the Second Republic and during the empire as well. He returned to Bordeaux in 1852 as the president of an appellate chamber.[190] His Orleanist past had not prevented the Provisional Government from appointing him as *procureur-général* at Bordeaux, and neither his choice of a wife nor his inability to win a conviction against Solidarité Républicaine ended his career as a member of the magistracy.

Troplong doubtless owed his professional survival to his brother. The elder Troplong had rallied to Louis Napoleon well before the coup d'état. On 3 December 1851 he was named to the president's consultative commission, which took the place of the Legislative Assembly.[191] Victor Hugo immortalized him, along with Baroche and Rouher, in *Les Châtiments* when he described all three jurists as "tramps" and "lackeys."[192]

Alcock, the first attorney general of Lyon after the revolution, was also no republican. He had been a leader of the dynastic opposition in that city and had presided over the local reform banquet.[193] Alcock belonged to the most moderate of the reform factions—the one led by Odilon Barrot, from which much of the leadership of the Party of Order was drawn during the Second Republic.

Alcock was also a veteran member of the judiciary, having assumed his first minor post (as *juge auditeur*) under Napoleon I. In 1820 he became a judge at Roanne, his birthplace, in the department of Loire. The July revolution gained him promotion to the office of presiding judge in that city, and in 1837 he moved to Lyon as a councilor at the appeals court, a position he held until the coming of the February revolution.[194]

The year 1848 was a remarkably busy one for Alcock. In March, the Provisional Government appointed him to head the Lyon *parquet*. A month later he was elected to the Constituent Assembly as a deputy for Loire.[195] He officially functioned in both capacities, *magistrat debout* within the Justice Ministry's provincial bureaucracy and active member of *la représentation nationale*, until the election of the Legislative Assembly in May 1849. Only then was Alcock officially transferred from his office in Lyon to a prestigious position as a councilor at the Cour de cassation in the capital.[196]

How was it possible for Alcock to fulfill his dual responsibilities for more than a year? Since his votes are recorded on several of the major issues decided by the Constituent Assembly, he must have spent a considerable amount of time in Paris.[197] The work of the *parquet* seems to have been carried out by the first advocate general and his staff assistants. Reports to the Justice Ministry from Lyon during Alcock's term are always signed by the first advocate general.

Perhaps Alcock's reputation as a prominent reformer under the July Monarchy was more important to the governments he served (the Provisional Government, the Executive Commission, Cavaignac's cabinet, and the Barrot ministry formed after Bonaparte's election) than the actual discharge of his duties as an attorney general. It is clear why he was kept on, even as an absentee, by Barrot. A reformer in 1847, like the new prime minister and justice minister, Alcock sat with the Party of Order in the assembly. He voted for the full package of repressive legislation presented in the wake of the June Days and supported the government on the Roman question.[198]

Alcock's combination of a bureaucratic and a political career illustrates, in an ironic manner, the crisis atmosphere of the years immediately following the 1848 revolution. One of the reforms demanded during the very banquet campaign in which he played an important part was the so-called incompatibility of functions. Guizot rewarded many of his supporters in the chamber with jobs in the administration; the reformers of 1847, members of the dynastic opposition and republicans alike, called for an end to such blatant corruption of parliamentary independence. Alcock's banquet in Lyon undoubtedly heard speeches and toasts on this precise subject. Yet the requirements of "order" led successive justice ministers to retain a deputy as *procureur-général* at Lyon.

Alcock's career, unique though it may have been, illustrates an important difference between the bureaucratic organization and procedure of the *parquet* and that of the prefecture. The prefect, even in the turbulent years of the Second Republic, has always been barred from holding elective office. The administration and policing of a department were (and are) considered tasks too sensitive to be placed in the hands of someone who enjoyed independent political power. And of course a prefect has no second in command to substitute for him; no office like that of the first advocate general exists in the prefectoral corps. Except for brief intervals between the departure of one prefect and the arrival of his replacement, and during very short prefectoral leaves, when the secretary general acts as a kind of caretaker, the administration of a department cannot be delegated.

The men who replaced Troplong and Alcock had pursued more conventional bureaucratic careers under the July Monarchy. Their appointment as *procureurs-généraux* after Louis Napoleon became president underscores the tendency of Orleanist professionals to return to the police bureaucracy once the republic had entered its counterrevolutionary phase.

Alphonse Gilardin, who took over the Lyon *parquet* in May 1849, had already served as attorney general at Algiers under the July Monarchy.[199] Dismissed by the Provisional Government in March 1848, he was reappointed as *procureur-général* of the Montpellier Appeals Court shortly after Bonaparte became president. A few months later, in June 1849, Gilardin was appointed to head the more important Lyon *parquet*.[200]

The new attorney general at Lyon had won his promotion against some strong local opposition. The personnel file of Gilardin's opponent for this sensitive post offers us a rare glimpse at the politics and judgments that went into the choice of a chief prosecutor. Henri-Antoine Lyson, the first advocate general since March 1848, had carried out the responsibilities of the post that Alcock filled in title only. A native of Alsace and a career magistrate, Loyson entered the Ministry of Justice in 1822 and had served in the Lyon *parquet* since 1838.[201] He was very well liked by the notables in

Lyon because of his activism in confronting the disorders that broke out during the early days of the Second Republic. Loyson had ridden side by side with General Gémeau against the Voraces in May and June 1848, personally directing the police, National Guard, and regular army. Elected to the municipal council by grateful conservatives, Loyson was nominated for the position of attorney general by General Gémeau, by the mayor of Lyon, by the first president of the appeals court, and by the dean of presiding justices.[202] His promotion was opposed, however, by the prefect, Tourangin. Loyson had failed to win a conviction against the city's major Montagnard newspaper, because he had not been careful enough to eliminate radicals from the jury.[203] Tourangin reported this "incompetence" to his minister, Léon Faucher, and added: "The *parquet* is administered in a manner that compromises the interests of society and those of the government."[204] Faucher, in turn, told Barrot, the justice minister, that "it is clear, unfortunately, that M. Loyson lacks the talent necessary to argue criminal cases with dignity and with success."[205] The prefect's advice was followed. Loyson was kept in Lyon as a public symbol of the government's commitment to order (he was even decorated with the Legion of Honor) but he was removed from the *parquet* and assigned to preside over an appellate chamber. The way was cleared for the more professional Gilardin to head the *parquet*.

Gilardin first entered the Justice Ministry in 1836 as an assistant (*substitut*) to the *procureur-général* of Lyon. He was acquainted both with his *chef de parquet* and with the minister himself.[206] Promoted to the position of *procureur du roi* in 1840, Gilardin advanced five years later to *procureur-général* of Algiers. Gilardin's service in this remote zone won him the affection of the Duc d'Aumale, son of the king and military commander of the colony. In fact, Gilardin remained as attorney general of this *ressort* at the duke's insistence.[207]

His Orleanist services and connections did not obstruct Gilardin's career under the republic or the empire. It is clear from his reports that he supported the president against the assembly, and he was rewarded for his performance in the particularly turbulent Lyon region with an appointment as first president of the Lyon Appeals Court in 1852.[208] In 1869 Gilardin became the first president of the Paris Appeals Court.[209]

The man who replaced Troplong at Bordeaux in February 1850 was, like Gilardin, a veteran magistrate. Adrien-Marie Devienne was first appointed to a judicial post in 1825. A native of Lyon, his career as a judge was limited to that city until the coming of the 1848 revolution. Devienne rose from the position of *juge auditeur* to that of president of a tribunal by May 1837. He held this latter judgeship until his resignation early in 1848.[210]

Devienne seems to have been a prominent member of the Lyon notability. An entry in his dossier (one of the few indications of private wealth I found in the Justice Ministry files) described him as "already rich and destined to have a very large fortune."[211] He was wealthy enough to serve a term in the Chamber of Deputies in the 1830s.[212]

Devienne owed his reinstatement as a magistrate, which came with his appointment as *procureur-général* at Bordeaux, to the intervention of another veteran civil servant of the July Monarchy whom we have studied in this chapter: Darcy, prefect of Rhône from June to December 1849 and undersecretary of state at the Interior Ministry from 1850 until just after the coup. Darcy wrote letters to the justice minister urging that Devienne be appointed to an important post.[213]

Unlike Darcy, however, Devienne went on to a brilliant career under the empire. In his reports, Devienne professed his support for Louis Napoleon, and he succeeded Gildarin as attorney general at Lyon in 1852. Six years later, Devienne became first president of the Paris Appeals Court, and in 1869 he succeeded to the most important judgeship in France: first president of the Cour de cassation.[214] Devienne's conversion to Bonapartism was rewarded, while Darcy was barred from the civil service throughout the empire.

Léon Thourel, who was appointed attorney general at Nîmes shortly after the election of Louis Napoleon, had also been a member of the July Monarchy's judiciary. He was president of a chamber in the Nîmes Appeal Court at the time of the February revolution.[215] Like Alcock, however, Thourel had made his reformist sentiments well known before February 1848, and he, also, plunged into the active political life of the republic's early months. Thourel edited a newspaper at Nîmes and sought election to the Constituent Assembly as a moderate republican. After his defeat, the Cavaignac government appointed him commissioner of Gard, a post he held for over a month.[216] But Thourel's family connections and friendships made it possible for him to shift his loyalties first to the Party of Order and then to the prince-president. Again appointed a presiding magistrate at Nîmes in May 1848, it is clear from Thourel's letter of acceptance that he was on very friendly terms with Adolphe Crémieux, the justice minister and former leader of the dynastic opposition. Thourel's official letter begins "Mon cher ami" and continues in the style of casual correspondence between men who knew each other well.[217] Crémieux was the only "republican of the day after" the revolution who served as a minister of both the Provisional Government and the Executive Commission. Later in 1848 Crémieux supported the candidacy of Louis Napoleon against Cavaignac, and, with Abbatucci and Mocquard, he wrote Bonaparte's presidential *profession de foi*.[218]

Thourel had even more convincing credentials as a Bonapartist. His maternal granduncle, Albisson, was a member of the Tribunate, author of the chapters on paternity and family in the Civil Code, and, most important, an eloquent advocate of giving Napoleon the title of emperor. Thourel's father had been a member of the Consulate's Council of Five Hundred before becoming an imperial *procureur-général*, a post also held by Thourel's paternal grandfather.[219] He quite literally earned his own spurs as an imperial *brave* at the tender age of sixteen. Thourel was a cadet officer and trooper in the Imperial Honor Guard through the final, desperate campaigns of 1813 and 1814.[220]

Without these past services to the first Napoleon and without Thourel's early (and probably sincere) rallying to the Bonaparte pretender, it is doubtful that his career could have survived. Thourel's younger brother, André, was the leader of the most radical wing of democratic socialism—the Young Mountain—in neighboring Vaucluse.[221] Despite a denunciation by no less a figure than General de Castellane, who complained in 1852 that Léon Thourel was the "softest" *procureur-général* in his district (implying fraternal complicity), Thourel continued as attorney general at Nîmes until 1869.[222]

The social strife of the Second Republic and the intense political conflict within the threatened governing elite itself did not seem to trouble the security of the magistrates in their careers. Even though the *procureurs-généraux* were key figures in carrying out repressive government policies after 1848, they escaped the political purges that swept through the prefectoral corps. Why were former Orleanist magistrates trusted by the Elysée while many prefects of the old regime were cast aside? Perhaps the attorneys general were spared because of their comparatively passive political role. Unlike the prefects, who administered and "policed" their departments, these protectors of the social order were not themselves vested with direct political power. The vague administrative "*impulsion*" of the prefect, which implied taking wide-ranging initiatives—even military action—against threats to the public order, contrasts dramatically with the clear legal rules and procedures that delimited the *procureur-général*'s field of action. In an emergency, the prefect could call out the National Guard and order divisions of the regular army into action to meet his very broad task of prevention and repression. The *procureur-général* had only his staff of magistrates and his skill as a lawyer with which to bring a case to trial. The attorney general acted only after the crime had been committed, whereas the prefect was responsible for preventing breaches of the peace and threats to the political system from developing at all. Although the role of the prosecutors is central to any understanding of the repressive policies directed against republicanism under the Second Republic, their actual role was a limited and technical one in comparison with that of the prefects. And it is probably these limits that kept the *procureur-général* safe in his career while the prefect faced all the insecurities of active political life in a time of stress.

Conclusion

The sample of prefects and attorneys general that we have studied in this chapter strongly suggests that the police agents who served after 1848 had learned their jobs and made their careers under the older order of the *juste milieu*. Charged by the government with confronting the new social and political forces unleashed by the overthrow of the July Monarchy and the establishment of universal manhood suffrage, these men were in fact Orleanist oligarchs. Their experience, interests, and instincts had all been formed during a period in which the social and political hierarchies were almost identical—and for seventeen years, they had been identically rigid in their resistance to change.

Under the stress of the crisis years of 1849, 1850, and 1851, it appears that discipline in one of these bureaucracies—the one with the greatest political power and active police responsibilities—broke down. The simultaneous threats to the world of the notables from previously disfranchised and mute social groups and from a disunity in the governing elite (manifested in the conflict between the president and the assembly for control of the republican legacy) required that prefects become politicians and choose sides. Most did not, and the prefectoral corps was thoroughly purged in the weeks before and after the coup d'état.

Procureurs-généraux were also politicized in the sense that they voiced support for Louis Napoleon in their reports. But they did not possess the power to overtly prove or disprove their loyalty to the Elysée.

Both state bureaucracies, the prefectoral corps and the *magistrature debout*, faithfully executed the repressive tasks they were assigned by the government. In the fight for the preservation of the world of the notables against the socially leveling tendencies of radical republicanism, all the bureaucrats were united: Bonapartists like Maupas, *attentistes* like Neveux, and even moderate republicans like Chanal. The Second Republic confronted the bureaucrats—men of the elite—with a new, unfamiliar, and inhospitable world of mass politics.

4 Reports from the Provinces

The political repression carried out by the *procureurs-généraux* and prefects is important evidence of the social fear and frustration experienced by the notables between 1848 and 1852 and also of the fear and stress experienced by the bureaucrats themselves. These matters have been acknowledged as significant by virtually all historians of the Second Republic, but they have never been subjected to systematic scrutiny.

The government and its agents were usually well aware that they were ineffective in suppressing the left. The ministers and the bureaucrats were not immune to the fear experienced by other notables, and when they did express apprehension it was because such a sentiment was appropriate. These men were faced by an entirely new situation, created not only by the surfacing of the social question in French political life but also by the appearance of a new kind of revolutionary crowd—one that had developed, in rudimentary forms, the organizing techniques of a modern mass movement and that was no longer limited to the cities, but had sunk permanent roots in certain regions of rural France. The prefects and prosecutors who were almost all trained in the quieter days of the July Monarchy were simply not equipped to measure or understand the nature, size, and dynamics of the radical threat they were ordered to destroy. That the notables were cool and effective in repressing the left is still a powerful myth in the historiography of the Second Republic (see Appendix 2). It is not borne out by the more than 25,000 arrests that took place in the weeks after the coup d'état, or by the rivers of blood shed twenty years later in founding the stalemate society of the Third Republic.

The Chronology of Repression—Action by the Central Government

The governments of the Second Republic were never satisfied with the success of their repressive policies. Having overthrown the repressive government of Louis Philippe, they were eventually forced to reestablish all the limitations on the freedoms of speech, press, and assembly that had been enforced under the censitary monarchy. The steady limitation of these rights, despite protests and guarantees, has been partially obscured by the attention historians have paid to the political struggles waged among republicans, legitimists, Orleanists, and Bonapartists for control of the republic. The turbulent fortunes of these groups and their champions must be carefully analyzed to reveal the common core of repressive legislation and ministerial decrees for which each group, republican and monarchist alike, shares a measure of responsibility.

As is so often the case, the first counterrevolutionary measures were taken by the revolutionaries themselves. We have already seen that it was the "republicans of the day before," the Executive Commission of the Constituent Assembly (including Ledru-Rollin), who unanimously proposed the first repressive measures passed under the Second Republic.[1] The Cavaignac government, composed exclusively of moderate republicans, accelerated the repressive process in the wake of the June Days.

Even when used by Louis Napoleon's monarchist ministers, and thus directed against moderate republicans and Montagnards alike, the Cavaignac laws did not satisfy the reactionary drive of the Party of Order. Although the conservatives had a clear majority in the new legislature, the elections of May 1849 returned a considerable delegation of radical republicans from the industrial cities and the countryside. And, in June 1849, the Mountain's Parisian protest of the Roman expedition set off an armed rising in Lyon and insurrectionary preparations in several rural departments, including Allier and Jura. Clearly the left was not a force in decline. The continuing spread of democratic socialism to many of the farms and small towns of a largely agricultural nation was a fearsome spectacle to the conservatives. The Mountain appeared unaffected by the laws of 1848. Louis Napoleon, in a proclamation published shortly after these troubles of 13 and 14 June, gave voice to the resolve of the Party of Order to crush the source of its fear and frustration: "This system of agitation in the nation feeds the political unease and the caution in economic investment which engender misery. It is time that the good take heart and that the evil tremble."[2]

In effect, the assembly declared a state of national emergency and took special measures, supposedly temporary, that further tightened the limitations on freedom adopted the year before. Paris, Lyon, and a number of departments surrounding those cities were placed in a state of siege. In these regions, the constitution and civil law were suspended. Nevertheless, the prefects and prosecutors continued to serve in their posts; indeed, they drew increased powers from their largely formal subordination to the military government. Acting in the name of the army, a prefect could decree the suspension of any newspaper or organization without bringing it to trial. A prosecutor could dispense with jury trials and bring political offenders before a court-martial. Jules Grévy, the moderate republican deputy from Jura, called this a "law of military dictatorship." The response of Dufaure, the minister of interior, clearly reflects the concern of the Party of Order: "Yes . . . but a parliamentary dictatorship, the temporary suspension of certain civil guarantees in a great social interest."[3] This "temporary" measure in the sixth military district, which included Lyon, lasted from June 1849 through the coup, which came two and half years later.

France as a whole was subjected to another emergency measure that effectively withdrew the freedoms of speech and assembly from the radicals. For one year, beginning in July 1849, the administration (that is, the prefectoral corps) was empowered to forbid any political meeting, public or private. The right of association had become a privilege subject to the discretionary authority of the police, just as it had been under the July Monarchy.[4] This "temporary" measure was renewed twice, in 1850 and 1851.

Moreover, a new press law was approved by the assembly in July 1849. This bill extended the definition of criminal libel to written attacks on Louis Napoleon and also punished attempts to demoralize or subvert the army. The latter provision was an obvious response to the many soldiers' votes the Mountain had received in May, and to the arrest on 17 June of one radical deputy who had been a sergeant in the Zouaves before being elected as a representative from Paris.[5] The army, after all, was largely made up of peasant conscripts, and peasants in certain regions were turning "red." The terrifying prospect of elements of the army, supposedly the buttress of order, turning against the social system remained a source of the notables' sense of insecurity until the coup d'état, when the army was called upon to support a dictator against the elected government.

Another provision of the press law of 1849 was aimed at restricting the circulation of Montagnard newspapers, pamphlets, and almanacs in the countryside. Itinerant peddlers sold these writings door-to-door in rural France along with their other wares. The assembly now gave the prefects the power to license these *colporteurs* and thus control the publications they could carry.[6]

The Falloux law, which was first introduced only five days after the troubles of 13 June 1849, was not passed until March 1850. It was assured support in the assembly because even the Orleanist anticlericals in the Party of Order, men like Thiers and Broglie, were frightened by the spread of republican ideas to the small towns and countryside. Although the more general aspects of this bill lie outside the scope of this study, one application was welcomed by conservatives as a repressive weapon to be used against the figure they considered to be a chief agent of subversion in rural France: the schoolteacher. The underpaid, young, and idealistic schoolmaster frequently was a figure of importance in the local secret society and often worked as the *adjoint* or the secretary of the republican mayor in his commune. Like Falloux, Montalembert, a spokesman for the Church, argued that there were two armies in rural France: the clergy, which stood for order, and the schoolteachers, who formed "the demoralizing and anarchist army."[7] Thiers supported the bill because it gave the prefect the right to dismiss schoolmasters and because he was "converted" to the clerical position "by a revolution in social conditions."[8]

Still another press law was passed in March 1850—one which Baroche, the minister of interior, called a "bold measure."[9] A stamp tax was levied on newspapers carrying serialized novels, which contributed so much to their increased circulation, and also on pamphlets that dealt with economics and "political economy." The categories of newspapers were also reclassified so that more of them would have to pay a higher bond.[10]

The final and most comprehensive act of repression taken by the assembly, the electoral law of 31 May 1850, was itself an indirect result of the demonstration of 13 June 1849. The special elections of 10 March 1850 held to replace the Montagnard deputies who had fled to England or had been arrested and condemned for treason sent another·wave of terror through the notables. In filling the thirty vacant places in the assembly, the electorate in widely scattered departments sent back twenty-one new members of the Mountain.[11] The election in Paris was a total victory for the re-

publican list: Paul Deflotte, a Fourierist convicted and transported
for his participation in the insurrection of June 1848; François Vidal,
a close friend of Louis Blanc; and Hippolyte Carnot, chosen as a
symbol of defiance to the Falloux law.[12] The discipline and vitality
of the left, despite the repressive legislation passed in 1848 and
1849 and its vigorous enforcement, were demonstrated unequiv-
ocally. In Paris, the republicans even won a majority of the votes
cast by the soldiers.[13] The garrison of the capital was "red." Would
it fight for the Party of Order?

The Parisian election also dramatized the unity that had been
achieved in the republican camp as a result of the repression exercised against moderates and radicals alike—two socialists and a
man of *Le National* ran on the same ticket. The "red" list also won
a complete victory in the March 1850 by-election in the agricultural
department of Saône-et-Loire.[14]

The final proof that the Party of Order's counterrevolution was
not successful came a few weeks later, when a second special
election was held in Paris because Vidal, simultaneously elected
in Bas-Rhin, opted to represent that department. The victor on 28
April was Eugène Sue, the socialist author of the *Mysteries of Paris*
and *The Wandering Jew*. On 31 May, after a heated debate in which
Montalembert called for a Roman expedition *"à l'intérieur"* and
Thiers attacked the "vile multitude," the assembly voted to require
proof of three years' continual residency in the canton as a qualification for voters.[15] Universal manhood suffrage was dead. Three
million voters were disfranchised, "this nomad population of town
workers, village artisans, of more or less temporary migrants, so
numerous in the France of the middle of the last century, and
which, in fact, played an essential role . . . in the spreading of
advanced ideas."[16]

The retreat from democracy at the polls was the last legislative
act of political repression taken by the assembly before the coup
d'état. But fear persisted after 31 May 1850 despite the compre-
hensiveness of the repressive apparatus constructed by the legislatures of the Second Republic. The Mountain still existed, and it
was preparing its forces for 1852, when elections for the presidency
and a new assembly would be held almost simultaneously. A retired prefect of the July Monarchy, Romieu, published *Le Spectre
rouge de 1852*, which enjoyed a considerable vogue in 1851 and was
quoted in much of the conservative press:

The indications accumulate. . . . The specter of 1852 which they did not wish to see and which I evoke again, appears before the eyes of a stupefied society. . . . Everything is laid out, concocted, commanded in the plan of conflagration which you will see implemented.[17]

Although undoubtedly a work of Bonapartist propaganda, this pamphlet captured an already existing sense of impending doom among many of the notables and attempted to turn it to account for the Elysée. As the assembly and the president fought over Louis Napoleon's reeligibility and as it became apparent that there simply were not enough votes to revise the constitution, the notables of all factions—legitimists, Orleanists, and Bonapartists—sensed the weakness of the government as it approached the unknown *échéance* of 1852. The discovery, in October 1850, of the conspiracy of Lyon showed that Pierre Dupont's menacing doggerel was no expression of empty rage:

C'est dans deux ans, deux ans à peine,
Que le coq gaulois chantera.
Entendez-vous ce qu'il dira?
Il dit aux enfants de la terre
Qui sont courbés sous leur fardeau:
'Voici la fin de la misère,
Mangeurs de pain noir, buveurs d'eau.'
Des monts sacrés où la lumière
Forge ses éclairs et ses feux,
Viens en déployant ta lumière,
Dix-huit cent cinquante-deux.

It is in two years, hardly two years,
That the Gallic cock will crow.
Do you already hear what he will say?
He says to the children of the land
Who are bent under their burden:
'Here is the end of misery,
Eaters of black bread, drinkers of water.'
From the sacred mounts where knowledge
Forges its lightning flashes and its fires,
Come in unfurling your enlightenment,
Eighteen hundred and fifty two.[18]

Under economic conditions of chronically low prices for their crops, the peasantry remained steadfastly committed to the Mountain in many departments of the east, center, and southeast of France. Would the peasants and artisans of a newly radicalized rural France take back the right to vote by force of arms? It was in this atmosphere of steadily intensifying apprehension that Louis Napoleon seized power on 2 December 1851.

The chronology of repression carried on "at the top"—by the legislatures and cabinets of the Second Republic—indicates a consistent counterrevolutionary trend. Yet this tendency has often been missed, because of the exclusive historical study of the volatile internecine political struggles within the Party of Order. This unflagging repressive drive is perhaps best emphasized by the fact that the ministers of interior and justice during the presidency of Louis Napoleon pursued the same vigorous course regardless of their recruitment from conflicting factions of the Party of Order. The circulars of Odilon Barrot, Faucher, and Dufaure, all members of the old dynastic opposition and men who remained jealous of the privileges of the assembly down to the day of the coup, charged the prefects and government's attorneys under their command with the same task of vigorous repression and painstaking surveillance as did the orders issued by Baroche, Rouher, and Ferdinand Barrot, men who had rallied to the Elysée.

Charles Seignobos and Adrien Dansette have allowed their focus on Parisian politics to obscure this aspect of similarity between Orleanist liberals and Bonapartists. They instead note a "changed" tenor in the conduct of repression between the Odilon Barrot cabinet, which reflected the Party of Order's majority in the Legislative Assembly, and the Hautpoul ministry, which replaced it in October 1849 and was made up of Bonaparte's personal appointees.[19]

Faucher, minister of interior in 1849 and again in the spring and summer of 1851, never ceased to be hostile to any dictatorial designs of Louis Napoleon.[20] On 8 March 1849 Faucher upbraided a prefect who had removed a red bonnet (the Phrygian cap reminiscent of the Terror) from the town square in the dead of night: "I will have you note that the government does not fear broad daylight for its acts, and *it is full face and resolutely* that its agents must attack the spirit of revolt."[21] In 1851 he ordered a prefect to make his circuit despite the political crisis that had broken out between the president and the assembly. "Each public functionary today is a missionary. Do not content yourself with defending the cause of order, it must be preached and its teachings must be propagated."[22] Odilon Barrot echoed this attitude toward the bureaucrats and their mission in April 1849 in a note to the attorney general at Nîmes. "Magistrates are, all at the same time, instruments of public action and apostles of morality and truth. This double mission, which ennobles and exalts its agents, imposes upon them the duty to defend alone, if necessary, the principles of order and justice in the midst of general weakness."[23]

I see no difference between these liberal attitudes of the time and what Dansette calls the "authoritarian, overtly anti-republican policy" of the Bonapartists Ferdinand Barrot and Rouher.[24] Ferdinand Barrot, dubbed "Cain" for his defection from his brother's liberal faction, called on the prefects to become the "first soldiers of order" and to "rally support for the government, act on public opinion, keep functionaries under an active surveillance."[25] This circular, which both Dansette and Seignobos use to show the "new" Bonapartist style of administration, reiterates the precise sentiments of liberals like Odilon Barrot and Léon Faucher. Although the Orleanists and the men of the Elysée certainly squared off against each other in the struggle for power between the president and the assembly, their style of command was the same. It was the result of a common enemy and a shared problem: the presence of a mass-based movement that threatened their social order, and the failure of both far-reaching legislation and energetic police action to conjure it away.

The consistency of tone and attitude shared by liberal and Bonapartist ministers in urging their subordinates on to greater repressive efforts raises serious questions about the quasi-plot theory of historians who argue that the red scare of 1849, 1850, and 1851 was simply too useful to the president's design to be based on real causes for social fear. Certainly the atmosphere of fear did win many adherents for the proposed revision of the constitution that would have permitted Louis Napoleon to run again. But fear does not necessarily imply panic or total surrender. Liberals in the Party of Order supported revision as preferable to an outright seizure of power by the president. Talk of a coup d'état had been widespread since 1850, and Orleanists like Odilon Barrot, Tocqueville, Broglie, and Faucher perhaps voted for revision more because of the immediate threat of a Bonapartist seizure of power than because of their chronic apprehension for the survival of the social system.[26]

The liberals were not the dupes of Louis Napoleon. Faucher continued to express alarm for the *échéance* of 1852 even after the proposed revision of the constitution had failed in the Assembly on 19 July 1851—when it was clear that such evocations of social fear played directly into the hands of Louis Napoleon and his widely rumored plans for a coup. Faucher opposed Bonaparte's plans and was forced to resign as part of the Elysée's preparations for the coup. Yet the reason for Faucher's resignation was not his liberalism, but his refusal to countenance Louis Napoleon's bid to reestablish universal manhood suffrage—his bid to remove the capstone of repression.[27] Before his cabinet fell, but after Bonaparte was denied the right to reelection, Faucher at first had given his full support to the prefect Maupas in his fight with the local *parquet* over the repression of a republican plot the prefect had "discovered" in Toulouse. As Maupas' superior, Faucher complained to the minister of justice in a tone that indicates his belief in the reality of a continuing threat to the social order, even if the red scare aided the plans of the Elysée:

> the absence of the attorney general is fatal. We have a conspiracy to repress and we cannot obtain authorization for a preventive arrest; the prefectoral administration will be powerless to save the country if the courts wish to let it be lost.[28]

Here is an example of the Orleanist Faucher upbraiding the Bonapartist Rouher for the weakness of the Justice Ministry's commitment to order, the watchword of Louis Napoleon himself. When Faucher finally did dismiss Maupas in September, it was not for giving a false alarm—both men suspected that a Montagnard plot had been under way in August 1851—but for going beyond the law and antagonizing the magistrates of Toulouse in his clumsy attempt to make arrests.

On the day of the coup, Faucher's closest political associates were arrested: Odilon Barrot, Tocqueville, and Dufaure. And in the first week of the new dictatorship he destroyed any chances of a political career under the empire by publicly refusing to serve on Louis Napoleon's sham consultative commission. The complexity of social fear as a factor in the struggle between the liberals in the Party of Order and the plotters around Louis Napoleon is evident in this letter of Faucher to an English friend, written a month after the coup.

> I write you, dear friend, from the bottom of the abyss. The February Revolution, that parody of the Revolution of 1789, will have its own period of despotism after having had its period of anarchy. The most genuine thing in all this is the humiliation and bitter pain of all those men sincerely attached to constitutional government. As far as the mob is concerned, the excesses of freedom have disposed it to tolerate all the excesses and all the abuses of order. . . . In the midst of this disaster we have some consolations. The head of society is intact.[29]

To a liberal like Faucher, a man who was at the center of things and was well informed of the state of the country in 1851, the threat to the social system posed by the Mountain was genuine. The fact that the threat to order might play a part in the post hoc justification of the coup d'état did not detract from its reality to this foe of the Eighteenth Brumaire of Louis Napoleon.

Faucher and other ministers of the Second Republic in the years 1849, 1850, and 1851—Bonapartists and Orleanists alike—based their apprehensions on the reports they receive from the prosecutors and prefects in provincial France. These documents show that bureaucratic communications were not orchestrated by Paris— that Seignobos, Dagnan, and many recent students of the period are mistaken in considering them mere exaggerations.

Bureaucratic Perception of Threat

There were many nuances to social fear under the Second Republic. Far from maintaining a uniformly alarmist party line in their reports, the bureaucrats in each department were describing the actual political and social conditions they saw and the real intensity of threat they perceived, which fluctuated with the fortunes of the local left.

The best sources in which to examine these bureaucratic definitions of the situation are the monthly reports submitted by the *procureurs-généraux* from November 1849, when Rouher first required them, until the coup d'état. I shall also refer to earlier quarterly reports addressed to Odilon Barrot. As we have already noted, the Justice Ministry's correspondence for the Second Republic has been largely preserved, whereas that of the Interior

Ministry exists only in fragments. On the basis of the few prefectoral documents that I have found in departmental archives, however, it is clear that the prefects and prosecutors based their reports
on the same shared sources and that, when they can be compared
for the same time periods and incidents discussed, they are remarkably similar in content and style.

The Quiet Departments

VENDÉE, CHARENTE-INFÉRIEURE, AND GIRONDE

If the red scare really was blown totally out of proportion by the
bureaucracy, the reports for departments in which the left was a
minor political factor might be expected to be full of exaggerated
dangers, and alarms and excursions over the small republican
groups that did exist in these jurisdictions. On the contrary, far
from the front in the repressive war waged against the enemies
of the notability, the prefects and prosecutors responsible for
Vendée, Charente-Inférieure, and Gironde did not attempt to en-
hance their careers by inventing dangers.

The reports of Damay, the attorney general at Poitiers with jurisdiction over Vendée and Charente-Inférieure, never once de-
parted from a tone of quiet confidence. From his first general report
of November 1849, Damay made clear that his problem in Vendée
was legitimism, not radicalism. He bemoaned the election of an
entirely legitimist delegation to the Legislative Assembly in May,
which divided the local Party of Order between whites and blues
(Orleanists).[30] The attorney general particularly regretted the defeat
of Luneau, the leader of the local Orleanists, and blamed this
setback on the power of the clergy, which "has caused the election
of representatives . . . quite worthy of esteem . . . but belonging
to an exclusive community of thought which is to be regretted in
a prudent assessment of the future."[31] Damay dismissed the possibility of a revived *Chouannerie* (legitimist army) in Vendée and
informed the ministry that the region would only rise in defense
of the Church. In his next report, the prosecutor went on to note
that while the legitimists criticized Louis Napoleon in their newspaper, *Le Publicateur Vendéen*, their "hostility remains within limits."[32]

In the light of the standard interpretation of the bureaucrats as
contributors to social fear under the Second Republic, it is important to note that the only time before 1851 that Damay evidenced

any irritation with the legitimists was when they tried to frighten the local population on the election of Eugène Sue in April 1850. The prosecutor reported that the white press, in an attempt to "recruit through fear," came close to breaking the press laws in their attacks on government "weakness."[33]

By 1851, however, in the midst of the president's campaign for the revision of the constitution, Damay began to view the legitimists in a less tolerant light. The petition in support of Louis Napoleon made scant headway in Vendée, and the vote for revision of the constitution failed in the assembly because of a combination of Montagnard and legitimist votes. Suddenly, in May 1851, the attorney general wrote of the legitimists in Vendée as potential subversives: "The partisans of Henry V say openly that it is the very force of things which will bring back this pretender in 1852; . . . they are quite determined to use the constitution against Napoleon."[34] He went on to describe them as "these dangerous auxiliaries who have become declared enemies."[35] Thus the échéance of 1852 was more of a white than a red scare in Vendée, although Damay never believed that the legitimists were actually capable of troubling the prevailing quiet in his ressort.[36]

Damay considered the republicans such a tiny force in Vendée that, aside from a few press prosecutions and the dismissal of republican functionaries, he did not even trouble to enforce the repressive legislation of 1848 or 1849 against the left. Generally, he treated the republican newspaper as a joke and wrote of it ironically: "the Démocrate Vendéen continues its experiment on public opinion. I am told that it has few chances of success."[37] Apparently neither the prefect nor the attorney general took any measures to prevent or prosecute republican banquets in Vendée as long as they took place in private.[38]

Charente-Inférieure presented the law-enforcement bureaucrats with a different political, social, and religious situation than did Vendée (see Appendix 1). In this largely Bonapartist enclave, legitimism was less of a force to be reckoned with in the internal politics of the Party of Order, and the left boasted more adherents than the tiny faction that existed in Vendée. According to Damay, writing in November 1849, Rochefort and La Rochelle were centers of "socialist activity" because, unlike the towns of Vendée, they were "places of concentrations of men whose existence depends on the vicissitudes of industrial labor."[39] But within a few months both Damay and the prefect, Brian, reported that the left presented no real threat to public order, though some secret societies continued to exist in the department. In December 1849 Damay informed the ministry that he had prosecuted a local branch of Solidarité Républicaine (the nationwide electoral committee that had worked for republican candidates) without getting a conviction, but he was satisfied that any local network had been broken up.[40] He also noted that the three thousand workers at the naval arsenal of Rochefort were organized into a secret society but that their political activity and the number of active militants were diminishing. Without expressing any serious fears about this bloc of republican voters, he pointed out that "In certain circumstances, a vulnerable point in public tranquility could develop there."[41] Yet in Damay's subsequent reports, and in those that I have found from the prefect, it is apparent that the law-enforcement bureaucrats felt that the situation was well in hand, even in Rochefort. The attorney general expressed no alarm even when a considerable amount of contraband lead and powder was discovered in September 1850 on the docks of La Rochelle, where a large number of arsenal workers were also employed.[42]

The prefect completely concurred with Damay in his judgment that no real threat to public order existed in the department. In his first report after taking up his duties, Brian informed the ministry of interior: "A great submission to the laws, a very decided love of order, a very marked sympathy for the general policy adopted by the government reign here."[43] In October 1850 Brian discovered a secret society at Jonzac, but his request for a secret police agent to infiltrate this club was based on national rather than departmental concerns for public order: "the number of members in it is limited, it is true, and can cause no serious worries for the present moment, but in a given circumstance it can become an embarrassment to the administration."[44] He asked for the agent "with *general* regard to the fact that higher authorities should be kept up to date on everything that takes place within this circle . . . because of the relations which the president of the group no doubt has with the demagogues of several parts of France."[45]

Both Brian and Damay clearly considered Charente-Inférieure a safe department. In February 1850 the prefect answered a ministerial circular warning of possible republican troubles on the anniversary of the revolution of 1848 by assuring his superiors that he was sure such demonstrations would not take place in his department.[46] A month later Damay characterized the department as dominated by "the Napoleonic spirit."[47]

Again, as in Vendée, prosecutions were directed almost exclusively against the press. Administrative and judicial actions were taken against republican schoolteachers and other "subversive" state employees, many of whom appear to have been natives of other regions of France. While the prefects and the attorney general responsible for Vendée and Charente-Inférieure were confident that order was assured in their jurisdictions, we shall see that they did exercise a painstaking surveillance over local republicans and the press, in order to avoid any damaging "embarrassments" to their careers.

The department of Gironde, which was far more urbanized than the two we have just discussed (see Appendix 1), nonetheless offered the law-enforcement bureaucrats similar guarantees that public order would not be seriously troubled by any massive local left-wing movement. As early as January 1849, Troplong, the attorney general, reported that almost all the political clubs in the department had been shut down and that he was now moving against the Solidarité Républicaine circle that still functioned in Bordeaux.[48] He added: "Finally, however, I see nothing seriously disquieting in the existence of the few clubs which still exist in the *ressort*."[49]

Republicanism in the department was limited to certain towns in the *vin ordinaire* and grain-farming *arrondissements* of La Réole, Lesparre, and Libourne. Throughout the period of the Second Republic La Réole, Bazas (*chef-lieu* of the *arrondissement* of Lesparre), and Libourne boasted Montagnard municipal councils. It was from the towns and villages of these areas—and from the few thousand republican voters in Bordeaux and environs—that Lagarde (the lone republican in Gironde's delegation to the assembly) and Tandonnet (leader of the small republican minority in the departmental general council) drew their support.[50]

The way in which incidents in these localities were reported provides an important insight into the tone of political repression in Gironde. On 10 August 1849, the first advocate general (acting in the absence of Troplong) reported "grave troubles in Libourne."[51] He attributed to political agitators a fight that broke out between a crowd of townspeople and elements of the National Guard and the army. However, the internal evidence in his report strongly suggests that a riot resulted when the troops broke up a prank (*charivari*) being played on a local woman. No sooner had Troplong returned from his summer vacation than he indirectly repudiated this exaggerated report. In his regular communication to the Ministry of Justice on the general state of public order in his *ressort* (26 August 1849), the attorney general did not even mention the incident and went on to say that "on the whole, the *political situation* provides every guarantee of order and security—it is evident that the social foundations are healing."[52]

The first advocate general seems to have learned his lesson, for in October 1849 he criticized the subprefect of La Réole and the local commandant of the Gendarmerie Nationale for reporting that "seditious cries" had been heard from troops of the regular army while they were drinking in a local cabaret.[53] The *juge d'instruction* dispatched to the scene of the crime discovered that nothing of the sort had occurred and that the gendarmerie reported the entire incident on the basis of hearsay, which had been accepted without question by the subprefect. The minister of justice passed along this complaint to his colleagues at the Interior and the War ministries. Both the police captain and the subprefect received sharp rebukes from their superiors for the "lightness" with which they had reported the incident.[54] This example hardly bears out the theory that both the ministers and the bureaucracy worked together to keep the red scare alive through overblown reports. The ministers involved in censuring the alarmism of their subordinates in this matter were General d'Hautpoul, the war minister, and Ferdinand Barrot, the interior minister. Both were men of the president's personal coterie, who, according to Dansette and Seignobos, presumably had an interest in maintaining an atmosphere of social fear among the notables.

Troplong's confidence that the left could not succeed in creating disorder in Gironde was echoed by the prefect, Neveux, in a circular to mayors dated 13 February 1850.

> The rumors spread on purpose throughout the countryside by the enemies of order have given rise to some restlessness in public opinion in anticipation of the forthcoming anniversary of the February Revolution. However the calm which has not ceased to reign in all the communes of Gironde must strengthen the population against such alarming rumors.[55]

As in Vendée and Charente-Inférieure, despite the absence of a serious threat from the left the law-enforcement bureaucrats in

Gironde exercised the closest surveillance over republican groups and newspapers. Numerous prosecutions were carried out against the republican press in Bordeaux by both Troplong and his successor, Devienne. In fact, Troplong was replaced as *chef de parquet* for his failure to obtain a conviction against the Bordeaux branch of Solidarité Républicaine, which he brought to trial in December 1849. But his dismissal was not based on any charge that he had underestimated the power of the left in his jurisdiction; it occurred because he mishandled the technical details of the case. Devienne's reports for 1850 and 1851, though they were worded more strongly than those of Troplong and made more ardent protestations of loyalty to the cause of order, made no exaggerated claims of a leftist danger in Gironde.

In fact, both Troplong and Devienne devoted considerable attention to the legitimist groups and newspapers in the department. Each directed prosecutions against the white press. And, in March 1850, Devienne worked together with the prefect to dissolve a legitimist club that the mayor of Bordeaux had allowed to function in the city.[56] Although Orleanists outnumbered whites in Gironde, the administration still had to deal with a rich and powerful legitimist minority, which by 1851 was outwardly hostile to Louis Napoleon Bonaparte. The legitimists were not quite alone in their opposition to the president. *Le Courrier de la Gironde*, which Devienne called the press organ of "extreme" Orleanism, was also an opponent of the Elysée's campaign to revise the constitution.[57] Indeed, if anything characterizes the chronology of repression in this department, it is the frustration experienced by the prosecutor and prefect in silencing a gadfly republican press that local juries (including legitimists and opposition Orleanists) consistently refused to convict.

Our overview of reports by those in charge of political repression where the left was weak clarifies certain important points, especially in light of the distrust that has been historians' standard attitude toward the prefects and prosecutors of the Second Republic. The law-enforcement bureaucrats in these three departments—without exception—evidently tried to make a calm assessment of the balance of political and social forces in their jurisdictions. Their calm tone suggests that their assessment was accurate. Most important, they did not attempt to color their reports with descriptions of nonexistent dangers. In fact, those officials who did indulge in overblown reports were promptly rebuked by their ministerial superiors. Republican newspapers and organizations existed in conservative western France, but the prefects and prosecutors did not use them as a pretext for the fabrication of a regional red menace. Police powers were exercised to attempt to put a halt to republican activity and propaganda in these departments, but the left was rarely taken seriously as a threat to public order.

In Vendée and in Gironde, the authorities devoted considerable attention to the role of the legitimists within the uneasy coalition of the Party of Order. Their hostility to the whites increased with the intensification of legitimist opposition to Louis Napoleon's candidacy for reelection. Charges were sometimes brought against legitimist newspapers and organizations, yet the supporters of Henry V were never dealt with harshly. Legitimists were simply too important to the cause of order in those regions where the Mountain was a real threat to the world of the notables.

The Troubled Departments

Gard, Rhône, Allier, and Jura were among the most turbulent departments in the France of the Second Republic (see Appendix 1). All but Rhône, which was under martial law, were scenes of rebellion against the coup d'état of 2 December 1851. Two and a half years earlier, on 13-14 June 1849, Rhône, Allier, and Jura each had serious insurrectionary movements when they received the news of the revolution-that-never-was in Paris. If any bureaucratically manufactured red scare, ordered from the capital, occurred in the years leading up to the Eighteenth Brumaire of Louis Bonaparte, these were the places that would have provided the highest quality of raw material. The witch-hunt atmosphere evoked by Seignobos and his followers—the magnification of insignificant republican activities into full-blown plots—ought to be evident, if it existed, in the reports submitted from the *parquets* and prefectures responsible for this group of departments.

The fact is, however, that the law-enforcement bureaucrats did not speak with a single, orchestrated voice on the serious problems they faced. Rather, there was a complex, shifting mixture of fear and confidence, replete, it seems, with all the nuances of the reality that the bureaucrats observed.

GARD

Gard had a legitimist majority in the elections for the Legislative Assembly. But the Protestant minority in the department proved to be a strong republican force, powerful enough to give Ledru-Rollin twenty-eight thousand votes in May 1849 and actually to elect a Montagnard deputy in a by-election in 1850, when the legitimists split their votes between two candidates (see Appendix 1). Yet in this setting, which offered a real threat from the left, and which was further charged with all the violence of traditional religious hatreds, neither the prefect nor the attorney general was prone to exaggerate the problems.

Thourel, the attorney general who had also been commissioner of Gard briefly in 1848, stands out among all the men we have studied as an extraordinarily candid, independent, and calm bureaucrat. His coolness in handling the political and religious divisions of his jurisdiction was also reflected in the attitude of his prefectoral opposite numbers, Chanal and Lagarde. The agents of the central government had to steer a course between significant extremist factions of the right and left in the Gard—between the uncompromising legitimists who followed the Abbé de Genoude, editor of the *Gazette de France* and leader of the so-called white Mountain, and the local partisans of democratic socialism. The general confidence expressed in bureaucratic reports contrasts starkly with the Wild West (*à l'américaine*) street brawls and gunfights that they sometimes described.

Thourel's unflappability as attorney general is evident in an early report dated 6 February 1849. Describing a meeting of the Nîmes branch of Solidarité Républicaine, he noted that the pure socialists and "red republicans" were now acting in concert and that they had greeted the current rumors of a move by Changarnier and Louis Napoleon against the Constituent Assembly with preparations of their own.

> I found out from completely confidential sources that they had agreed among themselves to carry loaded pistols on their persons and to try to take over the prefecture if the news encouraged them to do so. The president of the club . . . was chosen in advance to be the prefect; a carpenter . . . was to have been mayor.[58]

But Thourel went on:

I am hardly worried by the results of such a foolish endeavour. The harmony which reigns among the principal civil and military functionaries and the prudent preparations which we never abate could leave no chance for the disruptors to succeed in their *coup de main*.[59]

In a report submitted at the end of March 1849, Chanal agreed with the attorney general's estimation of the republicans of Nîmes: "there is nothing to fear in this regard."[60] Chanal went on, however, to emphasize a theme that would be reiterated for the rest of the period by his successor, Lagarde, and by Thourel. The prefect argued that radicalism was indeed a force to be reckoned with in the rural Protestant areas of the department and that the "provocations" of the legitimists made it easy for the reds to gain adherents in the countryside.

In November 1849 both Thourel and Lagarde sent optimistic reports to Paris. The *procureur-général* pointed out that violence in Gard had occurred only when the government favored one religion over the other.[61] He called for an administrative stance of "exact impartiality coupled with great energy in repression."[62] His repression had been impartial. Thourel reported that he had recently prosecuted both the Montagnard newspaper, *Le Républicaine du Gard*, and the organ of the extreme legitimists, *L'Etoile*.

Neither Thourel nor Lagarde saw the radical republican secret societies in the department as serious threats to public order. The attorney general dismissed them as a local force because of "their small number, their lack of consistency and the absurdity of their views."[63] The prefect reported that most of the clubs in his jurisdiction had been closed down and that "the most complete tranquility reigns in the department."[64]

Even the January 1850 election of a republican deputy to replace a legitimist who had died in office could not shake the confidence of Lagarde and Thourel in the basic political stability of Gard. Both bureaucrats blamed the victory of Favand, who had represented the department at the Constituent Assembly, on the divisive influence and violent rhetoric of the "white" Mountain. According to Thourel, "This violence of language bears its fruit and a large number of voters with moderate constitutional opinions preferred to vote for M. Favand, though they are far from approving his votes in the Constituent."[65] Lagarde noted that Favand's circuits of the department after his election had not troubled the local peace at all.[66] This administrative optimism was voiced despite the fact that both the attorney general and the prefect had thought Favand a moderate republican until they heard the successful candidate proclaim himself a Montagnard and a socialist.[67]

Only twice in the next two years did the reports of the attorney general betray a note of alarm over the potential strength and actions of the left. The first such expression of fear occurred in May 1850, just after the election of Eugène Sue in Paris and during a period when a republican petition campaign was being directed against the soon-to-be-passed revision of the electoral law. This was also the time when authorities throughout the east and southeast of France began to find evidence of the growth of a more militant offshoot of the democratic socialist movement, the Young Mountain. This new organization was already involved in the activities which came to be called the *complot* of Lyon and the Midi. An emergency dispatch from the minister of justice on the subject of the renewed energy of the secret societies provoked a frightened and frustrated answer from Thourel, which deserves to be quoted at length.

> The existence of the vast demagogic association that various seized letters lead us to suspect . . . is not a mystery to anyone, not only in the *arrondissements* of Orange and Avignon, but also in all of the South of France. The existing legislation on the right of association singularly favors the maneuvers of this dangerous party and makes it almost impossible for the magistrates to gather sufficient proof to undertake and also succeed in judicial prosecutions against these conspirators. Only a good police organization can obtain such a result, but in Provence it is not organized in such a manner as to arrive at such a goal.[68]

Thourel plainly felt the need to defend himself from any ministerial criticism of his own repressive efforts. He then went on to paint a fearful image of potential civil war. The attorney general foresaw a beacon for revolution in the countryside being relayed from Paris and Lyon by a system of bonfires:

> The same night and, as it were, at the same hour the insurrection could break out everywhere at once: authority could be surprised and paralyzed; the government forces, receiving no orders from civil officials, could hesitate when confronted with a new authority which would rapidly organize itself and which would show itself to be violent, resolute and bold.[69]

Yet Thourel does not conclude his letter on this note of unalloyed terror. He obviously feels that legislative and police action is required, but he seems to doubt that the Young Mountain can carry out its plan.

I am far from believing . . . that the execution will correspond with the dangerous skill of the plan, but I would not wish to hide the fact that, if this state of things continues, this militia of demagogy will finish by taking on such a solidity that civil war will become inevitable. It behooves the government, in concert with the National Assembly, to introduce necessary changes in the legislation so that the factions could no longer make light of the efforts of magistrates and abuse the rights that the constitution gives to citizens in order to prepare its overthow.[70]

Thourel, however, quickly overcame his fright. By July 1850 he was reporting a "very satisfying calm" in Gard and an apparent slackening in the strength of the left.[71] Recent municipal elections had resulted in many victories for the Party of Order (largely legitimist in Gard) and had left the Mountain in control only of certain village strongholds in the Protestant Cévennes.

Apparently, only two months after the Young Mountain episode both Thourel and Lagarde felt secure enough in the stability of the department to move against the extreme legitimists. For the first time, in July 1850, the prefect used the power given him in July 1849 by the "emergency" law on associations to decree the closure of extreme legitimist clubs that had held public banquets on the saint's name day of Henry V. Thourel saw this closure as a move favoring the more moderate supporters of the Bourbon pretender and one that deprived the local republicans of any pretext for protests and demonstrations of their own.[72] Throughout the rest of 1850, Thourel continued to describe Gard as a calm department, minimizing occasional outbreaks of violence between the "factions" of right and left as more religious and personal than political.[73] In December 1850, in the midst of the investigations and arrests (a few of which occurred in Gard) carried out in connection with the full discovery of the *complot* of Lyon in October, Thourel simply noted that he and Lagarde had been successful in shutting certain disguised republican clubs and expressed his conviction that the new electoral law ensured a conservative voting majority throughout his *ressort*.[74]

Thourel of course continued his surveillance and prosecutions of the left and remained wary of any future increase in republican strength or activity in Gard. At the end of 1850, he even recommended that the voting age be raised to twenty-five in order to assure the maturity and conservatism of the electorate.

The attorney general's caution did not, however, again become serious concern for the state of public order until February and April 1851. His renewed expressions of fear were very different from those of 1850. In 1851 Thourel was worried about the effects of the conflict between the assembly and the president on the fortunes of the left: the *échéance* of 1852. And his apprehensions were national rather than regional: they were couched in very general terms. He blamed the assembly for creating an atmosphere of insecurity that damaged the economy by limiting investments and by keeping the prices of agricultural products from rising to more profitable levels.[75] Thourel's particular concern, given his assignment in the Midi, were the legitimists who opposed Louis Napoleon: "people are alarmed above all by this occasional alliance between the legitimists and the Mountain; they fear that it may oblige the former more than they had expected and that from it may come great perils for the cause of order."[76]

According to the *procureur-général*, the left was again expressing optimism because of the new disunity and weakness demonstrated by the government.[77] The fate of order in the elections of 1852 depended on "the perception of the strength of government power and the sense of fear of anarchists. Until now these two feelings are too little developed to produce the effect which we must hope for in the interest of the country."[78]

On the local level, however, Thourel continued to seem satisfied with the future of public order. While he was expressing his fears about 1852 for the entire nation, Thourel was disputing with both the prefect and the minister of justice because of his unwillingness to prosecute a group of republicans who had met to establish a new Montagnard newspaper. The attorney general had argued that the prevention of such a business meeting would only make the authorities unpopular in the department, while advertising the republicans and their newspaper.[79] On the direct orders of the minister, Thourel finally agreed with Lagarde to send the police to break it up, but he refused to prosecute the republicans when they dispersed at the first request of the police commissioner.[80] The attorney general was certain that no jury would convict them under the circumstances, and he apparently convinced his superiors and the prefect that an administrative decree would suffice to prevent future meetings of this group. These were not the actions of a frightened man, nor of one who took part in a centrally directed conspiracy to create a witch-hunt atmosphere.

In fact, Thourel was reporting by June that Gard was quiet and that he had successfully prosecuted another republican club in the *arrondissement* of Uzès.[81] His outlook was optimistic for the cause of order and for the hopes of Louis Napoleon: "the resolute stand of the government on all the occasions in which the left has renewed its attacks against its policies brings the government new supporters every day."[82]

Once the assembly had defeated the president's attempt to revise the constitution, Thourel and Lagarde (like their colleagues in the west) began to crack down on previously tolerated legitimist clubs. Thourel reported numerous prosecutions and closures of Bourbonist associations in the department. Although this repression of the right was not undertaken with the same verve as that directed against the Mountain, it is clear that the central government had decided that the whites were no longer valuable members of the Party of Order, but a political force to be kept within convenient limits.

Thourel gave a final example of his independence in October 1851. He sent a strongly worded report to the Justice Ministry criticizing Louis Napoleon's recently stated intention of reestablishing universal manhood suffrage without any three-year residency requirement.[83] While he supported the president's drive for reelection, the attorney general made clear that a return to democracy would endanger the cause of order. In trying to dissuade the government from this new course, Thourel said he was well aware that by his frankness he risked his career. Yet he was still attorney general at Nîmes in 1852. Evidently the Elysée, after the coup d'état, continued to appreciate the coolness of this chief prosecutor in a divided and troubled region of France.

Gard was a department where the left, although a minority, was strong enough to be a constant concern for the law-enforcement bureaucrats. But both the prefect and the *procureur-général* responsible for Gard submitted reports that were essentially free of fear and of any exaggerated style of presentation. When Thourel did express alarm on two occasions, it was because he had ample reason to feel that the security of his *ressort* was temporarily threatened, first by the discovery of a secret-society network extending from Lyon into the Midi, and then, a year later, by the apparent breakup of the Party of Order over Louis Napoleon's reeligibility for the presidency, with the resulting weakness of the central government.

The Red Departments

The bureaucratic perception of potential threats to public order in Rhône, Allier, and Jura, and the attitudes of the prosecutors and the prefects over the years 1849, 1850, and 1851, are relatively easy to describe. In the presence of a widespread movement that challenged the existing social and political system, the bureaucrats expressed an appropriate sense of fear and frustration that did not dissipate until the Second Republic had been dismantled.

RHÔNE

The department of Rhône had been a police troublespot for years. before 1848. It remained the most danger-fraught assignment in provincial France for both its *procureur-général* and its prefect throughout the brief lifespan of the Second Republic. The city of Lyon and its hinterland had been a historic center of the radical secret societies since the time of the Carbonari. The newly radicalized rural departments to the south and east looked to Lyon for leadership and coordination of their nascent Montagnard movements. Rhône, with its metropolitan core, was second in importance only to Paris itself as the nerve center of French democratic socialism (see Appendix 1).

Unfortunately, prefectoral reports for this department are almost entirely lacking. But the correspondence of the appellate *parquet* provides us with a very rich and continuous record of bureaucratic evaluations of the local political situation. The tone of these documents is constant from the inauguration of Louis Napoleon as president until the coup d'état. Ever more stringent repressive laws and increasingly tough administrative practices—including placing the department under martial law in June 1849—failed to conjure away the menace of insurrection in Lyon and a revolutionary conflagration throughout the east and the Midi. The reports sent to Paris are filled with fearful descriptions of the local state of affairs. At no time during the years 1849, 1850, and 1851 did the bureaucrats cease to regard Lyon and its surrounding department as a powder keg. They were never satisfied with their work of repression and seem to have lived in expectation of a violent day of reckoning with the left.

The *procureur-général* in Lyon was responsible to a considerable extent for policing this very dangerous jurisdiction. Nothing in his reports suggests that he exaggerated the problems he faced. His fear, although sometimes expressed in vivid terms, seems never to have been communicated in a manner designed to create panic among the notables. In fact, the general sense of the reports submitted from the Lyon *parquet* under both Alcock and Gilardin was that, for the present, the law-enforcement bureaucrats had some degree of control over public order in Rhône. Each time they reported during 1849, 1850, and 1851, they looked to the near future with foreboding. Like the colonial administrators of some violent, exotic, and only vaguely understood territory, they could never predict what would happen next.

In February 1849 the first advocate general estimated the number of secret society militants in the department: 12,000 members of Solidarité Républicaine, 8,000 Mutualists (Proudhonians), 2,000 Carbonari, 2,000 Icariens (followers of Etienne Cabet), and 1,000 members of Solidarité Socialiste.[84] "All these associations," he declared, "preach the red Republic." They were growing, and not only in the city: "It follows, however, from information that I obtain daily that our socialists are gaining ground among the proletarians of the countryside."[85] The spread of radical doctrines worried this magistrate more than their well-known presence in Lyon itself. He was concerned about the activities of certain members of the secret societies, known as "propagandists," each one of whom was responsible for "preaching" socialism to the clubs just starting up in rural areas.

The first advocate general concluded his report by describing the preparations he had made for the mass arrest of the leaders of the leftist associations. He was eager to act on the slightest pretext.

> I was completely determined, during our unfortunate times in Lyon, to arrest eighty of the leaders reputed to be the most dangerous terrorists even before a clash had occurred. I would act in the same way today should the political circumstances in which we find ourselves become worse and present even the threat of a riot.[86]

By May 1849 he was reporting that the secret societies had grown considerably and regrouped themselves into three organizations: Les Voraces, Les Mutuellistes, and the revived Société des droits de l'homme. The latter had been the major republican secret society under the July Monarchy. He informed the Justice Ministry that he now had a list of 254 leaders and was ready to arrest them on the receipt of any news of an insurrection in Paris.[87] This dispatch was written on 28 May, the day the Legislative Assembly first convened. Led by Ledru-Rollin, the radical deputies began interpellating the government on the question of the Roman expedition while the secret societies both in Paris and Lyon were meeting in continuous session, awaiting word from their parliamentary leaders. These meetings were convened to show support of the Mountain's motion to impeach Louis Napoleon and the ministers.

The expected rebellion did not in fact break out in Paris until 13 June and, at Lyon, two days later. Heavy fighting occurred in the workers' districts of Lyon and its suburbs. The call to arms was sounded in La Croix Rousse at dawn on 15 June, and this slum neighborhood was not subdued until ten hours later.[88] Artillery and regular troops under the command of General Magnan finally crushed the rebellion. Eighty soldiers and 120 rebels were either killed or wounded; the department of Rhône was immediately placed under a state of siege. Military tribunals took the place of the civilian courts and at least 1,200 Montagnards were arrested and sentenced to hard labor and exile in the French colonies.[89] A number of soldiers from the garrison who had gone over to the side of the radicals were similarly tried and summarily executed.[90] Police powers in the department passed swiftly into military hands. Perhaps this is the reason why no attorney general's reports are available on the June rising.

Soon after these events Gilardin took up his post as *procureur-général*, and La Coste became the new prefect who was also to function as commissioner general for the entire region under martial law. At first, both Gilardin and La Coste seemed satisfied that the state of siege had crippled the left.

Reporting on a by-election held in the department in July, Gilardin noted that while the Montagnard, Jules Favre, had been elected, the left had received thirty thousand fewer votes than in the general elections two months earlier.[91] Gilardin warned that lifting the state of siege would simply re-create the conditions leading up to the rising of 15 June; yet he concluded his report on an optimistic note: "The facility with which the measures of the state of siege are accepted proves to me that our working class population, protected from the influence of a certain number of agitators, is disposed to accept the conditions of order."[92]

By December 1849, however, the attorney general was reporting, even under conditions of martial law, the frustration of his efforts to prevent the left from regrouping in legally permitted mutual aid and cooperative societies:

The socialist party puts down deep roots and holds a strong position among us, everywhere organizing associations imbued by its ideas and subject to its direction, organizations which some day could undertake formidable political actions and which, under the guise of simple mutual aid socieites, hide from the investigations of Justice. . . . Since the convulsive life of the clubs has ceased, agitation retreats into these centers; within them, they conspire just as dangerously to create disorder.[93]

Yet at this date he was still optimistic that he could close these associations with the cooperation of the prefectoral and military authorities. Gilardin was reporting, however, that even the military tribunals would not convict on the basis of the evidence he had gathered against the disguised secret societies. He called for the use of undercover agents as the only means to obtain solid evidence for convictions and went on to warn the ministry that these "small industrial armies . . . immediately turn into political armies, throwing their soldiers into the first insurrection which comes along and feeding the hottest furnace [*le plus incandescent foyer*] with evil passions [*mauvaises passions*] which seethe against the public peace."[94]

It was now apparent to Gilardin that the state of siege very tenuously held the left in check. Military rule could not prevent the secret societies from reappearing in the department or from growing in membership. To use the twentieth-century lingo of counterinsurgency, the government had not succeeded in "rooting out the infrastructure" of democratic socialism in Rhône. For the next two years, the reports of the attorney general maintained an almost constant tone of alarm.

In January and February 1850 (only six months after the defeat of the left on the barricades of La Croix Rousse), Gilardin reported that an apparent mass migration of workers into Lyon from the east and south, detected by other attorneys general and by the minister himself made him expect a new revolutionary "explosion" at Lyon.[95] In his March report he attributed the lack of an insurrectionary outburst on the anniversary of the February revolution to a growing discipline and organization among the diverse groups of the Mountain. He informed the ministry that unsigned placards had gone up throughout his jurisdiction recommending that the secret societies refrain from any violence—for the present.[96] To Gilardin, this was every bit as alarming as an actual rebellion. It demonstrated that democratic socialism had developed a new leadership since June 1849 and had created a system for the transmission of secret orders from the top down to the provincial—and neighborhood—sections of the movement. He also noted that the local pure socialists and radical republicans had joined forces.

> We are noticing here a certain tendency to abandon the extravagant conceptions of socialism in order to link up with a rigid and radical republicanism. This transformation does not take place, however, without putting a passion-blinded spirit of hostility to the government even more into the open; and revolutionary ideas are served with a cold and calculating fanaticism. . . .[97]

Four months later, Gilardin answered a question from the minister of justice on whether the government should lift the state of siege in his *ressort*. His response was a nuanced mixture of confidence in the ability of the civil authorities to police the rural areas surrounding Rhône and an absolute belief that military government in Lyon was the only barrier to an immediate insurrection. He argued that Lyon was "the holy city of socialism," the chosen starting point for a new French revolution.

> This situation will not cease until society has been armed with stronger laws, until the anarchical party has been better reduced to impotence, until the country has for a longer time been returned to the habits of steady government.[98]

Gilardin further warned the government that the state of siege at least had the effect of suppressing the subversive press in Lyon. Within a day of a return to jury trials, "we would see the resuscitation of this socialist press with its infernal boldness and its deadly malevolence which has corrupted public opinion here . . . and which created the June insurrection."[99] He added the optimistic observation that, although it was still socialist, the rural

population was less prone to violence than when it had been subjected to the propaganda of the Lyon press. The minister of justice
who was considering the return of normal administration to the
sixth military district was Rouher, a member of the so-called cabinet
of *commis* personally selected by Louis Napoleon. Far from being
instructed by the Elysée to frighten the notability, Gilardin actually
felt the need to retain the peace-keeping advantages of martial law
in Rhône. He was acting like a bureaucrat who had to inform a
superior bureaucrat of the truly menacing characteristics of his
local situation.

Again, after the discovery of the *complot* of Lyon, the attorney
general in Lyon reiterated his faith in the state of siege as the
government's only tenable line of defense. Gilardin maintained
that the insurrection was planned for the Midi because "the state
of siege, the only reason for our security," protected the region
around Lyon from similar developments.[100]

Given the state of siege, however, Gilardin became optimistic
in late 1850. Beginning with his report for October, when he said
that the uncovering of the plot and the arrest of many Montagnard
leaders had "clarified" the political situation, his reports employed
terms that indicate a degree of confidence. The apparent ease with
which the authorities tracked down and arrested the leadership
of the Young Mountain in October 1850 led Gilardin to coin a
confident and satisfied epigram: "Fear easily dissolves the gangs
which hatred recruits."[101] But he went on to warn that "it is a
serious symptom, however, and worthy of the government's attention."[102] Two and a half months later, in February 1851, he
reported that Lyon was externally calm although certain signs of
leftist activity "reveal the persistence of evil plans in the under-
world of demagogy."[103] He emphasized, however, that the secret
societies were discouraged by the arrests and convictions in the
wake of the *complot*. Thus, for a few months, Gilardin was not
worried about any immediate threats to the government in his
jurisdiction. And, for the rest of 1851, when he became alarmed
again his fears focused on 1852.

As the *échéance* of 1852 drew closer and while the assembly and
the Elysée clashed, the attorney general in Lyon again noted
(in April 1851) "a quite fiery agitation and a deep sense of dis-
quiet."[104] He blamed the legitimists for dividing the Party of Order
and for creating an atmosphere of apprehension among investors
and merchants that was aggravating the unemployment in Lyon.

This was the "real problem" that threatened public order. In this report, therefore, he asked the government to take measures before "the workshops close up and the famished multitude demands bread."[105] The Mountain was still as strong as ever in Lyon, according to the attorney general, but it had adopted a policy of watchful waiting.

Gilardin's report of June 1851, while it emphasized the dangerous possibilities inherent in the constitutional crisis, was hardly a counsel of despair. He added positive elements to his description of Rhône and its neighboring departments. According to the attorney general, the factory workers of Lyon, while they remained actively enrolled in the socialist movement, were effectively policed under the state of siege. The Mountain, he thought, was losing ground in the countryside. The peasants, despite the low prices for the goods they sold, were beginning to "open their eyes to the political madness." As for the lower-middle class, the artisans and shopkeepers were "tempered socialists" who would lean in the direction of the greater force of the masses in the large cities. Gilardin maintained that Louis Napoleon could guarantee order and win over most of these groups: "The people need to personalize their gratefulness, they are perplexed by such a sentiment when it only seems to be felt for an institution."[106]

Meanwhile, however, it was evident to Gilardin that the Mountain would wait until 1852 for any action of its own. No disorders had occurred on 4 May, the anniversary of the opening of the Constituent Assembly in 1848; and, again in placards appearing throughout the *ressort*, anonymous leaders of the left had urged restraint on the rank and file. The only effect of the radicals in the *ressort*, according to Gilardin was to prevent the petition in support of Louis Napoleon from gaining many signatures: "The Jacobin party has spoken so much of pillage and the guillotine that it has succeeded, in the face of the degeneracy of people's characters, in producing a real intimidation."[107]

By August, however, when it was clear that the conflict between the assembly and the president could not be solved and that Louis Napoleon could not legally run for reelection in 1852, Gilardin's fear for the future intensified. Not only did the Party of Order now appear to be a weakened and disunited force, but the left was becoming more unified and was arming itself to attain "that detestable goal: the overthrow of the present government."[108]

In October, Gilardin continued to describe the preparations of the secret societies for revolution in 1852.[109] He went on to deplore the attitude of the Party of Order in Rhône.

Under the protection of the state of siege, the conservative party is lulled into a sense of security. Without initiative, without energy, it waits and does not incite those decisive demonstrations of public opinion which win over those with hesitant convictions.[110]

If he had been trying to frighten the local notables into supporting Louis Napoleon, Gilardin had certainly failed. But his criticism of the conservatives sounds more like an appeal for help in confronting the approaching crisis of 1852 than like a public-relations pitch from the Elysée. It is apparent from his reports over an eighteen-month period that this bureaucrat was honestly afraid of the potential for revolution in his jurisdiction. Fear is not simply reiterated as a formula. It diminishes or grows with Gilardin's changing analysis of the situation.

ALLIER

The strength of the left in Rhône had been demonstrated years before 1848. In Allier, the development of a mass radical movement among a previously apolitical and deferential peasant population came in the wake of the February insurrection. This historically peaceful farming region suddenly became one of the most ardently radical departments of rural France. During the presidency of Louis Napoleon, Allier remained a constant source of concern for the police authorities; and their concern was intensified because they could never quite understand the strength and vitality of this nascent "populist" movement, which successfully resisted their repressive efforts down to the bitter, armed struggle that broke out on 3 December 1851.

The law-enforcement bureaucrats responsible for Allier, including Maupas, were not the harbingers of a manufactured red scare. In fact their communications with Paris during 1850 and early 1851 express a certain optimism about the success of their efforts to crush the Mountain in Allier.[111] If anything, the bureaucrats were somewhat overconfident in their assessment of the situation, as was proven by the massive rising there after the coup d'état.

In December 1849 the attorney general at Riom submitted a lengthy report on the state of his *ressort* that recapitulated his dispatches, and those of his predecessor, for the past year. The entire report was devoted to the department of Allier. Writing only six months after the local uprising of 15 June and only shortly after its leaders had been acquitted by the jury of Puy-de-Dôme, De Sèze painted a menacing picture of the department.

> Since the February events, a kind of intellectual work seems to have been carried out in the midst of the rural and indigent populations: vague aspirations for a better future. . . . Nowhere in my *ressort* could one have expected a faster and more widespread diffusion of the ideas of radical reform.[112]

He then went on to outline the economic and social factors that set Allier off from neighboring departments.

> The special nature of the area provided so many more chances for the propagation of socialist ideas because of the *exceptional* circumstances of property being concentrated here in the hands of a few wealthy residents and that the division of the land has not at all distributed it . . . to the more humble and more laborious tenants. These circumstances have been exploited with a carefulness, a boldness, an energy which have not been slow in bearing their fruit.[113]

Returning to the usual style of administrative reports, De Sèze did not see the economic situation of the department as the real cause for its sudden shift to the left. He blamed this on the work of the radical commissioner who had administered the department while Ledru-Rollin was interior minister, and who was presently a deputy to the Legislative Assembly and the leader of the Mountain in Allier—Félix Mathé. Mathé's direction of the department, his appointment of radicals to important administrative posts, and the support he gave to the republican press were the most important reasons, according to the attorney general, for the current deplorable state of affairs. Radical leaders had won over "the credulous inhabitants of the countryside" with the "banal promise" of redistributing the land and establishing a system of progressive taxation. Even worse, the red republicans had created an atmosphere of class conflict reminiscent of the Great Revolution.

> The agitators have made it a point to establish a fatal distinction, a dangerous antagonism between the several classes of which society is composed; they spread this abroad in the form of bitter recriminations, as violent reproofs to the *bourgeoisie* and, in order

to prepare for it the fate which the nobility suffered in 1793, they have given it the hostile designation of *new aristocracy*.[114]

De Séze pointed to the local events of 15 June 1849 as the index of how successful the radicals had been in winning the peasantry to their banner. The so-called *affaire* of La Brande des Mottes, in which more than a thousand armed peasants and townspeople gathered in preparation for an attack on Moulins when they heard of the risings in Paris and Lyon, provided clear evidence: "in the space of a few hours the hopes and passions of the multitude, deeds of violence, . . . violations of homes, pillage, were realized and permit us no doubt on the subject of the communist tendency of our agricultural populations."[115] This crowd, which dispersed when it learned that the Montagnard deputies had been arrested and that no revolution had broken out in Paris, was apparently led by the mayors of a number of communes in the department, "a rabble of men endowed with public office, mixing themselves up in these anarchical plots and showing themselves to be their most influential instigators. The municipalities have proven that . . . they are, for the most part, formidable centers of disorder."[116]

The verdict of the Assize Court of Puy-de-Dôme in this matter on 30 November was considered "calamitous" by the attorney general. All forty-three defendants were acquitted despite the fact that they had publicly stated "that they were acting in order to defend the constitution and to overthrow the government."[117] De Sèze reported that the conservatives in Allier, many of whom had testified for the prosecution, now feared reprisals; the radicals, for their part, greeted the verdict as a symbol of their future triumph.

In this summary of the state of public order in Allier at the end of 1849, the attorney general never mentioned the assault on Ledru-Rollin by the largely legitimist National Guard battalion of Moulins, which had occurred during the election campaign of May. Conservative violence was not viewed in the same light as radical agitation.

Within the two months after this alarming report was written, however, both Maupas and De Sèze were beginning to see a marked improvement in the local situation. In January, De Sèze informed Paris that the assembly's discussion of the Falloux law had inhibited the overt radicalism of many schoolteachers.[118] But he still considered the countryside a socialist stronghold because of the influence of the radical Parisian press, which the law allowed to circulate freely in the department. Among the three offending publications that he listed was *Le National*, the organ of moderate republicanism. And De Sèze was particularly worried about the recent reappearance of the republican newspaper in Allier, a newspaper he had shut down for seven months after a series of prosecutions. The tone of this report was wary, although the attorney general and his staff were pleased with the outward calm in Allier.

> All my *substituts*, in pointing out this change to me—this outward submission to the legal order—rejoice in it, but they all agree in believing that we must not see in it promises that are overly reassuring for the stability of the present or the safety of the future.[119]

The prefect, Maupas, submitted a more optimistic report at the end of February. Reporting on an incident in which a tax collector had been beaten and then forced to leave the town of Saint-Didier by the radical mayor and the commander of the local National Guard unit, Maupas first described the dangerous nature of the department "in which they only wait for the watchword to rise up and give themselves over to the most terrible excesses."[120] But he went on to relate, with some pride, the energy with which he had dealt with such attacks on governmental authority and the precautions he had taken to prevent any serious threats to public order. He had immediately revoked the mayor and the officers of the Saint-Didier National Guard and sent a squadron of cavalry to enforce his decree. After reporting this action, Mapaus turned his attention to the department as a whole.

> The precautionary measures that we have taken, above all the new garrison of Montluçon that keeps that turbulent population in check, the decree that I issued, with your authorization, to forbid banquets or demonstrations of such a kind as to trouble public tranquility, Citizen Mathé's counsels of prudence to his political friends, all converge today in assuring me that the socialist party will not dare to again take up arms this time. We are, moreover, perfectly prepared to resist at every point: at Moulins, where the population is subject to a certain disquietude—the inevitable consequence of our adversaries' threats— all the good citizens are preparing themselves for the struggle, more than eight hundred National Guardsmen hold themselves in readiness to defend threatened order and government alike at the risk of their lives.[121]

Two weeks later, De Sèze informed the Ministry of Justice that the "ever-growing firmness of government power" had created a return to law and order among the rural population.[122] Socialist propaganda no longer circulated freely, and the surveillance exercised on the local Montagnard leaders had made them more circumspect. The attorney general applauded Maupas' decree against all political meetings and was especially pleased by the condemnation of Fargin-Fayolle (a Montagnard deputy from Allier who had been arrested during the ill-fated Parisian protest against the Roman expedition), and by the impact of this decision on the morale of Fargin-Fayolle's supporters in Allier.

The attorney general's report for the month of April 1850, on the other hand, was an about-face. Writing soon after the election of Eugène Sue at Paris and after the radicals had won the municipal elections in the town of Cusset, De Sèze first bemoaned the fact that the Party of Order in Allier, which had succeeded in electing a conservative deputy to replace Fargin-Fayolle, was defeated at Cusset because it was divided by "a miserable question of local influence."[123] He now saw the left in his department as a unified force that was again growing in strength despite its defeat in the by-election of 10 March.

> But if order reigns on the surface, it hides beneath it a situation which should inspire serious concern. Since the election of 10 March, there are no more disorders in the streets. But the socialist party is more confident of the future. Its bearing shows increased security and boldness; and I am convinced that it gains ground every day. . . . All the nuances of the democratic opposition have arrayed themselves more or less under the socialist banner; and the very ones who viewed these doctrines as criminal insanity [des coupables folies], no longer have the courage to fight against them.[124]

Describing the growth of local secret societies, the attorney general informed Paris that rumors were circulating about the left's plans for an insurrection and that one club had received letters designating the victims "who must be delivered up to fire, to pillage and to the scaffold."[125] He did not, however, comment on the validity of such a story.

Why did this rapid alteration of tone occur in the reports of the attorney general? Probably because he was more worried about the power of the left in Paris, the revolutionary center of France, than by radicalism in his own *ressort*. The overwhelming victory of the capital's red list in March and April had the same impact on him as on frightened deputies like Montalembert. De Sèze concluded his report with statements about the centralization of France that are strikingly reminiscent of Tocqueville's work (written six years later) on the Revolution of 1789.

> The socialist party knows that the government cannot be overthrown except at Paris: but it also knows that there [Paris], where it disposes of a numerous army, there, where its leaders are . . . present, it can attack with success. . . . For sixty years the departments have allowed all the governments overthrown by Paris to fall and have accepted all those which Paris founded. They are struck by their impotence in the presence of this volcano in which all the revolutionary passions are in ferment and they remain convinced that they will no more stop the new eruption which threatens them than those which preceded it.[126]

Nonetheless, the final sentence of this fearful report reaffirmed the state's ability to weather the crisis. De Sèze was persuaded that the fear experienced by the notables (and obviously by himself) would diminish considerably if the government acted with firmness.

> But it is more into fear than into danger that the country is drifting. It is for the government to reassure it by energetic measures, and for the magistracy to support its action by the strength of its repressive justice.[127]

After the passage of the new electoral law at the end of May, De Sèze returned to a more confident outlook on the state of public order. From his report of July 1850 until after the assembly blocked the president's attempt to revise Article 45 a full year later, the attorney general at Riom, while fully cognizant that the left remained a considerable threat in Allier, seems to have been satisfied that the authorities were equal to their task of repression and capable, if necessary, of putting down a local insurrection.

In his July report De Sèze greeted the electoral law of 31 May as a show of unity between the Elysée and the assembly that demonstrated that the government was willing to take firm measures against the left. He saw the law as an important step in rebuilding the morale of the Party of Order and in stemming the tide of revolution: "The honest people, happy to feel themselves upheld, have regained their courage; the socialists, astonished by this vigorous act . . . have resigned themselves once again to awaiting a new chance."[128] The Mountain had sustained a major defeat: "The leaders of the party still try, either through the press, or by calumny, or by spreading false news reports, to excite political passions which have been somewhat calmed, but their efforts obtain few results of any consequence."[129]

In September he noted that the radicals were losing their hold over the peasant population.[130] In fact, his major concern at this time was that the improvement in the political situation in Allier would cause apathy among his and the prefect's subordinates. If their repressive zeal flagged, the left would again assert itself: "One instant of apathy and weakness could possibly suffice to stop the progress of public sanity [*raison publique*]."[131]

The news of the discovery of the *complot* of Lyon, far from frightening De Sèze, was welcomed as another indication of the left's growing desperation. The radicals were now in such disarray, according to the attorney general, that they were forced to trust their fortunes to the most risky enterprises.

I cannot refrain, given the present state of public opinion, from considering them as significant symptoms of the hopes and plans of a party that is disconcerted by the firmness of the government, that sees its chances diminish day by day due to the disillusionment of the population and that, accustomed to chance success, continues to dream of another chance at a 25 June [final battle of the June Days of 1848] and a dazzling reproduction of 24 February.[132]

He added that the authorities in his jurisdiction were in a position to deal with any uprisings.

In January 1851, in the midst of the growing conflict between the assembly and the president, De Sèze noted an increase in leftist activity but went on to reiterate his confidence in the ability of the police and the local Party of Order, which was unified in its support of Louis Napoleon, to maintain order.[133] De Sèze emphasized that the situation in Allier was not deteriorating as a result of the constitutional crisis. He concluded his report with a plea for unity in the Party of Order and for the cause of the president: "France at this moment wishes to be and feel itself to be governed. . . ."[134]

While De Sèze continued to inform Paris of the economic sufferings of the peasantry throughout 1851—a situation that he (and
the other law-enforcement bureaucrats) attributed to the political
uncertainties of the period—it was not until May that he reported
that the left was again making headway in the countryside.[135] He
wrote the ministry that the Mountain was more disciplined than
it had been in past years and that its members were carefully
avoiding any acts that could be prosecuted. But in July and September he still described a "satisfying calm" in the department.
The petitions supporting Louis Napoleon had been receiving support even in those areas of Allier where the Mountain was strongest.[136] In September, well after the revision had been defeated in
the Legislative Assembly and as the crisis year of 1852 loomed
closer, De Sèze asserted that "the defense of society against the
attacks of the factions would become easy, if everyone firmly resolved to give a courageous cooperation to the devotion of the
authorities."[137]

Finally, just a month before the coup d'état and the subsequent
outbreak of a desperate insurrection in the department, De Sèze
submitted a report strongly implying that both he and the prefect,
Charnailles, had seriously misunderstood the situation in Allier.
The attorney general in Riom asked Paris to send him a special
undercover police agent to gather evidence on the secret societies
in Allier, and particuarly around the town of Montluçon.[138] Completely contradicting the confidence of his reports for the past eighteen months, De Sèze was now asking the ministries of Justice and
Interior to consider an alarming request:

> I would, should I come to uncover the existence of secret soci-
> eties—which I have every reason to believe are organized in the
> department of Allier, ask you to propose to the cabinet that this
> department be placed under a state of siege. . . .[139]

It is apparent from this survey of the attorney general's descriptions of the balance of power in Allier that he was relatively untroubled by the very considerable strength of the Mountain there
and by its persistence despite the efforts to repress it. De Sèze had
been concerned about the left throughout the period 1849 to 1851,
but in the year and a half leading up to the coup d'état he had
refused to consider it as a "clear and present danger" to public
order. His regular reports to Paris were most definitely not the

chronicle of a red scare, either real, imagined, or faked. They indicated that the authorities were confounded by the very real power of the nascent radical movement in this part of rural France.

JURA

The secret societies were taken more seriously in Jura. The law-enforcement bureaucrats, despite some fluctuations in their outlook, continually informed Paris that this department contained an entrenched Montagnard movement, particularly in the wine- and grain-producing *arrondissements* of Dôle and Poligny (see Appendix 1).

The prefect and *procureur-général* responsible for Jura had a serious problem that bureaucrats in the other departments of our sample did not have to face. Jura is a border department. During the Second Republic, and especially after the events of 13 June 1849, the nearby city of Geneva sheltered a large community of radical exiles. Their communications with France had to be smuggled across the frontier into Jura before being sent south and west. In Jura, the agents of the central government had to worry constantly not only about the strong radical movement in the department, but also about the possibility that the exiles would come across the border to aid in any nationwide rising against the government. They also faced the frustration of seeing radical newspaper editors and the leaders of secret societies flee into Switzerland with relative ease whenever the authorities began to close in on them.

Like Allier, Jura responded to the appeal of the Montagnard deputies on 13 June 1849. In two towns of the *arrondissement* of Poligny—Salins and Arbois—and in Dôle, the *chef-lieu* of the neighboring *arrondissement*, meetings took place and volunteers were enrolled to go to the aid of a Parisian revolution.[140] But the crowds dispersed as soon as it became apparent that Paris had not rebelled. Although many republicans fled to Switzerland, some were arrested for this "*complot*." The authorities were unable, however, to obtain enough evidence to convict the participants.

Nevertheless, by November 1849 the attorney general at Besançon, Loiseau, was reporting that a semblance of order was returning, although republicanism was still a growing force on the agricultural plain of Jura. Outward peace was nonetheless a welcome improvement in the state of public order:

the enforcement of the laws is becoming easier and repression more severe; no more songs, no more outcries, no more public meetings, no more demonstrations; the authorities are regaining a little of the power which they had in earlier times and which was so difficult to give back to them after our late political commotions.[141]

Loiseau considered Jura the most turbulent department in his jurisdiction and devoted almost his entire report to a description of conditions there. The economic roots of radicalism among the debt-ridden small farmers he considered comparatively unimportant: "I think that the evil is more spread out than it is deep and that it comes from accidental causes."[142] Republican propaganda and an "immoderate" desire for material improvement were the real causes for the sudden growth of radicalism in this previously peaceful agricultural department. And the spread of republican ideas was beyond the reach of the authorities:

> evil has made some progress in several towns such as . . . Salins, Arbois and Poligny . . . with the help of a hidden and almost imperceptible propaganda—imperceptible because it is carried on less by writings and public speeches than within the intimacy of private communications. This propaganda, which seems to be redoubling its ardor at this moment, goes on neither with books nor with doctrines; it intrudes itself into families, it places itself within the home, it attracts the most evil passions [mauvaises passions]. . . . Often a single man who has the password within a town suffices to pervert [pervertir] practically the whole population of a commune, to dominate public opinion and direct the elections. Under the influence of a single person, or of a very small number, we have seen populations, once friendly to order, suddenly blinded and giving their votes to candidates endorsed by the anarchists.[143]

Loiseau described the local republicans as disciplined and well organized, but he was certain that Jura would never rise in revolt alone. It would only participate in an insurrection that had broken out elsewhere: in Alsace, at Lyon, or in a group of other neighboring departments. But to ensure the stability of the area and to police the frontier, he did ask Paris to station garrisons at Lons-le-Saunier, the departmental *chef-lieu*, and at Arbois and Poligny, the

most ardently republican towns. Soon thereafter, units of the Army
of the Alps were sent to these potential trouble spots.[144]

Jura was one of the few departments in France, and the only
one in our sample, in which moderate republicans, men of *Le
National*, played a leading role in the democratic movement
throughout the lifespan of the Second Republic. In two elections,
Jules Grévy came in first on a list that also included radical republicans. These were the elections for the Constituent and then
the Legislative Assembly. In a by-election held in July 1849, another
moderate beat a democratic socialist by over 2,000 votes.[145]

Yet throughout this period the attorney general in Besançon
persisted in lumping all republicans together as professed or disguised anarchists; at best, he sometimes described the moderates
as tools of the radicals. In January 1850 he noted a growing unity
on the left.

> I will limit myself at this time to drawing your full attention to
> the more and more complete rapprochement among the men
> who profess advanced opinions; the old nuances are giving way;
> the old republicans are identifying themselves with the socialists.
> On the other hand, the most extremist hide their plans and even
> their flag and efface themselves as much as possible. . . . They
> practice to the letter the well-known dictum: In revolution, it is
> necessary to hide the goal one wishes to reach.[146]

During December, Loiseau had received from his *substituts* reports of an improved situation in Jura. He traveled to Lons-le-
Saunier, Dôle, and Arbois to see for himself, but concluded from
his own observations that the improvement was more apparent
than real. The left still remained a potential threat to public order
although its size had been reduced to that of an "infinitesimal
minority" (except in the town of Salins, which it dominated). In
order for real stability to be achieved in the department, the authorities had to exercise "great efforts and an unflagging energy."[147]

The attorney general reserved the most bitter comments for the
local Party of Order. The conservative coalition in the Jura "does
nothing, absolutely nothing, to fight them off [the republicans]; it
is the most numerous and shows itself to be the weakest; it is
under the influence of a panic and does not even try to hide it;
voter, juror, national guardsman, they all flee from their duties
and their abstention is more and more evident."[148] The law-en-

forcement bureaucrat deplored the impact of the red scare on precisely those elements of the population that should have been aiding the authorities in their work of repression.

The next month, however, the attorney general in Besançon hoped that the fright of the elite would be strong enough to unify the legitimists and Orleanists in Jura, but he doubted that the two factions could ever overcome their local rivalries.[149] The beginnings of the conflict between Louis Napoleon and the assembly and the recent passage of a tax on wine consumption had caused an increase in radical activity in Jura, particularly in the wine-growing *arrondissement* of Dôle. Loiseau complained that the police forces in this department were totally ineffective against the growth of secret societies and the circulation of radical brochures and almanacs. The police commissioners were everywhere blocked in their investigations by the republican mayors of most of the communes. These mayors refused to act as agents of the central government and place themselves at the disposal of the prefect or the local prosecutors.[150]

Loiseau nonetheless expressed hope in a special report on Jura requested by the ministry during February. He praised the work of the prefectoral administration and described even the most radical parts of the department as calm.[151] Loiseau felt that the situation would improve markedly as soon as the prices of agricultural goods increased to their normal levels. "Do we have there a lost situation, or simply one which is very compromised? I am far from viewing it as hopeless despite the depth and extent of the evil. . . . Everywhere, the authorities are respected. I would not doubt the possibility of an amelioration of public opinion. . . ."[152]

The prefect, Vincent, agreed with the attorney general's wary optimism at this point. In response to a ministerial circular warning him of the possibility of troubles at Arbois on 24 February, the anniversary of the revolution, the prefect assured Paris that the greatest tranquility reigned throughout the department and that the authorities were prepared for any localized disturbances.[153] In a dispatch to the general commanding the local garrisons, Vincent made it clear that the *arrondissements* of Dôle and Poligny were centers of republican agitation, but he emphasized that no serious troubles had broken out for some time. While he was sure that the local radicals were just as militant as they had been in June 1849, he was equally confident that Jura would not be troubled on 24 February unless rebellion broke out elsewhere in France.[154]

In June the attorney general welcomed the revision of the electoral law as a sharp reverse to the morale of the local republicans.[155] But, unlike the bureaucrats responsible for Allier, the authorities in Jura never lost sight of the persistent activity of the secret societies that went on beyond their reach. Loiseau observed that "the evil is deep, immense; if the agitators confess their impotence today, it is only to take up their task for tomorrow with a new boldness. . . . This situation is less a return to the good than it is a breathing space in the progress of evil."[156] He was pleased, however, that he had succeeded in silencing all but one of the republican newspapers in the department.

Louis Napoleon visited Jura in September 1850 and received an enthusiastic welcome in Lons-le-Saunier, including many shouts of "Vive Napoléon!" This led the attorney general in Besançon to conclude that the destruction of the republican press had aided the administration in detaching the population from the influence of the radical leaders.[157] He was now certain that his prosecution of the surviving publication of the left, *La Tribune du Jura*, would also result in its going under. "Public spirit" was improving; Loiseau devoted most of his report to the actions of the local legitimists in the Conseil Général and to the reports in their newspaper, which were directed against Louis Napoleon's drive to revise the constitution. The whites had successfully blocked the petition campaign in Jura, and, because they were the majority in the departmental council, they had refused to pass a resolution asking for revision.

The prefect also noted an improvement. He reported that the radical republican deputies (Richardet, Jacqueau, and Versini) had made an unsuccessful tour of Jura, having been met with "indifference and coldness" from their old supporters.[158] His only worry, though he did not take it very seriously, was the possibility of an invasion by the Montagnard exiles across the Swiss border.

Beginning in December 1850, however, and continuing throughout 1851, the law-enforcement bureaucrats repeatedly warned Paris of the strength of local secret societies and of the increasing preparations and optimism among the republicans as 1852 drew nearer. In December Loiseau reported that the *complot* of Lyon did not seem to have extended its network into Jura.[159] Although quiet reigned in the department, he was frustrated in his work of repression by the underground work of the secret societies: "Beaten in armed insurrections, reduced to impotence in the press and by the latest legislative actions, anarchy would find itself at the end of its resources had it not found, in the organization and recruitment of secret societies, new nourishment for its activity."[160]

While their leaders publicly urged the radicals to put off all action until 1852, Loiseau still feared "an earlier movement." The divisions within the local Party of Order, which reflected the two sides of the conflict in the assembly over the revision of Article 45, and the weakening of the government's authority as a result of this clash, led the attorney general to observe that the gains made for "order" by the electoral law of 31 May were now in jeopardy.[161] The suffering of the peasants, due to consistently low prices for their crops, and the disharmony among the conservatives, created—in Loiseau's opinion—an atmosphere of potential revolution. And the militancy of the radical rank and file meant that it might sweep aside the cautions of its national and local leaders.

> At the moment when the cunning and ambitious within the demagogic party prepare themselves to profit from the victory of socialism, some very significant symptoms indicate that their authority would be powerless to hold back the movement which they are preparing, even if they wished to do so. . . . The hatred and jealousy of the lower classes for the upper classes knows no further limits.[162]

In June 1851 Loiseau again pointed out that the secret societies were disguising themselves as Masonic lodges or as charitable organizations and thus avoiding his efforts to gather incriminating evidence. Later in the summer, after failing once again to obtain convictions, he asked the prefect simply to decree that these groups, disguished as Bons Cousins (charity clubs), could no longer hold meetings in the department.[163] The prefect banned the meetings and then warned the mayors (who by now were mostly conservatives, since the administration had suspended many republican municipal administrations) to maintain a close surveillance on secret societies: "For some time now the department of Jura has enjoyed a happy tranquility, but . . . let us not fool ourselves, they work to compromise it, to make it disappear from among us and replace.it with agitation."[164]

Loiseau's concern intensified during the fall. In September the attorney general noted that, while some members of the left were preparing the departmental list in anticipation of the 1852 elections (a list headed by Grévy, whose role was to be a "passport" for the radicals), "others, more fervent, say that it is altogether useless to discuss such issues, and that it is necessary to prepare another struggle, the social revolution no longer being possible except by force of arms."[165] The concerns of the authorities were justified dramatically after the coup. On the night of 3-4 December 1851, hundreds of republicans from Salins and Arbois joined their comrades at Poligny, arrested the subprefect, and distributed arms in preparation for a march on Lons-le-Saunier.[166]

Conclusion

For each department we have studied, it appears that the law-enforcement bureaucrats made their reports without exaggeration and without any indication of a nationally orchestrated red scare. Their views changed as the local conditions changed and as the coalition of order deteriorated, both in the departments and in Paris. Only those police bureaucrats who had actual problems on their hands expressed alarm to their ministers. In the troubled departments of Allier and Gard, the police administration actually played down any radical threat to the government; yet serious risings in both these jurisdictions occurred in the wake of the coup d'état. In Jura and Rhône, the attorneys general were certainly not exaggerating the socialist peril. Both Gilardin and Loiseau often expressed fear of an imminent insurrection; but in both Rhône and Jura the secret societies controlled important urban and rural areas, and these societies were indeed armed and did indeed speak of revolution in their meetings. Moreover, the underground organizations of the left seemed to operate completely beyond the reach of the legal means of repression. They remained an imposing force-in-being (to borrow a phrase from Admiral Mahan) until Louis Napoleon transformed the Second Republic into a real police state. On the day after the coup, he placed more than a third of the country under martial law.

The problem of radicalism did not simply disappear after the June Days of 1848 or 1849. It persisted or even grew, not only in traditional centers of revolutionary activity like Paris and Lyon, but also in many other regions of urban and rural France. In Rhône, Allier, and Jura the radicals enjoyed the electoral support of the majority of citizens in the towns *and* the countryside. Meanwhile, the government itself began to break apart. By 1851, especially after the assembly's failure in July to amend the constitution, the executive and legislative branches no longer seemed capable of maintaining a united front, and yet the radical movement had won decisive electoral victories as recently as April 1850. Disunity seriously endangered the prestige of the government and thus its ability to maintain order in republican areas that it had viewed and administered almost as occupied territories since 1849. Furthermore the army, under Changarnier, had appeared to threaten Louis Napoleon with a coup d'état in 1850. If it now turned against the Elysée and supported the assembly, the bureaucrats would be serving an elite in total disarray; a mass-based and increasingly well-organized democratic socialist movement would confront a weakened government from many points in central, eastern, and southern France. The victory of the Mountain would represent the end of society as the notables knew it.

5 The Limits of Repressive Techniques before the Coup

With the major Marxist theorists of counterrevolution, from Marx himself to Mayer and Marcuse, historians of the Second Republic have believed that the leftward momentum of a revolution is spent, and counterrevolution is automatically triumphant, once the full force of the state is turned against the revolutionaries. The corollary to this "law" is that any fear professed by the ruling class is merely a calculated justification for obliterating the opposition, which was more an annoyance than a genuine threat. Yet the writers who have made these assumptions are surprisingly mute on the technical aspects of political repression, even though police work and prosecuting are technical matters. The rulers' purposes may be evaluated, but such an evaluation is empty if performance and effects are ignored. Too many assumptions have been made in the study of the reaction in France that began with the inauguration of Louis Napoleon and reached its climax with his seizure of dictatorial power. In fact, the state's power was limited in dealing with the new mass movement for political and social reform.

Between 1849 and 1851 the prosecutors and prefects were ineffective, despite comprehensive enabling laws, in destroying the radical threat to the world of the notables. Although the legislation of 1848, 1849, and 1850 had established the bases for wide-ranging police powers, the law-enforcement bureaucrats were hindered from carrying out their assigned tasks until the coup d'état finally swept away the considerable barriers to effective counterrevolution. Only when more than a third of France had been placed under martial law and the entire country subjected to the summary "justice" of the Mixed Commissions could the dictatorship of Louis Napoleon succeed in rooting out a mass-based radical movement that for three years had resisted the repressive drive of the prefects and prosecutors.

The obstacles to political repression under the Second Republic were consequences of both traditional and recent circumstances. In the first place, the police bureaucrats found themselves confronted by a radical movement that had taken root after 1848 among broad categories of a newly enfranchised (and politicized) citizenry in whole regions of France. Under the July Monarchy the prefects and prosecutors had been used to dealing with isolated republican sects in specific urban centers. Now they faced a "subversive" force that had not only greatly expanded its base in the cities but had also moved out into the countryside. The Mountain was now so large a movement and so well entrenched in certain urban neighborhoods (like La Croix Rousse) and in whole rural districts that its size was difficult to gauge and its underground organization, after 1849, almost impossible to penetrate.

In the second place, the left usually went about its activities beyond the ken of the law-enforcement bureaucrats. We have already seen an excellent example of this in the attorney general's reports on Allier. In a department where radical republicanism had demonstrated overwhelming strength at the polls in 1848 and 1849, it was not until late in 1851 that this bureaucrat actually took the secret societies seriously. The *procureur-général* was apparently unaware of the size and extent of the red menace he was supposed to suppress. The men responsible for Gard, Jura, and Rhône were more concerned about the radical underground than their colleague at Riom, but they too had great difficulty in estimating the size of the republican movement they faced and in finding out what the Mountain was planning to do in their jurisdictions. The law-enforcement bureaucrats could not bridge the gap that separated the social elites they defended (and to which they belonged) from the middle, lower-middle and lower-class "masses" that threatened them. Throughout the period, the prefects and prosecutors remained remarkably ignorant of what was going on among the politically awakened segments of the social classes beneath them. One of their major complaints, reiterated time and again, was that they did not possess the means to gather information on republicanism in their jurisdictions. In sum, the prosecutors and prefects were usually well aware of their ignorance of the actual strength, internal organization, and strategies of the radical movement they were supposed to police. The bureaucrats knew only that they faced a novel and unpredictable danger.

A third source of frustration to the prosecutors and prefects was the existing legal and administrative system itself. The liberal court procedures established after the Revolution of 1789 were not significantly changed by the dominant conservative coalition in the assemblies of the Second Republic. The most powerful group within the Party of Order, the Orleanists, was made up of classic liberals. They passed laws confining political freedom within the limits that had existed under the July Monarchy, but they did not tamper with a legal system that protected the individual against the untrammeled power of the state. Trial by jury remained a requirement for all offenses punishable by heavy fines or lengthy prison sentences. Thus a jury had to decide all cases involving serious breaches of the press and association laws promulgated under the republic. Jurors were chosen by lot from voting rolls, and universal manhood suffrage had opened the jury box to virtually all male citizens over the age of twenty-one.[1] Juries in republican departments refused to convict fellow radicals who were brought to trial. Legitimist jurors in Gard or western France were also tolerant of political offenders, even of the left, since their own leaders and newspaper editors were sometimes brought up on the same charges. Even in matters involving the press, in which the evidence of lawbreaking was printed for all to see, a considerable number of prosecutions were usually required to obtain a single conviction. As under the July Monarchy, the bureaucrats had to wage a long-term war of attrition against individual directors, editors, and printers in order to close down republican newspapers. They took cases into police courts (*tribunaux correctionnels*) where there were no juries, and directors were harrassed and sometimes bankrupted by a steady rhythm of press seizures, suspensions, small fines, and short jail sentences.

Judges continued to enjoy tenure for life, and they frequently demonstrated their independence of the political branches of the government by refusing to reverse unfavorable jury verdicts; if they did find a defendant guilty, they sometimes handed down very light sentences. To the dismay of the prefects and prosecutors, the judiciary rarely made allowances for the social crisis of the Second Republic: they refused to convict political offenders on shaky or circumstantial evidence. This was usually the only sort of information the authorities could gather against the secret societies. The men charged with participation in the *complot* of Lyon were not tried by the civilian courts. The republic's most successful prosecution of the secret societies took place before a court-martial.

In this chapter, we shall first consider the exceptional repressive activities—those measures that *were* to some degree effective. The most effective repression was directed against republican communal administrations and against members of the civil service who were suspected of harboring radical sentiments. The government's control over such officials was direct; their suspension or dismissal was a matter that could generally be handled within the administrative bureaucracies themselves.

Republican Mayors

The most important administrative impediment to repression was the Montagnard municipality. It was at least partially overcome during the course of the Second Republic, but only after playing a crucial role in establishing the nascent republican movement as the dominant force in many rural localities. In Gard, Jura, Allier, Rhône, and even in some districts of Gironde, with poor communications between the administrative *chefs-lieux* and many towns and hamlets, the prefect had to rely on the mayors to enforce his decrees and to issue their own orders barring republican activities in their communes. During the July Monarchy, the government (that is, the prefect) appointed the mayors of every city and town of France, regardless of size. Under the republic, in towns with no more than 6,000 inhabitants mayors were chosen by the democratically elected municipal councilors from among their own number.[2] The mayors of small republican towns were, therefore, the leaders of precisely those radical groups that the superior authorities wanted to disband. As long as they could stay in office, republican mayors simply defied the law-enforcement bureaucrats. They permitted illegal associations and sanctioned political meetings banned by prefectoral decrees.

According to the administrative code, mayors and their *adjoints* were required to take orders from the prefect and subprefect in police matters. As local officers of the *police judiciaire*, they were also subordinates of the prosecutor and *juge d'instruction* in reporting and investigating crimes. A refusal to submit to higher authority could result in the suspension or dismissal of the mayor or of the entire municipal council. Suspension could be ordered by a simple prefectoral decree; dismissal was a much more difficult process, requiring a decision by the Conseil d'état in Paris. As in any court procedure, this administrative supreme court heard both sides of the case. Proof of malfeasance or of lawbreaking was necessary before the Conseil d'état would dissolve a communal administration or remove mayors and *adjoints*. Perhaps the conservative councilors were inhibited from blatant political repression by the publication of their public deliberations, in the *Journal Officiel*. Or perhaps, like many other Orleanist jurists under the Second Republic, they were loath to compromise their sincerely held liberal principles by stretching the rules of evidence to convict republicans. Whatever the reasons, the outright dismissal of municipal administrations or mayors was rare, except in cases in which a town official was caught in the very act of breaking the political laws of the republic. The mayors of Allier who participated in the armed gathering that occurred on the night of 13-14 June 1849 were deprived of their offices for this reason, even though most of them had been acquitted of any criminal charges by the Puy-de-Dôme Assize Court.[3]

Nevertheless, during 1849 and 1850 the government succeeded in driving many republican town administrations from office for lengthy periods of time. This was done by repeatedly suspending mayors and *adjoints* on a variety of pretexts. The policing of municipal councils was the responsibility of the prefects; few documents describe this form of repression in detail. Georges Rougeron, who has studied the records of nearly every town in Allier, lists thirty-three mayors and *adjoints* who were suspended or removed between April 1849 and November 1850.[4] Only the five who had taken part in the June Days of 1849 were actually dismissed. By November 1850, fourteen mayors and ten *adjoints* were still temporarily barred from holding office. One mayor was suspended by Maupas for having publicly stated that priests and nobles were "enemies of the people." Another was suspended for having worked for Ledru-Rollin's candidacy for the Legislative Assembly in 1849. According to Maupas, this mayor had thus demonstrated "his hostility against the government of the republic."

Similar measures were taken in other departments where republicanism was an important local force. In Gard, the *adjoint* of Montjuin was suspended in July 1849 for participating in a "seditious demonstration."[5] In December 1850 the prefect suspended a mayor for displaying portraits of Barbès and Ledru-Rollin in the town hall.[6] The prefect of Jura in February 1850 was waiting for an excuse to suspend two mayors who were known to be Montagnard leaders.

Even this purely administrative form of repression was not entirely successful. Suspensions could remain in force only for a limited time, and republican mayors eventually took up their duties

again. Prefectorally appointed commissioners, replacing suspended town administrations, found it difficult to enforce repressive policies against the largely hostile citizenry of republican communes. Usually a conservative from the same commune, the
temporary commissioner had to work without the cooperation of
the town council, which had chosen the suspended mayor. The
local unit of the National Guard was similarly made up of republicans, if it had not already been disarmed and dissolved by the
government. The town that the commissioner administered was
often a considerable distance from the nearest gendarmerie garrison, and discrete unawareness frequently must have been the
better part of valor. Conservative mayors chosen after the revision
of the electoral law faced similar problems of being the isolated
agents of the Party of Order deep in enemy territory. In January
1850, six months after Rhône had been placed under martial law,
the attorney general in Lyon complained that the mayors in rural
areas were providing no help to his *substituts* or to the other police
authorities:

> From all sides I receive complaints about the mayors. . . . In the
> countryside there exist no judiciary police, no administrative
> police and no municipal police. . . . Since the republican con-
> stitution and universal suffrage have spread political activity and
> stirred up democratic sentiment in every last hamlet of the coun-
> try, it is clear that a counter-balance of authority has become
> more necessary than ever; and the municipal law has done ex-
> actly the opposite: it has weakened governmental authority in
> all the small towns of the countryside, which is to say, through-
> out the most extensive regions of France.[7]

Vincent, the prefect of Jura, dissolved the entire municipal council of Salins after it passed a resolution protesting the Roman expedition and then joined the other republicans of the city in preparing for an armed march on Paris in June 1849.[8] But the prefect
could find no group of conservatives who were willing to serve as
interim commissioners for this Montagnard town. From Besançon,
the attorney general wrote to Vincent in July:

> I have been informed that all the members designated to form
> the provisional town council of Salins have refused to accept this
> mission. The cause for their refusals is . . . the fear of being
> turned out of office in the next elections by a population which

is still saturated with the most subversive ideas, and in which exasperation can only increase from the very outset of their tenure in office.[9]

Finally, in October 1849, new elections were held, and the old Montagnard council was reelected in toto.[10] The prefect's only recourse was to call for a doubling of the garrison in the town. Vincent faced a similar problem in December. The mayor of Clairvaux, his *adjoint*, and his secretary (the schoolteacher) were brought to the prefect's attention by the interior minister as the leaders of the secret society in the *arrondissement*.[11] Vincent told Paris that removing the mayor would only lead to his replacement by other radical leaders.[12] He added that the government would have to rely on the gendarmerie brigade that was stationed in Clairvaux to keep the left under control. Finally, a month later, the administration tried to suspend the mayor of Clairvaux for the possession of contraband (untaxed) Swiss gunpowder.[13] We know that he was still in office in February, however; the attorney general in Besançon complained that he had refused to disperse a demonstration protesting the firing of the schoolteacher.

Despite the considerable number of dismissals and suspensions that had occurred in Allier, the attorney general in Riom reported in April 1850 that the mayors were not reporting republican schoolteachers in their communes.[14] The prefect of Charente-Inférieure succeeded in dissolving one of the few republican town councils in his department only in August 1851.[15] And in Lyon, now under a state of siege for almost two years, the municipal elections of 1851 were a total victory for the Mountain.[16]

The suspended or fired municipal authorities, using the facilities of the Montagnard press in their departments, were quick to use the repressive actions of the police bureaucrats as object lessons for fellow republicans. Their responses, however, were not those of beaten or isolated men, but rather those of political leaders who retained the support and respect of their communes. *Le Républicain de l'Allier* of 31 December 1848 published a sharp rejoinder of Georges Gallay, mayor of Donjon, to the prefect who had suspended him. Rather than accept the suspension, Gallay and his *adjoint* resigned both to underscore their protest and to force an early call for new town elections. Addressing himself to Coquet, the moderate republican prefect trying vainly to win favor with Louis Napoleon and Barrot, Gallay called his suspension "an act in which cowardice and servility compete for dominance" and an example of "low prostitution towards the new government."[17] Mixing irony and insouciance, he made clear to both the prefect and his readers that his suspension was a purely political act, punishment for his support of Ledru-Rollin against the presidential candidacies of Cavaignac and Louis Napoleon:

> I am not going to trifle with you by playing a game of false political modesty. Understand me? I will only remind you for the moment, Sir, that the commune of Donjon is one of the most "wicked" in the whole department; that its voters gave 574 out of 800 votes to Ledru-Rollin. Your declaration of war is therefore, in truth, thrown in the face of these 574 electors.[18]

Fined and jailed for publishing this letter, Gallay became the first radical martyr of Allier and was twice selected by the Mountain as its candidate in by-elections for the Legislative Assembly.

The revocation of the mayor of Libourne led *La Tribune de la Gironde* to observe that "it involved, quite simply, a⸳ attempt to throw our town, and with it the whole *arrondissement*, into the reactionary movement."[19] Like the radical town council of Donjon, that of Libourne was reelected within months.[20] The town council of Arbois, refusing to appoint a town policeman chosen by the prefect, resigned en masse. Its letter was not, however, addressed directly to the prefect of Jura, but published as a public notice in *La Démocratie Jurassienne*. The council refused to implement the decrees of "a magistrate, given his powers in the name of the democratic republic, . . . who has honored himself by calling himself a WHITE."[21]

The prefects were clearly dissatisifed with only suspensory powers over municipal governments. They wanted the right to appoint the mayors themselves—a power they had exercised under the July Monarchy. In response to a questionnaire sent to them by Vivien's Legislative Commission of the Conseil d'état in the summer of 1849, only six prefects in the entire corps defended the right of the small municipalities to choose their own mayors. Two of these nonconformists went so far as to argue that all towns, including the largest cities, should have the same democratic system of mayoral selection as that used in France's smaller communes under the republic. Only one of the prefects in the sample we analyzed in chapter 3 was in favor of the municipal selection of mayors, and he was one of the two who wanted to extend this right to all the cities of France: the moderate republican Chanal, who was then the prefect at Strasbourg (Bas-Rhin).[22] The other moderate republican who was still in service at this time, Wissocq, joined the majority of administrators in asking for a return to the prefectoral selection of mayors.[23]

Republican Civil Servants

The government was more successful in weeding out republicans from among its own appointees. The prefectoral corps was purged of moderate republicans in 1849, and throughout the presidency of Louis Napoleon a close surveillance was maintained on all civil servants. Those suspected of leftist sympathies were dealt with severely, from the most important members of the bureaucracy down to the humblest postmaster or rural policeman.

Historians generally agree in dating this administrative repression to the first *ministère des commis* (the cabinet appointed by Louis Bonaparte in October 1849, which was composed of relatively obscure friends of the Elysée), with Ferdinand Barrot at the Interior Ministry, Rouher at the Justice Ministry, and General d'Hautpoul at the War Ministry.[24] It is true that these three ministers sent out simultaneous circulars to their subordinates (the War Ministry commanded the Gendarmerie Nationale) asking for reports on all state functionaries in their jurisdiction. A secret circular from Rouher went to the *procureurs-généraux* asking them for "a careful estimation of the character, the behavior, and the political conduct of magistrates without permanent tenure."[25] He also requested information on functionaries belonging to other state services. The attorneys general were called upon to report "the shortcomings and bad inclinations" of all civil servants in their *ressorts*.[26] The circulars of the other ministers were written in the same terms.

As argued earlier, however, the repressive drive of Bonaparte's men differed in no way from that of members of the Party of Order who preceded them in office. In March 1849 Faucher wrote to his prefect at Nîmes: "Please point out those government officials who give you uncertain support: those who may falter in the fulfillment of their duty."[27] The first advocate general at Besançon wrote to Odilon Barrot before the fall of the liberal ministry:

You set us the example, Minister, and this example cannot fail to rouse a noble emulation. . . . However painful it may be for me, I would not hesitate to denounce the reprehensible acts of officials placed under my surveillance.[28]

This prosecutor went on to describe his investigations of civil servants who worked for other ministries: "rural postmen, rural policemen, drivers in the road and bridge service and, above all, employees of the local road maintenance service."[29] He added that schoolteachers and tax collectors were also being scrutinized for subversive tendencies.

In large part, we owe the state of tumult that still exists in the country to these functionaries. I have seen and questioned many of them. . . . These men know from experience that they live under a paternalistic administration which almost never employs harsh forms of discipline and they abuse this freedom.

The thought of criticizing the spirit of forebearance which characterizes the present government is far from my mind, but it is time . . . to replace indulgence with severity.[30]

Gilardin, the *procureur-général* in Lyon, similarly informed Odilon Barrot that he was carrying out a directive of 22 June 1849 calling for harsh measures against republican functionaries.[31]

Minor civil servants were not the only ones to suffer for their democratic political opinions. As soon as he took office in January 1849, Thourel, the attorney general in Nîmes, dismissed his two most important *substituts* in the department of Gard: the prosecutors at Nîmes and Uzès.[32] According to the attorney general, they had expressed "*opinions exaltées.*" A few months later Thourel dismissed an even more important official of the *parquet* for political reasons: his first advocate general.[33]

Ode, the prosecutor at Uzès, was apparently an active member of the local republican club. In February 1849, while he was awaiting his replacement, Ode participated in a street brawl between legitimists and republicans in which gunshots were exchanged.[34] Far from putting an end to the fight, the prosecutor, who had been drinking in the local republican café, joined in the melee. The prefect himself had to go to Uzès to quiet things down. Almost two years later, Ode was arrested as a key figure in the *complot* of Lyon. The former prosecutor had become a leader of the Young Mountain in Gard.

Thourel had more serious and chronic problems involving his personal staff in Nîmes. Despite his earlier dismissals, he was still complaining in May 1850 that his first advocate general, second advocate general, and another member of the *parquet* had been won over to radical republicanism.

> But . . . if the material order has not been disturbed around me, I cannot say the same for the *moral order* and I feel as much surprise as pity to see these intelligent—even rich—men, functionaries raised to the highest honors, permit themselves to be carried away into extremism, some because of fear, some because of ambition and, finally, others because of their vacillating and weak characters, drawing nearer to a party which will make them its first victims.[35]

He asked the minister to refuse to accept the proferred resignation of Demians, the first advocate general, which was couched in a letter composed as nothing less than an indictment of the political favoritism practiced by Thourel, of the Roman expedition, and of the "contempt for the constitution" shown by the government's restriction of the suffrage.[36] Instead, the *procureur-général* demanded Demians' dismissal sine die and his prosecution for insulting a public official: Thourel himself. He assured Rouher, the Justice Minister, that such an action would have a "salutary effect" on the two other republicans in his office and avoid the political embarrassment of firing all three at once.[37] Demians' greatest sin had been to publish his correspondence with Thourel and his resignation from the ministry in *Le Républicain du Gard*.[38] Though the publicity of the matter caused an enormous stir in Nîmes, Rouher refused to authorize any prosecution of Demians or the newspaper. Fearing that Thourel's "dignity" would be endangered, he merely fired the first advocate general.[39]

Among lesser civil servants, the government first moved against those directly responsible for law enforcement at the cantonal level: the justices of the peace. These local magistrates had the power to issue arrest warrants, open investigative proceedings against lawbreakers, judge minor misdemeanors, and, most important, oversee the electoral lists and preside at the polling place. As part-time members of the bureaucracy they were also required to report to the prefect and attorney general on potentially illegal political activities in their communes.[40]

The campaign to replace untrustworthy justices of the peace began soon after Louis Napoleon's inauguration. In Janury 1849 Thourel reported that he was dismissing a considerable number of these appointees who had permitted local disorders to take place or had participated in such demonstrations.[41] By November of that year, when Rouher first required that monthly *procureur-général* reports be submitted to the Justice Ministry, each prosecutor was informing his superiors that changes in the ranks of the justices of the peace had already been made.

Again the republican press publicized such measures. It used the protests of fired justices of the peace to attack the administration's abuse of technical powers to achieve political ends. Rather than remain, even temporarily, in an office that he had taken to aid Lebeuf, who had served as justice of the peace in Lesparre since February 1848, his friend and assistant wrote a scathing resignation letter that was published in *La Tribune de la Gironde*: "It was at his frankly republican point of view that they wished to strike. . . . It is up to all democrats to point out to the government the abyss which it is digging under its own feet."[42] *La Tribune's* editor pointed out that Lebeuf had been replaced at Lesparre by the July Monarchy's justice of the peace within the twenty-four hours preceding the presidential election; he decried a shabby electoral maneuver.[43] Just before the elections for the Legislative Assembly, *Le Républicain de l'Allier* reported the dismissal of four justices of the peace within the space of a single week and emphasized that their replacements were all members of the conservative parties and that two of them had fulfilled the same functions under Louis Philippe: "We had foreseen these dismissals: the presidency of polling places could not have been allowed to remain in hands stained with republicanism."[44]

Finding new justices of the peace who could be counted upon to aid the prosecutors proved to be a more difficult problem, particularly in the west of France. The government clearly wanted to keep extreme legitimists from exercising local police powers. In March 1849 Damay, the *procureur-général* in Poitiers, wrote to his *substitut* at Fontenay: "Regarding your work on the justices of the peace, I was happy to see that none of these magistrates can be suspected of hostility to our new institutions, and that their previous conduct offers us every guarantee of their independence of character, unselfishness and sincerity."[45] But Damay went on to criticize his subordinate's report for the vague political description of each justice of the peace, which the *procureur-général* was sure would be unacceptable to the ministry in Paris. He wanted to know what his assistant meant when he used the phrases "devoted to the republic," "honorable political antecedents," or "irreproach-able antecedents."[46] Damay cautioned his prosecutor to be more exact in rewriting his report: *"devoted to the republic* must, by itself, be inexact. . . . It is quite a different thing to be a legitimist who accepts the republic in the interests of social peace, or to be a liberal whose sympathies are with the Democratic Cause, or even to be a former opponent of the previous [Orleanist] government."[47] In 1850, while the justices of the peace were revising the electoral rolls to conform with the restriction of the suffrage, Damay again signaled his *substituts* to make sure that extreme legitimists were not involved in this process.[48] The "white" Mountain had opposed the electoral law of 31 May 1850 in the belief that democracy would aid the eventual restoration of the Bourbons.

Minor court officials were subjected to a similar scrutiny. In April 1849 Damay pleaded for the reinstatement of the court recorder at Napoléon-Vendée's tribunal. This clerk had been dismissed by the ministry for belonging to the tiny branch of Solidarité Républicaine in the town. Damay described the recorder as a town fool who was well loved in Napoléon-Vendée. He had been invited to join the republican club as a joke and had participated only out of vanity: "He has felt the full extent of his mistake and the fear which he experienced at being deprived of the position which gave him his livelihood has already been a severe punishment for him."[49] The clerk was reinstated.

I have found no political complaints against the officers of the Gendarmerie Nationale in the reports of the prefects and prose-cutors in our sample. The attorneys general, however, were un-happy with the failures of the local police to prevent republican activities or to gather evidence against the secret societies. Gilardin was particularly harsh in his criticism of the police force in Lyon, which provided him with no useful information on the clandestine republican groups in the city. The attorney general at Besançon went even further in his negative evaluation of the police in Jura. He claimed that the local police were easily bribed or cowed into permitting the republicans to hold meetings and to circulate their pamphlets and almanacs in many rural communes. These officials were supposed to carry out prefectoral orders, although they were appointed by the town councils. The government was powerless to replace them; and attorney general went on to demand a new municipal law that would give the prefects this right. According to Loiseau, only the central government could purge the local police: "The mayors who are devoted to us (and their number is remarkably small) [in Jura] dare not take the necessary measures against the police agents whom we point out to them for dismissal because they fear the influence of these village policemen, almost all of whom were born and raised in the localities where they hold their posts."[50]

Republican Schoolteachers

Next to mayors and justices of the peace, teachers were considered the most potentially dangerous government officials in France. We have already described how the Falloux law was welcomed by anticlerical conservatives as a blow against the "red army" of schoolmasters. The government, however, had moved against subversive primary schoolteachers and professors well before the passage of this measure. In October 1849 a schoolteacher at Saint-Jean-d'Angély (Charente-Inférieure) was dismissed by the city council for being a republican.[51] This was done despite the fact that a police search of his home had turned up no subversive literature or incriminating letters. A month later the attorney general in Poitiers reported that "several" lycée professors had been transferred out of the department of Charente-Inférieure because they were the principal members of a socialist club in La Rochelle.[52]

During late 1849 and early 1850, similar measures were taken in the other departments of our sample. In September 1849 the prefect of Gard asked the education minister to transfer a republican lycée professor to another department; the teacher had failed to reform after receiving a "severe warning" from the rector of his academy.[53]

A teacher in Jura was a source of special concern to the prefect and attorney general responsible for that jurisdiction. Basset, the primary-school teacher in Clairvaux, was considered a leader of the republican forces in the entire *arrondissment* of which that town was the *chef-lieu*. The prefect ordered an investigation of Basset and brought him before the local Primary Instruction Committee on serious charges of "immorality."[54] To the prefect's dismay, the committee merely suspended Basset for one month. As soon as Basset returned to his duties, he was dismissed by his ministry on the urgent recommendation of both the prefect and the minister of interior. According to the attorney general, this was done "not only because of his political opinions, but for facts which reveal this man's profound immorality."[55] Far from being a moral outcast in this small town of 1,240 inhabitants, Basset was the subject of a strong community protest against his dismissal.[56] Basset's "immorality" came to the prefect's attention through an article in the local Party of Order organ, *La Sentinelle du Jura*, which charged the teacher with an undefined "outrage" to a child or group of children during a republican banquet. The citizens of Clairvaux responded immediately. Three letters were published in *La Démocratie Jurassienne* defending the schoolteacher and labeling the charges a "political calumny."[57] They were signed by the mayor, the town council, the members of the republican committee responsible for the banquet, and by numerous citizens. The most moving of these petitions, signed by the heads of the families of the commune, called *La Sentinelle* "infamous" and "cowardly" for inventing an insult to their "honorable" schoolmaster: "the children were at the banquet with their own father and no one in the world would ever be able to interpose himself between the children and this paternal authority."[58] His pupils marched through the streets singing the "Marseillaise" and crying "Vive Basset!" with the approval of the mayor and town council.[59] The police response to this children's crusade was overwhelming. Three officers of the Gendarmerie Nationale were sent out from Lons-le-Saunier, and two companies of regular infantry were placed on alert; but no arrests were made, because the children and townspeople dispersed on the arrival of the police.

Dismissals of schoolteachers and protests in their defense were widespread with the passage of first the Parieu law of January 1850 (giving prefects the right to dismiss "subversive" schoolteachers) and then the Falloux law. In mid-1849 the radical newspaper in Allier had begun publishing a weekly feature entitled, simply and effectively, "Firings." One or two schoolteachers generally headed the list, but the Parieu law gave Maupas, the prefect, an opportunity to fire or suspend twenty teachers on a single politically significant day: 24 February 1850, the second anniversary of the Second Republic.[60] Even earlier, in April 1849, just before the elections for the Legislative Assembly, *La Tribune de la Gironde* was reporting house searches carried out by conservative mayors and *adjoints* against their town schoolmasters. The object of these searches was some kind of physical proof of republican sympathies: a copy of *La Tribune* in their lodgings.[61]

The Falloux law (which placed both the prefect and the *procureur de la république*, along with the ranking member of the local clergy, on each department's education council) was not the opening shot of the war against subversive schoolteachers. It was actually the institutionalization of a repressive process that had been under way during both the Odilon Barrot ministry and the Bonapartist *ministère des commis*, which took its place on 31 October 1849. The measure, of course, was uniformly welcomed by the attorneys general we have studied. All of them echoed the sentiments of De Sèze, the attorney general in Riom: "The draft bill, which the Assembly has just voted into law, has already made the school-teachers more circumspect and it will certainly do away with one of the most active and powerful sources of anarchistic propaganda."[62] While the bill was still being discussed in the assembly, the attorney general in Poitiers reported that the departmental administrations were taking other measures to insure the political reliability of their schoolteachers. The teachers in Vendée and Charente-Inférieure were offered jobs as part-time tax collectors, thus increasing their salary and hopefully reducing their dissatisfaction with the government and blunting the traditional anti-clericalism of the teachers. (The Falloux law gave the clergy considerable power over public education.) He concluded his discussion of this branch of the civil service by saying: "We can congratulate ourselves on the subject of the schoolteachers. We don't have to prosecute them anymore."[63] But a month later Boby de la Chapelle wrote the education minister (Parieu himself) that 31 of the 251 communal schoolteachers in Vendée were still "stained with socialism": the administration felt confident enough to let them off with "severe reprimands," perhaps because of their relative youth—half of them were under twenty-two years of age.[64]

The prosecutors carefully supervised the selection of the new academic councils created by the Falloux law. The attorney general in Poitiers asked his *substitut* at Napoléon-Vendée to send him a confidential report on the delegates selected to run the local schools.[65] A few days later the Justice Ministry asked the attorney general to be sure that a certain individual was passed over as a delegate because he offered "no guarantees of a political nature."[66]

The problem of republican teachers persisted despite the new structure for administering the educational system. We have already discussed the dismissal of a republican schoolteacher in the town of Saint-Jean-d'Angély in Charente-Inférieure. As late as July 1850 the prefect was complaining that the schoolmaster of nearby Jonzac was the real power behind the republican town administration (he was the mayor's secretary) and that the police were having difficulty in finding enough evidence to dismiss the teacher.[67]

But the Falloux law allowed the authorities to raise their sights in the struggle against republican ideas. University professors now came under fire. Devienne, the attorney general in Bordeaux, sent a police commissioner to attend the lectures of M. Rabanis, a historian who was the dean of the Bordeaux Faculty of Letters. Devienne informed his minister that the course was subversive, and he blamed the free speech and influence of such chaired professors on the liberalism of the July Monarchy.

> These courses have no other purpose than that of providing such gentlemen with a rostrum from which to expound their political ideas. . . . One of the paradoxes of our present government is this established institution, created in the midst of the monarchy, of these orators who teach nothing but insurrection against all authority.[68]

On 27 January 1851, less than two weeks after the receipt of Devienne's first report on these history lectures, Rabanis was removed as dean of the faculty and suspended from all teaching duties. The Education Ministry informed the attorney general of this action and the minister's *chef de cabinet* added:

> I hope that this measure will have the beneficial effect of making men, who might be tempted to stray from their line of duty, understand that the government will always be ready to repress fomentors of disorder, however high their position may be.[69]

The republican press and radical organizations—supposedly disbanded by law—protested with considerable political skill these dismissals of often beloved local figures. Each of the Montagnard newspapers in our sample of departments used this particular issue to appeal to anticlerical moderates who had not yet gravitated to the more radical republican position by late 1849. The by-election victories of Lagarde in Gironde and Favand in Gard may have resulted, at least in part, from the Parieu-Falloux assault on secular education. In both departments Cavaignac republicans now rallied to candidates committed to the democratic and social republic. The National Subscription for Schoolteachers Dismissed for Political Reasons, launched with a 500-franc contribution from the Mountain's deputies, enjoyed considerable success in the three instances in which I have been able to consult lists of contributions published in the departmental press (and preserved in the fragmentary holdings of the Bibliothèque Nationale). In less than two months *La Tribune de la Gironde* raised 2,390 francs from such sources (and in such denominations) as "a friend of order—1 franc" and "a poor devil who is a friend of legality—10 centimes".[70] *Le Travailleur* (Charente-Inférieure) collected 248 francs during the first weeks of its campaign to support local teachers under the banner: "To Educate Our Children, No Jesuits, No Ignoramuses."[71] Within two weeks the democrats of Jura, including "a converted 'white' " and "a converted moderate," had contributed 76 francs to the campaign.[72] And many fired schoolteachers, protected by republican mayors, stayed on in their towns as municipally licensed masters of "private" schools.[73] The suspended schoolmaster of Saint Pourçain (Allier) was elected mayor of the town in January 1851, but immediately removed by the prefect. The administration succeeded, nonetheless, in driving republicans from the public schools and lecture halls.

Minor Officials

The government also moved against a host of functionaries in the other branches of the civil service. A considerable number of minor officials—postal clerks, rural policemen, and the like—were summarily dismissed from their positions after they had participated in the disturbances of 14 June 1849 in Allier.[74] As in the case of the five mayors of this department who were removed at the same time, none of these individuals was convicted of any misdeeds by the assize court. In September 1849 the prefect of Jura requested and received powers of suspension and dismissal over a broad range of employees working for three other ministries: Justice, Public Works, and Finance.[75] Although no list of individuals was appended to this table, it is clear that the prefect, on direct ministerial orders, was about to take severe measures against eleven separate categories of minor officials in each of these bureaucracies, including *huissiers*, customs guards, tax collectors, maintenance crews of the Department of Bridges and Highways, forestry wardens, and postmasters. Many of these officials were suspected of aiding the Mountain in Jura to circulate its propaganda and transmit orders from Geneva to points throughout French territory. During the autumn of 1849 the prefect of Jura sent two separate lists of customs guards to Paris, demanding their immediate dismissal.[76] Late in 1850 he denounced the local director of the forestry service for his "neutrality" in refusing to dismiss one of his subordinates.[77] The prefect asked the Interior Ministry to investigate the political background of this director.

Actions of the same nature were taken against republican civil servants in all the departments of our sample. A few examples will suffice to demonstrate the thoroughness with which the government policed its own employees. The minister of public works dismissed a Bridges and Highways Department driver in Rochefort (Charente-Inférieure) when the prefect reported that this individual had privately stated that a cholera epidemic in the workers' neighborhood was caused by the government's poisoning of the water supply. A month later, in October 1849, the prefect of Charente-Inférieure was authorized by the finance minister to dismiss a number of officials who had expressed republican sentiments. Achille Fould, the minister, called such political opinions acts of treason against the state.[78] The prefect who carried out these dismissals was Wissocq, the moderate republican who had once been a member of republican secret societies under the Restoration and the July Monarchy. Wissocq's defense of "order" did not save his job.

His successor, Brian, continued to maintain a strict surveillance over civil servants in the department. In December 1849 he had several employees of the naval arsenal at Rochefort, including a captain of artillery, transferred to posts outside France.[79] Brian dismissed a minor official of the Finance Ministry in February 1850 for having thrown a bust of Louis Napoleon into the fireplace in the privacy of his own home—this punishment for a surveyor.[80]

Rougeron, in his exhaustive study of the municipal archives of Allier, has found documents describing the dismissal of thirty-two civil servants, apart from schoolteachers, from May 1849 through January 1850. Seven of these officials were in the service of the Finance Ministry, five were postmen (one of whom was dismissed for decorating his dog with a red collar and a white tail garland and walking the animal around town while shouting "à bas les blancs"). And no less than twenty of these "reds" worked on the road or canal crews of the Ministry of Public Works.[81]

Clearly the government, through its law-enforcement bureaucrats, was quite successful in extirpating republicanism from within the ranks of its own elected and appointed officials. The left, however, did not disappear as an imposing local force because of such an internal policing of the bureaucracy. It had forms of propaganda and organization that could only be repressed through the courts.

The Press

Of all the outward manifestations of republicanism under the Second Republic, law-enforcement bureaucrats considered the newspapers, pamphlets, and other publications of the left as its most powerful weapons. The actual organizations of the Mountain, although they were often viewed with great alarm, were believed by the attorneys general and prefects to be less threatening than the printed word. They attached great importance to the printing press as the genuine infernal machine of political democracy and of democratic socialism.

The men responsible for public order in those departments in which the left was a majority force uniformly gave priority to press matters. To Gilardin, De Sèze, and Loiseau, republican publications were more than simple symptoms of the strength of radicalism in Rhône, Allier, and Jura. To them, the press was the primary cause of the initial spread and the persistence of republican ideas in these departments. Baroche, the interior minister, and Rouher, the minister of justice, asked Gilardin in 1850 for his opinion on the feasibility of lifting the state of siege in his *ressort*. His main argument, in an impassioned brief for its maintenance, was that martial law prevented the circulation of radical newspapers and other writings. He was certain that the end of military government and of press control by administrative fiat would immediately be followed by a renaissance of the radical press in Lyon. He assured the cabinet that these publications would "pervert" the countryside around the city and draw departments like Ain and Loire "into the orbit of the evil press of Lyon."[82]

A few months before answering this questionnaire, Gilardin had written a special report to Rouher, dated 11 January 1850, requesting the passage of strong legislation to control cabarets. Again his central concern was not with these saloons as gathering places for secret societies, but as centers where newspapers were read aloud to illiterate peasants and workers. Citing the work of a contemporary historian, Hüron, on the influence of cabarets on the political life of the great cities of Europe, Gilardin argued that they were extending their revolutionary influence into the countryside.

Previously cabarets were only places to drink. Since the newspapers have pervaded them, the cabaret has almost always been transformed into something else. It has become a club-house in which to discuss political news. It should be noted above all that it is the evil newspapers and not the good ones which have reached this audience. . . . Thus the cabarets are henceforth a school for the propagation of immorality [*une école d'immoralisation*] among the people of the countryside.[83]

Gilardin's estimate of the power of the press was echoed by other bureaucrats in troubled departments. The attorney general in Riom explained the strength of republicanism in Allier by blaming it "above all" on "the organs of a wicked press."[84] Loiseau, the attorney general at Besançon, at first considered the press less important as a source of republicanism in Jura than the work of a few local organizers.[85] The prefect of Jura, who was closest to the problem, disagreed with the attorney general's analysis. In a report to the interior minister, written in December 1850—less than a month after the prosecutor had played down the importance of republican newspapers to his superiors—the prefect argued that

the over-excitement of public opinion at Salins since February 1848 is maintained principally by the publication in this town of *La Démocratie Jurassienne*: a certain number of copies of this newspaper are distributed free of charge to the wine-growing peasantry and the workers. It is quite probable that, without this dangerous publication, the population of Salins—as well as that of other towns in the department—would have been brought back to more moderate ideas.[86]

By February 1850 the attorney general had come to agree with the prefect on the crucial role played by the radical press in Salins. In describing the *arrondissement* of Poligny as "the sickest part [*la partie la plus malade*] of all Jura," with Salins as the republican headquarters of the region, Loiseau observed that *La Démocratie Jurassienne* was a principal cause of the strength of local radicalism and the source of "le plus grand mal."[87] When this publication reappeared in July 1850 after being closed down by a succession of fines, the attorney general sent a special dispatch to Paris.

We have seen a marked return to the ideas of order in the canton of Salins and even in the *arrondissement* of Poligny since the suspension of *La Démocratie Jurassienne*. . . . Its reappearance is certain to throw new troubles and ferments into the midst of the population and will especially revive political passions in Salins.[88]

Even the bureaucrats responsible for departments in which the left was a minority, as in Gard and Gironde, or a negligible factor, as in Charente-Inférieure and Vendée, sometimes viewed the republican press with great alarm. The main problem in the conservative west of France was *colportage*—the door-to-door peddling of radical pamphlets, almanacs, and even works of fiction (like the novels of Eugène Sue). The attorney general in Poitiers considered this a serious matter in Charente-Inférieure.[89] Troplong, when he was the attorney general in Bordeaux, reported in July 1849: "It is notorious that the party of disorder propagates dangerous doctrines through the distribution of tracts hostile to religion and to the principles which form the foundations of the social edifice."[90]

Troplong's successor, Devienne, believed the lone republican newspaper in Gironde to be so dangerous that he told the ministry in 1851 that this publication could, almost single-handedly, cause a republican victory in the elections of 1852.[91] And Thourel, who generally viewed the republicans in Gard and their single newspaper with equanimity, personally went to court in 1849 to argue a case against the editors of *Le Républicain du Gard*: "I have taken advantage of this occasion publicly to take issue with the prosecuted newspaper—with its odious doctrines, its vile lies and its repeated outrages against all that is most honorable and great in the nation."[92]

Because of the importance that the police bureaucrats attached to the proselytizing power of the republican press and to the laws of 1848, 1849, and 1850, which enabled them to move against it, one would think that their attack on seditious publications should have been effective. Irene Collins, a scholar who has specialized in the study of press control in France, so assumes in her treatment of the Second Republic.[93] Such a favorable estimate of the work of the prefects and prosecutors is simply inaccurate. The law-enforcement bureaucrats found the repression of the radical press to be a lengthy and frustrating business at best. Despite their legal resources and their own zeal, the prosecutors and prefects were often unsuccessful in preventing the circulation of republican publications. Until the second half of 1850, every department in our sample except for Rhône, which was under martial law, boasted at least one republican newspaper. On the eve of the coup d'état, the republican press still functioned in Jura, Vendée, Charente-Inférieure, Gironde, Gard, and Allier. *Colportage* continued unabated in most of these same areas until the republic had been overthrown.

Charente-Inférieure and Vendée

In their repressive campaign against the democratic press, the prefects and prosecutors apparently made no distinctions between radical and moderate republican newspapers. In separate reports, submitted almost a year apart, both the attorney general in Poitiers and the prefect of Charente-Inférieure described all the republican newspapers in their overlapping jurisdictions as "the press organs of the red party." They did so despite listing two newspapers in the department with the same nuance as *Le National*. According to the attorney general, three subversive newspapers circulated in Charente-Inférieure at the end of 1849: *Le Phare*, a socialist periodical published at La Rochelle; *L'Ami de la Constitution*, a moderate republican newspaper published in the same city and described as only "a bit more moderate" than *Le Phare*; and *L'Union Républicaine*, printed at Saintes and termed an "ultra democratic" sheet despite its likeness to *Le National*. Brian, the prefect, sent a table of newspapers in answer to a questionnaire from Baroche in October 1850. He added a socialist newspaper that had gone under and then reappeared in Rochefort: *Le Travailleur*. Only one journal in the department supported Louis Napoleon despite his overwhelming electoral victories there in 1848. All the rest were either legitimist or Orleanist.[94]

During 1849 no charges were brought against any of the republican newspapers in the department. Wissocq, the Cavaignac republican who was still the prefect, explained this in a general report submitted in June. He described one of the local moderate republican newspapers in his report, *L'Union Républicaine* of Saintes, as being extremist, but omitted mentioning a publication of the same nuance that was printed in La Rochelle, his own *chef-lieu*. Perhaps he was trying to avoid personal liability for failing to impede the circulation of a newspaper that his successor described a year later as "red." Wissocq remarked that "the newspapers in the department are all very moderate with the exception of three of them: *L'Union* of Saintes, *Le Travailleur* of Rochefort and *Le Phare* of La

Rochelle which represent quite an extreme point of view. Up to the present, however, they have not provided the basis for any action on the part of the judicial magistrates."[95] In a letter to his subprefect at Rochefort, Wissocq explained why the socialist *Travailleur* could not be charged with any breaches of the press laws. This newspaper simply reprinted clippings from the Parisian press and, however offensive these articles were to the departmental administration, no charges could be brought as long as the newspapers of the capital were not themselves prosecuted.[96] This complaint would be reiterated by law-enforcement bureaucrats in other departments who were limited by the unwillingness of the Paris *parquet* to offend the sophisticated and alert public opinion of the capital. The government would not prosecute the great dailies for anything but the most blatant infractions of the press laws. *Le National* continued to publish throughout the Second Republic, and if *La Réforme* eventually succumbed to a series of court actions, its Montagnard views were taken up immediately by a new daily, *Révolution,* and by Emile de Girardin (who had undergone a sudden, if temporary, conversion to radicalism) and his mass-circulation *La Presse,* with its 34,500 subscribers.[97] These latter two newspapers survived until the coup.

The attorney general in Poitiers lost his first case against a republican newspaper in Charente-Inférieure because the defense based its arguments on articles in the Parisian press that had not been prosecuted. Charges had been brought against *Le Phare* early in 1850 for the violence of its language in criticizing the High Court of Justice at Versailles. The trial of the Montagnard deputies involved in the events of 13 June 1849 was then underway. The actual charge under the press law of 1848 was that the socialist publication had excited its readers "to hate or scorn" the government. The attorneys for *Le Phare,* with a fine sense of irony, read even more violent criticisms of the government that had been printed in the two major conservative dailies of the capital: the extreme legitimist *Gazette de France* and the more liberal *Assemblée Nationale. Le Phare,* personified in its director, was acquitted by the jury. The author of the article was given a light prison sentence and fine only because he failed to appear in court (and thus pleaded guilty by default).[98]

The next press prosecutions were directed against *L'Union Républicaine* and *Le Travailleur.* In March 1850 both papers, one of which was moderate republican and the other socialist, were tried for the same offense by the same jury. They had each printed

Claude Durand's "Chanson des Vignerons" and were charged, under the law of August 1848, with "attacking the principle of property" and with inciting "hatred and contempt among citizens."[99] L'Union Républicaine defended itself at the Assize Court of Saintes and narrowly won an acquittal, the prosecution having failed by one vote to convince the necessary eight jurors (out of twelve) for a conviction. The director of Le Travailleur did not appear to defend himself against the same charges. He was therefore convicted and sentenced to six months in jail. His newspaper, however, continued to appear.[100]

The "Chanson des Vignerons" caused quite a stir in western France. Its author was one of the few republicans of Vendée, and his trial before the largely legitimist jury of Napoléon-Vendée was a severe defeat for the attorney general. By an overwhelming majority, Claude Durand was acquitted.[101] The government had attached considerable importance to this case and the related prosecutions of newspapers that had printed Durand's verses. In April 1850, Baroche wrote to Rouher:

> These songs . . . are designed to aggravate the hatred of the poor for the rich and for society itself. They enjoy a certain popularity which makes them extremely dangerous. Although, as regards form and composition, these writings are of a mediocrity which ought to condemn them to indifference or contempt, they produce the most vexatious effect on the masses because they are addressed to uneducated minds and an impassioned audience.[102]

The procureur-général in Poitiers considered the song an appeal to "civil war."[103] Yet the prosecutors were largely unsuccessful in suppressing it or in crushing the republican press for its publication. It is well worth quoting a few of the offending lines. Printed in moderate and socialist organs alike, they demonstrate that by mid-1850 the effect of government repression had been to drive the two wings of the democratic movement together.

> Good villagers, vote for the Mountain,
> There are the gods of the poor wine-growers,
> By joining with them, good people of the countryside,
> The wine taxes will be brought crashing down. . . .
>
> Impoverished worker, you build for your master
> Beautiful chateaux and sumptuous palaces.

But you also build the prisons for yourself,
Because you know well that the rich never end up there.[104]

The prison term of *Le Travailleur*'s director can hardly have been
a satisfactory penalty for Damay, the attorney general in Poitiers.
Republican newspaper directors expected to spend time in jail:
that was their journalistic role. Time behind bars was far more
acceptable than a heavy fine that would have shut down their
newspapers.

Damay's first really successful prosecution against the radical
press of Charente-Inférieure came in December 1850. *Le Phare* had
printed an article criticizing the Legislative Assembly for refusing
to discuss the maltreatment of political prisoners at Belle Isle and
Mont Saint Michel: "The Assembly began its work for the week
by giving its blessing to a serious blow against the constitution."[105]
The article also characterized the actions of the ministry, and those
of Baroche and Rouher in particular, as "arbitrary and odious."[106]
On 6 December 1850, Rouher told his *procureur-général* at Poitiers
that no jury would convict *Le Phare* for an "outrage to the Assembly" but that he should prosecute the newspaper for printing an
unsigned political article (a signature was required under the law
of July 1849).[107] *Le Phare* was found guilty and required to pay a
fine of 500 francs.[108]

Although this victory did not prevent *Le Phare* from continuing
to publish, it apparently was so long awaited and so rare in press
matters that the *procureur de la république* received a commendation from Damay couched in terms strikingly reminiscent of a battlefield citation: "M. Chaudreau, who argued this case before the
police court, has on this occasion completely justified his renown
as a talented man and completely justified my confidence in him
as a man devoted to the principles of order."[109] The case had probably been won because it was not tried before a jury. *Le Phare* had
been prosecuted before the police court magistrate on this relatively
minor charge.

Other prosecutions were brought against the republican newspapers of Charente-Inférieure, but only one other case resulted in
any penalties. In December 1850 the director of *L'Union* was found
guilty, again in police court, for defaming a local monk in an anticlerical article. He was forced to pay 300 francs damages, a 50-
franc fine, and spend eight days in jail.[110] An attempt to convict
the director of the moderate republican *Ami de la Constitution* for

having signed blank inspection copies of his newspaper so that it could legally appear while he was in Paris for three weeks resulted in an ordinance of *non-lieu* (no basis to proceed) by the local tribunal.[111] *L'Ami de la Constitution*, however, was the one republican newspaper in Charente-Inférieure that failed before the coup. The director skipped town to avoid his personal creditors, all of whom were fellow republicans, even before the case against him had been dismissed. His former friends immediately started a new republican journal in La Rochelle, *La Constitution*.[112] Thus the republican press of Charente-Inférieure survived intact until the coup d'état.

The same was true for the republican newspapers of Vendée. In 1849 only one such publication existed in the department: *L'Indicateur* of Fontenay. The attorney general described this journal as "quasi-socialist."[113] *L'Indicateur* was never prosecuted during the entire period 1849 through 1851, although in June 1850 it had published the "Chanson des Vignerons." When his *substitut* at Fontenay asked for permission to bring charges against this newspaper, Damay answered that a prosecution would be "inopportune."[114] The song's author was a wealthy landowner in the region, and, like Georges Clemenceau's father at Les Sables d'Olonne, Durand was well liked by his neighbors despite his radical leanings.[115]

Another republican newspaper was founded in 1850 at Napoléon-Vendée: *Le Démocrate Vendéen*. In October of that year, just at the time when the local republican committee was collecting funds to float *Le Démocrate*, Baroche ordered his prefect to devote meticulous attention to all the legal details required for the newspaper's actual appearance and to refuse his authorization until the bond had been paid in full.[116] When the journal did appear later in the month, the interior minister already knew that its editor, Napoléon Gallois, was Ledru-Rollin's former agent in his old electoral district of Le Mans and had been a member of the staff of *La Réforme*. Baroche called for a "close surveillance" of Gallois and his publication.[117] Nonetheless, *Le Démocrate Vendéen* was never prosecuted and survived until the coup.

The only serious blow directed against the republican press in Vendée and Charente-Inférieure came in June 1850, during the petition campaign against the limitation of universal suffrage. *L'Indicateur* circulated in Vendée but was actually printed by Siret in La Rochelle, who was also the printer of *L'Ami de la Constitution*. Siret had printed 800 copies of a petition protesting the law of 31

May 1850. The language of the petition, according to the attorney general, was perfectly legal; *one* of the 800 copies, however, did not bear Siret's name and address, for the paper had slipped as it went through the press. Siret was prosecuted for failing to print this information (required by a Restoration press law) and was found guilty in both the assize and appeals courts. He was forced to pay the enormous fine of 3,000 francs for perhaps the most expensive typographical error in French history.[118] Siret, however, did not go out of business. In October he began printing a third newspaper, *Le Démocrate Vendéen*, and he was still publishing all three republican organs in 1851.[119] It is quite probable that wealthy republicans in the region, men like Durand and Clemenceau, came to his aid.

No charges were ever brought against any of the legitimist newspapers in Charente-Inférieur and Vendée. When *La Gazette Vendéene* (the legitimist newspaper in Fontenay, which paid no bond because it claimed to be apolitical) illegally published a review of debates in the assembly, the *procureur de la république* told the attorney general that he would not prosecute. He argued that Fontenay needed a newspaper that countered the influence of *L'Indicateur*; both the *procureur-général* and the justice minister agreed.[120]

Gironde

Early in 1849 Bordeaux boasted two democratic newspapers: *Le Peuple Souverain* and *La Tribune de la Gironde*. *Le Peuple* was a socialist newspaper founded in March 1849 for the specific purpose of supporting the most radical republican candidates for the Legislative Assembly.[121] *La Tribune* was orginally a moderate republican organ, but after the events of 13 June 1849 it began to align itself with the more radical elements of the Mountain.[122]

Troplong, the *procureur-général* in Bordeaux until he was disgraced either for softness or for marrying the wrong kind of woman, was extraordinarily tough and successful in his first press prosecutions. *Le Peuple Souverain* was seized three times in its first month of publication.[123] (A seizure occurred when either the prefect or attorney general, having examined the legally required inspection copy that was delivered to their offices and having noted a possible breach of the press laws, sent the police to the printing plant to prevent a particular issue from circulating. Under the law, which dated from the Restoration, a seizure had to be followed by a prosecution.) *Le Peuple* was charged with three separate instances of inciting civil war among the citizenry (law of August 1848). Convicted on each count by the jury, the director was sentenced to two years in jail and a fine of 3,000 francs. *Le Peuple's* bond was absorbed by this case and the newspaper collapsed.

The lone republican newspaper in Gironde was now *La Tribune*. It became the object of an unsuccessful administrative vendetta that did not end until the coming of the coup d'état, when it was suppressed by decree. *La Tribune* was to survive at least ten separate attempts to shut it down between July 1849 and August 1851.

Troplong successfully prosecuted this newspaper in July 1849 for its attacks on the Legislative Assembly's acquiescence in the Roman expedition. The director did not defend himself before the jury of Bordeaux and was condemned to one month in prison and a fine of 100 francs.[124]

Troplong's successor, Devienne, opened a campaign against *La Tribune* in April 1850 in which he attempted to use every resource available to both the prefectoral administration and the *parquet*. In April he tried to prosecute the newspaper under the press law of July 1849 for insulting the president of the republic.[125] He failed. Later in the month Devienne and Neveux, the prefect, tried to orchestrate a maneuver by the ministries of Justice, Finance, and Interior in a serious bid to close down *La Tribune*. The original director of the newspaper, suffering undoubtedly from the legal fees and seizures that threatened to bankrupt him, sold *La Tribune* to a group of friends. The finance minister ordered Neveux to insist that a new bond be paid within three days of the registration of the bill of sale at the prefecture.[126] Neveux told the new proprietors that if this was not done he would decree "the suppression of their publication."[127] Since the old bond was on deposit in Paris and would not be returned for some time, this meant that the same small group of republicans in Bordeaux would have to raise an equivalent sum in only seventy-two hours. Somehow they succeeded, probably because of the great wealth of the new editor, a well-known lawyer named Tandonnet.

One month later Devienne again moved against *La Tribune*, this time on several fronts. First he attacked the newspaper in the same way that the attorney general in Poitiers had tried to undercut the republican publications of Fontenay and La Rochelle. Devienne brought charges against *La Tribune's* printer for failing to deposit with the *parquet* and the prefecture a copy of the petition against limiting the suffrage.[128] This prosecution came under the same law of 21 October 1814 that had been used against Siret. Tried in police court, Havel, *La Tribune*'s printer, was fined 5,025 francs.[129] But this did not succeed in closing down his shop or the newspaper he printed. Devienne then asked the interior minister to revoke Havel's license because he could see no other way of closing down *La Tribune*.

> This newspaper is all the more prudent because its editors are hardly the type of men prepared for jail sentences; rather they are two men of some substance in the community, one of whom [Tandonnet] is a member of the Conseil Général and possesses a rather considerable fortune. Because of the circumstances, it is not Havel we strike at in withdrawing his license, but Tandonnet himself, or more accurately, . . . *La Tribune*. Now if we evaluate just how severe . . . the danger of its evil-doing really is and the repression which should be brought against it, this particular newspaper deserves the least possible indulgence on our part. . . . It exploits the troubles of the people to the profit of the party of disorder.[130]

On 25 July Havel lost his license and did not recover it until well after the coup d'état.[131] At the same time the prefect informed the mayor of Bordeaux that Havel's condemnation had made the other printers in the city "very prudent" and that most of them were refusing to print "anarchist writings" (presumably including *La Tribune*).[132] He ordered the mayor to have the police commissioners begin a search for any clandestine presses. Yet Tandonnet found another printer, and *La Tribune* continued to appear.

At the same time as the Havel affair, Devienne prosecuted *La Tribune* for the sale of books (*colportage*) in its offices without having a license to run a bookstore. The police court fined the director the meaningless sum of twenty-five francs, and Devienne wrote a furious dispatch to Paris complaining that even "ordinary justice" (the nonjury trial) was not effective against the press.[133]

Seven more prosecutions were brought against *La Tribune* during 1850 and 1851. Only one resulted in a conviction. The director, who was not Tandonnet but a friend, was found guilty in July 1850 by the assize court jury of publishing an article that broke the law of 22 March 1822: *La Tribune* had been "deriding a recognized religion" (the Catholic church). The director was sentenced to three months in prison and a heavy fine of 3,000 francs.[134] Devienne's summer offensive of 1850 still failed to close down *La Tribune*. And this was the last conviction he would get against this stubborn thorn in his side.

Tandonnet, throughout what was literally a "time of trials," could still stand by his New Year's Day editorial of 1850. "*La Tribune de la Gironde*, whose demise has so often been announced, celebrates its fifteenth month of life. It has lived through some hard times. The wind of royalist reaction has raged against it with violence, but without succeeding in forcing it to lower its banner."[135] Indeed, by March of the same year he could treat Devienne the way a picador goads a bull: "France which is generous and truly honest, the France of enlightenment and progress, democratic France, to put it briefly, will not be defeated by these ridiculous pygmies."[136]

After the failure to win a few cases during October and December of 1850 and January of 1851, Devienne played his last card against *La Tribune* and promptly got into trouble with his minister. Beginning in February 1851, *La Tribune* had appeared with the following articles of the constitution as its masthead, with significant underlinings:

Article 1   Sovereignty resides in *the totality* of French citizens. It is an inalienable and irreducible right. No individual, no fraction of the people can make an exclusive claim to the use of it.

Article 24   The suffrage is direct and *universal*.

Article 25   All Frenchmen, without any requirement of a property qualification, are electors.

Article 110   The National Assembly entrusts the safekeeping of the present Constitution and of the rights which it sanctifies to the guardianship and patriotism of all Frenchmen.[137]

Although the attorney general realized that he could not prosecute for a simple printing of the republic's fundamental law, Devienne considered the masthead an appeal to revolution. He awaited the chance to link it to a political article in the newspaper and charge *La Tribune* with provocation to civil war. His chance came on Bastille Day 1851 when Tandonnet wrote an editorial defending the right of all Frenchmen to vote in 1852.

Unfortunately for the success of his case, Devienne lost his head and not only seized this issue of the newspaper but told Tandonnet that he would seize every future issue that carried the offending articles of the constitution.[138] Tandonnet immediately informed his friends in the Parisian press, and on 20 July 1850 Eugène Bareste, editor of *La République,* reported Devienne's threat and went on to exclaim, "What! Under the Republic it is prohibited to publish articles of the Republican Constitution in a Republican newspaper! There has been an error, no doubt, and M. *le ministre de la justice* will surely be eager to protest against the anticonstitutional inclinations of one of his prosecutors."[139] Bareste asked the Montagnard deputies to bring this matter before the assembly by interpellating Rouher, who had continued as justice minister in the Faucher cabinet.

At first Rouher did not respond. On 29 July he directed Devienne to prosecute Tandonnet for his article of 14 July, but made no mention of whether or not the case should also be based on *La Tribune*'s masthead.[140] Devienne enthusiastically welcomed this endorsement of his line of conduct. Rouher would, he declared, understand that destroying "this evil is worth some difficulties" if he could see "the evil caused by this drop of water that falls each day . . . , this voice saying that the constitution is violated [and] that—by law—insurrection is allowed."[141] Only five days later, Rouher sent an urgent message commanding his attorney general to withdraw his prosecution against the "simple" publication of articles from the constitution. The minister slapped Devienne's wrist for actions that had caused "sharp and numerous complaints" in the press and the assembly.[142]

Among these protests must be counted those of the provincial radical press throughout France. *Le Phare* of La Rochelle not only placed the offending articles of the constitution on its masthead as early as April 1851; it also published Tandonnet's reply to "this revolting and scandalously direct attack on the constitution" when the attorney general at Bordeaux threatened to silence *La Tribune.*[143] And the embattled *Travailleur de l'Allier et de la Creuse,* constantly on the brink of bankruptcy, did not flinch from running Tandonnet's constitutional articles (plus a few extra ones) on its own masthead.[144]

Finally, when the Chambre de mises en accusations (a grand jury composed of judges) refused to authorize a case against Tandonnet's defense of universal manhood suffrage, Rouher relented. He could only commisserate with his subordinate, complimenting him for his firmness and zeal.[145] *La Tribune* had survived a repressive war to the death and had succeeded in making a fool of the public prosecutor.

I have not been able to find any evidence of prosecutions brought against the Party of Order press in Gironde. Twice the Justice Ministry asked Devienne to bring charges against Bordeaux's two rival Orleanist newspapers: *Le Courrier de la Gironde*, which remained steadfast in its support of the antiBonaparte faction of the conservative coalition, and *Le Mémorial Bordelais*, which eventually came to support the Elysée.[146] Both offenses involved the use of violent language in criticizing certain actions taken by the Legislative Assembly during 1850. On both occasions the attorney general defended the newspaper in question against the anger of the central government, arguing that it was too important a defender of order in the department to be punished for rhetorical transgressions. Each time, Devienne convinced the ministry that no prosecution was necessary, because he could personally warn the editors to watch their copy more closely.[147]

Gard

Press control in Gard was far less dramatic than in the departments we have just discussed. Neither Thourel nor his prefectoral counterparts took republicanism very seriously as a potential revolutionary movement in the department. They were far more worried about the sporadic violence that broke out between Protestants (republicans) and Catholics (legitimists). During a time often bloody with religious strife, the political press did not excite the attention it commanded in the other departments in our sample. Besides, as Thourel discovered early in his service at Nîmes, there was little he could do to convince any jury to convict on practically any charge.

The *procureur-général* brought four prosecutions against newspapers before the end of February 1850 and then gave up. There was only one republican journal in the department, *Le Républicain du Gard*, which Thourel described as the combined organ of the local Montagnards and socialists. It was in competition with one Orleanist newspaper, one moderate legitimist publication, and *L'Etoile*, the local voice of the "white" Mountain.[148]

During 1849 Thourel seized *Le Républicain* twice. The issues of 13 and 14 July 1849 violently protested the Roman expedition and the arrest of the Montagnard deputies in Paris; Thourel charged the director with incitement to revolt, but the newspaper was acquitted by the Nîmes jury.[149] On this occasion, Thourel simply took the opportunity to attack the "odious" ideology of Le Républicain in the hope of swaying the courtroom audience to a better appreciation of the need for order. Later in the year he again seized an issue of the journal, this time for upbraiding the prefect for firings of schoolteachers, but the Chambre de mises en accusations immediately handed down an ordinance of non-lieu.[150] According to Thourel, this decision was based not on points of law but rather on the court's certainty that no local jury would vote a conviction in press matters. In January 1850 Le Républicain ceased publication, but Thourel bitterly assured the Justice Ministry that this closure had nothing to do with any action on his part. It had failed only because the director could not pay his debts to the printer.[151] When Le Républicain appeared again, Thourel tried one last time to convict the director, this time for printing a leaflet written by Ledru-Rollin, who by then was in exile in London. The attorney general charged that the pamphlet was an appeal to civil war, and, in order to combat the influential memory of the Montagnard chief, he again personally argued the government's case. For the second time, Thourel was so sure that he could not win the case that he chose to use the courtroom simply as a political forum. Tempering his argument to the deeply religious culture of Gard, both Protestant and Catholic, he maintained that the fundamental belief of the Mountain was "the necessity of uprooting from the human soul all religious belief."[152] The director was acquitted.

Thourel distinguished himself in several ways from the attorneys general in the west of France. This procureur-général actually attempted to prosecute a legitimist newspaper. In 1849 he seized the uncompromisingly white journal of Gard, L'Etoile, and charged its director with attacking republican institutions and with incitement to civil war. He too was acquitted by the jury.[153] Thourel also took a position with his ministry that contrasts starkly with the frenzied zeal of Devienne at Bordeaux. Thourel refused to prosecute a group of Montagnards that met in April 1851 to establish a new republican newspaper in Gard after Le Républicain definitively went out of business. He argued at that time, against the advice of Rouher, that such a move would only provide the new journal with good publicity.[154] Although the authorities did not allow the meeting to take place, no arrests were made, and the new *Journal Démocratique du Gard* continued to appear until the coup d'état.[155]

Rhône

Gilardin, the attorney general in Lyon after June 1849, had fewer press problems than any of the other prosecutors we have studied. With the establishment of martial law on 14 June 1849, the two republican newspapers of Lyon were shut down by decree.[156]

Le Républicain and *Le Peuple Souverain*, respectively the radical republican organ and the "pure" socialist newspaper of the city, had been repeatedly prosecuted by Gilardin's predecessor, Alcock (or rather this absentee prosecutor's first advocate general) in the early months of 1849. In each case, the newspaper was acquitted by the republican jury of Lyon. An excellent example is the case brought by the first advocate general against *Le Peuple Souverain* in March 1849. On 18 February the newspaper had printed an attack on Marshal Bugeaud, who had just been placed in command of the Army of the Alps, which had its headquarters in the city. "Old man, you horrify us! We wanted to leave Blaye, *la rue Trans-nonain* behind us . . . a past full of shame, blood and infamy: this is no longer within our power. . . . Old man, you promise us grapeshot and bullets. . . . We return the courtesy and give you hisses and boos."[157] Seized by the *parquet* for "insults, outrages and defamation" directed against a public functionary (law of August 1848), *Le Peuple Souverain* was acquitted by a jury vote of seven for conviction and five against, despite the flagrancy of the violation. According to the first advocate general, "This acquittal has created indignation among all the men of order and the honest population of Lyon."[158] Similar verdicts were handed down in such cases throughout April and May 1849.[159]

Gilardin's biggest problem under the state of siege was to prevent *Le Peuple Souverain* and *Le Républicain* from reappearing in disguised formats. The director and staff of the former newspaper had been jailed for their complicity in the insurrection of 14–15 June.[160] Their place was immediately taken by the journal's Paris correspondent, Gustave Naquet, who returned to Lyon late in the same month. During the by-election campaign, held in late June and early July 1849 to fill a vacant seat in the department's delegation to the Legislative Assembly, Naquet declared his candidacy for no other purpose than to republish *Le Peuple Souverain* in the form of periodic electoral circulars. The very first issue was seized, and Naquet was charged with provocation to civil war (law of August 1848).[161] Under the political and press laws of the republic, electoral meetings and literature were not subject to the same controls as those exercised between elections. But Gilardin felt it necessary to stop the disguised publication of a suspended newspaper and to punish Naquet for his attack on the state of siege. In deference to public opinion, however, the attorney general decided to try the case before the assize jury rather than exercise his option to bring Naquet before a court-martial.[162] The offending phrases of Naquet's *profession de foi* were all aimed at the existence of martial law in Lyon, a situation he criticized by quoting the words of the justice minister himself. Naquet recalled Odilon Barrot's speech for the defense before the Cour de cassation in 1832.

> The state of siege: is it a normal situation for defendants in a political trial? What! At this very moment—as I speak—I find myself subject to the attacks of the military jurisdiction, while you yourselves sit in judgment only because of the lofty tolerance of military justice which absorbs your own judicial authority.[163]

Naquet was acquitted by the jury, and this resourceful journalist immediately began publishing *Le Peuple Souverain* disguised as monthly reviews that, under different titles, appeared at least once a week during August and September.[164] According to Gilardin, these reviews were prosecuted on several occasions, but the cases failed. His only recourse was to have General Gémeau, the commander of the state of siege, seize the "monthlies" as they appeared.[165] Finally, in January 1850, Gilardin prosecuted Naquet and his printer, Madame Veuve Ayné, on the basis of technical clauses in the press law of August 1848. He charged them with publishing political periodicals without posting the required bond. At last, the jury handed down a conviction. Madame Ayné was forced to pay a fine of 400 francs; Naquet was sentenced to six months in jail and a 600-franc fine.[166] Naquet appealed his case and lost. Gilardin sent an urgent personal dispatch to the justice minister in Paris, where Naquet was currently acting as a delegate for the socialist clubs of Lyon, asking for a prompt arrest.

> I think it would be useful to arrest this convict immediately; he is busying himself at the moment with dangerous, demagogic

propaganda. The need for this measure is so great that I have decided to write directly to you. If handled by our ordinary procedures, I fear that some delay may occur.[167]

This was the importance a *procureur-général*, with all the resources of the state of siege at his disposal, attached to a six-month sentence against a newspaper editor and secret society leader. It indicates the rarity of successful repressive actions against both the press and the underground organizations of the left.

To ensure that there would be no more trouble from the widow Ayné's printing shop, the interior minister, at the request of Gilardin and Prefect La Coste, revoked her license in February 1850.[168] The radical press in Lyon had been completely crushed, but not without considerable embarrassment and difficulty—even under martial law. No Party of Order newspapers were suspended or prosecuted during this period.[169]

Allier

The department of Allier possessed two republican newspapers at the beginning of 1849: *La Constitution*; the moderate organ, and *Le Républicain de l'Allier*, the voice of the local Montagnards.[170] *La Constitution* was never prosecuted during 1849-1851 and continued to publish until the morning of 3 December 1851 when the police commissioner of Moulins arrested its editor and its printer.[171]

The more radical republican publication was the target of successive court actions in 1849. The attorney general and the prefect moved against *Le Républicain* in January for having published the "seditious" toast given by Georges Gallay, the mayor of Donjon, in December 1848 and later for having printed Gallay's insulting letter of resignation to Armand Coquet.[172] The prefect had suspended the mayor for having said that the Constituent Assembly had committed "treason" by creating the office of president of the republic "who, in the final analysis, is nothing but a kind of king elected every four years."[173]

On 3 January both the mayor and the editor of *Le Républicain* were tried in the Assize Court of Moulins for the publication of the angry letter to the prefect. The charge, the same one used against *Le Peuple Souverain* of Lyon for its attack on Marshal Bugeaud, was insulting a government official.[174] Both republicans were sentenced to one month in prison and fined 500 francs each.[175]

A month later the same two men were prosecuted for printing the antipresidential toast given at Donjon. They were charged with "serious attacks on the rights and authority of the National Assembly and against the Constitution" (law of August 1848), found guilty, sentenced to an additional month in jail, and again fined 500 francs each. The printer of this newspaper was also charged in this matter and sentenced to six days in prison and a fine of 200 francs.

The newspaper finally failed when, in April 1849, it was charged with three separate counts of seditious libel. These prosecutions were themselves the result of the earlier trial. *Le Républicain* greeted the summation of the *procureur de la république* and the testimony of Coquet with the words: "cowardly" and "ignoble."[176] The editor then went on to charge the prefect ("an official personage—even a *very official* personage") with assuring those present at a reception that he "would kill" *Le Républicain*.[177] After three trials before the assize jury, the director was sentenced to sixteen months in prison and 2,700 francs in fines. The attorney general in Riom reported that the director, Bandeau, had fled and that this "anarchist" publication was dead. But he saw no cause for rejoicing.

> My hope of seeing the department of Allier rid of this insurrectionary press has not come true. The socialist party was not about to deprive itself of such an organ, particularly at the moment of the elections. . . . A newspaper entitled *Le Républicain Démocrate de l'Allier* has just come out under the direction of a M. Marion—after payment of a new bond—in order to continue the propagation of Bandeau's doctrines. Despite the condemnations handed down against Bandeau, it has announced that its courage would not falter and that it would maintain the same ideas, but that it would be more clever in avoiding the actions of the prosecuting magistrates.[178]

The attorney general was clearly amazed that the Mountain possessed the financial resources and personnel to put out another newspaper immediately after the collapse of its first venture.

Le Républicain Démocrate de l'Allier was not successful in avoiding prosecution and conviction. Charged twice with libelous attacks on the government, in February and April 1850, it too succumbed.[179] In the fall of 1850 Félix Mathé, the leader of Allier's Montagnard delegation to the Legislative Assembly, made a tour of his home department and the neighboring department of Creuse in order to gather funds for the floating of a new newspaper.[180] It was a long and arduous process. *Le Travailleur de l'Allier et de la Creuse* did not come into existence until the middle of 1851, and the first meeting of its stockholders was prevented by the prefectoral fiat of Charnailles on 1 July 1851.[181] No meetings of this kind were to be allowed, but *Le Travailleur*, edited by Luc Desages, Pierre Leroux's son-in-law, continued to be published in Moulins until the coup d'état.[182]

I have found evidence of only one prosecution brought by the *procureur-général*, De Sèze, against a legitimist newspaper in Allier. In February 1849 he charged *Le Mémorial de l'Allier* with "exciting hatred and contempt of the republican government" (law of August 1848) for publishing the following passage and italicizing a significant phrase: "Rebellion, that supreme legitimacy of *les républicains quand-même*, has snuffed out all the hopes and illusions . . . of February by bringing terror into all hearts."[183]

De Sèze brought this attack on the Orleanists who supported the conservative republic to the Chambre de mises en accusations, and an ordinance of *non-lieu* was handed down. *Le Mémorial* had published a later issue professing support for the republic, and De Sèze welcomed both the *non-lieu* and the newspaper's change of tone: "In my judgment, both of these decisions are wise: given the present state of things, an acquittal would have been certain . . . and the journalist's spontaneous protestations of loyalty to the Republic will have more of a moral impact on his own party."[184] The *procureur-général* considered the coalition politics of the Party of Order more important at this early date than a successful prosecution of the anti-Bonapartist organ.

Jura

Perhaps because of the mountainous nature of this sparsely populated department and the distances (in terms of time) that separated one town from another, especially during the winter, Jura possessed two similarly oriented republican newspapers at the beginning of 1849. Both of them represented the radical wing of the movement: *La Tribune du Jura*, published at Lons-le-Saunier, and *La Démocratie Jurassienne*, which appeared in Salins.

An attempt was made in 1850 to float another republican journal in Lons-le-Saunier, one that was intended to be the voice for the moderate Grévy wing of the local movement, but the projected *Le*

Jura never appeared.[185] The effort to establish this new periodical by selling shares at one franc each failed when Bessard was haled before the police court of Lons-le-Saunier in January 1850 for distributing its prospectus without the permission of the prefect. Charged with *colportage* (law of July 1849), Bessard was fined but twenty-five francs. The attorney general's appeal raised his sentence to forty days in prison.[186]

Of the two Montagnard newspapers, *La Démocratie Jurassienne* was edited with the greater verve and became the object of numerous prosecutions. Founded in the summer of 1848, *La Démocratie* combined three earlier newspapers published in the *arrondissements* of Dôle and Poligny.[187] Its first editors, Victor Richardet and Antoine Sommier, were elected in May 1849 as Montagnard deputies to the Legislative Assembly. Their election saved them from the first prosecution brought against their newspaper. On 25 March 1849 they published an article, written by Sommier himself, that vilified the government for executing the men who killed General Bréa during the June Days of 1848. (The Provisional Government had abolished the death penalty in political matters.) Entitled "Restoration of the Political Scaffold," this piece attacked the alliance of moderate republicans and monarchists in the Constituent Assembly and insulted the president of the republic.

> They have restored the guillotine, overthrown with the throne by the people of February. It is but a prelude: from the restoration of the scaffold will come the restoration of the throne. . . . The executioner was always the king's pal. . . . Yes, the "moderates," this party which sees itself as so debonnaire and so benign—and which calls us the "reds"—has trampled the work of the people and the constitution under foot. . . . And what did the president of the Republic—that conspirator, that convict—do? What did he do while heads . . . rolled on the scaffold? The president! He rested . . . after the hardships of the ball of the previous evening to prepare himself for the work of the next day.[188]

Loiseau, the *procureur-général* at Besançon, asked the Legislative Assembly on 28 June 1849 to withdraw the deputies' immunity so that he could prosecute them for this article. Although Sommier and Richardet had just taken part in the protests of 13 June, the prosecutor's request was denied, despite its excellent timing.[189]

When Sommier and Richardet left for Paris the newspaper ceased publication, but it reappeared in August under the direction of their friend Paget, an extremely wealthy landowner in the *arrondissement* of Poligny.[190] Paget's holdings, mostly in vineyards, were estimated by the attorney general to be worth 50,000 francs.[191] The very first issue of the new *Démocratie*, according to the attorney general, contained three articles "whose violence went beyond all limits and which seemed to me to contain the felonies of grossly insulting the magistrates, attacking the Constitution, etc., etc."[192] Paget was prosecuted for the articles themselves and for his failure to deposit a signed copy of this first issue with the local *parquet*. Tried before the assize jury for the articles, Paget was found guilty and sentenced to four months in jail and a 500-franc fine. In the police court, Paget was also found guilty of neglecting to send an inspection copy of his newspaper to the tribunal at Arbois and was fined another 500 francs.[193] With Paget in prison and 1,000 francs of the bond absorbed by fines, *La Démocratie* still continued to appear. A new director, the newspaper's printer, was brought to trial in February 1850 for publishing without having repaid the bond in its entirety when he became *La Démocratie*'s legal proprietor. The police tribunal at Arbois found him guilty and Maréschal, the printer and director, was sentenced to one month in jail and a fine of 300 francs. A few days later he was also tried at the assize court for an article attacking the transportation of political prisoners to Belle Isle without trial. Maréschal was sentenced to an additional prison term and another heavy fine.[194] *La Démocratie Jurassienne* closed down.[195]

As soon as Paget was released from prison in June 1850, he sold 20,000 francs' worth of his property to pay off Maréschal's fines and put together a new bond. He started *La Démocratie Jurassienne* again. Once more the administration moved against the newspaper, this time avoiding the necessity of court action. On 5 July 1850 the *procureur-général* asked the Justice Ministry to bring Maréschal's two convictions to the attention of the Interior Ministry so that the license for his printshop could be withdrawn: "Maréschal is no ordinary printer here; no simple manufacturer, by his ideas and his actions, he belongs to the demagogy of Jura."[196] When Maréschal lost his printing license, Paget could find no other printer, and his newspaper collapsed definitively in August 1850.[197]

The history of *La Démocratie Jurassienne* shows that the tenacity of the prosecutors was matched by the stubbornness of the democratic socialists of a small town in rural France. The newspaper was finally closed, not by court action but by an administrative fiat that deprived it of the basic mechanical means for its publication.

La Tribune du Jura, although it was also a radical republican newspaper, was edited with greater prudence.[198] It was so radical, in fact, that the *procureur-général* reported its editors as considering the wealthy Paget a disguised legitimist. Yet Loiseau's only successful prosecution of *La Tribune* occurred in January 1851. Instead of printing verbatim the record of the trial of a legitimist society, *La Tribune* had interjected, at one point, the name of a particularly well-known defendant. However, the transcript only made a general reference to all the members of this club. Found guilty of this technicality by the jury of Lons-le-Saunier, the director of *La Tribune* was subjected to a very heavy penalty by the court: six months in prison and a fine of 2,000 francs.[199] Nonetheless, this newspaper, now entitled *La Tribune de l'Est*, continued to appear until its director, Barbier, was arrested on 4 December 1851.[200] The republican press of Jura, including the embattled *Démocratie Jurassienne*, had not been silenced by legal action but rather by the arbitrary power of the state administration.

In sum, the repressive action of the bureaucracy against the republican press under the Second Republic failed. Despite the ample legislative weaponry provided by the Constituent and Legislative assemblies, and regardless of the cooperation of such conservative juries as those of Moulins (Allier) and Lons-le-Saunier (Jura)—both of which were isolated Party of Order strongholds in overwhelmingly radical departments—republican newspapers continued to circulate in all of the provincial jurisdictions we have studied that were not under martial law. The resources of a mass-based republican movement were simply too great in Allier and Jura to be sapped by a legal war of attrition. And in most of the departments of our sample—Vendée, Charente-Inférieure, Gard, and Gironde—the jury system presented an insurmountable obstacle to the work of the prosecutors.

Irene Collins remarks that the government did not embark on a systematic attack on printers, yet in five of the departments we have studied, it attempted to destroy the republican press either by levying heavy fines against these small enterprises or by depriving them of their licenses.[201] The cases of Siret in Vendée and Charente-Inférieure, Havel in Gironde, Madame Veuve Ayné in Rhône, and Maréschal in Jura show that Collins' assertion is premature. It was precisely because legal repression was ineffective that the government moved against the printers in a last-ditch attempt to close down republican newspapers. Except in Rhône, which was ruled by fiat, and in Jura, where the attack on a printer worked against only one of two Montagnard newspapers, even this effort failed. Only the end of the republic spelled the doom of most of the newspapers we have studied. To a large extent, they owed their survival to the government's inability to gather them within effective reach of the law. Perhaps in larger measure, the republican press survived because its printers, its editors, and its directors were a remarkably tough breed of men and women who enjoyed the support and protection of large segments of the population in their departments.

Colportage

The regular publication of republican newspapers in many of the departments we have studied—especially in the rural ones—was an entirely new element in the local political situation. It reflected the sudden development of a massive radical movement in many previously "quiet" jurisdictions, which had been dominated by their notabilities for centuries. The elite had expanded under the impact of the Great Revolution and the empire, and until 1848 its rule had gone unquestioned. There was no appreciable radical press, designed to appeal to the "popular" audience of peasants, artisans, and industrial workers in rural France, before the February revolution. But suddenly, it functioned openly and was subject to all the controls and penalties embodied in the press legislation of 1848, 1849, and 1850. Yet the police bureaucrats of the Second Republic could not effectively control this decidedly aboveboard republican propaganda.

Given their inability to muzzle even this open radical agitation, it is not difficult to imagine the frustrations experienced by the prefects and prosecutors in dealing with the underground circulation of republican writings. These clandestine works were usually printed in Paris, or even outside of France, and sold or distributed door-to-door by itinerant peddlers. These publications included pamphlets, song books, almanacs, and especially issues of the radical Parisian dailies. One such Parisian newspaper, Pierre Joigneux's *La Feuille du Village*, was directed exclusively to a peasant readership. Given the administrative controls over the mail services and the unrelenting prefectoral and judicial attempts to bottle it up within Paris, its major means of circulation was *colportage*. Yet *La Feuille du Village*'s circulation grew throughout 1850 and 1851, with particular success in central France, Franche-Comté, and the Midi.[202] So popular were Joigneux's regular columns of "little lessons to villagers" on matters of both radical politics and progressive agronomy that his surname was significantly shortened in peasant parlance from Pierre to *père*.[203]

Their form of circulation, far from being as new as the republic itself, was as old as the rural tradition of the wandering tinker, backpack drygoods salesman, and the local poultry and egg man with his regular route. Embedded in the rural folkways of France, these itinerants became the carriers, under the Second Republic, of a most effective form of radical propaganda in the form of printed political tracts.

The problem was recognized early in the presidency of Louis Napoleon, and repeated legislative and administrative efforts were made to solve it. In February 1849 both Faucher, the interior minister, and Odilon Barrot, the justice minister, sent out strongly worded circulars on the subject of *colportage*. In a memorandum to Barrot, Faucher asked for vigorous action on the part of the prosecutors.

> Since the closing down of the principal clubs and the proposal of the bill whose purpose is to put an end to all these centers of anarchist preachings, the watchword of the socialist party is to put its greatest efforts into writing forms of propaganda. ... I hardly need to press this point with you, ... dear colleague, in order to bring your attention to bear on the danger to society and to order which would result if such ideas infiltrated the countryside. The prefectoral authorities are only empowered to provide surveillance; they would be condemned to remain powerless bystanders to these events if the judicial authorities did not come to their aid by prosecuting to the utmost writings which assault the principles of property, religious teachings and the family. The proposed legislation must give us these means.[204]

Barrot, quoting the interior minister's request verbatim, immediately ordered his attorneys general to crack down on *colportage* by bringing charges against those hawkers who sold writings forbidden by the press law of August 1848.[205]

This was more easily commanded than done. The attorney general in Poitiers, Damay, replied to Barrot's circular by pointing out that existing legislation was inadequate to the task of controlling *colportage*. Apparently the successful prosecution of peddlers on the basis of the content of the books they sold was not possible in his *ressort*; the juries of western France were quite tolerant of both the republican and legitimist press. Damay restricted his answer to a discussion of the purely technical laws of the July Monarchy and earlier regimes (which were still on the books)—legislation designed to control the peddlers themselves rather than the content of the writings they carried. Citing a law of 16 February 1834, the attorney general argued, "I therefore think that they will only be subject to punishment to the extent that they become hawkers, vendors or distributors on public thoroughfares under the pretense of doing their normal business."[206] Damay insisted that proving such a charge was almost impossible given the lack of policemen on the byways travelled by these merchants, and he asked for new legislation on the specific subject of *colportage*.

> I believe that I must inform you of this danger; it is real and it is urgent. Socialism is particularly redoubtable in the countryside. . . . If the laws that are presently in existence do not allow the prevention and repression of this *colportage*—which has had a frightening growth and which is carried out . . . by vagrants— is it not time to ask for . . . means to regulate it and to back them up with penal sanctions?[207]

A month later, Faucher sent out another circular to his prefects giving them a new legal basis for controlling book peddlers. Citing a Restoration law (21 October 1814) that permitted the sale of books only in licensed bookstores, the minister told his provincial agents that *colportage* was therefore illegal "in principle" and that they could eradicate it by administrative fiat.[208] Faucher's successor, Dufaure, soon discovered that this law was also ineffective. In a letter to Barrot, written in June 1849, he complained that the law of 21 October 1814 provided no real punishment for the unlicensed sale of books by peddlers and that, in 1844, the Cour de cassation had ruled that the only possible penalty was for the prefectoral administration to close down unlicensed bookshops without levying any fines or imposing any prison sentences.[209] Clearly such an administrative prerogative could have no effect on a *colporteur* who owned no shop and needed no license to hawk his wares.

Finally, a measure was passed by the Legislative Assembly specifically to end the circulation of seditious publications by door-to-door salesmen. Article 6 of the press law of 27 July 1849 gave the prefects the right to license all peddlers who carried pamphlets, books, and newspapers among their wares.[210] The prefects immediately used their new powers to investigate the "morality" (that is, the political persuasion) of peddlers in their departments and to license or bar them from selling books accordingly.[211] They also went one step further. Prefects established lists of publications that could or could not be sold door-to-door. A kind of prefectoral Index was, therefore, prepared in most departments. The attorney general in Poitiers complained that this latter practice could not be enforced even in the nonjury trials of the police courts. According to Damay, when a *colporteur* was caught selling seditious literature, he was ordinarily charged with a serious offense against public order that carried a stiff fine and prison term: violating the prefectoral decree that listed the particular books he was allowed to sell. The attorney general reported that defendants were never found guilty of this crime, but rather of the relatively minor transgression of having engaged in unauthorized bookselling.[212] The difference between the charges was considerable: the former charge is the equivalent of a felony under Anglo-Saxon law, whereas the latter is merely a misdemeanor.[213]

In reporting cases involving *colportage*, Damay actually agreed with the police court magistrates who refused to try the defendants for flouting a prefectoral order.

> One would think that, after investigation of the peddler's morality and the guarantees of good conduct which he presents, the prefect's power is then to deny or grant an authorization, but it is not the power to qualify the authorization by limiting it to only certain books. It seemed that it was the individuals concerned and not the books which the prefects were empowered to judge under the law of 27 July.[214]

The *procureur-général* was immediately rebuked by his minister. Odilon Barrot told Damay to continue arguing for the more severe penalty since, according to the justice minister, the prefectoral right to license peddlers implied the corollary prerogative to "define and limit" their activities.[215] Damay and his staff must have been dismayed by Barrot's lack of understanding for their plight. They simply could not convince the courts to levy serious sanctions against *colporteurs*. Damay has just reported a case tried in Vendée in which the police court had found a republican book hawker guilty of unlicensed *colportage* and fined him exactly one franc for his offense![216]

In fact, *colportage* was never brought under control during the years before the coup d'état. A few examples will suffice to demonstrate this point. In December 1849, six months after the state of siege was instituted in Lyon, Gilardin was still trying to stop the circulation of socialist almanacs in the rural parts of the department of Rhône. He could not rely on the provisions of the law of July 1849, even when they were enforced by military tribunals. But since martial law was in force, Gilardin had General Gémeau, the commander of the sixth military district, forbid the "printing, sale or peddling" of one particular almanac. Gilardin attached a particular importance to this forbidden *Almanach des Opprimés*, which was circulating freely throughout his *ressort*.

> A newspaper article is read and never looked at again; it is not read every day. . . . But an almanac is in their hands all year long. It is the book of common knowledge for the countryside. From the point of view of the existence of universal suffrage, there is an obvious, immense danger because this type of publication sows the detestable seeds of socialism.[217]

Because of the state of siege, this attorney general achieved more press control than his colleagues in other parts of France. Yet in reporting his activities against *colportage* throughout the period June 1849 through December 1851 (the entire "era" of martial law in his *ressort* during the Second Republic), Gilardin did not inform Paris of a single successful prosecution of a book peddler. Despite numerous seizures of almanacs and brochures carried out by the police and military authorities, no one appears to have been punished for distributing them.[218]

In March 1850 Gilardin reported that *Le National* was having a "bad influence" on the workers in Villefranche and could be seen in many cabarets, although he could not find out by what means this newspaper was being distributed.[219] Almost a year later he complained about the profuse circulation of "immoral novels at 20 centimes a copy."[220] Since he mentioned this in a political report, it is safe to assume that the attorney general in Lyon was referring to such radically oriented works of fiction as those written by Eugène Sue and George Sand rather than to pornography. The most frustrating evidence that subversive literature was circulating freely despite the state of siege came to Gilardin's attention in

January 1851. At that time, the police discovered that a "Seventh Bulletin of the Central Committee of Resistance" could be found all over Lyon, Villefranche, and the surrounding countryside.[221] Even martial law had not prevented the left from carrying on its propaganda activities or transmitting its orders, in printed form, to its mass of supporters.

Colportage also remained a problem endemic to those departments of our sample that still enjoyed a purely civilian administration. Months after the passage of the press law of July 1849, the attorney general in Riom, De Sèze, was complaining that in Allier, "repeated incidents of *colportage* reveal here, as elsewhere, the efforts of the socialists and the hostile leanings of the population."[222] The publications that most troubled De Sèze were the Parisian dailies: *La Réforme*, *Le National*, and the ever-present *Feuille du Village*. Although these newspapers could legally be distributed only to their subscribers, they were then circulated among the cabarets of many small towns and read by a larger audience. Such a form of circulation was illegal under the *colportage* clause of the July 1849 press law, since the people who delivered them were supposed to be licensed by the prefecture. Obviously, Maupas—then prefect of Allier—would not have given permits to the distributors of such subversive publications. Again, as was the case for Rhône, the attorney general reported no prosecutions of *colporteurs* in his monthly reports from December 1849 through November 1851. In fact, in January 1850 De Sèze concluded a discussion of the socialist newspapers and books that were often given to the peasants of Allier by remarking that

> the prefectoral administration has made fruitless attempts to uncover the people who receive and redistribute these inflammatory writings. . . . I receive not a single police citation of an infraction to act on. . . . This is the poisonous source, *Monsieur le ministre*, which infiltrates itself into public opinion and which has already taken hold of the countryside.[223]

In Jura, prosecutions were attempted for *colportage* and for the related crime of publishing a pamphlet. But these court actions, which came in 1850, seem only to have had the effect of harassing an activity that went on well beyond the reach of the law. In November 1849 Loiseau, the attorney general in Besançon, told the prefect that the entire *arrondissement* of Poligny was "inundated" with socialist pamphlets and almanacs and that the blame for this situation lay squarely with the ineffectiveness of the gendarmerie brigade stationed at Salins.[224] At the beginning of 1850 Loiseau reported to his ministry that the main sources for the distribution of radical literature in Jura were the private mail delivery services that flourished in this mountainous area. One such service was operated, under a license from the Finance Ministry, by the father-in-law of the chief of the secret societies of Dôle. According to Loiseau, this man already had been condemned once by the local tribunal for distributing socialist propaganda.[225] The sentence or fine must have been light, since his one-man operation continued without interruption. According to the attorney general, no further charges had been brought against this militant, because a circular of the Finance Ministry, dating from the July Monarchy, barred the police from searching the carriages and mail sacks carried by private agents. The policy apparently went unchanged; no further prosecutions occurred against this individual or another group of republicans who ran a similar service.

Two other successful prosecutions for *colportage* were reported by Loiseau. In December 1850 two men were charged with distributing the Parisian socialist daily, *La Voix du Peuple*, in the town of Dôle. The local police tribunal found Richard, one of the defendants and the leader of Dôle's secret society, guilty of unlicensed peddling and sentenced him to one month in prison. His accomplice was ordered to serve fifteen days behind bars.[226] The attorney general appealed these minimal penalties, but he warned the prefect that "I fall from Charybdis to Scylla, since the appeal will be heard by the court at Lons-le-Saunier: the softest one in the *ressort*."[227] Loiseau's worst fears were realized when the departmental appeals court reduced Richard's sentence to fifteen days and that of his friend to one day. Another case was tried at the same time, and a stiffer penalty was handed down by the police court of Dôle, perhaps because the defendant had twice been convicted of assaulting policemen. He was sentenced to five months in prison and a fifty-franc fine.[228]

Loiseau's final victory in a case involving the unlicensed circulation of radical publications came against Paget, the former director and editor of *La Démocratie Jurassienne*. Paget had written a Montagnard *Catechism for Everyone's Use*. The book was seized before it could be distributed, and in December 1850 Paget was sentenced to one year in prison and a fine of 2,000 francs.[229] Catching a pamphlet at its source seems to have been the only way to levy serious penalties against the circulation of radical literature. The fact that Paget was printing his book in Salins indicates that the means for its illegal distribution in Jura had not been disrupted by any repressive action of the bureaucracy.

Perhaps the only department in our sample in which the control of book peddling was even temporarily successful was Vendée. The prefect reported to the Ministry of Interior in March 1851 that *colportage* had been stopped for some time in his department. It had, however, sprung up again in the form of the unlicensed sale of seditious books in many small country stores, and a recent decision of the Cour de cassation had permitted the operation of an unlicensed bookstore in another department. The prefect of Vendée, therefore, felt unable to move against the general stores in his department. When he asked the Interior Ministry for instructions, he was told that the high court ruling applied only to shops that sold books exclusively. The prefect was ordered to bring the general stores, which carried pamphlets, newspapers, and books only as a sideline, to the attention of the prosecuting magistrates for violation of the press law of July 1849.[230] They were to be charged with unlicensed *colportage*, but I have found no evidence of any prosecutions of this nature in Vendée during 1851.

It appears that even the isolated republicans of this legitimist stronghold were able to circumvent the repressive action of the state. Indeed, *Le Démocrate Vendéen* reprinted one of Joigneux's "little lessons" on precisely this subject in May 1851. It attests to the irrepressible nature of *colportage*, not only in Vendée, but throughout the departments where père Joigneux's newspaper was popular. The editor of *La Feuille du Village* warned his readers not to welcome *licensed* peddlers into their homes or cabarets and to trust only those *colporteurs*—obviously the illegal ones—whom they knew from long association with their village. The others, he pointed out, were likely to be stool pigeons in the pay of the prefect.[231]

Colportage was never brought under control by the prefects and prosecutors of the Second Republic. The peddler, private postman, and small shopkeeper were familiar figures in the villages and poor urban neighborhoods of France. Embedded in the folk culture of their localities, protected by their familiarity with the landscape (urban and rural) and by the people they served, they carried on their activities beyond the reach of the "foreign" policeman and *juge d'instruction*. With the sudden growth of mass political movements in many of these neighborhoods, the *colporteur* was himself politicized. From a purveyor of essential goods and services he was transformed, in part, into a carrier of ideas that were in great demand. The democratic socialist movement had found powerful ideological auxiliaries in these "artful dodgers."

Thus, both the radical press and the means for its widespread distribution survived the reactionary phase of the Second Republic. Their continued existence and growth was possible because of two insurmountable obstacles to political repression: a liberal court system (which, as we have seen, even had to be used occasionally in Lyon as a sop to public opinion), and a vast social and cultural gap that separated the notables and their police from the middle- and lower-class constituents of the radical movement. The frequent verdicts of "not guilty," the light sentences usually imposed on those brought before the police courts, and even the decision taken by the Cour de cassation during 1851 (in the shadow of the *échéance* of 1852) in favor of unlicensed bookstores all indicate that judges and juries could not be convinced that press control necessitated the extreme measures voted by the conservative politicians of the Constituent and Legislative assemblies. The judiciary, whose members uniformly owed their appointments either to the July Monarchy or to ministers of the Party of Order, had no sympathy for radical ideas or for radicals. Yet it generally remained steadfast in its commitment to liberal legal procedures and to the traditional independence of the bench from the political organs of the state.

The juries, drawn under universal manhood suffrage from the full range of the local population, inhabited the same social universe as the political agitators they were called upon to judge. With few exceptions, jurors could not view the defendants, whether they agreed with them politically or not, as evil incarnate. In the face-to-face culture of the small rural town, and even in the urban neighborhood of mid-nineteenth-century France, the men at the bar of justice were known to the jurors as neighbors or at least as familiar faces in the street or cafe—not merely as defendants. Small wonder that the heated arguments of the attorney general did not often move them. Community feeling, the culture that existed beneath the rarefied stratum of the bureaucrats and the political elite, simply did not view political expression as a crime.

The other barrier to the work of the prefects and prosecutors was the distance that separated them from the very social elements they were supposed to police. They were simply unable to gather enough evidence in most cases of *colportage* to identify the malefactor. The rule of silence (*omerta*) is not geographically limited to Sicily or Corsica. It exists wherever a social and political elite, represented by police authorities, is viewed with hostility and distrust by a local population. This point, although it has been partly demonstrated in our discussion of *colportage*, can be shown most clearly by considering the almost total impotence of the authorities to suppress the actual Montagnard "force-in-being": the secret societies.

Secret Societies

As we demonstrated in our detailed survey of the estimates that the police bureaucrats made of the left's strength during the presidency of Louis Napoleon, it is apparent that they had completely failed to disrupt or dissolve republican organizations in their jurisdictions by the time of the coup d'état. The fear they expressed for the *échéance* of 1852 by the end of 1851 was not bogus. The prosecutors and prefects of Rhône, Jura, and Allier—jurisdictions in which the left was the dominant political force—were merely projecting into an uncertain future the consequences of their failure.

As in their campaign against the press, the police entered the battle against secret societies fully equipped with all the legislative weapons they needed. To help its prosecutors in preparing their cases, the Justice Ministry compiled a list of legislation pertaining to the clubs and associations and sent it to the attorneys general in July or August 1849. The jurists at the ministry began with a reference to the Constitution of 5 Fructidor of the year III. Article 360 of this document gave the government the right to prevent the formation of any clubs "contrary to public order." They bolstered their case for such political control by citing another Thermidorean antecedent to the legislation of the Second Republic. A decree of 25 Vendémiaire of the same year specifically outlawed all clubs, federations, and corresponding societies that had been created by the Jacobin Club. The ministry officials then listed the various decrees and laws passed in 1848 and 1849 (outlined above) and concluded their checklist with a significant quotation from the interior minister's circular to his prefects, which was dispatched on the very day the assembly voted to outlaw all political groups in France:

> The first use you will make of this law, *Monsieur le préfet*, will be to prohibit, everywhere in your department, and in the most absolute manner, clubs and public meetings in which people indulge in the discussion of "public affairs."[232]

The prefects dutifully decreed the end of political associations throughout France, and the prosecutors stood ready to enforce these laws and proclamations. This form of antirepublican prophylaxis, however, would never prove effective until France fell under a dictatorship two and a half years later. A study of all the available reports on secret societies submitted by the prosecutors and prefects responsible for our sample of seven departments has not revealed a single successful prosecution for a breach of the association laws of the republic. Yet these reports amply demonstrate that the law-enforcement bureaucrats were well aware that large underground republican organizations existed in their jurisdictions.

These groups flourished in a social milieu that was completely beyond the reach of the police. The secret societies enjoyed the support and protection of practically the entire middle- and lower-class population in their localities, and outsiders are easily noted and isolated in such provincial neighborhoods, where social activity is all face-to-face. If the environment in which these groups functioned was impenetrable, their simple but effective form of organization was an additional obstacle to police espionage. These were not mass organizations but rather coalitions of numerous small groups, each one composed of ten or twenty-five members. Each participant had probably known the others for years, so the potential spy, in order to gain entry to even the smallest unit of a secret society, had to pass the barrier erected against any "foreigner" in the neighborhood.

The information gap created by these circumstances troubled the attorneys general. In his first monthly report to the Justice Ministry, written in December 1849, Gilardin concluded a list of secret societies in the city of Lyon (with memberships numbering in the thousands) with a disgusted comment. "The police shed hardly any light on this situation. The police force here hardly knows those things which are almost public knowledge and it remains in ignorance of all that is secret."[233] A month later he complained that the state of siege itself, although it was absolutely necessary for the preservation of order, had "compressed" political activity beyond the reach of the police.

> The state of siege, by placing all public activities of the parties under constraint, has made it difficult to evaluate the political situation accurately. . . . The anarchist press is prohibited, the schemings of the agitators are lost in the shadows where police investigations try to find out what is happening. . . . In a word, we see all the outward appearances of calm reigning in the area. But what is the value of such appearances? . . . To what extent have the parties pulled back from taking violent action? No positive or observed information of any certainty will permit me to find out.[234]

This situation was never rectified, despite Gilardin's repeated calls for a thorough reorganization of the police in the zone placed under martial law.[235] Lyon and its environs formed a region in which the militants of the secret societies were experts. Many of the leaders were wily old veterans of the Carbonari who knew all about organizing their groups into a network of tiny *"ventes."*[236]

Gilardin's problem was echoed by his colleagues in other *ressorts.* Early in 1850 Loiseau told the ministry that the local police were "altogether lacking" in ability to provide the *parquet* and the prefecture with any intelligence on their adversaries.[237] Again in June 1851 he complained that he could never gather enough evidence to prosecute any of the secret societies in Jura, even though he estimated that Richard's group at Dôle, a small town, numbered at least four hundred members.[238] Thourel, at Nîmes, described the difficulties he faced by giving the dramatic example of a Phrygian cap that adorned the liberty tree of a town just outside the city, which the police were too frightened to take down (seditious symbols were illegal). According to him, "The police are almost everywhere either incompetent or complicit."[239]

The image of policemen visualized by most historians of the Second Republic must have been based on our own contemporary models of a Louis Lépine or the resourceful Inspector Maigret. The repression we are studying occurred in the middle of the last century, however, and police work had yet to become a craft, much less a science. The attorneys general and prefects gleaned their information about the internal organization and plans of the secret societies largely from informal personal sources and from rumor.

In very few cases was any "hard"evidence gathered by the grim modern and institutionalized methods of intercepting letters or by the use of secret agents.

Early in 1849 Thourel sent a report to Paris describing the plans made at a meeting of one of the secret societies of Gard. An "atrocious motion" had called for the preparation of incendiary devices, which, once a revolution had broken out in Paris or Lyon, would be used to burn down part of the city of Nîmes. This information came to him from an indignant and idealistic Montagnard, and Thourel bitterly remarked that

> the prefects are powerless to discover what takes place in the anarchists' cabals [conciliabules]. . . . The police in every town report nothing to the authorities. I have come to know of this fact only through a confidential and semiofficial communication from an honest homme du peuple who has extremely strong feelings against the use of violence.[240]

The first advocate general in Lyon similarly transmitted information from a private source, a person who claimed to have access to the Mountain Committee of the city. He dismissed this intelligence, which predicted a rising at Lyon shortly after the elections of May 1849, as mere alarmist rumors: "The workers lack courage and the leaders have neither the decisiveness nor the brains for it."[241] As the bloody struggle of 13-14 June 1849 clearly demonstrated, the first advocate was wrong. Later in the same year, after the events of June 1849, the parquet at Besançon learned from a "very honorable merchant from Dôle" that his friends in Lausanne had written him to urge that he cancel a business trip to Lyon because they had overheard some exiles discussing a new revolution in that city.[242] This rumor was immediately sent on to Paris.

In April 1850 the attorney general in Poitiers took a story in his local conservative newspaper seriously enough to ask the prefects in his ressort to begin investigations. L'Abeille de la Vienne had reported that peasants were busily stealing gunpowder and muskets from the National Guard in preparation for a red revolution in western France.[243] On the basis of this wild partisan rumor, Damay, the attorney general, quickly sent out a circular asking for confidential reports. Earlier in the year, Damay had ordered the subprefect at Saint-Jean-d'Angély (Charente-Inférieure) to close down a small singing society because neighbors had spread rumors that seditious songs were being sung.[244] And in August 1849 the police commissioner at Saintes had arrested a man said to own a model guillotine designed to lop off several heads at a time. The case was dismissed when the machine turned out to be a new design for a multiple pile driver.[245] *Le Phare* of La Rochelle reported the entire incident with relish. It described how the *procureur de la république, juge d'instruction*, process server, lieutenant and sergeant of the gendarmerie, and two town policemen had "erupted" into the home of Citizen Martinet, master carpenter, only to discover that his mass-production guillotine and the repeated comings and goings around his house had to do with nothing more than a new invention he was preparing for competition in the Paris Exposition.[246] *Le Phare* made clear that Martinet's crime was his outspoken republicanism.

The prefect of Jura informed the Interior Ministry in early February 1850 that rumors were circulating in Arbois and Poligny that predicted violent radical demonstrations for the second anniversary of the republic. These suppositions were based on the barroom conversations of Montagnard leaders that had been overheard by a local conservative. Although the prefect considered this story somewhat exaggerated, he was all too aware of his own ignorance of the secret societies' real plans to take any chances; the local garrisons were immediately placed on alert.[247]

Other information on the activities and plans of the left was based on similar fragmentary observations reported by the police or by citizens to the prefectures and *parquets*. In other words, the law-enforcement bureaucrats were reduced to decoding the meaning of scattered signs in order to predict the possible actions of the mass movement that confronted them. Their reports were exercises in speculation.

Early in 1850 the attorneys general and prefects of several jurisdictions warned Gilardin of an imminent revolution at Lyon. They had observed that many workers were requesting internal passports to this city and considered this a sign that the Mountain was gathering its troops for another battle. The justice minister immediately asked Gilardin for a special report, and the *procureur-général* answered that he had no access to the internal workings of the left but that "these symptoms are too serious and are seen too frequently for the authorities not to take them into account."[248] During 1849 Thourel had received reports of "perfectly constructed" signal towers on deserted hilltops in his *ressort*.[249] He concluded that this communications system ran from Paris into the

Midi and was part of a serious plot against the government. Yet this must have been another false alarm, since he did not mention it in later dispatches.

Many other reports were based on the observed comings and goings of known republican leaders. A dispatch from Loiseau, the *procureur-général* at Besançon, perfectly summarizes the frustration and speculation that this kind of marginal intelligence produced among the police bureaucrats. In September 1849 he reported that a meeting had taken place with all the republican chiefs of Jura in attendance—Sommier and Richardet representing the radicals and Jules Grévy's brother speaking for the moderates. But he added that "we are reduced to the purest conjecture about it, what's more, I will soon have the honor to discuss with you the inadequate police force at our disposal."[250] He prefaced his remarks by reporting an optimistic rumor that no agreement had been reached between the two factions, but he doubted its veracity and expected future troubles to result from the meeting.

The prefects and prosecutors were forced to clutch at the flimsiest straws in their search for information. In March 1850 a vagrant was arrested near the Swiss border in Jura. The police noted that this individual was acting oddly and took him to the local insane asylum for an examination. The doctors declared him insane. This appeared to close a minor matter until the vagabond incongruously claimed that he was on a mission for a radical deputy to the Legislative Assembly. This news aroused the interest of the prefect, and he had the mental patient questioned again by the police. The man then stated that his real name was Sentenac, that he had escaped from an asylum in France, and that he had joined the republican movement in which he now served as the "key" messenger between the exile communities in London and in Geneva. Sentenac then described a massive plot to assassinate every member of the conservative majority in the Legislative Assembly. He listed the names of his coconspirators in twenty-two departments of France. The attorney general at Besançon recognized that Sentenac was mentally ill but told the justice minister, "While we cannot accord these statements our fullest confidence, they nonetheless deserve very serious attention. Sentenac's madness does not prevent him from having lucid moments."[251]

The Paris prefecture of police was brought into the case, and a circular was sent to practically every *procureur-général* in France asking for verification of the names that Sentenac had listed. In

January 1851 Devienne informed the Justice Ministry that the person cited by Sentenac in Bordeaux was known to the *parquet* as a person "in financial ruin who would naturally get mixed up with the lowest kinds of political intrigue."[252] He added, however, that this person had left the city months ago. Thourel, less prone to accept this wild tale, told the ministry that those Montagnards identified by Sentenac in Gard could not possibly be connected with such a plot.[253] Finally, in March 1851, a full year after Sentenac had been discovered wandering the roads of Jura and after the most comprehensive police investigation of his tale, Gilardin submitted a report closing the case definitively. He reported that the lyonnais radicals mentioned in the madman's deposition were well-known leaders of the local Mountain and that they were presently implicated in the *complot* of Lyon. Their houses had been searched repeatedly during the investigation of this matter; no evidence of any assassination plot had been found in their effects. Gilardin concluded that

> the style of Sentenac's statements led me to believe, at the time, that his brain was sick. . . . It is most improbable that these men entered into any assassination pact. . . . A matter of this nature would not have been discussed with a confidant like Sentenac and it seems to me . . . that this whole account can be nothing but a fable.[254]

Thus, as late as 1851 the most important police bureaucrats were so ill-informed of the plans of their enemies that they spent considerable time and effort in investigating the story of a man recognized by all of them to be insane.[255]

Only rarely did the police bureaucrats have recourse to what may be considered modern investigative efforts. In the region placed under the state of siege, letters addressed to known radical leaders were often intercepted, but the only prosecution based even partly upon this information was the *complot* of Lyon.[256] I have also found evidence of several house searches other than those carried out in connection with the *complot* of Lyon. All of them either failed to turn up any evidence or resulted in acquittals.[257] In Jura, Paget's home was searched by the police in May 1849, but they discovered only the incomplete manuscript of his socialist catechism and a correspondence he had carried on with Proudhon.[258] Not until a full year later was Paget tried and convicted—when the *Catechism* had been completed, run off, readied for distribution, and finally seized at the printer's. In December 1849 a "domiciliary visit" occurred at the home of Bellion of La Rochelle. Evidence was found that he belonged to Solidarité Républicaine, but no conviction resulted. Bellion had come to the attention of the local authorities because, according to the attorney general, it was well known that he belonged to the Billaud-Varenne family (and was thus the descendant of a member of the Terror's Committee of Public Safety) and that he had made known "the extremism of his principles" in public statements.[259]

House searches were also undertaken by the prefect and *pro-cureur-général* responsible for Gard in April 1849. They took place simultaneously at Bagnols and Nîmes, and one man was arrested for belonging to a secret society. A notebook discovered at the home of the defendant included a speech he supposedly gave at a meeting.

> Yes, the future is storm-filled, the ground will be covered with blood and the rising tides will cast more heads on the land than all the sea shells it has ever left behind. Yes, in this not distant future, the wicked will pay fully his debt to the nation.[260]

Thourel considered this an example of "the extravagant atrocity of communist dreams."[261] He assured the ministry, however, that the Mountain had so few members at Nîmes that it would never become a serious threat to public order. Thourel also warned the minister that he could never convince the Assize Court of Nîmes that this speech had ever been made, but he said that he would use it as evidence of the plans of the secret society he intended to bring to trial.

On 3 December 1849 Thourel reported that the author of the sanguinary speech and his fellow members of a secret society which had branches both in Nîmes and Bagnols had been acquitted by the jury.[262] He brought two other radical groups before the Assize Court in February 1850, and they too were acquitted. The attorney general blamed this on "the weakness, I should even say, the fear of the jury."[263] These were the only cases he prosecuted against the left under the association laws before the coup d'état.

While Thourel was losing his first battle against the secret societies of Gard, Damay reported this failure to gain a conviction against Bellion and other members of Solidarité Républicaine in Charente-Inférieure.[264] Also in December 1849, Troplong lost his own case against Solidarité Républicaine in Bordeaux.[265] This defeat was partly responsible for Troplong's fall from grace, and his transfer to Nîmes came soon afterward. Troplong had brought eighteen individuals before the assize court and charged them, on the basis of the minutes of four meetings of their chapter, with belonging to a secret society (banned by the law of 28 July 1848). The jury acquitted them by a vote of five for "not guilty" and seven for conviction.[266] (Troplong lost his case by one vote.)

The presiding magistrate at the trial, a young councilor at the appeals court, immediately dispatched a letter to the justice minister accusing Troplong of bungling the case.[267] Rouher, the justice minister, wrote back to the councilor, Charles Henry, asking for a confidential report.[268] Henry's secret reply informed the minister that Troplong should not have prosecuted the republican group as a secret society, since the defense maintained that the law of July 1848 defined such illegal organizations as corresponding societies, not as groups that merely met to discuss politics.[269] According to Henry, the argument between Troplong and the defense attorneys on what actually constituted a secret society served only to confuse the jurors. And he pointed out to Rouher that the attorney general would have gained a conviction had he prosecuted the organization on the basis of the later law of 1849, which banned "unauthorized, nonpublic political meetings." After essentially accusing the chief of the appellate *parquet* of incompetence, Henry became modest: "I, one of youngest magistrates of the Court, will not dare to utter so serious a judgment about one of the leading figures of the Company to which I have the honor of belonging."[270]

The loss of this important political case before the jury of an overwhelmingly conservative city enraged Rouher. Immediately upon receiving Henry's critical report, the minister wrote a stern note to Troplong: "I regret that, in so important a case, the magistrates did not use all the means that were in their power to obtain a verdict that both Justice and Policy demanded."[271] Troplong tried in vain to defend himself by blaming the *juge d'instruction* and the Chambre de mises en accusations for forcing him to try the case under the law of 1848 on secret societies.[272]

The other prosecutions based on the association laws also ended in failure. Gilardin, a prosecutor who certainly enjoyed the confidence of the government, could not convince a police court to convict a group of Voraces—the largest secret society in Lyon—caught in the very act of holding a meeting in a café.[273] And Loiseau failed to gain a guilty verdict against a secret society that had disguised itself as a mutual aid society (a tactic that was common, and successful, in all the departments of our sample). Both the tribunal at Lons-le-Saunier and the Appeals Court at Besançon denied Loiseau a victory.[274] The government had failed to implement its repressive legislation against republican organizations.

Unable to enforce the association laws, the authorities could confront republicanism as a movement only when it came out from underground to fight election campaigns, to circulate petitions, to protest (peacefully or violently) the reactionary drive of the Party of Order and the bureaucracy, or, as with the *complot* of Lyon, when a schismatic group on the left attempted to orchestrate a rebellion in such a large region of France that it was virtually forced to conspire in public. In this latter case the authorities won one of their rare repressive victories over a republican group during the entire period following the June Days of 1849. As we shall see, however, the victory was illusory. The bureaucrats were so powerless to uproot republicanism as a mass force throughout whole departments of France that those involved in the *complot* of Lyon had to be tried by a carefully selected military tribunal in "besieged" Lyon in order to be convicted.

Universal manhood suffrage, in force for all the elections that actually took place during the Second Republic, left relatively little room for electoral manipulation on the part of the ministers or their provincial bureaucrats. The major attempt to rig elections during the four years following the revolution of 1848 was done in legislative fashion—through the wholesale disfranchisement of three million citizens by the law of 31 May 1850. As the continual victories of the Mountain through the by-elections of 1850 show, the electoral process remained basically uncorrupted in the new age of mass politics. The repressive tradition of the French bureaucracy, however, did not go into complete eclipse: the administration used electoral campaigns as a means of observing republicans in the open and, if possible, of bringing them up on charges based on their public acts.

The law of July 1848, which forbade certain forms of public political demonstrations, was to be suspended during the period immediately preceding an election. Both Barrot and Faucher, however, ordered their subordinates in March 1849 to maintain a strict and even secret surveillance on the temporarily legal public activities of the republicans. On 31 March 1849 the interior minister, Faucher, sent the following circular to his prefects:

The law frees preparatory electoral meetings from the restrictive measures required concerning clubs and public or nonpublic political meetings. But it would be easy for the artisans of disorder to evade these terms of the law and to organize real clubs, under the pretext of holding electoral meetings; clubs that would be all the more dangerous because they would not be subject to any police surveillance.[275]

Therefore, Faucher ordered the prefects to send a police agent to all electoral meetings to report all offenses against the political laws that remained in force. The minister emphasized that the policeman should attend the meetings in mufti.

It is not at all necessary for this policeman to wear any insignia of office: all the same, he must show these insignia and thus make known his mission and his presence at the meeting in the event that an incident occurs that requires official action on his part.[276]

The commissioner had to identify himself only if he was about to denounce a crime. This was necessary if the prosecution of the offense was to have any sound basis. Otherwise, he was sent to spy on legal, public meetings. The government obviously needed all the information it could get on the republican movement.

A few days later, Barrot sent a similar circular to the attorneys general asking them to pay particular attention to crimes denounced by the police authorities and ordering them to bring such cases into court immediately. The justice minister's intent was clear: denounce, try, and jail republican candidates before the electorate went to the polls. He emphasized this to his subordinates.

This is the time to proceed . . . with the greatest dispatch, so that repression follows the criminal act as soon as possible, and thus can become a useful warning to the citizens. It is above all during times of elections—when all opinions, all interests, all passions are in the struggle—that the cooperation of different kinds of officials is indispensable to the maintenance of order. The Magistracy, while remaining within that zone of independence and impartiality which is its special province, must give the example of vigilance and firmness.[277]

During the elections of 1849 and 1850, the bureaucrats tried to execute these instructions to the best of their abilities. A question addressed by the *procureur-général* in Riom to the Justice Ministry before the elections for the Legislative Assembly illustrates the extent of their repressive drive. The attorney general and the prefects wanted to know if they could remove republican posters, which announced electoral meetings, as violations of the press law. The ministry informed them that such announcements were permitted.[278]

I have found very few prosecutions that followed campaign speeches or *professions de foi*, dating from the campaign of April-May 1849. The few trials all ended in acquittals. The case of Naquet and his *profession de foi*, in the form of a revived socialist newspaper in Lyon, has been discussed above. In May 1849 Thourel arrested two candidates in Gard for giving seditious speeches at electoral meetings. The administration in this department, caught in a cross-fire between the red and "white" Mountains, struck in both directions. Thourel's actions, however, were tailored to the political exigencies of the situation: he jailed the republican at least temporarily, but allowed the legitimist to continue campaigning until his case came up. Encontre, the Montagnard bookseller and president of the Club socialiste of Nîmes, was arrested in late April for making a public statement against "the rich" and calling the local police bureaucrats "*canaille*." His opponent, Rivière, was charged, but not arrested, for breaking the same law of August 1848 (provocation to civil war, offense to the civil authorities, and attack on the form of government) when he promised the electors that the Legislative Assembly had the right to restore the Bourbon monarchy.[279] Both men were acquitted by the assize jury of Nîmes.[280]

Later, after the elections and the events of June 1849, the attorney general in Besançon did win a case against republicans who had prepared a "seditious" poster for a by-election held in late June 1849. The offending caption ran thus: "Does not the worker see everywhere that his own life and that of his family are placed at the mercy of the rich?"[281] The defendants—the author, the printer, and the man who hung these posters—were charged with violating the press law of 1848 (provocation to civil war among citizens and exciting hatred and scorn of the government) and with breaking a law of 1830 (having sought to trouble the public peace), which was a much less serious offense. The jury of Lons-le-Saunier found them guilty only of the latter charge. This assize jury, which had shown itself to be quite harsh in press matters, refused to enforce the Second Republic's political laws in an electoral matter. The penalties were relatively minor in comparison with those handed down by this court in other press cases: one defendant was given fifteen days and a fine of 200 francs, two others were sentenced to eight days and fined 150 francs.[282]

The attorneys general's lack of success in handling cases related to electoral activities apparently made them shy away from further prosecutions in 1850 and 1851. Thourel told the Justice Ministry that he was not bringing charges against Favand, the newly elected Montagnard deputy from Gard, despite his blatantly seditious public speech at Nîmes. The *procureur-général* argued that Favand's position as a member of the assembly made prosecution difficult and that such a case would surely stir up public opinion against the authorities.[283] Before the by-elections of March 1850, De Sèze, the attorney general in Riom, complained that he could not risk prosecuting Allier's Montagnard deputies, who were busily touring the department and appearing at illegal banquets, because of their legislative immunity and the support they enjoyed in the community.[284]

The government did attempt a few rather shady maneuvers during both national and municipal elections in 1849 and 1850. We have already seen that republican justices of the peace, largely because of their role as presidents of the cantonal election commissions, were replaced from the very outset of Louis Napoleon's presidency. On the very eve of the balloting for the Legislative Assembly, Faucher dispatched a circular to all the prefects denouncing a radical plot to interfere with the elections, and he ordered that the mayors and justices of the peace be informed of this nationwide cabal.[285] This alarmist prediction was clearly linked with another dispatch from Faucher, which he ordered posted in every commune. It listed the name of every deputy who had voted against the attack on the Roman Republic (that is, it listed the republican candidates for reelection). Faucher prefaced this official directory of undesirables with the following warning to the electorate: "The agitators await only a vote that is hostile to the government to rush to the barricades and renew the June troubles."[286] In all fairness to the conservatives in the Constituent Assembly, it must be noted that they rebuked Faucher's action by the overwhelming vote of 509 to 5, and he immediately gave up his portfolio. And to be just to Faucher, he was absolutely correct in his prediction that the Mountain would attempt to rouse Paris against a Legislative Assembly that supported the Roman expedition.

Nonetheless, the interior minister had attempted to influence the voters by using the resources of the state bureaucracy.

Faucher and Barrot used other maneuvers in April and May 1849. Both ministers told their subordinates in Gard to take an active role in the selection of the Party of Order's list of candidates. Faucher told the prefect, Chanal, to insist that certain Orleanist Protestants be included so that the department's delegation would not be entirely made up of Catholics and legitimists, thus driving the Protestant population further into the republican camp.[287] In May 1849 Barrot ordered Thourel to try to moderate the extremism of some of the legitimist candidates. (Chanal had failed, and the Party of Order list was made up exclusively of Catholics.) Barrot was disappointed, particularly since one of the Orleanists put forward was his own relative, and remarked: "I expected better things from the intelligent men who have led the Catholic party for such a long time."[288]

The ministers were willing to recognize the political predominance of legitimism in Gard and acted to win the support of the whites within the Party of Order. In April 1849 Chanal asked Faucher for permission to disarm and dissolve the National Guard units at Bagnols, Rocquemaire, and Uzès. The first two of these companies were made up of republicans; and, although they had caused no trouble, the prefect felt that it would be prudent to take away their muskets. The National Guard at Uzès, on the other hand, was composed of legitimists, and it had participated in a bloody brawl (the one involving Ode, the ex-*procureur de la république*) between Protestants and Catholics. Faucher informed his prefect that he was currently involved in delicate negotiations with the legitimists of Gard to prevent their endorsement of the Abbé de Genoude as a candidate in that department. Genoude was the leader of the most intransigent wing of the legitimist movement. Faucher therefore ordered Chanal to dissolve the republican Guard companies, which had caused no trouble, and to leave the legitimist unit at Uzès alone, despite its penchant for the anti-Protestant *farandole*. (The *farandole* was a traditional dance-demonstration and invitation to a fight; it had existed in Gard for centuries.) After the elections, the government rewarded the National Guard at Uzès with the gift of several carbines.[289]

Another maneuver undertaken by Faucher, one reminiscent of Tammany Hall practices, was evident in a telegram sent to the prefect of Gironde just a few hours before the polls closed in Paris.

He ordered Neveux to have the local unit of the Garde mobile, mostly recruited from Paris, send in its votes right away, even though the law was unclear on whether these men had the right to cast their ballots as absentees.[290]

Similar electoral maneuvers were attempted by Faucher's successors in 1849 and 1850, Dufaure and Ferdinand Barrot. Dufaure ordered all his prefects to actively support the lists of the Party of Order: "It is crucial that the election that will take place in your department become a brilliant demonstration in favor of the Constitution and order."[291] He told them to work with their local conservative groups to choose the best possible lists for the by-elections of July 1849. During the by-election campaign of 1850, Ferdinand Barrot told the prefects to have the conservative lists for all of France printed, at government expense, in their own jurisdiction so that the garrison troops away from home would know which candidates enjoyed the support of the Party of Order and the president of the republic.[292] After these elections were held in Allier, Maupas wrote the local military commander that the garrison had voted unanimously for the conservative candidate (who won) and asked that the captain of this regiment receive an immediate promotion.[293]

The captain, or another functionary loyal to the conservative cause, may well have earned a promotion by means more foul than fair. The republican candidate in Allier, Georges Gallay, was defeated by a mere 182 votes. The official returns list 274 ballots as "missing." *Le Républicain Démocrate de l'Allier* cried fraud and backed its charges by publishing letters and local reports that told of the army vote (the ballots of local conscripts) being counted with only Party of Order poll watchers permitted in the Moulins town hall and of republican voters being given the wrong ballots by conservative justices of the peace.[294]

The administration tried, by various devices, to influence communal elections in Jura and in Charente-Inférieure. Their efforts proved fruitless in both the cases we have been able to study.[295]

The government was also not averse to showing great leniency to those citizens who took it upon themselves to interfere with the electoral efforts of the Mountain. On 1 May 1849 Ledru-Rollin, who was carried at the top of the republican list for Allier, spoke at a banquet in Moulins. When he left the park in which the festivities had been held, his carriage was attacked by the town's conservative National Guard. Neither the prefect, the moderate

republican Armand Coquet, nor the local *procureur de la république*
intervened. Before certain officers of the guard brought their men
under control, rocks had been thrown through the windows of the
coach, sabre blows had been directed at Ledru-Rollin, Félix Mathé,
and Fargin-Fayolle, and bayonets had been run through the carriage walls. The radical deputies escaped only because the horses,
frightened by the tumult, simply ran off, drawing the coach beyond
the limits of the town. Odilon Barrot, fearing that this would turn
into a major election issue, ordered an immediate investigation.
In his report, the attorney general at Riom blamed the violence on
the seditious cries and speeches that had been heard by the National Guard outside the banquet tent. The case did not come to
trial until after the events of June 1849 and Ledru-Rollin's flight to
England, and the guardsmen were acquitted by the Assize Court
of Puy-de-Dôme. De Sèze welcomed this verdict.

> In light of the rash provocations that came from the demonstra-
> tions, which M. Ledru-Rollin permitted himself and those ac-
> companying him to express, in light, particularly, of the anar-
> chist cries so often uttered by them and publicly shouted in the
> crowded streets of Moulins, acquittal became an easily foreseen
> necessity; I almost said an act of justice.[296]

Although it is not within the scope of this study to add to the
historical literature on assassinations and attempted assassinations—and the plots and premeditations that may have preceded
them—it is interesting to note that there is evidence strongly sug-
gesting that the attack on Ledru-Rollin and the other deputies was
no spontaneous outpouring of righteous indignation. On 26 April
1849 (five days before the attack) *Le Républicain Démocrate de l'Allier*
ran, as its front-page lead article, a story in which a republican
reported overhearing a meeting of local conservatives. These were
the words he heard:

> —All right, it is fully agreed among us, says one of them, every-
> one must be ready for Tuesday [the day of the banquet]. — It
> is well understood that it won't be us who will start it? — Oh!
> Don't worry, *we have arranged it in such a way that we will be
> provoked.*[297]

So frustrated was De Sèze with the inability of the political and
judicial system to suppress radicalism that he endorsed the very
mob violence for which the left was usually labeled "anarchist."

The bureaucracy was plainly ineffective against most republican electoral activity in 1849 and 1850. And there were not enough policemen and soldiers in all of France to confront a mass descent on the voting places, at widely dispersed points, in the feared *échéance* of 1852. It is not difficult to understand the justifiable fears experienced by the prosecutors and prefects when they thought of enforcing the revised electoral law.

Another indication of the left's persistent strength in certain areas of France was the success of its petition campaign against the revised electoral law, an effort carried on throughout the latter half of 1850. These petitions circulated in seventy-seven departments, and at a time when a public declaration of republican sympathies could make an individual the target for various forms of government harassment; yet 527,000 signatures were collected. Vendée was the only department in our sample in which one of these petitions did not circulate. This petition campaign gave rise to numerous prosecutions and administrative actions, such as those we have already discussed in relation to printers in Charente-Inférieure and Gironde. Signers were questioned by the police, government employees and town officials were subjected to disciplinary action, printers were prosecuted for the content of certain petitions, and individuals were charged with forging signatures. The signed petitions, which had been addressed to the Legislative Assembly, were sent back to the appellate *parquets* to facilitate this repression.[298]

On 3 May 1851 the Justice Ministry collated the reports of its attorneys general and prepared a veritable scoreboard of prosecutions against printers. The results were far from encouraging. The two cases that carried the most serious penalties were those of Havel at Bordeaux and Siret at La Rochelle. Havel was driven out of business, but the goal sought by the *procureur-général* and prefect in withdrawing his license eluded them. *La Tribune de la Gironde* continued to appear. Siret was still printing at least three "red" newspapers for Vendée and Charente-Inférieure at the time of the coup. In the rest of France, forty cases were tried against printers for the same offenses that Havel and Siret had committed: the failure to have deposited a signed copy of the petition with the local *parquet* and prefecture. Nineteen resulted in ordinances of *non-lieu* or acquittals. Twenty-one cases ended with the conviction of fifty-one individuals with fines ranging from five to fifty francs and prison sentences of one to ten days.[299] Clearly the police prosecutions in the west of France, however unsuccessful they were in muzzling the republican press, had far more serious results than those in other regions.

The only other successful prosecutions connected with the petition campaign in our sample of departments occurred in Allier. In July 1850 the attorney general in Riom promised the ministry a considerable number of convictions for forgery.[300] Five individuals were charged with this crime, two women and three men. The results were one *non-lieu*, two acquittals, and only two convictions.[301] The penalties levied against the two men who were convicted were quite severe: one was sentenced to two years in jail and a fine of 1,000 francs, and the other had to serve fifteen months and pay 100 francs.

In Gard, Thourel reported that, despite the collection of 1,945 signatures, there were no legal grounds for him to bring charges against anyone. In his investigation of those who had signed the petition in his *ressort*, the *procureur-général* in Poitiers discovered the names of a few *fonctionnaires*, mayors, *adjoints*, and schoolteachers; but all of them avoided any punitive action by prudently claiming that they had been tricked or that their signatures had been forged. He did, however, dismiss one minor official of the Justice Ministry who had actually circulated the petition. Loiseau, at Besançon, took similar punitive measures against forest rangers, rural policemen, and schoolmasters. At least in Jura, and probably in Charente-Inférieur, the purge of the civil service that took place soon after the election of Louis Napoleon had not been totally effective.

The petition campaign infuriated the politicians of the Party of Order, the ministers, and the police bureaucrats. It clearly demonstrated the tremendous size of the movement they confronted. Despite the public nature of the protest and the zealous investigation of those who had printed, circulated, or signed these documents, no victory was won in the battle against republicanism.

Even when the left rose up in armed insurrection, the government's repression fell far short of crippling the local radical movements. All those involved in the armed gathering of 14 June 1849 at La Brande des Mottes in Allier were acquitted by the Assize Court except for the one man, the brother of the deputy Fargin-Fayolle, who had issued several signed calls to arms.[302] Again, when the assembly was discussing the limitation of the suffrage, the attorney general in Riom reported that a secret society in one of the towns of Allier had named a committee of public safety and had probably distributed arms, expecting an outbreak of revolution at Paris and Lyon. But in this dispatch of 5 April 1850, De Sèze made it quite clear to the ministry that he could not prove that such a plot had taken place.[303]

In October 1851 serious violence broke out in Allier, in the town of Commentry. The mayor, a conservative, had called in the police to break up a secret society meeting that was being held in a local restaurant. The chairman of the meeting was the radical deputy Sartin; when the gendarmes attempted to arrest him, they were attacked by a crowd of villagers that had gathered to defend the republicans. The police were forced to retreat. Two days later they returned in force to arrest one of the more effective rioters. They brought him to the town hall. A crowd of several hundred people soon surrounded the building and began pelting it and its occupants with a "hail of stones." Despite volleys of carbine fire directed at the crowd, the police remained besieged, until they were relieved by a column of cavalry at dawn the next day. The army detachment, commanded by a general and accompanied by the prefect and the commandant of the local Gendarmerie Nationale, succeeded in arresting only fifteen members of this insurrectionary crowd. Sartin, who was clearly the leader of this fight, was still a free man when the assembly reconvened in November 1851. The trial of the Commentry rebels did not occur until after the coup.[304]

Preparations for a rising in Jura in June 1849 similarly went unpunished. Its organizer had fled Arbois for Switzerland when the news reached Jura that no general rebellion had broken out. He returned in December bearing a forged passport and was immediately arrested and brought before the tribunal at Saint-Claude. The attorney general felt that he could gain a conviction only on the false passport charge; he did not prosecute this Montagnard leader for rebellion. The magistrature won its case, and the court levied the ridiculously trivial penalty of twelve days in jail. The rebel's sentence was upheld by the court at Lons-le-Saunier.[305]

In July 1849 a street battle broke out between many of the townspeople of Arbois and a detachment of troops that was passing through the town. The crowd, which was fighting with the pickets around the battalion encampment and shouting "Vive Barbès!" and "You think you can do here what you did in Lyon" was dispersed only when the troops formed a line of battle and drove them from the streets at bayonet point. The first advocate general informed the ministry that a prosecution of this case would be difficult; the soldiers had started the fight by pummeling a teamster who had insulted them and had then broken into several houses in their pursuit of the crowd that attacked their campsite. Six people were arrested the next day by the gendarmerie of Poligny. The defendants were tried before the assize jury for their physical assault on the troops and for "seditious shouts." Two were acquitted, two were sentenced to six days in prison, and two received the heaviest penalty handed down—only ten days in jail.[306]

Thourel's reports, which contain numerous descriptions of fights between Protestant Montagnards and Catholic legitimists, show the same ease with which republicans escaped the consequences for any of their violent deeds. Finally, in the spring of 1851, Thourel began to bring secret society members who had been involved in *farandoles* and brawls before the police tribunal, and he was pleased to report that one group of thirteen Montagnards had been sentenced to terms varying from four to eight days in prison.[307]

Even the *procureur-général* in Lyon, where the barricade fighters of June 1849 were tried by court-martial, complained about the softness with which these insurrectionists were treated. In December 1849 he reported:

I am obliged to say that the spectacle of Justice, too softly rendered by our courts-martial, may have contributed singularly to increase the boldness of the anarchists. Healthy public opinion [*la saine opinion publique*] deplored many of the decisions issued by these courts-martial. They have, in general, borne the imprint of the most unfortunate leniency. There have been inexplicable acquittals and sentences of just a few months in prison inflicted on participants in the civil war. By what means are we to keep them under control when so many enticements [*séductions*] accompany their idea of victory and so little fear is connected with their defeat.[308]

Gilardin's finest hour would come with the successful prosecution of the *complot* of Lyon in 1851. This affair has been described in detail by Dutacq.[309] In demonstrating the ineffectiveness of political repression under the Second Republic, our concern is not with the plot itself, but with the special circumstances that made possible its discovery and with the subsequent unwillingness of the government to bring its case before a civil court. We shall also try to answer the related question of the government's inability to capitalize on its capture of Gent and his accomplices. It never destroyed the secret society network they supposedly headed.

The *complot* of Lyon, which ended with the transportation of Alphonse Gent, Ode, and Longomazino, and with prison terms ranging from six months to fifteen years for thirty-three others, was the work of an upstart group within the French left: the Young Mountain.[310] Supported by the exile committees of London and Paris, Gent's group had no popular base within France itself, at least at first.[311] Seeking to inject a new militancy into the Mountain, Gent paradoxically had to operate openly in the world of the underground.

The minister of interior informed the prefect of Gard on 29 December 1849, almost a year before the discovery and arrest of Gent and his accomplices, that rumors were circulating in Geneva, London, and Paris of an insurrection that would break out in the east and south in 1850.[312] In April, documents were discovered in the possession of a messenger from Geneva to Dijon. The courier must have belonged to Gent's group, since he was so unknown to the chiefs of the secret societies in the east and the south that he was actually carrying letters of introduction from the exiles in Geneva.[313] The underground was coordinated by face-to-face communication between messengers who knew each other well, not by strangers carrying stiff middle-class and businesslike endorsements. Later, in his summary of the case, Gilardin would remark on the upper-class manner of Gent and his friends.

> Gent is an elegant conspirator with aristocratic manners. In so fine a wrapping, in this form, our working population does not see a democrat. . . . Moreover, at Lyon, he ran up against a compact organization. . . . It was among that kind of society that he would have had to seek his recruits to his own organization: he could not.[314]

In June, well before the authorities were on to the plot, they began to find public evidence of a split in the Mountain. Gent, incapable of gaining a foothold among the lyonnais secret societies, placarded the city with vituperative criticism of the Mountain's French leadership.

> Yes, *PEUPLE*, you have been expecting decisiveness and energy from those of your representatives who sit with the Mountain;

you have been waiting for the signal to rise and render justice. You are still waiting for that decision!—Weakness or cowardice, for which soon, one day, you will demand an accounting.[315]

Gent, Ode, and the others in the Young Mountain existed at the margin of the movement. The watchword of the Mountain's leaders was to organize and wait for 1852, and most local groups followed this advice. Even Gent's old friends from his native department of Vaucluse were against his plan. The leader of the Mountain at Apt attended a meeting presided over by Gent at Valence; the ideas of the Young Mountain so worried him that he reported the projected insurrection to the subprefect. He had been ordered by Gent to gather six thousand men for this action, and when he refused Gent had him deposed as president of the Montagnard society in his town. No doubt he informed on the Young Mountain as much from offended vanity as from any political scruples about the survival of his own organization. Gilardin described him, however, as "a man hardly disposed to serve the plans of a revolutionary *coup de force*."[316]

By the time of the so-called Congress of Valence, which was held on 29 June 1850 and was attended by representatives from fourteen departments, Gent's "general staff" was already penetrated by an informer. Gent was so unfamiliar with the Montagnards and so desperate for supporters that he took a M. Lombard, a man with an arrest record for lock picking, into his confidence and gave him command of fifty-seven men. According to Dutacq, Lombard was known to the secret societies of Marseille as a stool pigeon, but apparently Gent was unaware of this until it was too late. Another informer, who was never a member of the Young Mountain, heard enough second- and third-hand information on Gent's desperately open attempts to split the movement that he too warned the authorities in July 1850.[317]

As early as August 1850, three months before the police actually arrested Gent, the Justice Ministry sent out a circular asking for information on his whereabouts and describing the plan for a rising in the Midi in some detail.[318] When Gent was finally apprehended on 24 October 1850, his address had been known to the police for at least a month, and his mail had been intercepted since 13 September.[319] The official leadership of the Mountain also knew of his plans, and on the day before Gent's arrest a circular from Raspail went up all over Lyon:

While waiting, my good friends, continue to maintain the worthy and firm line of conduct which you have shown up to the present; and if some mercenary, some bogeyman brandishing his big sabre, some inventor of orders of the day—all a sham—tries hurling provocations at you—don't trust him.[320]

Gent's capture was soon followed by the arrests of fifty-one other people mentioned in his correspondence. For once the government was in a position to try them all, on the basis of a wealth of seized documents and the testimony of at least two informers. Gilardin recognized that the Young Mountain was an amateur operation at best and that it would be difficult to convince a jury, especially the jury of Rhône, that the *complot* was a serious matter.

They will only see . . . Gent, surrounded by a low quality of followers, drawing to himself the dregs of the secret societies, having recourse to no other resources, and setting up his conspiracy without a military leader, without any opening into the army, without any careful plans. . . . It will be difficult to convince public opinion that a plot thrown together like this could have set off any great danger to public order.[321]

Gilardin argued that the assize jury at Lyon would never convict the defendants, regardless of the evidence: "Given the inequality in size of the classes within the population, we know which elements will make up the jury and how much sympathy for the demagogic cause is shown by the voting under universal suffrage."[322] He also urged against bringing the case before the High Court of Justice because that tribunal was designed to handle matters of "historic" importance—plots that really jeopardized the security of the state and of society. On the contrary, Gilardin evaluated the *complot* as a relatively minor affair: "Nothing particularly noteworthy will be revealed, neither by the stature of the persons involved, nor by the nature of the acts they planned or carried out, which will satisfy a keen and widespread interest."[323] The attorney general also doubted if the informers and the documents provided enough solid evidence to win a treason conviction from the high court. But Gilardin wanted a victory and he wanted to impress upon the public the danger represented by the secret societies. He recommended that the case be tried at Lyon by a court-martial. The attorney general desired a forum in which he could demonstrate that "the Gent conspiracy, denied by the radical press and treated by them as the subject for derisive disbelief, was no police specter, but a serious and menacing reality."[324] He even asked that a particular regiment be kept in Lyon because he knew its court-martial to be tougher than those of the other units in the city.[325]

The history of this important case and of how it was brought to trial reveals several important points about the quality of the red scare and about political repression under the Second Republic. Dutacq has seen the entire affair as a hoax. To him, the *complot* was a "non-event" created by government provocateurs to win the support of the notables for the revision of the constitution. It is clear that Gilardin, who was ultimately responsible for handling the case, did not view the *complot* of Lyon as a major threat to French society. He did understand that it had some public relations value, but it appears that the *procureur-général* wanted to alert public opinion to a threat he sincerely believed existed—not in the form of the Young Mountain, but in the secret society network that he and every other prosecutor knew to be a very real menace to the social order. They had been incapable of uprooting this hardy organization by any form of legal or police action. Like the other attorneys general, Gilardin was frustrated by his inability to win important cases against either the republican press or republican organizations, and he quite understandably wanted to strike at least a minor blow at the enemy. As the *procureur-général* in the region under martial law, he had the opportunity to do this by an appeal to the military authorities, in itself a declaration of his own inability as a civil official in a liberal legal framework to save a social system that he believed was in grave danger. Nonetheless, as his future reports to the ministry were to show very clearly, Gilardin entertained no illusions about the impact of his successful prosecution of Gent and his accomplices on the republican movement as a whole. Only the desperation and incompetence of Gent had allowed the authorities to penetrate a small part of the left—to capture and try fifty-one marginal figures in a movement that numbered in the thousands.

Aside from the unbridgeable social gap that cut off the law-enforcement bureaucrats from the information they needed in order to move against the republicans, the greatest obstacle to their repressive drive was the court system itself. In the preceding pages we have seen their estimates of the impact of universal manhood suffrage on the juries and of the effect that a seemingly outmoded liberalism had on the magistrates on the bench. Rouher, in a circular to the attorneys general sent out in December 1850, echoed their sentiments clearly. On the democratized jury, he stated:

> Some see in it a real improvement, and believe they find in the new jury more guarantees of a good and precise justice than could be found in the old censitary jurors. . . . Popular common sense seduces them, they have confidence in that instinct to do good that generally moves the masses when they are not carried away by evil passions [*mauvaises passions*]. . . . On the contrary, the new composition of the jury presents no guarantees of security to society; the ignorance of most of those called on to fulfill these duties . . . deprives them of any independence of mind and . . . gives them over . . . as the prey of all the wicked influences that rage so often outside—and even in the midst— of the Assize Courts.[326]

To Rouher and to the *procureurs-généraux* from whom he received monthly reports, justice and society itself were subverted in the jury box. As the justice minister's last sentence implies, with very little subtlety, he was none too happy with the leniency of the judges themselves.

The prefects and prosecutors often could not understand why the judges, members of their own social class, did not share their concern for the future of society. A typical case was a complaint made by the prefect of Jura against a presiding magistrate in the Assize Court of Lons-le-Saunier. He charged this judge with being too lenient in political cases by allowing the defense attorneys to speak freely in court. Loiseau, the *procureur-général*, defended the judge without, however, defending the magistracy as a whole. He called the president of the court one of the best judges in his *ressort* and added, "and you know their number is extremely small."[327] The *procureur-général* then went on to describe the majority of presiding magistrates as liberal anachronisms who were ill-suited to the pressing needs of the elite in a time of crisis: "The presiding judges of the *Assises*, because of old habits of never interrupting the lawyers, permit them a latitude that causes no problems in ordinary criminal cases, but that has very serious consequences in political cases."[328]

Officers of a police state that had taken form, after the June Days of 1848, within the shell of a liberal legal system, the prosecutors and prefects could not suppress the radical republican movement under the rule of law. From having been liberals and legalitarians they rapidy evolved into advocates of rule by force. The bureaucrats did this because a new and powerful opposition to the dominance of the notables had developed in such a way as to remain persistently beyond the reach of the law.

6 From Frustration to a Totalitarian Revolution

The extralegal powers given the police bureaucrats from the date of the coup through the end of March 1852 mark a watershed in French history. Far from being a mere culmination of the repression carried out during the brief constitutional existence of the Second Republic, the mass arrests, the courts-martial, and finally the Mixed Commissions were an explosion of rage against those who had threatened the social order of nineteenth-century France. The sheer numbers involved (more than 26,000 arrests officially recorded), the kangaroo court procedures (defense attorneys were never present at a hearing, no witnesses were heard, and the defendant himself was physically absent from the "court" room), the total disregard for civil or criminal law in determining guilt or innocence in the vast majority of cases (only 2 percent of those arrested were remanded to the civil courts for trial), and the severity of the sentences imposed—all indicate, quite convincingly, that the new wave of repression was an extremist measure. Dictatorial repression was a radical break with old procedures and methods that was consciously designed to achieve a thorough—and final—solution to the social and democratic-socialist problem.[1] But the rage was far from blind: it took institutional form and followed patterns that show just how frustrated the police bureaucrats had been during the past four years.

Neither the obsessive witch hunters depicted by Seignobos nor the frightened "neurotics" of more recent scholars, the prefects and *procureurs-généraux* were simply the harsh and angry enforcers of a social vision that made perfect sense to them.[2] Though officially and publicly justified as a response to the risings that greeted Louis Napoleon's coup, the four months of massive, untrammeled repression were a settling of accounts between the police bureaucrats and the enemies who had eluded their grasp. The attacks were a full-scale assault on those the bureaucrats held responsible for haunting their future for at least two years: the fomenters and the organizers of the feared *échéance* of 1852. Unlike the quarry of the repression after the June Days of 1848, the targets for harsh punishment in 1852 were not the barricade fighters—the participants in the risings of December 1851—but those who had won them over to a new ideology of protest and social change.

Much of the material used in this chapter has been drawn from a case-by-case study of the work of the Mixed Commissions in our sample of departments: a total of 2,189 arrests and decisions.[3] Although this volume of information required statistical study, two points must be emphasized from the outset: first, statistics of this nature have usually been used to elucidate "history from below," but our purpose is to demonstrate that the arrest, trial, and punishment of so large a population tells us much more about those making the arrests and fixing the penalties than it may disclose about the "revolutionary crowd" itself; and second, the trends and priorities suggested, however strongly, by the statistics contribute to the interpretations presented in these pages, but the responsibility for these judgments is the author's.

The registers and lists examined in this study of the Mixed Commissions contain not only the name, place of birth, home, profession, age, and sentence of the defendant, but also brief statements by the Mixed Commission (usually written by the *procureur-général* or his *substitut*) describing the defendant's political background, opinions, influence, actions, degree of threat to public order, and often his "morality." Such attitudes, expressed in relatively ordinary language and with all the variations of meaning and nuance that can exist among differing officials in different settings, can be grouped and quantified only at great peril.[4] Despite these difficulties and despite the variations in conditions and in numbers of arrests and trials among our sample of departments—indeed, despite the disorganized, heterogeneous, ramshackle process of retributive "justice" throughout France—certain uniform trends emerge.

As we shall see below, the most severe penalties handed down by the police bureaucrats were called forth by the long-term political activities and influence of the defendant, rather than by the immediate and palpable crime of insurrection against the authorities. The higher one's social class, the more one was seen by the prefects and prosecutors as a leader of the radical movement or as a local organizer. And the more one was perceived as a threat (often with a notation of "dangerous" or "very dangerous" and even more often by one or more moral judgments written in a "comments" column on the register), the more severe the sentence—even if one had taken no part in the insurrection.[5] The real culprits, in the eyes of the authorities, were precisely those they had failed to punish for years before the coup. Nothing illustrates the bureaucrats' frustration better than a comparison of defendants arrested *before* the coup with those ultimately tried under the virtually unlimited authority of the Mixed Commissions. Only 141 people of the 2,189 rounded up in our sample after the coup had ever been arrested and charged with a political offense (slightly over 6 percent of the total).[6] At the same time, more than 20 percent of the 2,189 had been *suspected* by the police bureaucrats of illegal political activity before the coup (448 people), yet less than a third of them were ever arrested and charged.[7]

Radical Rebellion and Police Repression: The Setting for the Mixed Commissions

The repression that came in the wake of the coup was officially justified as a direct response to the armed risings that occurred in at least eighteen departments on receipt of the news of Louis Napoleon's seizure of power. The main centers of insurrectionary activity were in the center, the south, and, to a lesser extent, in the mountainous east. The Sixth Military District (Rhône and surrounding departments) had been under military rule since 1849. By mid-December 1851, thirty-two additional departments were placed under a state of siege; the authorities had already begun extending unlimited police powers to departments in which no uprisings had occurred. By 18 January 1852 each department of France would have a Mixed Commission, dispensing only a mildly diluted form of drumhead "justice."[8]

The insurrections, therefore, were only the pretexts for mass repression. While these risings temporarily heightened the police bureaucrats' fears by showing the imposing size and militancy of the left in certain departments, they were scattered, rural upheavals that never received the indispensable support of revolution in the great cities. Like other, less serious, incidents during the period of the Second Republic, they were seen by the prefects and prosecutors as symptoms of a graver, more profound and chronic danger to the social order.

Three departments in our sample were scenes of insurrection:

Gard, Allier, and Jura. Lyon and its historically combative poor suburbs did not rise; the Army of the Alps, under the vigorous command of General de Castellane (who, together with the prefect, may have been privy to the timing of the coup), moved in force to block any gathering of angry radicals before word of the Parisian events reached the general populace. Indeed, the only violent events in Rhône reported by the prefect and attorney general were isolated attacks on dispatch coaches by small bands of Montagnards anxious for news of a Parisian rising.[9]

On the night of 4-5 December 1851, three poorly coordinated risings occurred in Gard. They were limited to the areas of the Vaunage and Gardonnenque (near Nîmes), the villages around Uzès, and those near Vigan—all heavily Protestant regions. Each area sent an armed column in the direction of the closest *chef-lieu*. Those converging on Nîmes counted on the support of Montagnards within the city. But a regular army regiment prevented any armed gathering in Nîmes while a column of hussars came up behind the rural insurrectionists poised just outside the city and dispersed the rebellion. Other troop movements stopped the separate marches on Alès and Uzès.[10]

A day earlier the radicals of Donjon (Allier) responded to news of the coup by overthrowing the conservative municipal administration imposed on them by the prefect. The mayor, city council, and justice of the peace were arrested and replaced by republicans who had held the same posts before being removed for their participation in the armed gathering at La Brande des Mottes in 1849. Forming a column of more than one hundred, thirty of them armed with rifles stolen from the town hall, the Montagnards of Donjon resolved to march on the subprefecture at La Palisse. By dawn of the fourth they had taken their objective and arrested the subprefect. They turned the town square of La Palisse into a defensive strongpoint on hearing of the approach of a mounted column of the Gendarmerie Nationale. The mounted police led a much larger force—the conservative National Guard battalion of La Palisse, which had fled the city—and rode directly toward the town hall. They were greeted by a volley of musket and shotgun fire that killed one gendarme and wounded five other members of the "forces of order." The guardsmen again took to their heels, and the mounted police withdrew. Finally, faced by a conservative population and the imminent arrival of a cavalry squadron, the donjonnais abandoned La Palisse and returned to their home town.

Around midnight of the same day they set out for Moulins itself, only to be turned back by regular army forces patrolling the roads.[11]

A similar rebellion broke out in Jura. Poligny, long a center of democratic socialist strength, rose on the night of 3-4 December 1851. The tocsin was sounded; peasants from neighboring villages took up arms and joined the Montagnards of this *chef-lieu*. They arrested the subprefect, mayor, tax collector, and other officials. A smaller rising occurred in the villages around Lons-le-Saunier, but the column that was to march on the prefecture was easily broken up by the prefect, who headed a company of regular infantry. Chambrun then gathered a larger force of troops and marched on Poligny. The rebels scattered, many of the leaders crossing into Switzerland, before the prefect arrived.[12]

By 5 December Gard, Allier, and Jura had seen the end of their two- or three-day insurrections. Each department was placed under a state of siege, and the manhunt for radicals, whether they had participated in the rebellion or not, began.

No such dramas were played out in Gironde, Charente-Inférieure, or Vendée. In Bordeaux the republican leaders decided to forego any armed resistance to the coup unless Paris rose first. But hundreds of republicans gathered outside the prefecture, awaiting news from the capital and crying "Vive la République!" On 6 December Haussmann, only recently arrived, issued a prefectoral decree warning the crowd that any demonstration would be broken up—without warning (*sommation*)—by cavalry charges and musket volleys.[13] Twenty-four hours later the city was quiet. Charente-Inférieure and Vendée remained completely untroubled.

Nevertheless, insurrection was everywhere invoked to track down and arrest republicans. When the prefect and *procureur de la république* of Vendée asked the Justice Ministry if they could prosecute Napoléon Gallois, editor of the local republican newspaper, and his friend, Doctor Clemenceau—despite the fact that both had been "politically quiet" since the coup—they were told to bring them (or rather their names) before the Mixed Commission. The *procureur de la république* wrote that both of them had carried on an "active socialist propaganda" in the department and that they should be punished for its "deadly" (*funeste*) influence.[14]

The attorney general at Besançon complained that the court-martial of Jura had freed Doctor Jean-Baptiste Noir because there was no evidence at all that he had participated in the rising, but he is notorious as one of the most active and most dangerous leaders of Jura's secret societies; he has aided ultrasocialist propaganda with his enormous efforts on its behalf and he helped establish every demagogic newspaper in Jura. . . . Finally, the justice of the peace of his canton tells me that his arrest created an excellent effect and that the men of order fear his return.[15]

Noir was kept in custody and tried by the Mixed Commission. He was only one of many noninsurrectionaries to be swept up in the net. The same *procureur-général* reported that "the examination of the dossiers proves that the evil ran deeper in Jura, even deeper than we could have thought; material order is reestablished, but only energetic measures can . . . definitively guarantee moral order in the department."[16]

Thourel, reporting from Nîmes, argued that the uprising was only "a brief troubling" of public order, but that the real problem was that the "demagogues" had "penetrated every commune of Gard."[17] And Gilardin saw Lyon, despite its quiescence after the coup, as the hub of radical activity throughout the south and center and therefore as the center of insurrection for most of France. He wanted the local radicals treated accordingly. The real "moral ravages" of republicanism only became evident as radicals were arrested, often at home.

Each time that police investigation brings us into their homes we find portraits of revolutionaries hanging on the wall as if they were the house deities, a thick and fermenting pile of filthy pamphlets or socialist newspapers, disgusting songs, sordid writings: in a word, all that combination of things that lead the heart and the mind into error.[18]

What began as the repression of scattered rebellions quickly developed into a wholesale attack on radicalism itself. The courts-martial that began operating in December 1851 became a "sort of combined or mixed court" in January 1852 and finally took the full-fledged, though still ad hoc, form of Mixed Commissions by early February.[19] The administration was confronting two simultaneous problems of organization until the Mixed Commissions took their definitive form. First, the prefectoral and judicial authorities were jealous of the military's complete control of repression under the state of siege. Second, they did not trust the military to do a thorough job, because the punishments at the disposal of the courts-martial were extremely severe: either deportation to the penal colony of Cayenne in French Guiana or to an only slightly less terrifying servitude in North Africa-Lambessa—or nothing at all. A thorough and general repression required greater cooperation among all police authorities and a greater range of penalties, which would ensure that no heart grew faint at the choice between sending someone to Devil's Island or setting him free. The answer was a commission enjoying all the freedoms from legal procedures that made the court-martial such an effective tool, but on which both the prefect and the prosecuting magistrate sat as equal partners with the departmental military commander: the extralegal, triune Mixed Commission. It also involved a list of punishments that gave the "judges" the broadest possible range of choice:

(1) Freedom
(2) Parole in home town or place of one's choice, requiring bimonthly meetings between the convict and an officer of the new Ministry of National Police
(3) Parole "at least 50 leagues distant" from one's home department, requiring even more stringent surveillance by Maupas' ministry
(4) Jail sentence in a penitentiary and/or a fine
(5) "*Algérie moins*," or exile to Algeria, but with an opportunity to live with one's family and carry on one's usual occupation in a place of one's choosing (although residence in Algiers itself required special permission from the Ministry of National Police)
(6) Exile from France: permanent for foreigners who had been involved in radical activities and temporary for moderate republican and conservative deputies and notables who were seen as threats to the new regime, but who could someday apply for a pardon
(7) "*Algérie plus*," or exile to a place of forced residence under military authority in Algeria: a lesser form of penal colony involving clearing and farming land
(8) Lambessa
(9) Cayenne[20]

In addition, those charged with minor felonies or misdemeanors could be remanded to the civil courts for trial. But those charged with murder or attempted murder in the course of an insurrection were to be tried by special courts-martial empowered to levy capital punishment for "acts of civil war." The entire process of sentencing was almost complete by the end of March.[21]

Our sample comprises seven departments with variations in the number of recorded arrests ranging from 9 in Vendée to more than 800 in Allier. Three of the seven departments witnessed insurrections and a fourth, Rhône, was treated as the nerve center of revolution. (In France's eighty-three departments, however, only eighteen were scenes of similar events.) Finally, one of our departments, Jura, shared a border with Switzerland, permitting many Montagnards to avoid arrest. Yet our 2,189 cases are reasonably representative of the 26,885 tried by all the Mixed Commissions, especially when we look at the larger groups subjected to arrest and sentencing. Although no claim is made to an exact depiction of the national scene, it is worth noting that our sample departments do remain quite close to national averages when we compare the size of the artisan-worker population to the size of the agricultural population (see table 1), or when we compare the proportions of the various sentences handed down most frequently.[22]

TABLE 1

Class by Department

Department	Peasant %	Unskilled %	Artisan %	Petit Bourg. %	Elite %	N
Vendée	0	0	25.0	0	75.0	4
Char.-Inf.	5.9	11.8	64.7	5.9	11.8	17
Gironde	4.7	1.2	30.2	22.1	41.9	86
Gard	28.4	2.5	28.4	19.7	20.9	359
Jura	44.3	1.4	22.4	8.1	23.8	361
Allier	18.7	2.6	51.6	11.1	16.0	731
Rhône	1.5	6.7	60.7	20.6	9.5	252
N	410	53	751	253	343	
	22.7%	2.9%	41.5%	13.9%	19.0%	

Missing cases = 379

ACTION: Did the punishment fit the "crime"?

Participation in an insurrection, even armed participation (and such an important detail was recorded for 213 individuals in our sample), did *not* lead to severe punishment in the majority of cases. Indeed, the defendants most likely to be freed were the armed participants: almost 30 percent of them were set free. An additional 10 percent were given the lightest possible sentence: parole in their home town. Furthermore, those recorded simply as participants (without any qualification) were given this lightest sentence more than half the time. They formed the group most likely to be paroled in their home town. However, more than one-fourth of the participants were sent to Algeria; the majority of them were permitted to settle where they wished. A slightly larger proportion of armed participants than participants was sent to Algeria, but the majority of armed participants also received the milder punishment of *Algérie moins*.[23]

In examining table 2, however, we can see that those groups most often given severe sentences (*Algérie plus*, Cayenne, or Lambessa) were those seen as having influence over the insurrectionary mass—whether or not they actually participated in the risings. Those accused of no overt activity at all were sentenced to Cayenne or Lambessa at the highest rate of all groups: more than 18 percent of them were sent to the penal colonies as opposed to only 6 percent of the armed participants. Of the 275 people in our sample charged with nothing more than membership in a secret society (and no act of insurrection at all), 30 were sent to Cayenne or Lambessa. They made up 26.5 percent of all those given this harsh sentence, which was given to an average of only 5.5 percent in all the "action" categories combined. Though substantial numbers in the "no overt" or "member" groups were set free or received comparatively light sentences, they shared the greatest risk of harsh sentencing with those seen as "organizers" of the insurrections.

TABLE 2

Sentence by Action

Action	Freed %	Parole %	Jail %	Algérie Moins %	Exiled %	Algérie Plus %	Cayenne-Lambessa %	N
Organize	1.3	5.3	4.0	34.7	1.3	41.3	12.0	75
Incite	13.6	9.1	8.0	38.1	2.8	23.9	4.5	176
Armed part.	29.1	11.3	11.7	24.9	.5	16.4	6.1	213
Participant	9.4	53.5	3.6	17.9	1.1	10.7	3.9	363
Sedition	16.0	.34.0	14.0	14.0	11.3	3.3	7.3	150
Member	12.7	33.4	5.1	24.7	4.4	8.7	10.9	275
No overt act	9.1	33.4	13.6	10.6	9.1	6.1	18.2	66
N	186	489	99	307	46	180	97	
	13.2%	34.8%	7.1%	21.9%	3.3%	12.8%	6.9%	

Missing cases = 871

"Organizers" (only seventy-five people in our sample for whom I have found sentences recorded) pose a major problem for an analysis of the bureaucrats' perception of threat and the severity with which they repressed it. Our only source for determining membership in this category, as with the other "action" categories, is the written word of the Mixed Commissions. They dealt quite severely with organizers: nine were sent to Cayenne or Lambessa and thirty-one (41.3 percent) were given *Algérie plus* as their punishment. In fact, they form the only group in our "action" analysis that was sent to penal colonies in Algeria more often than it was sentenced to the "freer" form of North African exile. But who were they? Did they really organize the insurrections, or were they seen as longer-term organizers of radical groups that may or may not have rebelled?

The first clue that the latter answer may be correct can be seen in table 2 itself. "Inciters" (those charged with actually setting off a rising) were treated far more leniently than the organizers. Among all the 483 people freed, only 1 organizer can be found as against 24 inciters. Inciters were paroled in their home towns far more often than organizers, and a clear majority of inciters were sentenced to *Algérie moins*. If we are dealing with two related forms of power being exercized over an insurrectionary mass, then the sentences should be similar. But the divergence in the way inciters and organizers were viewed and treated is simply too great for the relationship to hold. A second indication that organizers may not necessarily be linked with insurrection is that 3 of the 75 organizers were identified in Gironde, and 15 (or almost 20 percent of them) were similarly categorized in Rhône, both relatively quiet areas after the coup.

But the most persuasive explanation for the severity of sentences passed on organizers, members, and "no overts" alike can be seen in table 3. Although we are dealing with slightly different numbers of individuals (because of missing data) when we move from a comparison of action broken down by sentence to action analyzed by class, it is clear that almost half of all organizers came from the petite bourgeoisie and the elite. The same proportion of petit bourgeois and elite representation (or rather overrepresentation) is present in the "no overt" category. This proportion declines considerably for members, though more than one-fourth of them also came from the more elevated social strata. Class, along with action, was clearly an important factor in the total picture which the police bureaucrats constructed of, or projected upon, those they judged.[24]

TABLE 3

Class by Action

Action	Peasant %	Unskilled %	Artisan %	Petit Bourg. %	Elite %	N
Organize	7.7	1.5	38.5	23.1	29.2	65
Incite	21.5	1.2	44.2	12.7	20.6	165
Armed part.	28.2	2.3	49.8	9.0	10.8	213
Participant	31.0	3.1	37.1	15.6	13.2	326
Sedition	19.0	2.4	31.7	12.7	34.1	126
Member	5.4	3.6	57.7	16.7	16.7	222
No overt act	10.5	3.5	28.1	26.3	31.6	57
N	243	31	509	174	217	
	20.7%	2.6%	43.4%	14.8%	18.5%	

Missing cases = 1,015

CLASS: The face of the enemy

There is considerable variation in the social-class proportions arrested and tried in the departments of our sample. The thorniest problem is represented by the artisans—our largest single category that was explicitly called "skilled," or labeled as containing specialists requiring skills.[25] Totaling more than 40 percent of our 1,810 cases (for which profession was noted), this group makes any clear analysis by class extremely difficult. The registers give no indication of whether any particular artisan was a master, journeyman, or apprentice. They provide no indication of relative wealth or number of employees. Artisans, therefore, lie athwart much of the social spectrum, ranging from poor, part-time craftsmen of the villages to well-off masters in towns and large cities. With this very important caveat in mind, however, we can still make an adequate approximation of which broad sectors of the population in each department were over- or underrepresented in the pool of arrestees. Furthermore, we can see some fairly clear trends in the political activity and sentencing of these groups. Finally, with some trepidation, we can estimate the impact of social class on sentence while holding action and departmental setting constant.

Table 1 shows the folly of estimating over- and underrepresentation of individual social classes for Vendée, Charente-Inférieure, and probably for Gironde as well. It is enough to note that peasants are almost absent from the sample in these departments and that the elite was a preferred target in both Vendée and Gironde. Interestingly, the proportion of artisans and unskilled workers arrested in Gironde corresponds almost exactly with their percentage of the working male population recorded in the 1851 census: 29.3 percent.[26] Clearly, Tandonnet and his cohorts had been reaching the city and village workers of Gironde with *La Tribune*.

In Gard, the 102 peasants arrested form a much smaller group among those brought before the Mixed Commission (26.9 percent) than they form among the population at large (58.7 percent). Artisans and unskilled workers again correspond almost exactly to their proportion of the adult working population: about 28 percent in each tabulation. Members of the elite (professionals and wealthy landowners) are overrepresented among arrestees in Gard, but not as dramatically as in the departments described above. Whereas they comprised slightly under a fourth of those arrested, they were only 10 percent of the population.[27]

The enormous number of arrests we can document for Allier, almost half of which never led to a trial before the Mixed Commission, provides us with some indications of why peasants were so underrepresented throughout our sample (and in national figures as well). The majority of them were simply let off—regardless of original charge—before final sentence was passed: Fifty-seven were tried by the Mixed Commission, and eighty were released. Those given a final sentence account for only 13.6 percent of all defendants tried by the Mixed Commission; yet peasants made up almost 75 percent of the department's working male population. Artisans and unskilled workers, however, were overrepresented by almost three to one compared with the census figures. And members of the elite were more than three times as likely to appear before the Mixed Commission than to be counted in the department's general census.

Rhône—largely Lyon, its suburbs, and the department's towns—provides us with only six peasants. The artisan and unskilled worker category, however, is amost 15 percent larger among the arrestees than its proportion within the department's working population. Lyon's history of worker uprisings had a "chilling" effect on radicalism among loftier social groups. The elites are *underrepresented* by more than half, the reverse of trends in our other departments.

Jura, on the other hand, conforms more closely to the trends seen in other departments. Professionals and wealthy proprietors (elites) were twice as likely to be arrested than to appear in the general population. Artisans are somewhat overrepresented: 22.6 percent of the arrestees compared with about 18 percent of the department's adult males. Peasants are again a smaller group among those tried than among the census totals: 43.5 percent as against 70 percent.

It is important to avoid a possible error arising from this department-by-department overview. Given that no one was turning himself in for trial, the choices of those to arrest (in the first place) and those to punish (in the final analysis) were made by the police bureaucrats. Peasants most certainly voted for the Mountain in Jura, Allier, Rhône, and the Protestant regions of Gard. They participated to a large degree in the uprisings that broke out in Jura, Allier, and Gard. Peasants account for more than half of those charged with direct participation in the insurrection. The totals for all departments in table 3 show that they provided one-fifth of the inciters and more than one-fourth of the participants and armed participants. But peasants fall far behind artisans, the petite bourgeoisie, and members of the elite among organizers, members of secret societies, and "no overts." And, as we have seen above, these were the actions that received the heaviest penalties. Seen in terms of social class (table 4), leniency increases as one moves "down" in status; sentences generally become more and more severe as the arrestee's position "rises." Peasants were simply of far less interest to the Mixed Commissions than were the skilled, the urban, the literate, and the influential.

When we examine the sentences given to members of different social classes in the same department for the same action, the pattern of repression emerges more clearly, though our conclusions here can only be suggested by the statistics available from our sample.[28] Two departments will suffice for this risky enterprise: Allier and Jura. Both departments provide us with reasonable numbers of cases in comparable conditions of insurrection (and without the religious complications in Gard).

Of the forty-two peasants in Jura for whom we have complete information on action and sentence, nineteen were participants. The majority of them (twelve) were given light sentences. The remaining seven received the moderately heavy sentence of exile to Algeria. The single armed participant received a light sentence. One of the two members was exiled to Algeria and the other got off with no more than a fine or jail term. Both "no overts" received

TABLE 4

Sentence by Class

Class	Freed %	Parole %	Jail %	Algérie Moins %	Exiled %	Algérie Plus %	Cayenne-Lambessa %	N
Peasant	21.7	41.7	3.7	19.8	.7	9.1	3.2	405
Unskilled	19.2	36.5	9.6	17.3	3.8	7.7	5.8	52
Artisan	28.7	28.4	7.0	19.9	1.8	9.7	4.5	732
Petit bourg.	20.9	30.9	5.6	18.5	4.8	11.2	8.0	249
Elite	13.1	24.7	11.9	17.0	12.5	12.5	8.3	336
N	404	556	125	338	72	182	97	
	22.8%	31.3%	7.0%	19.1%	4.1%	10.3%	5.5%	

Missing cases = 415

light sentences, but all four peasant organizers or inciters were transported to Algeria. Finally, because we are dealing with a single department, we shall introduce that broad but fuzzy charge used so widely and indiscriminately throughout France: sedition. Whatever it meant to the Mixed Commission of Jura and to the attorney general at Besançon who dictated the final register, half of the fourteen peasant "seditionists" were treated lightly, and the other seven were transported to Algeria.

Either "sedition" meant something very different for members of Jura's elite sentenced by the same Mixed Commission, or the defendants' social status charged the word with far more frightening power. Nine of ten upper-class "seditionists" were transported; only one was given a light sentence. (This was the largest single group among the elite for whom we have found both charge and sentence in Jura: ten of twenty.) The three elite participants were also treated with greater severity than peasants: all of them were transported to Algeria. The single inciter from the elite was also sent to North Africa. Only elite organizers were treated somewhat more leniently than their peasant counterparts: one received a light sentence, but the other three followed the peasants to Algeria.

A similar pattern emerges in Allier. From a peasant grouping of twenty-two and an elite category of ten, it can be suggested that an elite participant ran more than four times the risk of being sent to Algeria than a peasant charged with the same crime. Elite participants were sentenced to Cayenne or Lambessa 20 percent of the time while peasant participants, though also treated with more severity than we saw for Jura, went to the penal colonies 13.6 percent of the time. Of the forty armed peasant participants, only 27 percent received sentences of exile or Cayenne or Lambessa (three were transported to Algeria and three received the heaviest sentence). But more than 45 percent of the elite armed participants (five of eleven) received sentences of this severity, and two of them went to the penal colonies. Four of five peasant members received light sentences, while seven of fourteen elite members were sent to Cayenne or Lambessa, and two more were exiled to Algeria. Two-thirds of peasant "no overts" got off lightly while more than two-thirds of the elite "no overts" were sent to Algeria (five) or Cayenne or Lambessa (two). Finally, the charge of sedition returns to tantalize us when it was used for different social classes by the same Mixed Commission: five of seven peasants received light sentences, while only nine of sixteen elite seditionists received equal treatment. Exile to Algeria was imposed on two of the remaining seven, and the other five (more than 30 percent of the largest single action category for Allier's elite) faced Cayenne or Lambessa.

Higher class status meant leadership of the left to the Mixed Commission. This is suggested from our analysis of sentencing trends by both action and class, particularly in the ambiguous action-categories of organizer and seditionist.

LEADERSHIP: The elite perceives threat among its own, or those just beneath it

More than 474 members in our sample (21.6 percent) were either described by the Mixed Commissions as leaders of one kind or another, or held elective office as victorious—if often removed or suspended—radical candidates.[29] Using entries in the registers, we have divided them into two categories: national/regional leaders, and local leaders. There is considerable variation in the number (and probably the bureaucrats' definition) of leader among our seven departments. Table 5 shows that the percentage of leaders within the full sample ranges from 4 percent in Jura, where many of the left's acknowledged spokesmen sought exile in Switzerland, to almost 40 percent in Gard. Certain clear distinctions between leaders and followers can be seen, however, when we consider these two groups across the complete sample.

Class appears to be a major factor in determining leadership.

TABLE 5

Leaders by Department

Department	National Leaders %	Local Leaders %	Nonleaders %	N
Vendée	11.1	0	88.9	9
Char.-Inf.	4.8	0	95.2	21
Gironde	11.1	15.2	73.7	99
Gard	8.2	31.6	60.3	380
Jura	.8	3.2	96.0	373
Allier	1.8	20.9	77.3	846
Rhône	3.3	18.2	78.5	461
N	77	408	1,704	
	3.5%	18.6%	77.8%	

Missing cases = 0

While the largest and, necessarily, the vaguest social grouping in the sample is made up of artisans (41.5 percent), they provided only about one-fourth of the national and regional leaders and slightly over one-third of the local leaders. The elite, with only 343 identifiable individuals (19.1 percent of the sample), provided 44 percent of the national and regional leaders and 30 percent of the local leaders. Indeed, petit bourgeois and elite local leaders together account for more than 40 percent of that leadership group.

While the presence of sixty-one local peasant leaders should not be ignored, two points must be emphasized. First, it seems fairly clear that imposing men—like the fifteen wealthy landowners, the sixteen doctors, the thirteen lawyers, down to the nine schoolmasters and fifteen minor functionaries listed as leaders—enjoyed the deference and support of the great mass of the Mountain. They possessed the most powerful organizing tools of the time: literacy, fluency in speech, and, perhaps most important of all, facility with the pen. The wealthiest among them, like Tandonnet in Gironde or Paget in Jura, could deploy resources that protected less prosperous or influential radicals from the full force of repression, thus winning respect for their courage in the face of prosecutions and fines.

Second, the prefects and attorneys general understood the power of such respected local figures in binding together the radical movement, spreading its message, and directing it with practiced political skills. In fact, though leadership alone made an individual suspect, those against whom the Mixed Commission recorded additional notations of suspicion were generaly considered chronic "propagandists" or influential members of a secret society. Before the coup, leaders were prosecuted somewhat more often than others eventually brought before the Mixed Commissions, but they were found guilty far less often than the rank and file: only one-eighth of the ordinary radicals (nine people out of the sixty-seven for whom such verdicts are known) were acquitted, whereas one-third of national leaders (four men) and more than one-fourth of local leaders (ten men) were acquitted of obviously minor charges.

The reckoning came after the coup. More than half of those sentenced to Cayenne or Lambessa by the Mixed Commissions were national or local leaders; leaders received 61 of 113 such penalties handed down in our sample. Again, more than half of those sentenced to *Algérie plus* (114 of 210) in our study were leaders. The proportions begin to shift in the other direction—away from the leaders—as we descend in severity to *Algérie moins*; leaders account for only slightly over one-third of those given this sentence. Finally, only 8 percent of those permitted parole in their home towns were leaders, a considerable variation from the 25 percent of the entire sample given this sentence. Yet leaders who were arrested were charged with direct participation in the insurrections following the coup in only 60 percent of the cases, a surprisingly low figure considering the high number of leaders contributed by Gard and Allier alone. They were really detained and punished for being what they were: neither images of neurotic fear nor illusive threats, but the very image of the *échéance* of 1852. As organizers and spokesmen for the "red specter," the leaders were more likely than their followers to be labeled "very dangerous" or "dangerous." Whereas the Mixed Commissions made such notations for 24 percent of all individuals tried in our sample, leaders received these comments almost 43 percent of the time. Although 63.5 percent of followers avoided a broader lexicon of adjectives, expletives, and comments (which I have called moral judgments in our analysis) that Mixed Commissions showered onto their registers, leaders were described by at least one such extra notation more than two-thirds of the time.[30]

THREAT AND MORAL JUDGMENT: The overlapping categories of social fear

Although moral judgments cannot be considered the "causes" for sentences, it is evident from table 6 that receiving at least one such description placed the defendants in considerably more trouble than having none at all.

We have already seen how often the term "evil passion" was used as a shorthand description of leftist ideas in general. More than 43 percent of our 2,189 defendants were the subjects of similar stigmas, almost 20 percent more than those who received a notation of dangerous or very dangerous. Rather than being seen as causes, moral judgments should be viewed as an enormously rich body of clues to the mental structure through which the police bureaucrats viewed their social enemies and thus their threatened world of 1848 through 1851.

TABLE 6

Moral Judgments by Sentence

Sentence	One or More Moral Judgments %	No Moral Judgments %	N
Freed	13.7	86.3	483
Parole	32.6	67.4	644
Jail	65.0	35.0	143
Algérie moins	66.8	33.2	395
Exile	70.7	29.3	82
Algérie plus	69.0	31.0	210
Cay.-Lambessa	85.8	14.2	113
N	1,137	933	
	54.9%	45.1%	

Missing cases = 119

Eleven categories of moral judgments were established for this analysis. The categories were necessary because, if 389 individuals received only one judgment, an additional 323 received two different ones, 149 more received three distinct moral judgments, and 93 others were the subjects of four separate kinds of descriptions. The eleven categories did not establish any clear pattern of language use by the Mixed Commissions for specific actions, classes, or sentences. But they were useful in showing how often seemingly distinct kinds of language overlapped when applied to those individuals who received multiple moral judgments. In the order of the number of times they were used (and with examples in the often curiously spelled French of the period), the categories are:

(1) Troublemaker: *influent; redouté; actif-énergique; influence funeste; intrigeux; a fait un mal affreux;* etc.—369 uses

(2) Demagogue—250 uses

(3) *Exalté*—214 uses

(4) Wicked: *a perverti les habitants de sa commune; corrupteur de l'esprit de la population; sans moeurs, sans moralité;* etc.—169 uses

(5) Moral vices: *envieux; haineux; vaniteux; ambitieux; orgeuiex;* etc.—167 uses

(6) Dangerous ideas: *ayant des opinions détestables; idées subversives; mépris pour l'autorité; avancé dans ses opinions;* etc.—145 uses

(7) Violent: *violent; visieux;* etc.—103 uses

(8) Barbaric: *brutal; capable de tout; des idées de meurtre et de pillage; terreur du pays;* etc.—84 uses

(9) Socialist or anarchist—68 uses

(10) Bad background: *mal famé; mal élevé; odieux; vivant dans la crapule;* etc.—66 uses

(11) Criminal: *repris de justice; braconnier; pillard; brigand;* etc.—38 uses

A twelfth category, for miscellaneous remarks, includes 58 entries.

Table 7 shows the often understandable, but usually puzzling, overlay of moral, political, medical, common-law, criminal, and even sexual terms. *Exalté* was commonly used at this time as a clinical description of fever, especially of "brain fever" and hysteria.[31] The judges most often used it together with such seemingly political expressions as "dangerous ideas" and "troublemaker." "Moral vices," nothing less than the seven deadly sins, were usually found in tandem with "troublemaker," "demagogue," and *exalté.* "Socialist or anarchist" and "wicked" crop up an interesting number of times. "Wicked" is the category that comes closest to the more generic *mauvaises passions,* and its linkage with "troublemaker" and "barbaric" suggest just how closely the police bureaucrats connected morality, politics, and criminality when viewing the left. The sexual and moral connotations of the verb *pervertir,* a major element of the "wicked" category, require no labored explanation.

CONCLUSION: Counterrevolution and Social Mentality

The social fear experienced by the bureaucrats cannot be described fully in neat categories of stimulus and response. It was, to be both

TABLE 7

Moral Judgments by Moral Judgments
(Percentages)

	Exalté	Wicked	Barbaric	Moral vices	Demagogue	Bad background	Violent	Troublemaker	Dangerous ideas	Criminal	Socialist	Other
Exalté	—	7.9	5.6	11.7	34.6	3.7	11.7	15.9	26.2	1.4	12.6	2.8
Wicked	10.1	—	10.1	12.4	12.4	8.9	5.9	38.5	8.3	3.0	7.1	5.3
Barbaric	14.3	20.2	—	23.8	16.7	13.1	29.8	32.1	8.3	9.5	2.4	8.3
Moral vices	15.0	12.6	12.0	—	19.2	6.6	7.8	26.9	11.4	3.0	4.2	6.0
Demagogue	29.6	8.4	5.6	12.8	—	3.6	14.4	33.6	5.2	2.0	2.0	12.1
Bad background	12.1	22.7	16.7	16.7	13.6	—	7.6	16.7	9.1	4.5	1.5	3.0
Violent	24.3	9.7	24.3	12.6	35.0	4.9	—	26.2	8.7	5.8	1.0	4.9
Troublemaker	9.2	17.6	7.3	12.2	22.8	3.0	7.3	—	10.0	3.0	6.2	4.1
Dangerous ideas	38.6	9.7	4.8	13.1	9.0	4.1	6.2	25.5	—	1.4	4.8	2.1
Criminal	7.9	13.2	21.1	13.2	13.2	7.9	15.8	28.9	5.3	—	7.9	2.6
Socialist	39.7	17.6	2.9	10.3	7.4	1.5	1.5	33.8	10.3	4.4	—	1.5
Other	10.3	15.5	12.1	17.2	12.1	3.4	8.6	25.9	5.2	1.7	1.7	—
N	214	169	84	167	250	66	103	369	145	38	68	58

precise and evocative, a gestalt. The upper-class outside agitator was seen as a carrier of lethal social contagion. His newspapers, speeches, pamphlets ("fermenting pamphlets"), and very influence over the peasant and artisan masses, so mute until the explosion of 1848, continued to assault the social order throughout 1849, 1850, and 1851. And democratic socialism, though defeated on the barricades of June 1848, could not be uprooted from its centers of mass support by normal legal procedures. Beheaded on the national level by the arrest and exile of its most prominent leaders, often floundering on the local level because of press prosecutions, firings of republican bureaucrats and teachers, and suspensions of municipal administrations, the Mountain stood its ground. Its survival—even growth—during the crisis years of the Second Republic was the main reason for the radical response of the prefects and *procureurs-généraux* who rallied to the coup and relished the unlimited powers afforded by the Mixed Commissions. By surviving in the present, the Mountain threatened their future: 1852. Although we might conclude that the left was never strong enough, or well organized enough, or well armed enough to create this year of revolution that never was, we cannot ignore the fact that these possible weaknesses were *not* the particular attributes that frightened the bureaucrats.

They were concerned for the future because the left seemed to flourish when it was forced underground. In Allier, Jura, Gard, and especially in Lyon, they felt that they faced an army of the night that put up its placards, circulated its pamphlets, and planned its actions beyond their ken and outside their repressive reach. Even worse, the content of the Mountain's ideas and programs was even more fearful than its often unknown, but imposing, size.

The police bureaucrats of the Second Republic were not the Manchester bourgeoisie that Marx knew best. The prosecutors and prefects held a mixture of ideas, one that is not as peculiar as it may seem at first sight. Trained under the bourgeois-aristocratic-Bonapartist oligarchy of Louis Philippe, they were members of a bourgeoisie that placed greater emphasis on landed property and order than on dynamism and industrial growth. These *procureurs-généraux* and prefects, jealous of any title they could claim from king or emperor, represented the continental bourgeoisie that Michels and then Gramsci would later study. The police bureaucrats combined the classic liberal view of slow, steady, and rational progress in a reasonable world (the view that was so dear to Guizot) with a view of an organic, hierarchic, even deeply religious society (if the cause of order required orthodox observance) learned from their aristocratic "fencing master." The radical disruption of a reasonable world in progressive equilibrium was an irrational project. The tearing apart of an organic hierarchy by rousing natural inferiors against traditional superiors (the bourgeoisie did not like to remember its violent entry into the upper reaches of the hierarchy) was the introduction of disease into a healthy body politic (and social). *Exalté, mauvaises passions*, "moral vice," and "barbaric," when applied to the left, all reflected this dual meaning of order: half rationalist and half traditional.

The police bureaucrats' support for Louis Napoleon's imperial pretensions even before the coup, their support for a suspension of parliament and courts, and their work on the Mixed Commissions were all part of a single radical dynamic: defense of a threatened future by a total social prophylaxis that secured the present and effaced the recent past. In the interest of maintaining a hierarchy and avoiding an uninhabitable future, the insecurities of the Second Republic were swept away: liberalism, constitutional government, civil court procedure, and of course any form of democracy with any real political meaning for the voter. *The New Age of Caesar*, preached by Romieu, the Elysée's propagandist, expressed more than the political opportunism of the president's personal coterie. It was a radical counterrevolutionary program enforced with genuine conviction by the prefects and attorneys general. Its institutionalized extremism of January to March 1852 would not be seen again until the Commune. And perhaps Caesarism's combination of mock populism and repressive ferocity in 1852 would not be fully realized until our own century.

Appendix 1
The Prefects and Their Departments

Paris

JURA
● Lons-le-Saunier

La Roche-sur-Yon ●
VENDÉE

Moulins ●
ALLIER

RHÔNE
●Lyon

La Rochelle●

CHARENTE-INFÉRIEURE

Bordeaux ●
GIRONDE

GARD
● Nîmes

The Sample Departments and *Chefs-Lieux*

Personal and Career Data for Prefects in the Sample Departments

Prefects, in sequence of service in department	Date of birth	Place of birth	Father's occupation at time of birth	Private wealth of prefect evaluated in yearly revenues
ALLIER				
Coquet, Armand-Alexis (10 July 1848-23 Nov. 1849)	1814	Troyes	Merchant	2,000 francs
Maupas, Charlemagne-Emile de (Nov. 1849-7 Mar. 1851)	1818	Bar-sur-Aube	Proprietor	25,000 francs in 1851; he expected his inheritance and that of his wife to triple this revenue
Charnailles, Gabriel-Léonce Cortois, vicomte de (Mar. 1851-May 1852)	1816	Paris	Not available	12,000 francs
CHARENTE-INFERIEURE				
Wissocq, Paul-Emile (12 June 1848-Nov. 1849)	1804	Boulogne-sur-Mer	Former judge at the Tribunal for Appeals; in 1804 *magistrat de sûreté* for the *arrondissement* of Boulogne	3,000 francs
Brian, Charles-Jean (Nov. 1849-Nov. 1856)	1799	Seine-St. Denis	Former *adjoint* to one of the mayors of Paris	20,000 francs
GARD				
Chanal, François-Victor-Adolphe de (29 Aug. 1848-28 June 1849)	1811	Paris	chief of bureau, *Intendance Générale de la Maison de l' Empereur*	6,000 francs

Date enters Ministry of Interior	People from whom he received recommendations at his entry into service and for promotion	Positions held before appointment to this prefecture	Service after term at this prefecture
10 July 1848	Marie, minister of public works in the Provisional Govt.	Lawyer at Paris Court of Appeals; *chef de cabinet* Feb.- July 1848 for the ministers of public works, Marie and Trélat	Never assigned to other duties
1840		Joins Paris bar 1840; *attaché* at M. of I. 1840-44; S.P., four posts 1844-48; out of service Feb. 1848-Jan. 1849; S.P. Jan. 1849-Nov. 1849	P. Haute-Garonne Mar. 1851; P. of police Oct. 1851; minister of police Jan. 1852
9 Aug. 1848	General Baraguey d' Hilliers (his wife's uncle); Countess de Danremont (his mother-in-law)	No previous service or training cited in dossier, only: proprietor *fortune-aisé* S.P. (three posts) Aug. 1848-Mar. 1851	P. Mayenne 1852; P. Aube 1857; P. Eure-et-Toir 1861-69
12 June 1848	Garnier-Pagès, member of the Provisional Govt. and of the Executive Commission; Buchez, pres. of Constituent Assembly; Drouyn de Lhuys, rep. of Pas de Calais, recommended that he be kept on in 1849	Graduate of the Ecole Polytechnique; hydrographic engineer at M. of Marine 1823-37; Proprietor 1837-48	Never assigned to other duties
1837	Baron Dupont-Delporte, P. of Seine-Inf.; Admiral Amauret, minister of marine	*Maître de requêtes* 1837; S.G. Seine-Inf. 1837; P. of Aude 1841; P. of Vienne 1847; Out of service Feb. 1848-Nov. 1849	Replaced as P. of Charente-Inf. 1856; no other assignments
Mar. 1848	Froussard, rep. to the Constituent Assembly, former commissioner general under Ledru-Rollin; reinstated Mar. 1851 seemingly by Louis Napoleon	Graduate of Ecole Polytechnique 1831; licensed to practice law 1841; captain of artillery 1841-48; commissioner of Hautes-Alpes 1848	P. of Bas-Rhin June 1849; removed May 1850; reinstated Mar. 1851, as P. of Ain; resigns 3 Dec. 1851 in protest against coup; mission to America during

Personal and Career Data for Prefects in the Sample Departments (*cont'd.*)

Prefects, in sequence of service in department	Date of birth	Place of birth	Father's occupation at time of birth	Private wealth of prefect evaluated in yearly revenues
Lagarde, Eugène (28 June 1849-26 Nov. 1851)	1801	Cahors (Lot)	Proprietor	10,000 francs
Pougeard du Limbert, Henri-François (Dec. 1851-at least 1856)	1817	Limoges (Haute-Vienne)	General, former imperial prefect	6,000 francs
GIRONDE				
Neveux, Baron (23 July 1848-27 Nov. 1851)	1805	Montier-en-der (Haute-Marne)	Postmaster (of the town)	Not available
Haussmann, Georges (27 Nov. 1851-June 1853)	1809	Paris	*Commissaire de guerre;* grandfather had been a textile manufacturer in Alsace	22,000 francs
JURA				
Pagès, Bonaventure (1848-Jan. 1849)	1806	Ceret (Pyrénées Orientales)	Proprietor	25,000 francs

Date enters Ministry of Interior	People from whom he received recommendations at his entry into service and for promotion	Positions held before appointment to this prefecture	Service after term at this prefecture
			the Civil War for emperor, 1861-65; S.P. of Gex (Ain) 1870 for Govt. of National Defense
1841	Joseph Périer (brother of Casimir Périer); J. Calmon, deputy of Lot (1841) and director general of Bureau for Land Registration; Comte de Mosbourg, peer of France	File says only "attaché à Casimir Périer"; S.P. (three posts) 1841-48	P. of Gers Nov. 1851; removed and never reassigned 1852
1849	General Baron Pougeard du Limbert (his father), soldier, P. under Napoleon I and Bonapartist deputy from Charente 1848-49	S.P. Beziers	Remained a prefect until his dismissal by Ollivier in 1870
1838	Baron Greiner, colonel of artillery, member of the Imperial Guard (ret.) (his father-in-law); J. J. Rousseau, peer of France, "doyen" of the mayors of Paris, mayor of the Third *Arrondissement*; M. de Failly, deputy of Haute-Marne 1848; Richier, rep. of Gironde at Constituent Assembly	*Chef des bureaux*, Third *Arrondissement* Paris, 1831; S.G. Loire-et-Cher, 1838; S.P. (three posts) 1841-48; subcommissioner of Provisional Govt. at Rethel	Removed Nov. 1851
1831	Duc d'Orléans, heir to the throne; Comte de Montalivert; Nicolas Haussmann (his father), who worked for Casimir Périer, the minister of interior	Licensed in law 1830; S.G. at Poitiers 1831; S.P. (four posts) 1832-48; councilor at prefecture of Gironde, Feb.-Dec. 1848; P. of Var, Dec. 1848; P. of Yonne, May 1850	P. of the Seine (Paris) 1853-69
1831	M. Etienne, deputy of Meuse; the entire delegation from Pyrénées-Orientales	S.P. (four posts) 1830-39; P. of Haute-Loire 1838-41; P. of Lozère 1841-43; removed in 1843	P. of Côte d'Or 1849; P. of Ille-et-Vilaine 1851

Personal and Career Data for Prefects in the Sample Departments (*cont'd.*)

Prefects, in sequence of service in department	Date of birth	Place of birth	Father's occupation at time of birth	Private wealth of prefect evaluated in yearly revenues
Besson, Charles Jean Olympie (10 Jan. 1849- Sept. 1849)	1799	Rouen	*Commissaire de guerre;* later a prefect under July Monarchy	9,000 francs
Vincent, Louis-Charles Marie, baron de (Sept. 1849- Mar. 1851)	1793	Cap Français Saint Dominique (Antilles)	Colonel, later general and *maréchal de camp* under Napoleon I	12,000 francs
Becquey, Charles (7 Mar. 1851-27 Nov. 1851)	1797	Chalons-sur-Marne	Not available; His uncle is referred to as a former director general of Ponts et Chaussées	20,000 francs
Chambrun, Aldebert, vicomte de (Dec. 1851-1854)	1821	Paris	Proprietor	80-90,000 francs

Date enters Ministry of Interior	People from whom he received recommendations at his entry into service and for promotion	Positions held before appointment to this prefecture	Service after term at this prefecture
831	General Fabvier, commander Paris military district and head of Commission des Récompenses Nationales for participants in July 1830 revolution; his father, P. of Charente 1830 and S.P. (removed) under Restoration; Devienne, judge at Lyon Civil Tribunal (1830); Deputies of Ain demand his reinstatement (1849)	S.G. Finistère 1831; S.P. Vassy 1832; S.G. Rhône 1840; P. Ain 1846; out of service Mar. 1848-Jan. 1849	P. Maine-et-Loire 1849; P. Haute-Garonne 1850; P. Nord 1851; P. Bouches du Rhône 1857
835	Thiers; General Baudrand, peer of France; General Jacqueminot; Duc d'Orléans supports him for a prefecture in 1843; Count de la Morlière, his brother-in-law, writes to Louis Napoleon in 1849	S.P. Toul 1835; out of service Mar. 1848-July 1848; S.P. Aix 1848; S.P. Le Havre 1848; P. Lot 1849	P. Rhône Nov. 1851; later councilor of state and senator of Second Empire
821	M. De Valory, receveur-général at Mâcon (his wife's uncle); J. Calmon, deputy of Lot, director general of the Bureau of Land Registration, requests his promotion to P. in 1840; Drouyn de Lhuys, rep. to Constituent Assembly and Legislative Assembly, requests a prefecture for him in 1850	Lawyer at the Paris Court of Appeals, 1820; attaché at M. of I. 1821-27; S.P. (two posts) 1827-48; out of service Feb. 1848-June 1850; S.P. St.-Etienne June 1850	Removed Nov. 1851
850	Portalis, member of the personal entourage of Louis Napoleon and the P.G. of Paris; Godart, director general of Baccaret Crystal (his father-in-law)	Proprietor; S.P. Toulon 1850; S.P. St.-Etienne 1851	Resigned as P. of Jura 1854 because he had received no promotions

Personal and Career Data for Prefects in the Sample Departments (*cont'd.*)

Prefects, in sequence of service in department	Date of birth	Place of birth	Father's occupation at time of birth	Private wealth of prefect evaluated in yearly revenues
RHÔNE				
Ambert (3 July 1848- 24 Jan. 1849)	1801	Not available	Not available	"Without fortune," his dossier specifically notes
Tourangin, Denis-Victor (24 Jan. 1849- 29 June 1849)	1788	Issoudun (Indre)	Not available	12,000 francs
Darcy, Hugues-Iéna (29 June 1849- 2 Dec. 1849)	1807	Not available	Not available	12-15,000 francs
La Coste du Vivier, Charles-Aristide de (2 Dec. 1849- Nov. 1851)	1794	Nancy	Cavalry officer; became general-baron under Napoleon I	25,000 francs
Vincent (Nov. 1851-1853)		See above (Jura)		
VENDEE				
Bonnin, Casimir Jean Baptiste (3 Jan. 1849- 16 Sept. 1851)	1806	Bussière (Haute-Vienne)	Proprietor *adjoint* to mayor	3,500 francs

Date enters Ministry of Interior	People from whom he received recommendations at his entry into service and for promotion	Positions held before appointment to this prefecture	Service after term at this prefecture
3 July 1848	Rep. of Lot (his cousin); he was also well known to the men of *Le National*, having been a close friend of Carrel	Lawyer in private practice in Paris	Removed
1830	Comte de Gasparin, close friend of Guizot; Guizot writes him in familiar tone (1833)	Lawyer at Bourges (Cher); P. of Sarthe 1830; P. of Doubs 1833-48; out of service Feb. 1848-Jan. 1849	Retired June 1849 for reasons of health; councilor of state; senator of Second Empire
1830	Referred to in an unsigned memorandum written sometime after 1848 as "one of the two or three prefects of the greatest ability"	Doctor of Law; Prefectoral councilor, 1830; S.P. Sens 1834; P. of Tarn-et-Garonne 1838; P. of Aube 1839; P. of Gard 1843-48; out of service Feb. 1848-Jan. 1849; P. of Moselle, Jan. 1849	Undersecretary of state at M. of I. until the coup
1816	Thouvenel, deputy of Meurthe, wrote letters for him in 1818 and 1828; General Baron De la Coste (his father)	S.G. Creuse, 1816; S.P. (two posts) 1819-22; removed 1822; P. of Gard 1830; P. of Tarn-et-Garonne; P. of Somme; P. of Gironde; P. of Bouches-du-Rhône 1836-48; councilor of state, 1833-48	Retired
	See above (Jura)		
1830	Vicomte de Beaumont, vice pres. of chamber at end of Restoration and moderate-liberal deputy throughout July Monarchy; His brother, notary and deputy from Vienne (1848-49)	Private secretary of Beaumont, before July Days; prefectoral councilor Basses Pyrénées 1830; S.P. Fontenay 1834-Dec. 1848 (one of only ten S.P.'s	Removed

Personal and Career Data for Prefects in the Sample Departments (*cont'd.*)

Prefects, in sequence of service in department	Date of birth	Place of birth	Father's occupation at time of birth	Private wealth of prefect evaluated in yearly revenues
Boby de la Chapelle, Alphonse-Charles (Sept. 1851-1862)	1812	Provins (Seine-et-Marne)	Inspector of local roads, later prefect	5,100 francs in 1851, when both father and father-in-law were living; 10,000 francs at death of father (1866)

Date enters Ministry of Interior	People from whom he received recommendations at his entry into service and for promotion	Positions held before appointment to this prefecture	Service after term at this prefecture
		of July Monarchy to keep his post after 1848 revolution)	
1838	His father, P. of Lot-et-Garonne; His father-in-law, Baron Boullé, S.P. under Napoleon I and P. of Finistère under July Monarchy; J. Calmon, deputy and director, Bureau of Land Registration	Prefectoral councilor, Finistère, 1838; S.P. Chateaulin 1841; S.P. Dinan 1846; S.P. Saumur 1847-48; out of service Feb. 1848-Nov. 1848; S.P. Saumur 1848	P. of Aveyron 1862; P. of Haute-Vienne 1863; retires as honorary P. 1867

Sociopolitical Sketches of the Sample Departments

Vendée, Charente-Inférieure, and Gironde: The Conservative Departments

VENDÉE

Of all the departments in France, Vendée gave the lowest proportion of its vote in 1849 to republican candidates: slightly more than 5 percent. All the deputies elected from Vendée to the Legislative Assembly were legitimists. They defeated their republican opponents by an average vote per candidate of 40,500 to 6,000.[1]

With a population in 1851 of approximately 380,000 dispersed over 681,700 hectares, the department possessed no large towns. Napoléon-Vendée (modern name: La Roche-sur-Yon), the largest town and the administrative *chef-lieu* of the department (the seat of the prefecture), had only 7,500 inhabitants in 1851.[2] Vendée was an almost entirely agricultural department with only a few artisanal shops and lime furnaces (for fertilizer production) scattered among its hamlets. A small center of shipbuilding and fishing existed in the coastal town of Les Sables d'Olonne. Grain growing and cattle raising were the major farming occupations in Vendée; the soil of the department was either too marshy or too sandy for the cultivation of more lucrative cash crops.[3]

Most of Vendée is located in the swampy wooded region along France's Atlantic coast. At mid-nineteenth century, most of the land in this region belonged to large landholding aristocrats. The peasants were usually sharecroppers or landless farm laborers. Dependent upon the old nobility for their livelihood and sharing the deeply religious culture of the traditionally legitimist west, this population followed the lead of the local aristocrats and clergy. It was enthusiastically legitimist in its political outlook under the Second Republic. The only part of the department in which peasants owned their own small parcels of land was the sandy plain southeast of Napoléon-Vendée. Here, the local farmers and a few professional men and artisans of the towns formed the tiny Orleanist and republican constituencies in the department.[4]

CHARENTE-INFÉRIEURE

Located just south of Vendée on the Atlantic coast, Charente-Inférieure was one of the few departments under the Second Republic that was dominated by a purely Bonapartist political movement. As in Vendée, the peasants of this department generally followed the political lead of the local large landowners. In Charente-Inférieure, these local notables were often distinguished veterans of the first Napoleon's Grand Army, or their heirs. Louis Napoleon defeated both an Orleanist and a moderate republican (Charles Thomas, candidate of *Le National* who received support from prominent Parisian leaders) in by-elections to the Constituent Assembly held on 9 June 1848. His greatest electoral strength was in the agricultural *arrondissements* of Saintes and Saint-Jean-d'Angély. Bonaparte carried the latter district with over 80 percent of the vote. A student of this election has attributed Louis Napoleon's tremendous majority in the rural *arrondissements* of Charente-Inférieure to the local influence of General Regnault de Saint-Jean-d'Angély.[5] The son of an early supporter of Napoleon Bonaparte who was ennobled under the First Empire, Regnault himself won a battlefield promotion at Waterloo.[6]

In May 1849 the department supported the entire slate backed by the Comité électoral Napoléonien. Two important politicians who had rallied to the personal banner of Louis Napoleon, Jules Baroche and Jules Dufaure, led the delegation to the Legislative Assembly. Both of these men were to serve the president as his spokesmen in the assembly and as ministers of justice and interior. The victorious list also included the names of local Bonapartist luminaries, including two men who had shared Napoleon's exile on Elba and Saint Helena and the elderly marshal of France and former Napoleonic general, Thomas-Robert Bugeaud d'Isly. The opponents of the Bonapartists, a coalition of moderate and radical republicans, garnered less than 15 percent of the vote in these elections.[7]

At the time of the Second Republic, Charente-Inférieure had a population of approximately 470,000 in an area of nearly 655,000 hectares: a population more than one-fourth greater than that of Vendée in a somewhat smaller total area. Although it was primarily an agricultural region, the department boasted two port towns that were centers of commercial and industrial activity. Rochefort, with its important naval arsenal employing 2,000 workers, had a total population in 1851 of 24,330. La Rochelle, the departmental *chef-lieu*, was a shipbuilding, fishing, and commercial center with a population of 16,507.[8]

The main economic activity of Charente-Inférieure, however, was viticulture. Almost the entire inland plain of the department was planted in vines (nearly one-fifth of the farming land in Charente-Inférieure). The regions closest to the sea were centers of grain production. Aside from the large estates belonging to the Napoleonic nobility, most of the department's farms were small holdings worked by their peasant proprietors. Because of the intensive seasonal labor required by the vines, however, a considerable proportion of the agricultural population was made up of landless laborers.[9]

Finally, Charente-Inférieure differed from most French departments because it had a small Protestant population that exercised considerable political influence over the two towns in which it was concentrated: La Rochelle and the smaller port of Marennes. The Protestants in these communities generally supported Orleanist candidates and made Marennes and La Rochelle important centers of resistance to the overwhelming Bonapartism of the rest of the department.[10]

GIRONDE

Situated just south of Charente-Inférieure, Gironde was one of the richest departments of France.[11] Bordeaux, with approximately 131,000 inhabitants in 1851, was one of only five French cities with a population over 100,000 during the period of the Second Republic. Yet Gironde remained a predominantly rural department. The majority of its working population engaged in agriculture and lived in 542 communes, dispersed over 980,000 hectares, with less than 5,000 inhabitants in each. Only Bordeaux and the small city of Libourne can be considered urban centers in this department of 614,387 inhabitants.

The Party of Order dominated the elections to the Legislative Assembly here, winning almost 65 percent of the vote in its victory over a list composed mainly of moderate republicans. The major conservative faction in Gironde was Orleanist. However, legitimism was so important a minority faith among the department's elite that two prominent "whites" were included in the Party of Order's list in May 1849. When the Orleanists and legitimists broke with each other during a by-election later in the year, neither of the competing conservative candidates was elected. A well-known moderate republican, Barthélemy Lagarde, won with barely 50 percent of the ballots cast: 35,245 votes to 25,766 for the Orleanist and 9,379 for the legitimist. The department's lone republican deputy in a delegation of thirteen owed his election to a turnout of less than half of Gironde's 176,000 registered voters.

Despite the large number of people concentrated in Bordeaux, it was not an industrial city like Lyon or Lille. The city itself possessed only three large manufacturing enterprises: a pottery plant with 600 workers, a wool spinnery with 200 workers, and a furniture factory with a work force of only 50. The most important industries in the department—shipbuilding, sugar refining, and cooperage—depended on the commercial port of Bordeaux and on the rich wine growing region near the city. One large shipyard, located outside of Bordeaux, employed more than 400 artisans and unskilled workers. The three other such enterprises in Gironde employed less than 100 workers each. The department's forty sugar refineries were relatively small operations employing between 25 and 50 workers. The manufacture of barrels was carried out in many small shops employing 10 to 12 craftsmen. While Bordeaux had 131 such enterprises, most of the cooperage shops in Gironde were located in Libourne.

In marked contrast with the elites of the French industrial cities, the Girondin notables were foes of protective tariffs and passionate propagandists for free trade. What a recent student of Gironde under the Second Republic calls the *"timocratie"* of Bordeaux (the city's bankers, merchants, and shipping magnates) united with the great viticultural interests of the department in their dependence on international trade. Wine exports and wool and raw sugar imports were their sources of wealth. Cosmopolitan in its outlook and imbedded in a cash nexus that extended far beyond France's frontiers, the department's notability largely eschewed the traditionalism of the legitimists and embraced the more modern "get rich" ethos of Orleanism. And Gironde boasted one of the richest groups of notables in France. In 1846 almost 9 citizens in every thousand in the department paid the 200 francs in direct taxation (levied largely on real estate) that carried with it the right to vote under the July Monarchy. The national average at this time was only 6.7 electors per thousand. In Bordeaux alone, the proportion of electors (all men of considerable wealth) to the citizenry as a whole was more than twice the average for the nation. More than one-fourth of the department's voters paid more than 500 francs per year in these taxes, a figure that represented a great fortune indeed.

The richest farmland in Gironde was concentrated in the hands of a few proprietors, who owned the estates on which the department's "noble" wines were produced. Blanqui, the local liberal economist and brother of the revolutionary, estimated that certain vineyards in the Médoc region northwest of Bordeaux produced wine worth 25,500 francs per hectare of vines every year. An enormous sum, 1,000 francs per year, was paid by one-third of the tax-paying electorate in a single commune of the Médoc. As the employers and political leaders of most of the department's landless agricultural laborers (almost 30 percent of Gironde's total farming population), these great landowners ensured that their localities consistently voted for the candidates of the Party of Order.

Property was more evenly dispersed in the *arrondissements* that produced grain and *vin ordinaire*, Libourne and La Réole, and in the poorer two-thirds of the department taken up by salt bogs, sandy moors, and scrub pine forests. Landowners, mostly the peasant proprietors of small parcels in these regions, made up 43 percent of the Gironde's agricultural population at mid-nineteenth century. Despite the dire impact on wine prices of the trade crisis that began in 1846 and continued through the Second Republic, most of Gironde's peasants deferred either to the Orleanist or legitimist notables in their localities. Republicanism in this department was limited in its support to the lower-middle class and to the artisans of Bordeaux, Libourne, and a few smaller towns.

Gard—a Contested Department

With a small coastline on the Mediterranean and the bulk of its territory (592,000 hectares) extending northward along the right bank of the Rhône river and westward into the Cévennes Mountains, Gard shared the religiously and politically divided heritage of the Midi. Along with its neighboring departments (and those of Alsace), Gard possessed large and geographically concentrated Protestant communities. The poor farmland of the forbidding highlands that form the western third of the department was—and is today—almost entirely inhabited by Protestant peasants.[12] Nonconformist strength existed in a belt through the middle of the department: from St.-Jean-du-Gard in the northwest through Nîmes and then further southeast to the villages of the Vaunage. In 1851 more than one-fourth of Nîmes' 54,000 residents were Protestants.[13]

The majority of Gard's population (400,000 in 1851) was Catholic, however, and was concentrated on the rich agricultural plain along the Rhône river.[14] Its political outlook was legitimist, whereas that of the Protestant minority was Orleanist or republican. Relations between the two groups had frequently taken on the characteristics of a religious war. At mid-nineteenth century, interdenominational hatreds were still very much alive, and Gard was notorious for the violence that broke out intermittently between the sects. Under the July Monarchy, the political abstention of the legitimist, or "white," aristocracy had left power in the department largely in the hands of a Protestant notability. The Second Republic, by extending the vote to the population as a whole, made possible a reassertion of Catholic and therefore legitimist dominance in Gard. The considerable size of the Protestant minority, however, ensured that local elections under the new republic would be hotly contested. The violence of legitimist rhetoric and the menacing development of an extremist wing among the Bourbonist leadership (the so-called white Mountain, which revived memories of the antiProtestant terror of 1815) had a singular impact on the nonconformist community in Gard. Most Protestants, despite their widely varying social and economic conditions, united behind one banner—democratic socialism, the most radical wing of the republican movement. Following the lead of the artisans and peasants of the Alès basin and the Cévennes, Protestants who had once been Orleanists or moderate republicans began in 1849 to cast their votes for the Mountain. Political radicalism became their protest against the religious intolerance of their local opponents and against the increasingly pronounced clericalism of the Party of Order's leaders in the republic's assemblies.

In May 1849 the legitimists carried the department with approximately 65 percent of the vote.[15] The opposition to the white list, which was overwhelmingly Protestant, had given its vote almost en bloc to a coalition slate of moderate and radical republicans.[16] In January 1850 the legitimists split into two hostile camps; both a moderate and an extremist candidate contested a by-election to the Legislative Assembly. The Protestants of Gard meanwhile united behind a moderate republican turned Montagnard, Etienne Favand, and won their only major victory under the Second Republic.[17] The only republican in a departmental delegation of ten, Favand became an important voice for the local radical movement both in the assembly and in the national leadership of democratic socialism.[18] But perhaps the most important indication of the burgeoning radical strength among the Protestant minority in Gard was the growth of a large network of secret societies where the Protestant population was most highly concentrated. These clandestine radical groups had their head-quarters in Nîmes and in Alès (the administrative and manufacturing center of the department's northern *arrondissement*). Their peasant support was concentrated in the Protestant highlands of the *arrondissements* of Alès and Le Vigan and in the Protestant villages of the Vaunages. After the coup of 2 December 1851, the Protestant peasants and townspeople of Gard rose against the authorities in the western part of the department and attempted in vain to march on Nîmes and seize the prefecture. Three centuries of religious hatred, compounded by the arrogance and extrem-ism of the newly enfranchised legitimist majority, had culminated in the birth of a mass radical movement among the Protestants of Gard—a leftist tradition that continues into the present.

Economics played an important role in the development of left- and right-wing extremisms in Gard during the period of the Second Republic. The main cash crops of this largely agricultural department were silk and wine. The trade crisis that began in the mid-forties had a severe impact on the demand for silk, causing a sharp drop in prices for the cocoons harvested by the peasants and widespread unemployment in the weaving shops of Nîmes and other towns in the department. The sales tax on wine voted by the Constituent Assembly in 1848 reduced demand throughout France, especially among the poor. And Gard was an area in which *vin ordinaire* was the almost exclusive product of the local vineyards.[19] The commercial wine crisis was further intensified in 1849 by a vine disease that reduced the department's crop by one-third, but despite this decline in supply prices fell to a twenty-year low.[20] While the Catholic peasants of the wine-growing region south of Nîmes and those of the more diver-sified agricultural area along the Rhône suffered considerably, they turned to their traditional leaders among the nobility and clergy and remained in the conservative camp. The nonconformist peasants, most of whom owned their small farms, generally inhabited land so poor that their daily diet often consisted exclusively of chestnuts. For the market, they raised hogs and cultivated olive trees, vines, and mulberry trees (for feeding silkworms).[21] To supplement family income, women worked domestic looms throughout the year while the entire family turned to weaving during the winter months. This chronically impoverished peasantry pro-vided the backbone of the Montagnard movement in Gard.

Gard also possessed industries of national importance. The manufacture of silk thread and cloth and the production of gloves, hats, and other luxury goods were the major economic activities of Nîmes.[22] The religious tensions in the city were reflected in the factories, where the owners were usually Protestants and the workers were generally Catholics. Silk spin-ning and weaving were also dispersed in the small shops and cottages of the Protestant region northwest of Nîmes.

A growing coal and iron industry was developing around the city of Alès (population 18,871 in 1851) by the time of the 1848 revolution. In Alès alone, 540 workers were employed in the foundries and 110 labored in the nearby coal mines. Until 1847 the Rochebille mines, located just outside the city, produced as much as five million kilograms of coal per year. Shortly after the revolution, however, production declined to only three-fifths of this earlier figure because of the paralysis of credit and industry throughout France.[23] Among the workers of the Alès basin, religious differences played the same divisive role that they did among the farming population. The Catholic miners supported legitimism, whereas the Protestant ironworkers with greater skills and literacy, formed a powerful Montagnard constituency.[24]

Another center of republicanism in the department was the shipping town of Beaucaire, located where the River Gard joins the Rhône. The teamsters, sailors, and artisans exercised a considerable influence on the numerous day laborers who worked in the immediate vicinity of the town.[25]

Jura, Allier, and Rhône: The Republican Departments

Republicanism, in both its moderate and radical forms, became a force to be reckoned with under the Second Republic largely because of the extension of its appeal beyond the confines of the great cities and into the countryside. In the period immediately following the 1848 revolution, rural France experienced the growth of a "red" peasant movement that carried many previously quiescent departments into the democratic camp. Jacques Bouillon, in his study of the electoral sociology of France in May 1849, argues that the elections for the Legislative Assembly mark the first appearance of a regional "regrouping" of political forces. This division of the nation into conservative and radical spheres of influence was to survive the Second Empire and continue into the twentieth century.

According to Bouillon, the sudden appearance in May 1849 of "red" regions on France's electoral map was caused by the agricultural crisis. He describes the farming areas in which the Mountain established itself as the dominant electoral force as those in which the soil was generally unproductive and poor: regions of "starving cantons." The peasantry of these areas suffered intensely from the poor harvests of the July Monarchy's final years and from the low agricultural prices following the paralysis of credit and commerce under the new republic. The lack of rural credit after February 1848 placed numerous small landowners in jeopardy of losing their heavily mortgaged holdings. The poor prices paid for the relatively good harvests of the republican period deprived the peasants of needed cash income. The high taxes levied on wine by the Constituent Assembly depressed the market even further and ate away at the real earnings of many small holders, renters, and sharecroppers throughout the years leading up to the coup. Consequently, the peasantry of much of eastern, southeastern, and central France turned to the Mountain, with its program of free rural credit and tax relief for the poor, as the answer to its chronic suffering.[26]

Bouillon was concerned with the more general findings of electoral sociology; other students of the radicalization of rural France have noted other factors that contributed to the electoral results of 1849. Ernest Labrousse and Rémi Gossez, in studying the rural riots that accompanied the agricultural crisis of 1846-1847, point out that the most explosive regions were those in which a farming population was mixed with concentrated minorities of artisans, miners, or industrial workers.[27] In such settings, the combined impact of industrial depression and of wild fluctuations in harvest sizes and agricultural prices intensified discontent. The more literate artisans and workers shared wider political horizons because of their participation in enterprises with regional or national markets. They were in constant communication with the great cities. As Maurice Agulhon, Leo Loubère, and Philippe Vigier have shown in their local studies, these more advanced elements of rural society, many of them still part-time farmers or only recently removed from peasant life, transmitted the shock that galvanized their neighbors into a sudden shift to the left. They were the go-betweens in the democratic socialist alliance that linked the petite bourgeoisie with a peasantry only beginning its awakening to political consciousness.

JURA

Neither utopian socialism nor moderate republicanism were entirely new political forces in this mountainous and sparsely populated department on the Swiss border (population in 1851: 313,000; territory: approximately 500,000 hectares).[28] Joseph-Louis-Etienne Cordier, a native of the department, was one of the deputies to France's legislative bodies from 1827 until his death in 1849. For eighteen years he consistently voted with the democratic opposition to the censitary regime of Louis Philippe.[29] Jules Grévy, the scion of a prominent bourgeois family in Jura, was an important member of the moderate republican circle in Paris before the 1848 revolution. He made his legal debut in 1839 as the defense attorney for two members of a radical secret society who had been charged with treason. Grévy, eventually president of the Third Republic, was already the most popular politician in Jura during the years 1848 through 1851. In March 1848 the Provisional Government appointed him as *commissaire* (temporary administrator) of Jura. Twice—in April 1848 and May 1849—Grévy came in first on the republican slate elected by the department.[30] His influence, and that of Cordier, ensured that Jura's political complexion would differ from that of other republicanized departments in one very important respect. Here, moderate republicanism remained an important wing of the democratic movement despite its national decline in 1849.

By May 1849, however, democratic socialism had become as powerful a local political movement as moderate republicanism. The moderates monopolized the department's victorious republican list in the 1848 elections for the Constituent Assembly. Only a year later, three of the seven republican candidates for the Legislative Assembly were outspoken radicals, and they received approximately the same number of votes as their moderate allies. With more than 60 percent of the vote, this coalition list won a decisive victory over the Party of Order.[31]

The rapid growth of socialism within the republican camp in Jura had two local sources: the utopian socialism of the farmer-artisans in the mountains and the desperation of the peasants on the plain. The ideas of Charles Fourier, Victor Considérant, and Pierre-Joseph Proudhon (both Fourier and Proudhon were born in nearby Besançon) found a small but significant following among the department's watchmakers and dairy farmers during the years before the 1848 revolution. Concentrated in the villages of the mountainous parts of the department, these artisan-agriculturalists (dairy farmers generally worked as watchmakers during the winter months) already enjoyed the benefits of self-help organizations: cooperative dairies and associations for the production and marketing of their clocks and watches. While some of them followed the individualist and apolitical teachings of Proudhon and remained in the moderate republican camp, others joined the democratic socialists in a political pursuit of their goals. Grévy's closest associate among the moderates was a Fourierist. But Louis-Adolphe Derriey, the leading radical vote-getter in 1849, was an ardent disciple of Victor Considérant.[32]

Derriey was the president of the agricultural society in the *arrondissement* of Dôle. His electoral success and that of his fellow socialists from the other relatively low-lying *arrondissement* of Poligny points up the second crucial element in the rise of radicalism in Jura. Under the republic, democratic socialism became the political creed of the peasants who farmed the department's central and southern plain. This region rapidly became the center of the most militant Montagnard movement in the department. It was soon a hotbed of secret society activity and the home of Jura's most radical newspapers. Here the peasantry made preparations for an armed rising against the government in June 1849, and a small rebellion actually did break out when the news of the coup d'état reached Jura on 3 December 1851.

The department's plain, a wine- and grain-growing region, became a Montagnard stronghold because of the local pattern of land tenure and the agricultural depression that plagued the republic. Prior to 1830 the *arrondissements* of Dôle and Poligny had been areas of large landholding; most of the peasant population either rented small farms or worked as landless laborers. The landlords, most of whom were absentees, sold the bulk of their properties in order to cash in on the stock-market boom of the early forties. By 1848 most of the peasants on the plain had gone heavily into debt in order to purchase their own small holdings. The collapse of credit and prices after February 1848 presented these humble proprietors with the disastrous possibility of being forced off their newly acquired farms. A significant minority of the peasants in this region were renters. Their lack of cash and credit made it difficult for them to meet the regular payments required by their leases.[33]

The extent of the problem is readily apparent in the landholding pattern of the department as a whole in 1851: 46 percent of the agricultural population owned their farms, 24 percent were renters, 4 percent were sharecroppers, and 16 percent were landless laborers.[34] With the small proprietors deep in debt and almost a fourth of the farmers tied down to cash rental agreements at a time when neither loans nor sales of crops would be expected to provide enough cash, it is small wonder that the authorities considered Jura among the most politically combustible departments in France.

Scattered among the farming population of Jura's plateau were small concentrations of artisans and industrial workers employed in the exploitation of iron ore deposits and extensive forests. At Champagnole, near Poligny, more than 300 men, women, and children produced iron (284,000 kilograms in 1847-1848) at numerous local furnaces; and a similar number worked in forest-related industries such as woodcutting and charcoal and plank production. Close to 400 worked to transport these goods to market.[35] The manufacture of ceramic tiles was a small shop operation scattered throughout the *arrondissements* of Poligny, Dôle, and Lons-le-Saunier.

The mountainous region of the department was a center of viticulture, dairy farming, lumbering, and cottage industries. Aside from the *vin ordinaire* produced on the plains, Jura's most important articles of commerce—Gruyère cheese and timepieces—were produced in these highlands. The population that was engaged in the seasonal production of both commodities lived in Jura's least populous *arrondissement* of Saint-Claude. Centered around the town of Morez, more than 2,500 men, women, and children made clocks and watches during the winter. In prosperous times, they produced more than one million francs' worth of timepieces in a single year. Dairy farming became the primary occupation of three-fourths of these artisans during the warmer months. The land on their small holdings was suitable only for the growing of barley and oats and for pasturage.[36]

Like the peasants of the plain, the mountain dwellers of Jura suffered a heavy blow in the economic crisis of the republic. The demand for cheese fell off considerably, and prices declined by 30 percent in 1848. In the same year, only half the watches and other manufactured goods produced in the region around Morez were actually sold.[37]

The authorities responsible for public order in Jura were hindered by two formidable obstacles to their task of repressing the left in this department. Only Dôle and Lons-le-Saunier (the *chef-lieu*) were much larger than villages: each had about 10,000 inhabitants in 1851.[38] More than 90 percent of the department's population was dispersed in villages and hamlets separated from the administrative centers (and each other) by roads that were often impassable in winter. Jura's climate, terrain, and poor communications made it a uniquely difficult department to police.

Secondly, Jura lies just across mountain passes from the Swiss canton of Geneva. Under the presidency of James Fazy, a veteran radical, Geneva was one of the few hospitable areas for democratic and democratic-socialist activity in Europe at the time of the Second Republic. Along with London, Geneva was the major command post for the French secret societies. Orders, printed propaganda, gunpowder, and weapons were carried over the border into Jura by Montagnard messengers. Jurassiens wanted by the police for their subversive activities often avoided arrest simply by walking across the frontier into Switzerland. The judicial and police authorities responsible for this department found themselves involved not only with domestic law enforcement but also with patrolling a border and "running" secret agents into Geneva in order to gather information on their local political antagonists.

ALLIER

Although its terrain is not as forbidding as that of Jura, its moors, forests, and sandy soil made Allier an even more sparsely populated department in 1851: 336,558 inhabitants dispersed over 723,981 hectares.[39] By 1848 economic conditions were so desperate in this region of unprofitable agriculture that Allier quickly became an important focal point of democratic socialism in central France. The department was a notoriously difficult assignment for law-enforcement bureaucrats throughout the period of the Second Republic. Charlemagne-Emile de Maupas, whose brilliant career as a prefect began here in 1849, described Allier in his memoirs as the headquarters of seditious activity among its six neighboring departments.[40] Eugène Ténot, who in 1865 published a remarkably careful survey of provincial France on the eve of the coup, characterized Allier as the department in central France that inspired the greatest fear among the authorities.[41]

Moderate republicanism was not a new political force in Allier, even among the limited group of large taxpayers allowed the vote under the July Monarchy.[42] In 1846 the department elected two champions of political reform to the Chamber of Deputies: Maurice Bureaux de Puzy and the retired General de Courtais. Since 1815, in fact, Allier and the entire region on the northeastern edge of the massif Central had been centers of opposition to the governments of the Restoration and the July Monarchy.

Local friction between an ancient landowning aristocracy and a new class of proprietors who had purchased nationalized lands during the Great Revolution divided the region's elite. This divided elite faced strong opposition. By 1848 a series of three disastrous harvests in central France created agitation for political and economic reform among important groups outside of the Orleanist regime's political class. Small landlords, lawyers, doctors, and pharmacists of Allier's rural communes began to agitate not only for an extension of the suffrage beyond the censitary elite but for important social reforms. They spread the socialist ideas of left-wing republicanism to the department's small population of town-dwelling industrial workers, to the miners and artisans of the villages, and ultimately to the impoverished peasants.

Although the first commissioners appointed after the 1848 revolution to administer the department were moderate republicans, they were soon replaced by Félix Mathé, an outspoken local radical and a close associate of Alexandre Auguste Ledru-Rollin. The new commissioner promptly began to establish republicanism in Allier on a more radical footing by encouraging the formation of socialist clubs among the peasantry. His local popularity, and that of other new men who had embraced democratic socialism, would establish advanced republicanism as the preponderant political force in the department by 1849.

The first electoral list presented by the republicans in April 1848 was a coalition of moderates and radicals. Mathé had encouraged its formation in order to combat the unified legitimist forces in Allier, which controlled the local Party of Order. The republican ticket was headed by the familiar names of the department's former deputies, but it included an equal number of relatively unknown radicals. A recent local historian, Georges Rougeron, has called this an early experiment in popular-front tactics. It was enormously successful among Allier's largely illiterate peasantry. The four moderates on the list, led by Courtais, polled between 52,000 and 71,000 of the 72,223 ballots cast. The four radicals were also victorious, but by a substantially smaller plurality. Mathé himself, despite his tenure as temporary prefect, came in only fifth, with 51,989 votes. The rest of the radicals received an average of less than 48,000 votes. The Party of Order, however, was crushed in this first democratic election in Allier. The most popular conservative candidate came in more than 24,000 votes behind the eighth (and last) man elected on the republican slate.

The coalition of moderate and radical republicans did not survive the lifespan of the Constituent Assembly. Allier's moderate deputies played important roles in drafting the republic's constitution and in the ministry formed by General Cavaignac. The radicals became staunch opponents of the Cavaignac government and of the repressive measures it introduced after the June Days of 1848. By early 1849 Allier's popular front had split into rival camps. Two prominent moderate republicans allied themselves with legitimists and Orleanists on a rather eclectic "list of order." This broad conservative coalition came into being, according to its founding charter, in order to protect society, defend the republic, and support the policies of Louis Napoleon. It specifically excluded "fanatic republicans, arrogant socialists, revolutionaries, and enthusiasts."[43]

In the elections of May 1849, this Party of Order list faced a republican slate made up exclusively of democratic socialists. The radical ticket was led by the Mountain's national leader, Ledru-Rollin, and by Félix Mathé. When the ballots were counted, Allier had been swept into the radical column by more than 60 percent of the vote. The moderate republicans, who led the democratic list in 1848, now came in first on the Party of Order's slate, but more than 15,000 votes behind their victorious socialist opponents.

The Montagnard clubs in Allier, though banned and operating underground, had delivered a decisive majority to their leaders. A month later, these same secret societies armed themselves and prepared to march on the administrative centers of the department to protest the Roman expedition and to join a revolution they believed had broken out in Paris. In June 1849 the radical peasants dispersed before taking any action. But on 3 December 1851 they participated in one of the most serious rural rebellions against Louis Napoleon's coup d'état.

The major reason for the rapid growth and militant stance of this local radical movement was the exceptional poverty of Allier's peasantry. The department's rural population—more than 90 percent of its inhabitants—was made up largely of peasants who owned no land. They depended on a small group of proprietors for seasonal work as day laborers or for the rental of small farms. So intense, in fact, was the land hunger among the peasants of Allier that many had signed extremely disadvantageous leases for their farms before the onset of the agricultural depression of 1846. These contracts required the yearly payment of a fixed cash rental *plus* a share of their harvest. The peasants of Allier produced *vin ordinaire* and wheat for the national market. Other grains (barley and rye) and bran were produced for home consumption. The disastrous harvests of the last years of the July Monarchy and the low prices for wine during the republican era threatened to drive sharecroppers and tenants off the land and left the day laborers without work. Only 24 percent of Allier's agricultural population owned land. About 6 percent were reported as tenants; 26 percent were officially listed as sharecroppers, although many of them must have paid an additional cash rental for their farms. The largest group of peasants was made up of landless laborers: 28 percent of the department's farm population. Rougeron describes the misery and backwardness of the Mountain's constituency in Allier in terms reminiscent of a feudal society: "Placed under the domination of great landed proprietors, sometimes owners of whole communes, masters of things and people, the rural population lived, for the most part, in veritable serfdom permitting one to believe that '89 never took place."[44] Only these large landholders could afford the investment and provide the forage for raising livestock, the agricultural enterprise best suited to the department's poor soil.[45]

The only town in Allier with a population over 10,000 in 1851 was Moulins, the departmental *chef-lieu*, with 17,318 inhabitants. Montluçon, the department's second town, had a population of only 8,922. The few industries in Allier were largely artisanal: shoemaking, weaving, tanning, and stone masonry. They were concentrated around Montluçon, on the newly opened Canal du Berry.[46] More advanced forms of industry had sprung up because of the canal. A new boat-building industry at Montluçon employed 400 men and women. The nearby coal deposits, at Commentry, could now reach a national market; and two coke furnaces had recently been established, with 327 workers in 1848.[47]

RHÔNE—THE URBAN RADICALISM OF LYON

With a population in 1851 of 574,745 concentrated on only 279,081 hectares, Rhône was preeminently an urban department. Its economic, social, and political life was dominated by the great manufacturing and commercial city of Lyon (population in 1851: 177,190) and its working-class suburbs of La Croix Rousse, La Guillotière, and Vaïse.[48]

The impact of this urban agglomeration—its commerce and industry—on the department's rural hinterland was to create an unusually specialized village population of weavers, artisans, and farmers. In fact, the census of 1851 found that only one-seventh of the department's population was primarily engaged in agriculture and that 50 percent of these peasants owned some land.[49] But a recent student of rural Rhône, Gilbert Garrier, points out that the average landholding was less than half a hectare and that most of the peasantry was involved in some form of sharecropping, renting, or wage labor to survive in a landscape "overloaded" with people.[50] Two activities dominated rural Rhône at mid-nineteenth century: weaving and viticulture. The weaving of cotton, and then of silk, had spread beyond Lyon to the point that it was absent in only three cantons by 1848. In some areas of Rhône, almost half the male population was at the loom full-time in periods of great demand.[51] According to Garrier, the weaver-peasant, neither completely removed from the land nor capable of surviving by farming alone, became the representative rural figure in Rhône.

The department's poor soil, however, was ideal for the production of quality wine of considerable commercial value. From the great bourgeois and aristocratic properties of the Beaujolais (north of Lyon), worked by prosperous sharecroppers, to the small proprietors of the plain around Lyon, to the tenants of the mountains south of the city, wine was the cash crop whose quality and quantity determined whether whole regions would have good or bad years. A considerable population of landless day laborers (20 percent of the agricultural population) and artisans engaged in cooperage, wine pressing, and transportation depended on the vines for their livelihood as well.[52] Unlike the poorer peasants of Allier and Jura, the farmers of Rhône were dependent on commercial transactions and wages for basic survival. The department did not even grow enough grain for the sustenance of its own rural population, let alone the urban masses of Lyon.

The collapse in the late forties of the textile trade *and* of the wine market began a peasant exodus in Rhône that continued through the empire and the Third Republic. If the crisis radicalized some artisans and peasant-weavers in the villages, the bulk of the rural population remained too dependent on the textile merchants and the landlords of the "noble" viticultural areas to move decisively left during the Second Republic: "The rejection of the 'red republic' of the democratic socialists had its origins in the very structure of property: the confiscation of the land by big property had prevented the formation and coming to consciousness of small peasant proprietors."[53] While scattered villages did shift to the left, it was the massive political abstention of the peasantry that gave political control of the department to "red" Lyon.

Located at the confluence of the Saône and Rhône rivers, Lyon was the natural shipping center of eastern, central, and southern France. Here the raw materials and finished goods of whole regions were brought together for transshipment to the rest of the nation or to Marseille for export. In 1841 the prefect of Rhône described the enormous quantity of goods that passed through the city:

> We find more than 200,000 tons of coal coming down the Rhône, destined for the cities along the river, 100 to 120,000 [tons] going up the Saône being distributed along its entire course as far as Mulhouse, 150 to 160,000 hectoliters of wine embarked . . . for Paris, . . . 18 to 19 million kilograms of salt crossing the department, merchandise entering or leaving the port . . . representing several millions in value, finally 350 to 400 tons of all kinds of products transshipped every day. . . . [54]

In 1832 a railroad line had been completed linking Lyon with the city of Saint-Etienne. It was extended further westward to Roanne in 1843, thereby establishing a rapid overland system of transportation (by train and stagecoach) between Lyon and Paris. This rail line carried so much freight and so many passengers in the latter years of the July Monarchy that its stockholders realized a yearly dividend of 10 percent on their initial investment.

Commerce was an important and enduring source of the city's economic importance, but the prosperity and social stability of Lyon in 1848 remained primarily dependent on a single fragile industry: silk weaving.

The silk thread of the Midi was brought to Lyon to be woven, dyed, printed, and often made into finished articles of clothing before being sold on the domestic and foreign markets. (The United States was a particularly important consumer of lyonnais silks.) A luxury trade, the manufacture of silk products depended on a steady demand from among the most wealthy classes in France and other countries. An economic depression, a political crisis, or even a change in fashion could knock the bottom out of the silk market. The thousands of weavers employed in the numerous small shops of Lyon and its suburbs would then be thrown out of work.

Indeed, the silk weavers of Lyon experienced a chronic economic depression that began early in the era of the July Monarchy and continued under the Second Republic. While the production of silk cloth more than tripled (from 440,000 kilograms in 1825 to 1,500,000 in 1847), the industry suffered several severe setbacks. When the American market for silk collapsed in 1837, fifteen-thousand looms were left idle in Lyon, and thirty-five-thousand people in the city and its suburbs were supported by charity for almost two years. American demand improved during the early forties but fell off sharply again in 1845. Only a fourth of the city's looms remained in operation, and the paralysis of the French economy during the last two years of the July Monarchy prevented the silk industry from making a recovery. Lyon, its suburbs, and the many small weaving towns of the department remained areas of unemployment and widespread misery at time of the February revolution and thoughout the period of the Second Republic.

Republicanism, socialism, and secret societies flourished in Lyon long before the revolution of 1848 broke out. The low wages and frequent unemployment of the weavers during the reign of Louis Philippe led to a tremendous growth of mutual aid societies in the workers' quarters of the city and in the densely populated suburbs. These groups included both the masters and the workers of the small shops, and their aim was to unite against the clothing manufacturers and wholesale merchants who set the piece rate for bolts of woven silk. In the early thirties, Lyon was twice the scene of armed weavers' uprisings against the city's notables and the government that protected their interests. By 1848 the nascent labor unions of the thirties had been transformed into socialist secret societies. These underground groups—the Voraces, Carbonari, Ventres Creux, Vautours, and Unionistes—were composed of relatively small numbers of active members. But in 1848 and 1849 they proved themselves capable of mobilizing thousands of supporters in the shops and slums of Lyon and its suburbs. Years of illegal existence gave these organizations an internal cohesion and discipline; Lyon was guaranteed a radical leadership under the republic made up primarily of artisans and masters. Their militant outlook, formed by years of economic depression and by experience on the barricades, was a major cause of the violence in the city's history after February 1848.

No sooner had the July Monarchy collapsed than the secret societies of Lyon came out of hiding and armed themselves. Thousands of muskets, tens of thousands of cartridges, and several cannons were taken from the city's surrounding forts and hidden in working-class neighborhoods. The Voraces completely supplanted the civil authorities in La Croix Rousse and held the suburb for three months. They patrolled the streets, delivered the mail, and even garrisoned the forts temporarily. In an effort to reduce unemployment in Lyon and to calm a population inflamed by the radical clubs' insistent demands for sweeping economic reforms, the Provisional Government opened National Workshops in the city during March 1848. A month later it ordered thousands of silk flags and ceremonial sashes from the local weavers. These measures were unsuccessful. While the suffering of the workers was temporarily alleviated, the February revolution had raised their expectations to such a pitch that Lyon remained in ferment throughout March and April 1848. In late March a mutiny led by radical soldiers broke out in the city's garrison. Early in April the Voraces and other groups marched across the border in a ragtag and abortive campaign to spread the French revolution to Savoy.

The elections of 23 April 1848 took place, therefore, in an atmosphere of continuing violence and political confusion throughout the department of Rhône. The radical groups banded together in a socialist Club Central, and the conservatives formed their own electoral committee. The lists of candidates presented to the department's voters were, however, hopelessly tangled mixtures of names and ideologies. The local legitimists and Orleanists managed to attract a considerable number of rural voters to their standards, but the urban vote was almost evenly divided between moderate and advanced republicans. Of the fourteen deputies elected to the Constituent Assembly, seven were republicans (four socialists and three moderates) and seven were conservatives. The victorious candidates were led by the moderate republican mayor of Lyon, who won 126,000 of the 130,000 ballots cast. A socialist printer came in second with 104,000 votes.

The June Days in Paris did not lead to a similar outburst in Lyon. The new government of General Cavaignac took advantage of the Parisian events to appoint a moderate republican prefect to replace the socialist commissioner of Rhône. The new administration immediately dissolved the National Guard of Lyon and its suburbs. House-to-house searches were carried out, and thirty-four thousand rifles and much of the ammunition distributed in February were returned to government hands. The military strength of the clubs appeared to have been broken in Lyon. The political activities and the propaganda of the radicals became more and more circumscribed by government repression.

Despite these blows suffered by the radical movement in Rhône, 1849 was to be a year of heady socialist victory in the elections to the Legislative

Assembly and of bloody rebellion against the government of Louis Napoleon. In May 1849 the department elected the socialist list in toto with well over half the vote. The Montagnard candidates received between 69,000 and 72,000 of the 120,000 ballots cast. The most successful of the Party of Order's candidates came in almost 10,000 votes behind the least popular member of the radical slate. Seven of the department's new deputies were artisans. Of the four other members of the delegation, two were national leaders of the Mountain (Mathieu de la Drôme and Raspail *fils*) and two were lawyers with long service to the secret societies.

Only a few weeks later, the Voraces led the workers of La Croix Rousse in a tragic repetition of the Parisian June Days of the previous year. The isolated lyonnais insurrection of June 1849 was put down by the regular army. Rhône and its neighboring departments were placed under martial law for the duration of the republic.

Lyon and its hinterland thus afforded a preview of the empire's garrison state long before Louis Napoleon's coup. Rhône and its metropolis, however, remained sources of acute concern among the police authorities and the conservative elite during the remainder of the republican era.

Appendix 2
The Standard Interpretation: Social Fear after 1849 as a Hoax

Marxism-Tocquevilleism dominates the historiography of the Second Republic. The work of Seignobos in the 1920s, of quasi Marxists like Duveau in the period surrounding the centennial of the revolution, and of such recent contributors as Tudesq, Girard, Guillemin, Price, Machin, and Merriman, despite many other differences, speaks with a single voice on the phenomenon of social fear and on the activity of the prefects and *procureurs-généraux* during the presidency of Louis Napoleon.[1] They all agree in seeing the actual threat of the "democratic and social" republic decisively defeated on the barricades in June 1848 and reduced to a pathetic shambles by the abject failure of the demonstrations against the Roman expedition in June 1849. The social fear that persisted after 1849 is therefore characterized as unreasonable: there was no real menace to the social order. These historians then shift their sights to the internal politics of the Party of Order and to the relations between the Legislative Assembly and the president, and offer their different explanations for the failure of the notables to preserve their conservative republic against Louis Napoleon's imperial pretensions.

Historians with methodologies and assumptions as diverse as those of Seignobos and Tudesq unite in concentrating on the political uses of fear after the June Days rather than on the sources and internal dynamics of the fear itself. Tudesq, writing in the contemporary vein of Marxist sociology, argues that the anxiety of the notables is significant only in explaining the formation of the Party of Order out of legitimist and Orleanist factions, which had warred for seventeen years under the July Monarchy.[2] The only scholar who has devoted a whole chapter to the notables' fear, Tudesq identifies fear only with the confusion and passivity of the social elite immediately after the February revolution. He argues that it disappeared even before the June Days: "stupor paralyzed energies for more or less lengthy periods of time: a few hours at Bordeaux; some months at Lyon."[3]

Seignobos takes an ambivalent position on the persistence of social fear in 1849, 1850, and 1851. He acknowledges that the notables remained apprehensive of the electoral strength of the democratic socialists during these years, but argues that the Elysée fanned this anxiety into outright terror as a calculated political maneuver to panic the assembly into revising the constitution so that Louis Napoleon could run for reelection. To Seignobos and to other scholars who were influenced by his work, notably F. Dutacq and Emile Dagnan, the villains were none other than the prefects and attorneys general themselves.

Seignobos, Dutacq, and Dagnan were the first historians to use the collection of bureaucratic reports for the period in the Archives Nationales. They charged the authors of these documents with exaggeration and deceit in describing conditions in their jurisdictions. To them, the red scare, which continued from June 1849 until the coup, was a hysterical obsession (even a hoax) perpetrated on a notability that should have been allowed to recover from its fears of 1848. Seignobos wrote:

> Republican secret societies were created. . . . No means remain for us to know the number of members, but official reports exaggerated it to the point of absurdity. Like judges in a witch-hunt, the magistrates, obsessed by an *idée fixe*, interpreted the facts reported by their subordinates by using a preconceived system. Any group of democratic electors meeting in a café or a house to work on an election campaign, sign a petition, or discuss the political situation appeared to them to be a secret society, called together by leaders to prepare an armed rising. . . . Red belts, ties or caps transformed themselves into rallying signals; a scuffle with policemen in a cabaret became a rebellion against the Police.[4]

Dutacq argued that the *complot* of Lyon of 1850 was really an elaborate government publicity stunt complete with *agents provocateurs* and "stool pigeons." Dagnan, in a series of articles on government repression in the west, center, and south of France, maintained that the attorneys general "stuffed" their reports with "unbelievable childishness."[5]

Three recent scholars—Adrien Dansette, Philippe Vigier, and Howard Payne—have taken the red scare more seriously and have even discussed a fear "psychosis" that took hold of the notables but was independent of any action by the bureaucracy.[6] They implicitly disagree with the view of social fear held by Seignobos and his contemporaries; yet neither Vigier, Payne, nor Dansette directly confronts the distrust with which these earlier scholars approached the reports and actions of the bureaucrats. Vigier, in fact, accuses the prefects and prosecutors of playing upon the existing fears of the notables.[7]

Without relating their observations to the veracity of bureaucratic reports, and without giving sufficient attention to the actual dynamic of social fear, these scholars point out that there was genuine cause for alarm on the part of the notables in the years between June 1849 and December 1851. They simply note that in the three days following the coup d'état, thousands of armed and organized Frenchmen rose in rebellion against Louis Napoleon Bonaparte in many places throughout France. This fact suggests the obvious corollary that "subversive activities" had been going on unimpeded by the vigor and vigilance of the police authorities.[8] In other words, perhaps the prefects and prosecutors were not exaggerating their problems in suppressing the left: perhaps, in fact, the political repression carried out under the Second Republic was not successful enough to satisfy the police authorities themselves. These are points that neither Vigier nor Dansette nor Payne nor any other historian of the Second Republic has made.

Until the last few years, American and British scholars have shown scant interest in the counterrevolutionary side of the Second Republic. Unfortunately, recent work on the period, while it sheds new light on the republic's "history from below," avoids the crucial issues of motivation and ideology (or collective *mentalité*) in describing the bureaucratic repression of 1849, 1850, and 1851. This apparent lack of concern with the causes of counterrevolution (as perceived and recorded by the prefects and *procureurs-généraux* themselves) is all the more striking since an American, Howard C. Payne, suggested the importance of social fear as a factor leading to the coup, in a pioneering article published almost fifteen years ago.[9] Yet recent attempts to explore the social history of the republic's political crisis by Roger Price, John M. Merriman, Ted W. Margadant, Howard Machin, and Vincent Wright continue the tradition of denying any dynamism and, therefore, any causal background to the bureaucrats' repressive drive.[10] Counterrevolution remains a reflex; the coup represents an evolution, not a revolution.

The scholars whose articles appear in Roger Price's collection *Revolution and Reaction* have, to their credit, worked together on various aspects of a complicated and challenging historical period. They represent a school of thought in social history that is strongly influenced by the work of Charles Tilly. In "How Protest Modernized in France: 1845-1855" and other essays, Tilly attempts to place the Second Republic within a long-term continuum of changing modes of lower-class mobilization leading to the mass parties and trade unions of modern times.[11] Placed between the "archaism" of eighteenth-century forms of protest and the "modernism" of twentieth-century political institutions, the Mountain of the Second Republic is seen as a significant, but doomed, instance of slow change in the French social system. Tilly's approach is an example of how a behavioral methodology leads some historians to quite traditional conclusions (à la Tocqueville and Marx) on the significance and thrust of repression during this troubled period. Indeed, the very lexicon of Tilly's behavioral modernization theory masks the intensity of the republic's social conflict and substitutes remarkably weak (though "clinical") words for the dramatic and necessarily radical drive of counterrevolution:

Although the process of revolution draws people into political consciousness, the process is not irreversible. From 1849 through 1851, we witness the gradual, deliberate demobilisation of most groups in the initial revolutionary coalition: the repression of the great insurrection of 1851 completed the demobilisation.[12]

Applications of Tilly's model to the Second Republic, while often challenging and always enlightening, curiously depoliticize this period of intense political and ideological stress. Placing due emphasis on "changing forms of protest" in rural France, they take little account of how a threatened elite responded to a novel situation of universal manhood suffrage and a mass democratic-socialist movement. They tell us a great deal about the ways and means by which radical ideas penetrated the countryside, but almost nothing about the terror, frustration, and ferocity of the notables.

Social fear or, for that matter, any other motivation for the "demobilization" of the left remain outside the bounds of behavioral explanation. Price argues that Louis Napoleon merely "posed" as a "saviour of society," cleverly manipulating a public opinion irrationally "obsessed" with a red menace that somehow never was.[13] Howard Machin maintains that the conservatives experienced a "neurotic anxiety," while Vincent Wright describes reports from prefects and prosecutors in the months following the coup as "replete with neurotic warnings."[14] In his larger study of four departments, *The Agony of the Republic*, John M. Merriman states at the outset: "First, I will not attempt to tell explicitly the story of the countermobilization of conservatives after the February revolution or of the evolution of a Bonapartist government staffed by civil servants who served loyally although they were not necessarily Bonapartist. The counterrevolution is not problematic."[15] Frequently reading prefectoral intentions for genuine police accomplishments, Merriman considers the repression a success *before* the coup.[16] The republic's final "agony," rather painless in Merriman's estimation, is portrayed as a final "mopping up" of an intimidated, often leaderless, and usually isolated and localized democratic-socialist remnant. Despite scattered mention of bureaucratic reports voicing concern about the size and strength of the Mountain, he consistently concludes (or assumes) that the police machinery was more "modern" and more "efficient" than the evolving organization of the left. Intent as he is on measuring the success or failure of police behavior in terms of the Mountain's behavior, Merriman has studied a great deal of bureaucratic correspondence without taking seriously the concerns and fears constantly expressed by the prefects and *procureurs-généraux* themselves. Like others applying Tilly's model, he has preferred his own "modern" judgment of police efficiency to the explicitly stated doubts and fears of the historical actors who wrote the documents.

Notes

The following abbreviations have been used throughout the notes. See the Bibliography under "General Reference Sources" for the reference works abbreviated here.

A.D.	Archives Départementales
A.N.	Achives Nationales
B.N.	Bibliothèque Nationale
D.B.F.	*Dictionnaire de biographie française*
D.B.M.O.F.	*Dictionnaire biographique du mouvement ouvrier français*
D.P.F.	*Dictionnaire des parlementaires français*
M.I.	Ministry of the Interior
M.J.	Ministry of Justice
P.	prefect
P.G.	*procureur-général* (attorney general)
P.R.	*procureur de la république*
S.G.F.	*Statistique Générale de la France*
S.P.	subprefect

Introduction

1. Frederick F. Ridley and Jean Blondel, *French Administration* (London, 1969), p. 160.
2. Alexandre-François Vivien, président de la section de législation du Conseil d'état, *Rapport sur le projet de loi relatif à l'administration intérieure* (Paris, n.d.), found in pamphlet form in A.D. Allier, M643³.
3. Ibid.
4. Pierre Legendre, *Histoire de l'administration de 1750 à nos jours* (Paris, 1968), p. 250.
5. Chiappe, a twentieth-century prefect of police, quoted in Legendre, *Histoire de l'administration*, p. 259.
6. See for example Adrien Dansette, *Louis-Napoléon à la conquête du pouvoir* (Paris, 1961, and Henri Guillemin, *Le Coup du 2 décembre* (Paris, 1951).
7. Max Weber, *The Theory of Social and Economic Organization*, ed. Talcott Parsons, trans. A.M. Henderson and Talcott Parsons (New York, 1969), pp. 333-334.
8. Michel Crozier, *The Bureaucratic Phenomenon*, (Chicago, 1964), pp. 89-112.
9. Arno J. Mayer, *Dynamics of Counterrevolution in Europe, 1870-1956* (New York, 1971), p. 72.

10. Charles Seignobos, *La Révolution de 1848—le second empire* (Paris, 1921); François Goguel, *L'Influence des systèmes électoraux sur la vie politique* (Paris, n.d.); Gaston Génique, *L'Election de l'assemblée législative en 1849* (Paris, 1921); and Jacques Bouillon "Les Démocrates socialistes aux élections de 1849," *Revue française de science politique*, VI (1956), 70-95.
11. Gougel, *L'Influence*, p. 74.
12. Bouillon, "Les Démocrates socialistes," p. 81.
13. Ibid.

1 An Anatomy of a Permanent Counterrevolution

1. Arno J. Mayer, *Dynamics*, p. 35
2. Charles Tilly, *The Vendée* (Cambridge, 1964), and Jacques Godechot, *La Contre-révolution: doctrine et action (1789-1804)* (Paris, 1961).
3. Mayer, *Dynamics*, p. 35.
4. Ibid., p. 36.
5. René Rémond, *The Right Wing in France from 1815 to de Gaulle*, trans. James M. Laux (Philadelphia, 1968).
6. François Goguel, *La Politique des partis sous la IIIᵉ république*, 3rd ed. (Paris, 1957).
7. Stanley Hoffmann, "Paradoxes of the French Political Community," in *In Search of France*, ed. Stanley Hoffmann, et al. (Cambridge, 1965), p. 8.
8. Ibid., p. 7
9. Ibid., pp. 13-14.
10. Ibid., p. 14.
11. See for example Howard C. Payne, *The Police State of Louis Napoleon Bonaparte* (Seattle, 1966), pp. 3-33; Legendre, *Histoire de l'administration*, pp. 246-282; Marcel Le Clère, *Histoire de la police* (Paris, 1971), passim; and Irene Collins, *The Government and the Newspaper Press in France: 1814-1881* (Oxford, 1959), passim.
12. The theme of "permanent counterrevolutionary" mobilization of political institutions, economic structure, and social strata has been central to the formation of the "Common Program" of 1972 and to the literature accompanying this troubled union of communists, socialists, and left radicals. See especially Jean Fabre, François Hincker, and Luciene Sève, *Les Communistes et l' état* (Paris, 1977); and Jean-Pierre Chevènement, *Les Socialistes, les communistes et les autres* (Paris, 1977). Work on specific crises in French history since 1870 is frequently suggestive, but a general consideration of this theme remains to be written. See Sanford Elwitt, *The Making of the Third Republic: Class and Politics in France, 1868-1884* (Baton Rouge, 1975). See also the difference in approach to the events of May-June 1968 in Stanley Hoffmann, "Confrontation in May 1968," in *Decline or Renewal: France*

Since the 1930s, ed. Stanley Hoffmann (New York, 1974); Henri Lefebvre, *L'Explosion* (Paris, 1970); and Alfred Williner, *The Action Image of Society*, trans. A.M. Sheridan Smith (New York, 1970).

13. Alexis de Tocqueville, *Recollections*, ed. J.P. Mayer and A.P. Kerr, trans. George Lawrence (Garden City, 1971); idem, *The Old Regime and the French Revolution*, trans. Stuart Gilbert (Garden City, 1955); Karl Marx, *The Eighteenth Brumaire of Louis Bonaparte*, trans. anon. (New York, 1969); and idem, *Class Struggles in France*, trans. anon. (New York, 1964).

14 Classics of the genre include A. Rossi (Angelo Tasca), *The Rise of Italian Fascism* (London, 1939); Barrington Moore Jr., *Social Origins of Totalitarianism and Democracy: Lord and Peasant in the Making of the Modern World* (Boston, 1966) and Franz Neumann, *Behemoth* (New York, 1942).

15. Tocqueville, *Recollections*, p. 265.

16. Tocqueville, *Old Regime*, p. xiii.

17. Alexis de Tocqueville, "Letter of December 11, 1851, to the London *Times*," in *December 2, 1851*, ed. John B. Halsted (Garden City, 1971).

18. Marx, *Brumaire*, p. 19.

19. Friedrich Engels, "Introduction" (1895), in Marx, *Class Struggles*, p. 11.

20. Marx, *Brumaire*, pp. 122-123. In *Class Struggles*, Marx saw this freeing of revolutionary potential within the short-term crisis itself.

21. Marx, *Class Struggles*, p. 33.

22. Marx, *Brumaire*, pp. 131-135.

23. Ibid., p. 135.

24. Marx, *Brumaire*, p. 106.

25. Ibid., pp. 56-59.

26. Ibid., pp. 74, 77, 127-130. It is a common misunderstanding among modern scholars to see *Brumaire* as a pioneering analysis of the role of the petty bourgeosie in supporting authoritarian regimes. Marx places most of the lower-middle class squarely, and accurately, in the radical camp under the Second Republic.

27. See especially Louis Chevalier, *Laboring Classes, Dangerous Classes in Paris During the First Half of the Nineteenth Century*, trans. Frank Jellinek (New York, 1973).

28. Marx, *Brumaire*, pp. 45, 64.

29. Ibid., pp. 129-130.

30. Ibid., p. 123.

31. Ibid., p. 124.

32. Ibid., p. 125.

33. Robert Michels, *Political Parties: A Sociological Study of the Oligarchic Tendencies of Modern Democracy*, trans. Eden Paul and Cedar Paul (Glencoe, 1962), p. 15.

34. Ibid., p. 228.

35. Ibid., pp. 227-253.

36. Ibid., p. 55.
37. Ibid., p. 52.
38. Charles de Rémusat, *Mémoires de ma vie*, introduced and annotated by Charles H. Pouthas (Paris, 1962), III, 255.
39. Ibid., p. 269.
40. See Antonio Gramsci, *Selections from the Prison Notebooks*, ed. and trans. Quintin Hoare and Geoffrey Nowell Smith (New York, 1975), and Georg Lukács, *History and Class Consciousness: Studies in Marxist Dialectics*, trans. Rodney Livingstone (Cambridge, 1971).
41. Neil J. Smelser, *Theory of Collective Behavior* (London, 1962), p. 120. Smelser uses Clyde Kluckhohn's definition of values.
42. Ibid., p. 356.
43. Gustave Flaubert, *Sentimental Education*, trans. Robert Baldick (London, 1972), p. 334.
44. Ibid., pp. 409-410.

2 The Contending Social Factions ca. 1840-1848

1. See chapter 3 for the career patterns of the prefects and *procureurs-généraux*.
2. Vincent E. Starzinger, *Juste-Milieu Political Theory in France and England* (Charlottesville, 1965), pp. 14-15 (his emphasis).
3. Rémond, *The Right in France*, pp. 101-106.
4. Ibid., p. 125.
5. Ibid., pp. 113-114.
6. See especially Félix Ponteil, *La Monarchie parlementaire: 1815-1848* (Paris, 1949); André-Jean Tudesq, *Les Grands notables en France (1840-1849); étude historique d'une psychologie sociale*, 2 vols. (Paris, 1964); and two contemporary accounts: Tocqueville, *Recollections;* and Rémusat, *Mémoires*, III.
7. Tudesq, *Les Grands notables*, I, 98.
8. Ibid., I, 88.
9. Rémond, *The Right in France*, pp. 123-124.
10. See Paul Bastid, *Doctrines et institutions politiques de la seconde république*, 2 vols. (Paris, 1945).
11. Tudesq, *Les Grands notables*, I, 88-89.
12. Rémond, *The Right in France*, p. 123.
13. Félix Ponteil, *Les Classes Bourgeoises et l'avènement de la démocratie 1815-1914* (Paris, 1968), p. 95.
14. Georges Weill, *Histoire du parti républicain en France (1814-1870)* (Paris, 1928), pp. 93-94.
15. Louis Girard, *Le Libéralisme en France de 1814 à 1848: doctrine et mouvement* (Paris, 1967), p. 35.
16. Collins, *Government and Press*, p. 82.

17. Ibid., pp. 82-83.
18. Ibid.
19. Ibid., p. 85.
20. Ibid., p. 84; and Frederick A. De Luna, *The French Republic Under Cavaignac: 1848* (Princeton, 1969), p. 21.
21. A. Jardin and A.-J. Tudesq, *La France des Notables* (Paris, 1973), I, 141.
22. Collins, *Government and Press*, p. 83.
23. William L. Langer, *Political and Social Upheaval: 1832-1852* (New York, 1969), p. 42.
24. Barante quoted in Starzinger, *Juste-Milieu*, p. 64.
25. Benjamin Constant, "On Popular Sovereignty and its Limits," in *French Liberalism 1789-1848*, ed. W.M. Simon (New York, 1972), pp. 64-66; and Girard, *Libéralisme*, pp. 13-25.
26. Langer, *Upheaval*, p. 54.
27. Frederick B. Artz, *Reaction and Revolution: 1814-1832* (New York, 1934), p. 94.
28. Guizot quoted by Starzinger, *Juste-Milieu*, pp. 64-64.
29. Langer, *Upheaval*, p. 74.
30. Tudesq, *Les Grands notables*, II, 567.
31. Léon Epszstein, *L'Economie et la morale aux débuts du capitalisme industriel en France et en Grande Bretagne* (Paris, 1966), p. 70.
32. Shepard Bancroft Clough, *France, A History of National Economics* (New York, 1964), p. 158.
33. Epszstein, *L'Economie et la morale*, p. 73.
34. Ibid.
35. Chevalier, *Dangerous Classes*, pt. 2, passim.
36. Epszstein, *L'Economie et la morale*, p. 76.
37. Ibid., p. 77.
38. Chevalier, *Dangerous Classes*, pt. 2, and Tudesq, *Les Grands notables*, II, chap. 1.
39. Epszstein, *L'Economie et la morale*, p. 82.
40. Tudesq, *Les Grands notables*, II, 569.
41. Girard, *Libéralisme*, p. 118.
42. Weill, *Parti républicain*, pp. 139-140.
43. De Luna, *French Republic*, pp. 27-28.
44. Bastid, *Doctrines et institutions*, I, 46.
45. De Luna, *French Republic*, p. 28.
46. Maurice Agulhon, *1848 ou l'apprentissage de la République* (Paris, 1973), p. 19, on the exceptional characteristics of Le Mans, a constituency radicalized by its proximity to Vendéen *chouannerie*.
47. Bastid, *Doctrines et institutions*, I, 68.
48. Girard, *Libéralisme*, p. 130.
49. Arthur Rosenberg, *Democracy and Socialism* (Boston, 1965), pp. 46-47.
50. See D.C. Charlton, *Secular Religions in France, 1815-1870* (New York, 1963); Frank E. Manuel, *The Prophets of Paris* (Cambridge, 1962); Eliz-

abeth Eisenstein, *The First Professional Revolutionary: Filippo Buonarotti* (Cambridge, 1959); Alan B. Spitzer, *The Revolutionary Theories of Louis Auguste Blanqui* (New York, 1957); and Bastid, *Doctrines et institutions,* I, 55.

51. Bastid, *Doctrines et institutions,* I, 55.
52. Langer, *Upheaval,* p. 216.
53. Bastid, *Doctrines et institutions,* I, 69, and Rosenberg, *Democracy and Socialism,* p. 35.
54. Collins, *Government and Press,* p. 90. The large-circulation daily newspapers of France date back to Girardin's *La Presse* and Dr. Véron's *Le Constitutionnel.* Founded in the forties, both journals marked a revolution in mass-circulation, cheap-newspaper production by accepting advertisements (and charging substantial fees for the service) and by serializing the latest works of popular novelists *before* these novels were published in book form.
55. See Georges Duveau, *1848: The Making of a Revolution,* trans. Ann Carter (New York, 1968), pp. 203-230.
56. Ibid., pp. 224-225.
57. Girard, *Libéralisme,* p. 120, and Spitzer, *Blanqui,* passim.
58. Langer, *Upheaval,* p. 336, and Peter Amann, *Revolution and Mass Democracy: The Paris Club Movement of 1848* (Princeton, 1975), chap. 1.
59. Agulhon, *1848,* p. 7.
60. This section is based on the treatments of legitimism in Girard, *Libéralisme,* and in Rémond, *The Right in France.*
61. See Stendhal's *The Green Huntsman.*
62. Rémond, *The Right in France,* p. 93.
63. Tudesq, *Les Grands notables,* II, 697-727.
64. Girard, *Libéralisme,* pp. 67-68.
65. André-Jean Tudesq, *L'Election présidentielle de Louis-Napoléon Bonaparte: 10 décembre 1848* (Paris, 1965), pp. 18, 23-24.
66. De Luna, *French Republic,* p. 72.
67. Dansette, *Louis-Napoléon,* p. 188.
68. Ibid., pp. 188-189.
69. Ibid., p. 145.
70. François-Pierre-Guillaume Guizot, *Memoirs to Illustrate the History of My Time* (London, n.d.), VIII, 4-8.
71. Tocqueville, *Recollections,* pp. 7-9.
72. Ibid., p. 6.
73. Rémond, *The Right in France,* p. 107.
74. Gordon Wright, *France in Modern Times* (New York, 1968), p. 154.
75. Girard, *Libéralisme,* p. 48.
76. Sherman Kent, *Electoral Procedure Under Louis Philippe* (New Haven, 1937), pp. 190-191.
77. Jardin and Tudesq, *La France des Notables,* I, 245.
78. Gaetano Mosca, *The Ruling Class, Elementi di scienza politica,* ed. A.

Livingston, trans. Hannah D. Kahn (New York, 1939), chaps. 15 and 16; Michels, *Political Parties*, pt. 2, chap. 6.

79. Tudesq, *Les Grands notables*, II, 966-970.
80. Jardin and Tudesq, *La France des Notables*, I, 246.
81. Tocqueville, *Recollections*, pp. 16-17.
82. For a more detailed discussion of this period and the social fears of the notables see Tudesq, *Les Grands notables*, II, pt. 3. I do not share his categorization of fear as first "physical" and then "social" and disagree with his dating of the notables' reassurance and reassertion to 1849; yet his work remains a pioneering effort to apply social psychology to the crisis of an oligarchy.
83. Tocqueville, *Recollections*, p. 82.
84. Ibid., pp. 72-74.
85. Docteur Véron, *Mémoires d'un bourgeois de Paris* (Paris, 1896), VI, 41.
86. Prosper Mérimée, *Correspondance générale*, ed. by Maurice Parturier, Pierre Josserand, and Jean Mallion (Paris, 1946), V, 258.
87. Justin Godart, *A Lyon en 1848: Les Voraces* (Paris, 1948), p. 62.
88. Joseph Bergier, *Le Journal d'un bourgeois de Lyon en 1848*, published and annotated by Justin Godart (Paris, 1924).
89. *Le Constitutionnel*, 12 March 1848.
90. Quoted in Tudesq, *Les Grands notables*, II, 1006.
91. *Le Constitutionnel*, 4 April 1848.
92. Tudesq, *Les Grands notables*, II, 1018.
93. Ibid., p. 1020.
94. Tocqueville, *Recollections*, p. 83.
95. Ibid., p. 86.
96. *Le Courrier de la Gironde*, 14 March 1848.
97. De Luna, *French Republic*, pp. 110-112.
98. *La Réforme*, 1 May 1848.
99. Tocqueville, *Recollections*, pp. 124-125.
100. See Amann, *Revolution and Mass Democracy*, pp. 233-235, and Agulhon, *1848*, pp. 62-64.
101. Amann, *Revolution and Mass Democracy*, p. 285.
102. Rémusat, *Mémoires*, III, 312.
103. *Journal des Débats*, 18 May 1848.
104. Quoted in Tudesq, *Les Grands notables*, II, 1076.
105. *Le Courrier de la Gironde*, 21 May 1848.
106. Odilon Barrot, *Mémoires Posthumes* (Paris, 1875), II, 206.
107. Charles Schmidt, *Des Ateliers Nationaux aux Barricades de Juin* (Paris, 1948), p. 21.
108. Rémusat, *Mémoires*, II, 322.
109. Schmidt, *Barricades de Juin*, p. 27.
110. Alvin R. Calman, *Ledru-Rollin and the Second French Republic* (New York, 1922), p. 206.
111. Tocqueville, *Recollections*, p. 168.

112. Ibid., p. 169.
113. *La Gazette des Tribunaux*, 1 July 1848.
114. Lord Normanby, *Year of Revolution: From a Journal Kept in Paris in 1848* (London, 1857), pp. 74-75. For "atrocities" "reported" in the press and mentioned in this paragraph, see *Le Constitutionnel*, 28-29 June 1848, and *La Gazette des Tribunaux*, 25, 27, 28, 30 June 1848.
115. *La Réforme*, 1 July 1848.
116. *Le Courrier de la Gironde*, 1 July 1848.
117. *Le Courrier de Lyon*, 2 July 1848.
118. Calman, *Ledru-Rollin*, p. 221.
119. De Luna, *French Republic*, pp. 204-205.
120. Ibid., p. 205.
121. Seignobos, *Révolution de 1848*, p. 110.
122. Collins, *Government and Press*, p. 102.
123. Ibid., p. 105.
124. Ibid., p. 106.
125. Seignobos, *Révolution de 1848*, p. 110.
126. Both De Luna and Collins are suprisingly weak in their descriptions of the dynamics, technicalities, and effectiveness of press control. This description is based on my own research; see chapter 5.

3 Career Patterns of the Prefects and *Procureurs-Généraux*

1. Legendre, *Histoire de l'administration*, p. 53.
2. Ibid., p. 114.
3. Ibid., p. 117.
4. Ibid., p. 118.
5. Ibid.
6. Ibid.
7. Ibid., p. 141.
8. Ibid.
9. Ibid., p. 140.
10. Ibid., pp. 135-143.
11. Pierre Henry, *Histoire des préfets—cent cinquante ans d'administration provinciale: 1800-1950* (Paris, 1950), p. 155.
12. Ibid.
13. Ridley and Blondel, *French Administration*, p. 97.
14. Legendre, *Histoire de l'administration*, p. 140.
15. See Ridley and Blondel, *French Administration*, pp. 125-159.
16. Legendre, *Histoire de l'administration*, p. 254.
17. Tudesq, *Les Grands notables*, I, 401.
18. This description of the "chain of command" under the attorneys general is based on my own research.
19. Henry, *Histoire des préfets*, p. 155.

20. Girard, *Libéralisme*, pp. 189-191.
21. Bernard Le Clère and Vincent Wright, *Les Préfets du Second Empire* (Paris, 1973), p. 191.
22. Henry, *Histoire des préfets*, p. 156.
23. Calman, *Ledru-Rollin*, p. 112.
24. Ibid.
25. Ibid., pp. 114-115.
26. Ibid., p. 129.
27. Albert Charles, *La Révolution de 1848 et la seconde république à Bordeaux et dans le département de la Gironde* (Bordeaux, 1945), p. 112.
28. Ibid., pp. 112-123.
29. De Luna, *French Republic*, pp. 110-115.
30. Henry, *Histoire des préfets*, p. 158.
31. Ibid.
32. Ibid.
33. Ibid.
34. Ibid., p. 159.
35. On Cazavan's ephemeral tenure as prefect of Vendée, see L. Morauzeau, "Aspects vendéens de la Seconde République," in *Revue d'études historiques et archéologiques*, ed. Société d'émulation de la Vendée (Luçon, 1960), p. 67.
36. A.N., F^{1b1}, Coquet dossier, M.I. to Coquet, 23 November 1849; A.N., F^{1b1}, Wissocq dossier, M.I. to Wissocq, 23 November 1849.
37. Wissocq dossier, memorandum of interview between M.I. and M. Drouyn de Lhuys, 9 January 1849. Drouyn de Lhuys said: "M. de Wissocq . . . a su conquérir l'estime et l'affection des habitants par son zèle, sa capacité et ses manières douces et conciliantes."
38. Coquet dossier, Marie to M.I., 8 July 1848.
39. Coquet dossier, Marie to M.I., 8 July 1848.
40. Wissocq dossier, Wissocq to M.I., 24 May 1848.
41. Ibid.
42. Ibid.
43. A.N., F^{1b1}, Ambert dossier, undated and unsigned memorandum.
44. Ambert dossier, undated and unsigned memorandum; Coquet dossier, undated and unsigned memorandum.
45. Wissocq dossier, Wissocq to M.I., 24 May 1848.
46. Ibid.
47. Coquet dossier, undated and unsigned memorandum; Wissocq dossier, undated *Notice individuelle*; Ambert dossier, undated and unsigned memorandum.
48. I have not included Chambrun and Haussmann in this calculation. Both were extremely wealthy and increased the average to over 20,000 francs.
49. A.N., F^{1b1}, Chanal dossier, Chanal to M.I., letter asking for a prefectoral post, n.d.

50. Ibid.
51. Ibid., unsigned service memorandum written in 1850; Henry, *Histoire des préfets*, p. 158.
52. Chanal dossier, unsigned memorandum of 1850.
53. Ibid., another unsigned memorandum of 1850 charging Chanal with "sinon infidélité à ses devoirs, du moins l'inexpérience."
54. Ibid., *Notice individuelle* for 1851.
55. Ibid., copy of *registre des actes de naissance*, 1811, 1ᵉ *Arrondissement* of Paris, 22 June 1811.
56. Ibid., unsigned memorandum of 1850 explaining Chanal's dismissal.
57. Ibid., Prince Napoleon to M.I., 17 January 1870.
58. Ibid.
59. Ibid., *Notice individuelle* for 1849.
60. A.N., F1b1, Neveux dossier, Neveux to M.I., 2 August 1831. See also Albert Charles, "Un exemple de carrière administrative dans la première moitié du siècle dernier: le Baron Neveux," *Revue historique de Bordeaux*, XLIII (1954), 229-240.
61. Charles, "Un exemple de carrière," p. 230.
62. Ibid., pp. 230-231.
63. Ibid., p. 233.
64. Ibid.
65. Ibid., p. 234.
66. A.N., F1b1, Pagès dossier, unsigned memorandum of 1830. Only the year is written on the document.
67. Tudesq, *Les Grands notables*, I, 516.
68. Pagès dossier, Pagès to M.I., request for assignment, 20 October 1848.
69. Ibid.
70. Ibid., letter of seven deputies to M.I., 21 October 1848; ibid., undated service memorandum.
71. A.N., F1b1, Charnailles dossier, passim. For General Baraguey d'Hilliers, see *D.B.F.*, v, 169-172.
72. A.N., F1b1, Brian dossier, *Notice individuelle* for 1837.
73. Ibid., minister of the navy and colonies, Vice Admiral Amauret to M.I., 13 May 1837; ibid., prefect of Seine-Inférieure, Baron Dupont-Delporte, to M.I., 22 March 1838.
74. Ibid., *Notice individuelle* for 1849.
75. A.N., F1b1, Maupas dossier, *Notice individuelle* for 1840; and Georges Rougeron, *Les Administrateurs du département de l'Allier* (Montluçon, 1959), p. 51.
76. Maupas dossier, *Notice individuelle* for 1851.
77. Rougeron, *Les Administrateurs*, p. 52.
78. Charlemagne-Emile de Maupas, *Memoirs of the Coup d'Etat*, trans. Lord Kerry (London, n.d.), p. 179.

79. Ibid.
80. Ibid., p. 181.
81. A.N., F¹ᵇ¹, Tourangin dossier, personal note M.I. to Tourangin, 27 September 1833.
82. Ibid., M.I. to Tourangin, 24 May 1849.
83. Ibid., Tourangin to M.I., 11 June 1849.
84. A.N., F¹ᵇ¹, Arthur Tourangin dossier, report on subprefect, prefect Eure-et-Loire to M.I. for 1856.
85. A.N., F¹ᵇ¹, Darcy dossier, unsigned and undated memorandum.
86. Ibid.
87. Ibid.
88. A.N., F¹ᵇ¹, La Coste dossier, *Bulletin de renseignements* for 1836.
89. Ibid.
90. Ibid., *Rapport au président de la république* from M.I., 1849.
91. Ibid.
92. Ibid., *Bulletin de renseignements* for 1836.
93. Morauzeau, "Aspects vendéens," p. 68.
94. A.N. F¹ᵇ¹, Bonnin dossier, Fontenay City Council, mayor, National Guard officers letter to M.I., 8 March 1848.
95. Ibid.
96. Henry, *Histoire des préfets*, p. 158.
97. Bonnin dossier, unsigned M.I. memorandum, 12 February 1852.
98. Ibid., prefect of police to M.I., 22 April 1863.
99. Ibid., prefect of Basses-Pyrénées (Beaumont) to M.I., n.d. 1832 and n.d. 1834.
100. Ibid., prefect of police to M.I., 22 April 1863.
101. A.N., F¹ᵇ¹, Besson dossier, M.I. "Note" (date illegible).
102. Ibid., *Bulletin de renseignements* for 1860.
103. Ibid., General Fabvier to M.I., 24 April 1831.
104. Ibid., Devienne to M.I., n.d. 1846; ibid., prefect of Rhône to M.I., report on his secretary general for 1846.
105. Ibid., *Bulletin de renseignements* for 1860.
106. A.N., F¹ᵇ¹, Vincent dossier, General Baudrand to Count Duchatel (M.I.), 6 May 1843.
107. Ibid., Vincent to M.I., May 1848; ibid., *Bulletin de renseignements* for 1849.
108. Ibid., Vincent to M.I., 22 March 1845.
109. Ibid.
110. Ibid., General Baudrand to M.I., 6 May 1843.
111. Ibid., prefect of Meurthe to M.I., 5 October 1840.
112. Ibid., Vincent to M.I., May 1848.
113. Ibid., *Notice individuelle* of 1849.
114. Ibid., Count de La Morlière to President Louis Napoleon Bonaparte, 19 February 1849.

115. Ibid.
116. Ibid., minister of public works to M.I., 20 August 1850 (while on *tournée* with president).
117. A.N., F[1b1], Becquey dossier, passim.
118. A.N., F[1b1], Lagarde dossier, passim.
119. Becquey dossier, Jean Calmon to M.I., 12 March 1840.
120. Ibid.
121. Ibid., Drouyn de Lhuys to M.I., n.d.
122. Ibid., Joseph Périer to M.I., 18 November 1838; ibid., Joseph Périer to M.I., 10 March 1841; ibid., Comte de Mosbourg to M.I., 24 September 1841; ibid., Jean Calmon to M.I., 13 September 1841.
123. Charnailles dossier, *Bulletin de renseignements* for 1849.
124. Ibid., Countess de Danremont and General Baraguey d'Hilliers to M.I., 12 January 1849.
125. Tudesq, *Les Grands notables*, II, 1095-1096.
126. Rougeron, *Les Administrateurs*, p. 53.
127. Dansette, *Louis-Napoléon*, p. 302.
128. For General Baraguey d'Hilliers, see *D.B.F.*, v, 169-172.
129. Ibid.
130. Dansette, *Louis-Napoléon*, p. 306.
131. A.N., F[1b1], Boby de la Chapelle dossier, *Bulletin de renseignements* for 1860.
132. Tudesq, *Les Grands notables*, I, 431.
133. Boby de la Chapelle dossier, copy of *registre des actes de naissance* Provins (Seine-et-Marne), 11 October 1812. His uncle, Nicolas-Claude-François Simon, subprefect at Provins, was a witness.
134. Ibid., Jean Calmon, director general, Bureau of Land Registration to M.I., 5 April 1840.
135. Ibid., *Bulletin de renseignements* for 1841.
136. Ibid., Boby de la Chapelle to M.I., 28 February 1848.
137. Ibid., M.I. memorandum, n.d. 1849, and minister of war to M.I., 13 January 1849.
138. Dansette, *Louis-Napoléon*, pp. 325-341.
139. Ibid.
140. Bonnin dossier, unsigned M.I. memorandum, 12 February 1852.
141. Ibid., prefect of police to M.I., 22 April 1863.
142. Morauzeau, "Aspects vendéens," p. 71.
143. La Coste dossier, La Coste to M.I., 26 October 1851.
144. Dansette, *Louis-Napoléon*, p. 367.
145. Dutacq and A. Latreille, *Histoire de Lyon de 1814 à 1940* (Lyon, 1952), p. 166.
146. Ibid.
147. Neveux dossier, M.I. to Neveux, 27 November 1851.
148. Charles, "Un exemple de carrière," pp. 236-237.

149. Ibid., p. 238.
150. Becquey dossier, P.G. of Paris to M.I., 17 December 1851.
151. Pagès dossier, unsigned and undated memorandum.
152. Darcy dossier, unsigned and undated memorandum.
153. Ibid.
154. Lagarde dossier, memorandum drafted for M.I. in margin of letter of Lagarde to M.I., 13 December 1852.
155. Le Clère and Wright, *Les Préfets*, p. 27.
156. Chanal dossier, Chanal (prefect of Ain) to M.I., 5 December 1851, in which Chanal reiterated his resignation submitted 3 December.
157. Ibid., passim., and le Clère and Wright, *Les Préfets*, p. 23.
158. Henry, *Histoire des préfets*, p. 105.
159. Besson dossier, Besson to M.I., 28 February 1848.
160. Ibid., M.I. to Besson, 22 December 1850.
161. Morauzeau, "Aspects vendéens," p. 71.
162. Maupas, *Memoirs*, p. 135.
163. Ibid.
164. Ibid., p. 136. Lord Kerry's translation, although accurate, is awkward. The reader should consult Charlemagne-Emile de Maupas, *Mémoires sur le second empire*, 2 vols., (Paris, 1884), I.
165. Maupas, *Memoirs*, p. 136.
166. Emile Levasseur, "Un épisode du second ministère de Léon Faucher," *La Révolution de 1848*, III (1906), 3-13.
167. Ibid., p. 11.
168. Maupas, *Memoirs*, p. 139.
169. See Le Clère and Wright, *Les Préfets*, pp. 19-29. Unfortunately the authors are at pains to avoid such a conclusion despite their admirable presentation of the evidence. It is not until much later in the study, when they describe the final days of the Second Empire, that they discuss *"La dépolitisation des préfets."* See pp. 206-209.
170. A.N., F1b1, Haussmann dossier, passim., and Baron Haussmann, *Mémoires*, 3 vols. (Paris, 1890-1893), I and II.
171. A.N., F1b1, Pougeard du Limbert dossier, *Bulletins de renseignements* for 1848, 1849.
172. A.N., F1b1, Chambrun dossier, *Bulletin de renseignements* 1850.
173. Ibid., Portalis to M.I., n.d. 1850.
174. On Chambrun's subsequent career, see *D.B.F.*, VIII, 267-268.
175. Le Clère and Wright, *Les Préfets*, pp. 280-281.
176. A.N., F1b1, La Hante dossier, *Bulletin de renseignements* for 1852, P. of Morbihan to M.I., 5 April 1852.
177. Quoted in Le Clère and Wright, *Les Préfets*, p. 184.
178. Ibid., *annexe 5*.
179. Tudesq, *Les Grands notables*, I, 141.
180. *Almanach National* (Paris, 1850), passim; *Almanach National* (Paris, 1852), passim.

181. Jean Maurain, *Baroche, ministre de Napoleon III: un bourgeois français au XIXᵉ siècle, d'après ses papiers inédits* (Paris, 1936), p. 45.
182. Tudesq, *Les Grands notables*, i, 250.
183. See *Almanach National* for 1850 and 1852.
184. A.N., BB⁶ ii, Troplong dossier, *Notice individuelle* for 1850.
185. Ibid., Troplong's brother to M.J., 15 March 1847.
186. *Almanach National*, 1850.
187. Troplong dossier, Troplong to M.J., 7 January 1850; ibid., Devienne to M.J., 2 December 1851.
188. Ibid., memorandum to M.J. from personnel section, 26 January 1852.
189. Ibid., M.I. to M.J., 28 December 1849.
190. Ibid., memorandum of 26 January 1852.
191. Dansette, *Louis-Napoléon*, p. 353.
192. Quoted in Maurain, *Baroche*, p. 103.
193. Dutacq and Latreille, *Histoire de Lyon*, p. 140.
194. A.N., BB⁶ ii, Alcock dossier, service list, n.d.
195. *D.B.F.*, i, 1336.
196. Alcock dossier, service list, n.d.
197. Charles Raginel, *Histoire des votes des représentants du peuple dans nos assemblées nationales depuis la révolution de 1848*, 2 vols. (Paris, 1851), i, see entry for Loire, pages are not numbered.
198. Ibid.
199. A.N., BB⁶ ii, Gilardin dossier, service list, n.d.
200. Ibid.
201. A.N., BB⁶ ii, Loyson dossier, service list, n.d.
202. Ibid., first president of Lyon Appeals Court to M.J., 1 June 1849, expresses support of mayor and General Gémeau and that of the first president; ibid., M. Archer, *doyen des présidents de Chambre à Lyon* to M.J., 10 February 1849.
203. Ibid., P. of Rhône to M.I. (copy sent to M.J.), 27 March 1849.
204. Ibid.
205. Ibid., M.I. (Faucher) to M.J. (cover letter to prefect's report), 27 March 1849.
206. Gilardin dossier, undated memorandum of M.J.: "il était présenté en première ligne par M. Duplan [the P.G.] . . . sans aucun note: 'Je nomme M. Gilardin, disait-il, sans ajouter un mot sur lui: vous le connaissez.' "
207. Ibid., Gilardin to secretary general of M.J., 9 September 1847.
208. Ibid., service list, n.d.
209. Ibid.
210. A.N., BB⁶ ii, Devienne dossier, service list, n.d.
211. Ibid., M. de Belbeuf, first president at Lyon to M.J., 16 June 1847.
212. Ibid., memorandum of conversation between F. Barrot and M.J., n.d.
213. Ibid., Darcy to M.J., 5 December 1849, in which he refers to other letters.

214. Ibid., service record, n.d.

215. A.N., BB⁶ II, Thourel dossier, service list, n.d.

216. Ibid., *Notes des services de M. Thourel*, in letter requesting that Thourel's personal good wishes be expressed to the emperor, Thourel to M.J., 30 December 1854. See also H. de Montféal, *Notice biographique sur M. Thourel* (Paris, 1855), a pamphlet enclosed in Thourel's request for the title of baron, Thourel to M.J., 21 February 1856.

217. A.N., BB³⁰ 363, Thourel as commissioner of Gard to M.J., 26 May 1848.

218. Dansette, *Louis-Napoléon*, p. 246.

219. Thourel dossier, Thourel to M.J., 21 February 1856.

220. Ibid.

221. *D.B.M.O.F.*, pt. 1, III, 452, entry for André Thourel.

222. Thourel dossier, General de Castellane to minister of war (copy sent to minister of police and M.J.), 17 March 1852.

4 Reports from the Provinces

1. Calman, *Ledru-Rollin*, pp. 183-187, 191.

2. Seignobos, *Révolution de 1848*, p. 139.

3. Ibid., p. 140.

4. Ibid., p. 139.

5. *D.P.F.*, v, 93.

6. Seignobos, *Révolution de 1848*, p. 140.

7. Ibid., p. 148.

8. Ibid., p. 141.

9. Collins, *Government and Press*, p. 110.

10. Ibid.

11. Philippe Vigier, *La Seconde république* (Paris, 1967), p. 78.

12. Ibid., and Seignobos, *Révolution de 1848*, p. 153.

13. Ibid.

14. Vigier, *Seconde république*, p. 78.

15. Ibid., p. 79.

16. Ibid.

17. M.A. Romieu, *Le Spectre rouge de 1852* (Paris, 1851), p. 1.

18. Dansette, *Louis-Napoléon*, p. 317. My translation.

19. Seignobos, *Révolution de 1848*, pp. 146-148, and Dansette, *Louis-Napoléon*, pp. 386-387.

20. Léon Faucher, *Correspondance* (Paris, 1868), passim, and Levasseur, "Un épisode," pp. 3-13.

21. Faucher, *Correspondance*, p. 245.

22. Ibid., p. 289.

23. A.D. Gard, 4 U 5/102, M.J. to P.G.

24. Dansette, *Louis-Napoléon*, p. 287.

25. Ibid.

26. Ibid., p. 323.
27. Ibid., p. 330.
28. Levasseur, "Un épisode," p. 6.
29. Faucher, *Correspondance*, Letter to Reeve, 31 December 1851, p. 296.
30. A.N., BB[30] 385, P.G. to M.J., 27 November 1849.
31. Ibid.
32. A.N., BB[30] 385, P.G. to M.J., 30 December 1849.
33. A.N., BB[30] 385, P.G. to M.J., 15 May 1851.
34. A.N., BB[30] 385, P.G. to M.J., 30 May 1851.
35. Ibid.
36. A.N., BB[30] 385, P.G. to M.J., 20 January 1851 and 9 September 1851.
37. A.N., BB[30] 385, P.G. to M.J., 20 January 1851.
38. A.N., BB[30] 385, P.G. to M.J., 27 November 1849.
39. Ibid.
40. A.N., BB[30] 385, P.G. to M.J., 30 December 1849.
41. Ibid.
42. A.N., BB[30] 385, P.G. to M.J., 15 September 1850.
43. A.D. Charente-Maritime, 4 M 4/3, P. to M.I., 25 December 1849.
44. A.D. Charente-Maritime, 4 M 2/20, P. to M.I., October 1850.
45. Ibid., *his* emphasis.
46. A.D. Charente-Maritime, 4 M 2/20, P. to M.I., 11 February 1850.
47. A.N., BB[30] 385, P.G. to M.J., 9 March 1850.
48. A.N., BB[18] 1472, dossier 6733, P.G. to M.J., 20 January 1849. This prosecution, which failed, would cost him his job.
49. Ibid.
50. Charles, *La Révolution de 1848*, p. 16.
51. A.N., BB[30] 359, first advocate general to M.J., 10 August 1849.
52. A.N., BB[30] 359, P.G. to M.J., 26 August 1849.
53. A.N., BB[30] 359, first advocate general to M.J., 27 October 1849.
54. A.N., BB[30] 359, M.J. to P.G., 15 November 1849.
55. A.D. Gironde, 1 M 330, P. to mayors, 13 February 1850.
56. A.N., BB[18] 1474[1], P.G. to M.J., 8 March 1850.
57. Charles, "Un exemple de carrière," pp. 229-240, and A.N., BB[30] 374, P.G. to M.J., 30 November 1851.
58. A.N., BB[18] 1474[2], P.G. to M.J., 6 February 1849.
59. Ibid.
60. A.D. Gard, 6 M 376 bis, P. to M.I., 31 March 1849.
61. A.N., bB[30] 382, P.G. to M.J., November 1849.
62. Ibid.
63. Ibid.
64. A.D. Gard, 6 M 376 bis, P. to M.I., November 1849.
65. A.N., BB[30] 382, P.G. to M.J., 23 January 1850.
66. A.D. Gard, 6 M 615, P. to M.I., 9 February 1850.
67. Ibid., and A.N., BB[30] 334, P.G. to M.J., 16 January 1850.

68. A.N., BB^{18} 1485^2, dossier 8729A, P.G. to M.J., 6 May 1850.
69. Ibid.
70. Ibid.
71. A.N., BB^{30} 382, P.G. to M.J., 21 July 1850.
72. Ibid.
73. A.N., BB^{30} 382, P.G. to M.J., 27 July 1850 and October 1850.
74. A.N., BB^{30} 382, P.G. to M.J., 11 December 1850.
75. A.N., BB^{30} 382, P.G. to M.J., 17 April 1851.
76. A.N., BB^{30} 382, P.G. to M.J., 28 February 1851.
77. A.N., BB^{30} 382, P.G. to M.J., 17 April 1851.
78. Ibid.
79. A.N., BB^{18} 1494, dossier 509, P.G. to M.J., 14 April 1851.
80. A.N., BB^{18} 1494, dossier 509, P.G. to M.J., 1 May 1851.
81. A.N., BB^{30} 382, P.G. to M.J., 8 June 1851.
82. Ibid.
83. A.N., BB^{30} 382, P.G. to M.J., 14 October 1851.
84. A.N., BB^{18} 1474^2, first advocate general to M.J., 19 February 1849.
85. Ibid.
86. Ibid.
87. A.N., BB^{18} 1474^2, first advocate general to M.J., 28 May 1849.
88. Dutacq and Latrielle, *Histoire de Lyon*, p. 162.
89. Seignobos, *Révolution de 1848*, p. 139.
90. Dutacq and Latrielle, *Histoire de Lyon*, p. 163.
91. A.N., BB^{18} 1468, dossier 6355, P.G. to M.J., 2 August 1849.
92. Ibid.
93. A.N., BB^{18} 1474^2, P.G. to M.J., 20 December 1849.
94. Ibid.
95. A.N., BB^{30} 379, P.G. to M.J., 2 February 1850.
96. A.N., BB^{30} 379, P.G. to M.J., 4 March 1850.
97. Ibid.
98. A.N., BB^{30} 379, P.G. to M.J., 2 July 1850.
99. Ibid.
100. A.N., BB^{30} 379, P.G. to M.J., 6 November 1850.
101. A.N., BB^{30} 379, P.G. to M.J., 26 November 1850.
102. Ibid.
103. A.N., BB^{30} 379, P.G. to M.J., 7 February 1851.
104. A.N., BB^{30} 379, P.G. to M.J., 23 April 1851.
105. Ibid.
106. A.N., BB^{30} 379, P.G. to M.J., 2 June 1851.
107. Ibid.
108. A.N., BB^{30} 379, P.G. to M.J., 2 August 1851.
109. A.N., BB^{30} 379, P.G. to M.J., 8 October 1851.
110. Ibid.
111. Maupas, as minister of police, may have culled out his correspond-

ence dating from his tenure at Moulins for his personal use. Though reports from the prefects are largely lacking from the departmental archives of Allier, the local archivist was extremely helpful in finding an uncatalogued box of first drafts for some reports.

112. A.N., BB³⁰ 386, P.G. to M.J., 13 December 1849.
113. Ibid.
114. Ibid.
115. Ibid.
116. Ibid.
117. Ibid.
118. A.N., BB³⁰ 386, P.G. to M.J., 15 January 1850.
119. Ibid.
120. A.N., BB³⁰ 386, P. to M.I., 22 February 1850.
121. Ibid.
122. A.N., BB³⁰ 386, P.G. to M.J., 5 March 1850.
123. A.N., BB³⁰ 386, P.G. to M.J., 5 May 1850.
124. Ibid.
125. Ibid.
126. Ibid.
127. Ibid.
128. A.N., BB³⁰ 386, P.G. to M.J., 10 July 1850.
129. Ibid.
130. A.N., BB³⁰ 386, P.G. to M.J., 16 September 1850.
131. Ibid.
132. A.N., BB³⁰ 386, P.G. to M.J., 11 November 1850.
133. A.N., BB³⁰ 386, P.G. to M.J., 11 January 1851.
134. Ibid.
135. A.N., BB³⁰ 386, P.G. to M.J., 13 May 1851.
136. A.N., BB³⁰ 386, P.G. to M.J., 2 July 1851.
137. A.N., BB³⁰ 386, P.G. to M.J., [no day] September 1851.
138. A.N., BB³⁰ 386, P.G. to M.J., 4 November 1851.
139. Ibid.
140. A.D. Jura, M 40, P. to M.I., 5 July 1849.
141. A.N., BB³⁰ 373, P.G. to M.J., 30 November 1849.
142. Ibid.
143. Ibid.
144. A.N., BB¹⁸ 1470², minister of war to P.G., 26 November 1849.
145. The moderate was Claude Valette. See *D.P.F.*, v, 493.
146. A.N., BB³⁰ 373, P.G. to M.J., 4 January 1850.
147. Ibid.
148. Ibid.
149. A.N., BB³⁰ 373, P.G. to M.J., 1 February 1850.
150. Ibid.
151. A.N., BB³⁰ 373, P.G. to M.J., special report on Jura, 5 February 1850.

152. Ibid.
153. A.D. Jura, M 37, P. to M.I., 9 February 1850.
154. A.D. Jura, M 37, P. to general commanding third subdivision of fifth military district, 16 February 1850.
155. A.N., BB³⁰ 373, P.G. to M.J., 11 June 1850.
156. Ibid.
157. A.N., BB³⁰ 373, P.G. to M.J., 10 September 1850.
158. A.D. Jura, M 37, P. to M.I., 24 October 1850.
159. A.N., BB³⁰ 373, P.G. to M.J., 10 December 1850.
160. Ibid.
161. A.N., BB³⁰ 373, P.G. to M.J., 26 April 1851.
162. Ibid.
163. A.N., BB³⁰ 373, P.G. to M.J., 7 August 1851.
164. A.D. Jura, M 67, P. to mayors, 12 August 1851.
165. A.N., BB³⁰ 373, P.G. to M.J., 8 September 1851.
166. Eugène Ténot, *La Province en décembre 1851* (Paris 1865), pp. 39-40.

5 The Limits of Repressive Techniques before the Coup

1. See A.N., BB¹⁸ 1467², dossier 6335, M.J. to P.'s circular on organization of jury under universal manhood suffrage, n.d.
2. Charles H. Pouthas, "Une enquête sur la réforme administrative sous la seconde république," *Revue historique*, CXCIII (1943), 1-11.
3. Georges Rougeron, "De la révolution de février au 2 décembre," in *La Révolution de 1848 à Moulins et dans le département de l'Allier*, ed. Comité départementale du centenaire de la révolution de 1848 (Moulins, 1950), p. 57.
4. Ibid., pp. 57-58. The facts and quotations in the rest of this paragraph are drawn from Rougeron's work.
5. A.D. Gard, 6 M 376 bis, M.I. to *conseiller de préfecture*, 25 July 1849.
6. A.N., BB³⁰ 382, P.G. to M.J., 11 December 1850.
7. A.N., BB³⁰ 379, P.G. to M.J., 11 January 1850.
8. A.D. Jura, M 34, P.G. to P., 29 July 1849.
9. Ibid.
10. A.D. Jura, M 34, P. to M.I., 7 November 1849.
11. A.D. Jura, M 40, M.I. to P., 22 December 1849.
12. A.D. Jura, M 40, P. to M.I., 28 December 1849.
13. A.N., BB³⁰ 359, P.G. to M.J., 8 February 1850.
14. A.N., BB¹⁸ 1484, dossier 8556A, P.G. to M.J., 10 April 1850.
15. A.D. Charente-Maritime, 4 M 2/20, S.P. to P., 25 August 1851.
16. A.N., BB³⁰ 369, P.G. to M.J., 28 April 1851.
17. *Le Républicain de l'Allier*, 31 December 1848.
18. Ibid.
19. *La Tribune de la Gironde*, 19 April 1849.

20. A.N., BB³⁰ 374 P.G. to M.J., 7 December 1849.
21. *La Démocratie Jurassienne*, 8 December 1849, their emphasis.
22. A.N., F¹ᵃ 598, Chanal (P. of Bas-Rhin) to Conseil d'état, n.d.
23. A.N., F¹ᵃ 598, Wissocq (P. of Charente-Inférieure) to Conseil d'état, n.d.
24. Dansette, *Louis-Napoléon*, pp. 286-287.
25. Ibid.
26. Ibid.
27. A.D. Gard, 6 M 376 bis, M.I. to P., 10 March 1849.
28. A.N., BB³⁰ 359, first advocate general to M.J., 20 October 1849.
29. Ibid.
30. Ibid.
31. A.N., BB³⁰ 361, P.G. to M.J., *accusé de réception*, 27 June 1849.
32. A.N., BB³⁰ 382, P.G. to M.J., December 1849.
33. A.N., BB³⁰ 382, P.G. to M.J., 12 May 1850.
34. A.N., BB³⁰ 363, P.G. to M.J., 22 February 1849.
35. A.N., BB³⁰ 382, P.G. to M.J., 12 May 1850. Thourel's emphasis.
36. A.N., BB⁶ ɪɪ, Thourel personnel dossier, Demians to M.J., 15 May 1850.
37. Ibid, P.G. (Thourel) to M.J., (day illegible) October 1850.
38. *Le Républicain du Gard*, 27 September and 18 October 1850.
39. A.N., BB⁶ ɪɪ, Thourel personnel dossier, marginal notation drawn up by secretary general for personnel matters and initialed by Rouher for transmission to Thourel, P.G. to M.J., (day illegible) October 1850.
40. A.D. Jura, M 40, justice of the peace at Champagnolles to P., 15 December 1849.
41. A.N., BB³⁰ 333, P.G. to M.J., 5 January 1849.
42. *La Tribune de la Gironde*, 17 December 1848.
43. Ibid.
44. *Le Républicain de l'Allier*, 6 May 1849.
45. A.D. Vendée, 4 U 2/212, P.G. to P.R., 22 March 1849.
46. Ibid.
47. Ibid.
48. A.D. Vendée, 4 U 1/165, P.G. circular to *procureurs de la république* in his *ressort*, 7 July 1850.
49. A.N., BB¹⁸ 1472, dossier 6733, P.G. to M.J., 17 April 1849.
50. A.N., BB³⁰ 373, P.G. to M.J., 4 January 1850.
51. A.N., BB³⁰ 385, P.G. to M.J., 27 November 1849.
52. A.N., BB³⁰ 385, P.G. to M.J., 30 December 1849.
53. A.D. Gard, 6 M 376 bis, P. to minister of education, September 1849.
54. A.D. Jura, M unclassified, P. to M.I., September 1849.
55. A.N., BB³⁰ 359, P.G. to M.J., 8 February 1850.
56. A.D. Jura, M. unclassified, P. to M.I., 22 December 1849.
57. *La Démocratie Jurassienne*, 20 May 1850.

58. Ibid.
59. A.N., BB³⁰ 359, P.G. to M.J., 8 February 1850.
60. *Le Républicain Démocrate de l'Allier*, 28 February 1850.
61. *La Tribune de la Gironde*, 19 April 1849.
62. A.N., BB³⁰ 385, P.G. to M.J., February 1850.
63. A.N., BB³⁰ 385, P.G. to M.J., 20 January 1850.
64. A.D. Vendée, 2 M 30, P. to Ministry of Education, 20 February 1850.
65. A.D. Vendée, 4 U 1/165, P.G. to P.R., 2 December 1850.
66. A.D. Vendée, 4 U 1/165, M.J. to P.G., 10 December 1850.
67. A.D. Charente-Maritime, 4 M 2/15, P. to M.I., 21 July 1850.
68. A.N., BB³⁰ 391, P.G. to M.J., 16 January 1851.
69. A.N., BB³⁰ 391, *chef de cabinet* of minister of education to P.G., 27 January 1851.
70. *La Tribune de la Gironde*, 26 March 1850.
71. *Le Travailleur* (Rochefort), 6 July 1850.
72. *La Démocratie Jurassienne*, 4 May 1850.
73. See, for example: *Le Républicain Démocrate de l'Allier*, 17 January 1850, and *La Démocratie Jurassienne*, 4 May 1850.
74. A.N., BB³⁰ 386, P.G. to M.J., 30 December 1849.
75. A.D. Jura, M 40, undated table in answer to M.I. circular of 24 December 1849.
76. A.D. Jura, M 34 P. to M.I., 19 October and 7 December 1849.
77. A.D. Jura, M 34, P. to M.I., 12 October 1850.
78. A.D. Charente-Maritime, 4 M 2/15, minister of finance to P., 9 November 1849.
79. A.D. Charente-Maritime, 4 M 2/15, P. to M.I., 23 December 1849.
80. A.N., BB³⁰ 385, P.G. to M.J., 9 March 1850.
81. Rougeron, "De la révolution," pp. 60-62.
82. A.N., BB³⁰ 379, P.G. to M.J., 2 July 1850.
83. A.N., BB¹⁸ 1481, dossier 8169A, P.G. to M.J., 11 January 1850.
84. A.N., BB³⁰ 386, P.G. to M.J., 13 December 1849.
85. A.N., BB³⁰ 373, P.G. to M.J., 30 November 1849.
86. A.D. Jura, M 34, P. to M.I., 26 December 1849.
87. A.N., BB³⁰ 386, P.G. to M.J., 5 February 1850.
88. A.N., BB³⁰ 359, P.G. to M.J., 5 July 1850.
89. A.N., BB³⁰ 385, P.G. to M.J., November 1849.
90. A.N., BB³⁰ 359, P.G. to M.J., 18 July 1849.
91. A.N., BB¹⁸ 1489, dossier 9290, P.G. to M.J., 2 January 1851.
92. A.N., BB³⁰ 382, P.G. to M.J., 3 December 1849.
93. See Collins, *Government and Press*, chap. 9.
94. For entire paragraph, see A.N., BB³⁰ 385, P.G. to M.J., 27 November 1849, and A.D. Charente-Maritime, 4 M 10/4, P. to M.I., 1 October 1850.
95. A.D. Charente-Maritime, 4 M 4/3, P. to M.I., 28 June 1849.

96. A.D. Charente-Maritime, 4 M 2/15, P. to S.P., 30 June 1849.
97. Collins, *Government and Press*, p. 113.
98. For entire paragraph, see A.N., BB³⁰ 385, P.G. to M.J., 9 March 1850. See also *Le Phare*, 20 February 1850.
99. Ibid., and A.D. Vendée, 4 U 2/212 no. 2, P.G. to P.R., 14 May 1850.
100. A.D. Charente-Maritime, 4 M 10/4, P. to M.I., 1 October 1850.
101. A.N. BB¹⁸ 1487, dossier 9127, P.G. to M.J., 16 August 1850.
102. A.N., BB³⁰ 364, M.I. to M.J., 9 April 1850.
103. A.N., BB³⁰ 385, P.G. to M.J., 9 March 1850.
104. A.N., BB¹⁸ 1487, dossier 9127, P.G. to M.J., 16 August 1850. Enclosed is an *exemplaire* of *L'Echo de l'Ouest* of 15 August 1850. My translation.
105. A.N., BB¹⁸ 1490, dossier 48, P.G. to M.J., 24 November 1850. Enclosed is an *exemplaire* of *Le Phare* underlined by the P.G.
106. Ibid.
107. A.N., BB¹⁸ 1490, dossier 48, M.J. to P.G., 6 December 1850.
108. A.N., BB¹⁸ 1490, dossier 48, P.G. to M.J., 22 December 1850.
109. Ibid.
110. A.N., BB¹⁸ 1490, dossier 49, P.G. to M.J., 18 December 1850.
111. A.N., BB¹⁸ 1490, dossier 49, P.G. to M.J., 31 December 1850.
112. Ibid., and A.N., BB³⁰ 385, P.G. to M.J., 20 January 1851.
113. A.N., BB³⁰ 385, P.G. to M.J., 30 December 1849.
114. A.D. Vendée, 4 U 2/212 no. 2, P.G. to P.R., 19 June 1850.
115. Durand's wealth and local standing are described in *L'Echo de l'Ouest* of 15 August 1850 enclosed in A.N., BB¹⁸ 1487, dossier 9127, P.G. to M.J., 16 August 1850.
116. A.D. Vendée, 4 M 25, M.I. to P., 17 October 1850.
117. A.D. Vendée, 4 M 25, M.I. to P., 23 October 1850.
118. A.N., BB³⁰ 385, P.G. to M.J., 15 July 1850, and A.N., BB¹⁸ 1485², dossier 8730A, P.G. to M.J., 7 November 1850.
119. A.D. Charente-Maritime, 4 M 2/20, P. to M.I., 22 March 1851.
120. A.D. Vendée, 4 U 2/212 P.R. to P.G., 15 December 1849, and A.D. Vendée, 4 U 212, P.G. to P.R., 27 December 1849.
121. A.N., BB³⁰ 359, P.G. to M.J., 26 April 1849.
122. A.N., BB³⁰ 359, trimestrial report, 18 July 1849.
123. For the prosecutions of *Le Peuple Souverain*, see A.N., BB³⁰ 359, P.G. to M.J., 26 April 1849.
124. A.N., BB³⁰ 359, P.G. to M.J., 18 July 1849.
125. A.N., BB¹⁸ 1470², P.G. to M.J., 12 April 1850.
126. A.N., BB¹⁸ 1470², P.G. to M.J., [no day] June 1850.
127. Ibid.
128. A.N., BB¹⁸ 1483, dossier 8325, P.G. to M.J., 8 July 1850.
129. A.N., BB¹⁸ 1485², M.J. circular to P.G.'s, 24 October 1850.
130. A.N., BB¹⁸ 1483, dossier 8525, P.G. to M.J., 8 July 1850.
131. A.N., BB¹⁸ 1483, dossier 8525, M.I. to M.J., 25 July 1850.

132. A.D. Gironde, 1 M 330, P. to mayors, n.d.

133. A.N., BB¹⁸ 1483, dossier 8525, P.G. to M.J., 8 July 1850.

134. A.N., BB¹⁸ 1470², P.G. to M.J., 17 July 1850.

135. *La Tribune de la Gironde*, 1 January 1850.

136. Ibid., 26 March 1850.

137. A.N., BB³⁰ 334, P.G. to M.J., 15 February 1851. Enclosed is an *exemplaire* of *La Tribune*.

138. A.N., BB¹⁸ 1489, dossier 9290, P.G. to M.J., 16 July 1851.

139. A.N., BB¹⁸ 1489, dossier 9290, P.G. to M.J., 20 July 1851. Enclosed is an *exemplaire* of *La République*.

140. A.N., BB¹⁸ 1489, dossier 9290, M.J. to P.G., 29 July 1851.

141. A.N., BB¹⁸ 1489, dossier 9290, P.G. to M.J., 31 July 1851.

142. A.N., BB¹⁸ 1489, dossier 9290, M.J. to P.G., 5 August 1851.

143. *Le Phare* (La Rochelle), 19 July 1851.

144. *Le Travailleur de l'Allier et de la Creuse*, 1 August 1851.

145. A.N., BB¹⁸ 1489, dossier 9290, M.J. to P.G., 14 August 1851.

146. For characterization of newspapers, see Charles, "Un exemple de carrière," p. 237.

147. For the case of *Le Courrier*, see A.N., BB¹⁸ 1488, dossier 9211, P.G. to M.J., 6 and 7 August 1850; for the case of *Le Mémorial*, see A.N., BB¹⁸ 1470², P.G. to M.J., 30 April 1850.

148. A.N., BB³⁰ 382, P.G. to M.J., 3 December 1849.

149. Ibid.

150. *Le Républicaine du Gard*, 23 September 1849.

151. A.N., BB³⁰ 382, P.G. to M.J., 23 January 1850.

152. A.N. BB³⁰ 382, P.G. to M.J., 8 March 1850.

153. A.N., BB³⁰ 382, P.G. to M.J., 3 December 1849.

154. A.N., BB¹⁸ 1494, dossier 509, P.G. to M.J., 1 May 1851.

155. Adolphe Pieyre, *Histoire de la ville de Nîmes depuis 1830 jusqu'à nos jours*, 2 vols. (Nîmes, 1886), II, 122.

156. A.N., BB³⁰ 379, P.G. to M.J., 1 December 1849.

157. A.N., BB¹⁸ 1470³, dossier 6170A, P.G. to M.J., 18 February 1849. Enclosed is an *exemplaire* of *Le Peuple Souverain*.

158. A.N., BB¹⁸ 1470³, dossier 6170A, first advocate general to M.J., 18 March 1849.

159. A.N., BB¹⁸ 1470³, dossier 6170A, first advocate general to M.J., 29 April and 5 May 1849.

160. A.N., BB¹⁸ 1483, dossier 8525A, P.G. to M.J., 28 January 1850.

161. A.N., BB³⁰ 361, P.G. to M.J., 26 June 1849.

162. Ibid.

163. Naquet's *profession de foi*, quoted in A.N., BB³⁰ 361, P.G. to M.J., 30 June 1849.

164. *La Revue Démocratique, numéro unique*, B.N., Jo 3932, August 1849.

165. A.N., BB³⁰ 379, P.G. to M.J., 11 December 1850.

166. A.N., BB¹⁸ 1483, dossier 8525A, P.G. to M.J., 28 January 1850.
167. A.N., BB¹⁸ 1483, dossier 8525A, P.G. to M.J., 4 March 1850.
168. Ibid.
169. Dutacq and Latrielle, *Histoire de Lyon*, chap. 1, passim.
170. Rougeron, "De la révolution," p. 51.
171. Ibid., pp. 75 and 91.
172. A.N., BB¹⁸ 1470³, dossier 6701A, P.G. to M.J., 9 January 1849.
173. Rougeron, "De la révolution," p. 37.
174. A.N., BB¹⁸ 1470³, dossier 6701A, P.G. to M.J., 9 January 1849.
175. For prosecution of *Le Républicain*, see Rougeron, "De la révolution," p. 37.
176. *Le Républicain de l'Allier*, 4 February 1849.
177. Ibid., 5 March 1849.
178. A.N., BB¹⁸ 1470³, dossier 6701A, P.G. to M.J., 4 May 1849.
179. A.N., BB¹⁸ 1470³, dossier 6701A, P.G. to M.J., 21 February 1850, and Rougeron, "De la révolution," p. 75.
180. Leguai, "Félix Mathé," in *La Révolution de 1848 à Moulins et dans le département de l'Allier*, ed. Comité départementale du centenaire de la révolution de 1848 (Moulins, 1950), p. 154.
181. Rougeron, "De la révolution," pp. 77-78.
182. Leguai, "Félix Mathé," p. 158.
183. A.N., BB¹⁸ 1470³, 6701A, P.G. to M.J., n.d., report received at M.J. 5 February 1849. Enclosed is a clipping from *Le Mémorial*.
184. A.N., BB¹⁸ 1470³, dossier 6701A, P.G. to M.J., 5 February 1849.
185. A.N., BB³⁰ 373, P.G. to M.J., 4 January and 10 September 1850.
186. A.N., BB³⁰ 373, P.G. to M.J., 5 February 1850.
187. Charles Mangolte, "La Presse en 1848 dans le Jura," in *Volume du centenaire de la révolution de 1848 dans le Jura*, ed. Société d'émulation du Jura (Lons-le-Saunier, 1948), pp. 41-45.
188. A.N., BB¹⁸ 1470², P.G. to M.J., 20 March 1849. Enclosed is an *exemplaire* of *La Démocratie*.
189. A.N., BB¹⁸ 1470², P.G. to M.J., 28 June 1849.
190. A.N., BB¹⁸ 1470², P.G. to M.J., 9 September 1849.
191. A.N., BB¹⁸ 1470², P.G. to M.J., 11 June 1850.
192. A.N., BB¹⁸ 1470², P.G. to M.J., 12 August 1849.
193. Ibid.
194. A.N., BB¹⁸, 1470², P.G. to M.J., 25 February 1850.
195. A.N., BB³⁰ 359, P.G. to M.J., 5 July 1850.
196. Ibid.
197. A.N., BB¹⁸ 1489, dossier 9428, P.G. to M.J., 8 December 1850.
198. A.N., BB³⁰ 373, P.G. to M.J., 11 June 1850.
199. A.N., BB¹⁸ 1490, dossier 24, P.G. to M.J., 6 January 1851.
200. Ténot, *La Province*, p. 39.
201. Collins, *Government and Press*, p. 111.

202. *D.B.M.O.F.*, ii, 381, entry for Pierre Joigneux.
203. *Le Démocrate Vendéen*, 21 May 1851, and *Le Républicain Démocrate de l'Allier*, 30 December 1849.
204. A.N., BB[18] 1449, dossier 3160A, M.I. to M.J., 10 February 1849.
205. A.N., BB[18] 1449, dossier 3160A, M.J. to P.G.'s, 15 February 1849.
206. A.N., BB[18] 1449, dossier 3160A, P.G. to M.J., 27 February 1849.
207. Ibid.
208. A.N., BB[18] 1449, dossier 3160A, M.I. to P.'s, 28 March 1849.
209. A.N., BB[18] 1449, dossier 3160A, M.I. to M.J., 19 June 1849.
210. A.N., BB[18] 1470[2], M.J. to P.G.'s, 16 August 1849.
211. A.N., BB[18] 1449, dossier 3160A, P.G. to M.J., 27 December 1849.
212. Ibid.
213. For examples of distinctions, in press matters, among *attentats, crimes, délits*, and *contraventions*, see Collins, *Government and Press*, Introduction; on the use of police courts, see chap. 14.
214. A.N., BB[18] 1449, dossier 3160A, P.G. to M.J., 27 December 1849.
215. A.N., BB[18] 1449, dossier 3160A, M.J. to P.G., 7 January 1850.
216. A.N., BB[18] 1449, dossier 3160A, P.G. to M.J., 27 December 1849.
217. A.N., BB[18] 1449, dossier 3160A, P.G. to M.J., 11 December 1849.
218. A.N., BB[30] 373, P.G. to M.J., 11 January 1850. Gilardin reports multiple press seizures in Lyon and environs but mentions no arrests or trials.
219. A.N., BB[30] 373, P.G. to M.J., 4 March 1850.
220. A.N., BB[30] 373, P.G. to M.J., 7 February 1851.
221. Ibid.
222. A.N., BB[30] 386, P.G. to M.J., 10 February 1850.
223. A.N., BB[30] 386, P.G. to M.J., 15 January 1850.
224. A.D. Jura, M 34, P.G. to P., 29 November 1849.
225. A.N., BB[30] 373, P.G. to M.J., 4 January 1850.
226. A.N., BB[30] 373, P.G. to M.J., 5 February 1850.
227. A.D. Jura, M 34, P.G. to P., 16 December 1849.
228. A.N., BB[30] 373, P.G. to M.J., 5 February 1850.
229. A.N., BB[18] 1449, dossier 3160A, P.G. to M.J., 8 December 1850.
230. A.D. Vendée, 4 M 25, M.I. to P., 11 April 1851.
231. *Le Démocrate Vendéen*, 15 May 1851.
232. A.N., BB[18] 1474[1], dossier 1, M.J. to P.G., "législation: Clubs et Associations," n.d., but the list ends with a quotation from a ministerial circular of June 1849.
233. A.N., BB[30] 379, P.G. to M.J., 11 December 1849.
234. A.N., BB[30] 379, P.G. to M.J., 11 January 1850.
235. A.N.. BB[30] 379, P.G. to M.J., 11 December 1849-October 1851.
236. See Godart, *A Lyon*, chap. 1.
237. A.N., BB[30] 373, P.G. to M.J., 1 February 1850.
238. A.N., BB[30] 373, P.G. to M.J., 5 February 1850 and 7 June 1851.

239. A.N., BB[18] 1472, P.G. to M.J., 10 February 1849.
240. Ibid.
241. A.N., BB[30] 361, first advocate general to M.J., 15 May 1849.
242. A.N., BB[30] 359, first advocate general to M.J., 20 October 1849.
243. A.D. Charente-Maritime, 4 M 2/20, P.G. to P., 20 April 1850.
244. A.N., BB[18] 1474[2], P.G. to M.J., 18 January 1850.
245. A.N., BB[30] 364, P.G. to M.J., 1 August 1849.
246. *Le Phare* (La Rochelle), 25 July 1849.
247. A.D. Jura, M 37, P. to M.I., 9 February 1850.
248. A.N., BB[30] 379, P.G. to M.J., 1 February 1850.
249. A.N., BB[30] 363, P.G. to M.J., 1 June 1849.
250. A.N., BB[18] 1470[2], P.G. to M.J., 20 September 1849.
251. A.N., BB[30] 391, P.G. to M.J., 15 November 1850.
252. A.N., BB[30] 391, P.G. to M.J., 24 January 1851.
253. A.N., BB[30] 391, P.G. to M.J., 27 January 1851.
254. A.N., BB[30] 391, P.G. to M.J., 8 March 1851.
255. For the Sentenac *Affaire*, see unnumbered file "Révélation du con-damné Sentenac," A.N., BB[30] 390.
256. For other mail intercepts in Lyon, see A.N., BB[30] 361, P.G. to M.J., 11 February 1850, and A.N., BB[30] 359, General de Castellane to M.J., n.d.
257. See A.N., BB[30] 364, P.G. to M.J., 3 December 1849 (Vendée); A.N., BB[18] 1472, P.G. to M.J., 7 April 1849 (Gard); and A.D. Jura, M 40, P. to M.I., 25 May 1849.
258. A.D. Jura, M 40, P. to M.I., 25 May 1849.
259. A.N., BB[30] 364, P.G. to M.J., 3 December 1849.
260. A.N., BB[18] 1472, P.G. to M.J., 7 April 1849.
261. Ibid.
262. A.N., BB[30] 382, P.G. to M.J., 3 December 1850.
263. A.N., BB[30] 382, P.G. to M.J., 8 March 1850.
264. A.N., BB[30] 385, P.G. to M.J., 30 December 1849.
265. A.N., BB[18] 1474[1], Charles Henry, *conseiller à la cour d'appel*, to M.J., 23 December 1849.
266. A.N., BB[18] 1474[1], P.G. to M.J., 27 December 1849.
267. A.N., BB[18] 1474[1], Charles Henry to M.J., 23 December 1849.
268. A.N., BB[18] 1474[1], M.J. to Charles Henry, 2 January 1850.
269. A.N., BB[18] 1474[1], Charles Henry to M.J. (confidential), 5 January 1850.
270. Ibid.
271. A.N., BB[18] 1474[1], M.J. to P.G., 5 January 1850.
272. A.N., BB[18] 1474[1], P.G. to M.J., 8 January 1850.
273. A.N., BB[30] 379, P.G. to M.J., 7 February 1851.
274. A.N., BB[30] 373, P.G. to M.J., 7 August 1851.
275. A.N., BB[18] 1476, dossier 7285A, M.I. to P.'s, 31 March 1849.
276. Ibid.

277. A.N., BB^{18} 1476, dossier 7285A, M.J. to P.G.'s, n.d. (probably early April) 1849.
278. A.N., BB^{18} 1476, dossier 7285A, P.G. to M.J., n.d. 1849.
279. A.N., BB^{30} 363, P.G. to M.J. (confidential), 3 May 1849.
280. A.N., BB^{30} 363, P.G. to M.J., 17 August 1849.
281. A.N., BB^{18} 1449, dossier 3160A, P.G. to M.J., 2 July and 5 September 1849.
282. Ibid.
283. A.N., BB^{30} 363, P.G. to M.J., 5 February 1850.
284. A.N., BB^{30} 386, P.G. to M.J., March 1850.
285. A.N., BB^{18} 1468, dossier 6355, M.I. to P.'s, sent to P.G. at Poitiers 11 May 1849, and A.D. Charente-Maritime, 2 M 4/14, M.I. to P., 13 May 1849.
286. Seignobos, *Révolution de 1848*, pp. 132-133.
287. A.D. Gard, 6 M 376 bis, M.I. to P., 5 April 1849.
288. A.N., BB^{30} 363, M.J. to M.I., 10 May 1850.
289. For the entire paragraph, see A.D. Gard, 6 M 376 bis, confidential correspondence between P. and M.I., 6 April to 3 October 1849.
290. A.D. Gironde, 3 M 207, M.I. to P. (telegram), "3:00h du soir," 13 May 1849.
291. A.D. Charente-Maritime, 4 M 2/15, M.I. to P.'s, 23 June 1849.
292. A.D. Charente-Maritime, 4 M 2/20, P. to S.P.'s, 27 February 1850.
293. A.D. Allier, M. 643^{3}, P. to General Pellion, n.d. 1850.
294. *Le Républicain Démocrate de l'Allier*, 17 March 1850.
295. A.D. Jura, M 67, P. to M.I., 8 August 1851. The prefect dispersed the voting places from the center to the suburbs of Salins, but the left won handily.
     A.D. Charente-Maritime, 4 M 2/15, P. to S.P., 20 September 1850. The prefect nullified an election at Surgères, which the republicans had won, because the voting lists had not been changed in accordance with the law of 31 May 1850. New elections again resulted in a republican victory.
296. A.N., BB^{30} 365, P.G. to M.J., 20 August 1849. For paragraph, see A.N., BB^{30} 365, P.G. to M.J., 3 and 10 May 1849.
297. *Le Républicain Démocrate de l'Allier*, 26 April 1849. Their emphasis.
298. A.N., BB^{18} 1485^{2}, dossier 8730A, unsigned M.J. memorandum, 10 May 1851.
299. A.N., BB^{18} 1485^{2}, dossier 8730A, unsigned M.J. memorandum on printers, 3 May 1851.
300. A.N., BB^{30} 386, P.G. to M.J., 10 July 1850.
301. For the rest of the information in the paragraph, see A.N., BB^{18} 1485^{2}, dossier 8370A, unsigned M.J. memorandum, 10 May 1851.
302. A.N., BB^{18} 1486, dossier 8854, P.G. to M.J., 19 July 1849; and A.N., BB^{30} 334, P.G. to M.J., 24 February 1850.

303. A.N., BB³⁰, "Complot à l'occasion du réforme électoral en mai 1850," P.G. to M.J., 5 April 1850.
304. For entire paragraph, see Rougeron, "De la révolution," pp. 83-84.
305. A.N., BB³⁰ 373, P.G. to M.J., 4 January and 5 February 1850.
306. For paragraph, see Gabriel Perreux, *Arbois: première cité républicaine de la France* (Paris, 1932), and A.N., BB³⁰ 365, first advocate general to M.J., 11 July 1849.
307. A.N., BB³⁰ 379, P.G. to M.J., 8 June 1851.
308. A.N., BB³⁰ 379, P.G. to M.J., 1 December 1849.
309. F. Dutacq, "Notes et documents sur le complot du sud-est (1850-1851)," *Révolution de 1848*, XI (1925), passim.
310. For prison sentences, ibid., p. 351.
311. Dansette, *Louis-Napoléon*, pp. 315-359.
312. A.D. Gard, 6 M 376, M.I. to P., 29 December 1849.
313. A.N., BB¹⁸ 1485¹, dossier 8729, M.J. to M.I., 19 April 1850.
314. A.N., BB¹⁸ 1488, dossier 9262A, P.G. to M.J., "*complot de Lyon*," 31 March 1851.
315. A.N., BB³⁰ 366, P.G. to M.J., 20 June 1850. A placard is enclosed.
316. A.N., BB¹⁸ 1488, dossier 9262A, P.G. to M.J., "*complot de Lyon*," 31 March 1851.
317. Dutacq, "Notes et documents," p. 352.
318. A.N., BB³⁰ 363, P.G. to M.J., *accusé de réception*, 3 August 1850.
319. A.N., BB³⁰ 334, P.G. to P., 13 September 1850.
320. A.N., BB¹⁸ 1488, dossier 9262A, P.G. to M.J., n.d. Enclosed is a circular from Raspail to the Montagnards of Lyon, 23 October 1850.
321. A.N., BB¹⁸ 1488, dossier 9262A, P.G. to M.J., "*complot de Lyon*," 31 March 1851.
322. Ibid.
323. A.N., BB¹⁸ 1488, dossier 9262A, P.G. to M.J., "*complot de Lyon*," 31 March 1851.
324. Ibid.
325. A.N., BB³⁰ 334, P.G. to M.J., 21 April 1851.
326. A.N., BB³⁰ 1161, M.J. to P.G.'s, December 1850.
327. A.N., BB¹⁸ 1490, dossier 24, P.G. to M.J., 29 December 1850.
328. Ibid.

6 From Frustration to a Totalitarian Revolution

1. The figure of 2 percent (645 cases of 26,885) can be found in the list of final sentences in the Justice Ministry's register of all cases in France: A.N., BB³⁰* 424. Practically the same percentage emerges in our own study of the 3,189 people arrested in the seven departments of our sample: 1.6 percent. For very recent interpretations which

present the post-coup experience as a "culmination" or continuation" of the repression carried on during the more legalistic phase of the Second Republic, see John M. Merriman, "Radicalisation and Repression: A Study of the Demobilisation of the '*Démoc-Socs*' during the French Second Republic," and Vincent Wright, "The *Coup d'état* of December 1851: Repression and the Limits to Repression" both in Roger Price, ed., *Revolution and Reaction: 1848 and the Second French Republic* (New York, 1975).

2. For what I consider inappropriate (and misleading) uses of such terminology, see Roger Price, *The French Second Republic: A Social History* (London, 1972), passim.; Wright, "The *Coup d'état*"; and Howard Machin, "The Prefects and Political Repression: February 1848 to December 1851," in Price, ed., *Revolution and Reaction*. See also John M. Merriman, *The Agony of the Republic: The Repression of the Left in Revolutionary France 1848-1851* (New Haven, 1978). The most balanced and suggestive treatments of the subject of post-coup repression are in Payne, *The Police State*, pp. 34-73, and in Maurice Agulhon's *La République au village: les populations du Var de la Révolution à la Seconde République* (Paris, 1970), pp. 436-483.

3. The Justice Ministry compilation of these cases (on a department-by-department basis) can be found in the BB[30]* 402 series at the A.N. This material for our seven departments was supplemented by and checked against the alphabetical listings of all cases in France kept by the Interior Ministry, A.N. F[7] 2588 through 2595.

4. This chapter (and particularly those sections dealing with descriptive language used by the bureaucrats) summarizes major trends found in our sample. A more precise study of the "language of fear" present in many entries in the BB[30]* 402 series lies outside the scope of this work and will be the subject of articles I am preparing with the indispensable statistical guidance and "cliometric" insight of John Reynolds and the equally valued help of a linguistic analyst, Dr. Johanna De Stefano.

5. See tables in this chapter.

6. Seventy-eight percent of them were found guilty, usually of such minor charges as "rebellion against an official" (that is, scuffling with a policeman), "seditious shouts and apparel" or offenses so unimportant that they were left unspecified in the Mixed Commission register. These political types fared better than the 109 people who had been tried for criminal acts (ranging from vagrancy through murder) for whom verdicts were recorded: more than 96 percent were found guilty.

7. The very fact of having been prosecuted for a political offense made one a suspect, of course, by the time the Mixed Commission met. In

addition, our suspect category includes only those cases where an explicit statement of suspicion appeared in the registers, or where being removed from a bureaucratic or elective post indicated that one's political sympathies were known to the authorities.

8. A.N., BB³⁰ 397, M.J. to P.G.'s, circular on state of siege and "military commissions," 18 December 1851, and circular on setting up Mixed Commissions, countermanding earlier circular, 18 January 1852. The Justice Minister was Rouher.

9. A.N., BB³⁰, 396, P.G. to M.J. (incorporating prefectoral reports), February 1852. This is a forty-page document of enormous value for understanding the mentality of those sitting on the Mixed Commission.

10. Ténot, *La Province*, pp. 124-125.

11. Ibid., pp. 14-15.

12. Ibid., pp. 20-21.

13. Ibid., p. 53.

14. Morauzeau, "Aspects vendéens," pp. 89-90.

15. A N., BB³⁰ 396, P.G. to M.J., 17 January 1852.

16. Ibid., P.G. to M.J., 7 January 1852.

17. Ibid., P.G. to M.J., 27 January 1852.

18. Ibid., P.G. to M.J., general report cited above; see note 9.

19. A.N., BB³⁰ 397, circulars of M.J. to P.G.'s, 18 December 1851 and 18 January 1852; and report of Laton, *juge d'instruction*, acting as Rouher's inspector general of Mixed Commissions, 12 February 1852.

20. Ibid. See also BB³⁰* 402 registers for lists of sentences.

21. See A.N., BB³⁰* 402 registers for dates of final reports. The earliest innovation (before the full list of sentences) was the addition of Algiers city as an option.

22. Comparing our figures to the national statistics presented by Price from Interior Ministry records and keeping in mind the quirks of French census takers of the period (not to mention police record keepers), which included listing wealthy landowners as *agriculteurs*, we find our agricultural population to be 27.2 percent of the total: half a percent below the national figure. Despite the presence in our sample of three large cities (Lyon, Nîmes, and Bordeaux), our artisan-worker population was only 2 percent above the national average. See Price, *The French Second Republic*, tables on pp. 291-293.

    Comparing our figures for sentence to those presented by V. Wright, and keeping in mind that he combines Lambessa with *Algérie plus*, we find that those given these two sentences in our sample form just under 15 percent of the total, 1.5 percent below his national figure. Similarly, our figures for *Algérie moins* (19.1 percent) differ only slightly from his national 18.9 percent. For the other large groupings (freed and parole in home town), our figures are within 2 percent of the national groupings. See Vincent Wright, *"The Coup d'état,"* table on p. 308.

23. Action, as a category in our analysis, was grouped by descriptive statements of circumstances of arrest, sequence of actions taken by those involved in risings, and by statements of "charges" when and if they appeared on the registers. Missing data, combinations of actions (the most frequent was membership in a secret society *and* insurrection *and* sedition) that could not be grouped with any accuracy, and the 297 arrestees from Allier who received no notation on their dossiers because they were among the 366 released before trial by the Mixed Commission account for the 752 cases in the "unknown" category.

24. I have not dealt with "sedition" in this discussion because, quite frankly, it is impossible to "decode" what the Mixed Commission meant by the term. It is almost evenly spread among social classes and does not cluster very strongly under any particular sentence. As we shall see, however, the class of the seditionist (which could mean a differing social definition of "sedition") and his department had some impact on sentence.

25. My definition of artisan is considerably broader and, I feel, more accurate than the Interior Ministry figures presented by Price. It includes all skilled trades, including textile, construction, and transport, which are left separate in police statistics but are combined with all "workers" in a very useful table of the 1851 professional census of adult males. See *S.G.F.*, ii, table 37.

26. Ibid. The figure in the census table is 29.13 percent.

27. *Propriétaires* and professionals included factory owners in the census table cited throughout this discussion of the proportionality of class in each department.

28. The data missing from the registers, my concern with limiting "action" definitions of cases only to those for which register entries give clear evidence of a single major act (thus eliminating many "combination" cases), and the limited number of cases for each department make the actual "numbers" dealt with rather small. In order to see trends as clearly as possible by grouping cases, sentences were combined into three categories: "light sentence" (freed, paroled in home town or outside department, or jail and/or fine), "moderately severe sentence" (exile to Algeria, *moins* or *plus*), and "very severe sentence" (Cayenne or Lambessa).

29. The leadership category is based on entries in the registers that call someone a leader (either local or regional/national) or on elective positions held that would indicate to the authorities that an individual was a radical leader. It was exclusive enough as a category to be "surprised" by those who often surfaced only as organizers.

30. All registers in the Justice Ministry's department-by-department series on the Mixed Commissions and in the Interior Ministry's alphabetical and national registers provided space for such comments.

31. For contemporary medical terms for madness, see Stanley Loomis, *A Crime of Passion* (New York, 1967).

Appendix 1
The Prefects and Their Departments

1. Génique, *L'Election de 1849*, pp. 42-45.

2. *S.G.F.*, II, tables 19 and 45.

3. A.N., C 967, responses for Vendée to "L'Enquête sur le travail agricole et industriel," Constituent Assembly decree of 25 May 1848. The "Enquête" for France as a whole is conserved in C 942-967. The answers to the assembly's questionnaire were prepared by a committee in each canton under the presidency of the justice of the peace and including—ideally—both workers and proprietors. The results are incomplete (of all the cities of France, only Marseille provided answers from each of its wards). The "Enquête," however, is an invaluable source for the study of rural France under the republic.

4. For the information in this paragraph, see A.N., BB[30] 385, P.G. to M.J., 27 November 1849.

5. J.-G. Gaussens,"Essai sur le comportement politique charentais 1848-1870," D.E.S. (Paris, 1851), and Tudesq, *Les Grands notables*, II, 1180.

6. *D.P.F.*, V, 106.

7. Marie-Hélène Pont, "La Seconde république en Charente-Inférieure," D.E.S. (Bordeaux, 1960), chap. 7; and *D.P.F.*, I, 528-529; III, 480 (Etienne de Laborde); and IV, 418 (Charles-Tristan, comte de Montholon).

8. Pont, "La République en Charente-Inférieure," pp. 3-5; and *S.G.F.*, II, table 45.

9. Pont, "La République en Charente-Inférieure," p. 3, and *S.G.F.*, II, table 27.

10. Pont, "La République en Charente-Inférieure," p. 4.

11. This section based on information in Charles, *La Révolution de 1848*.

12. See especially Stuart R. Schram, *Protestantism and Politics in France* (Alençon, 1954), chap. 9, and Leo Loubère, "The Emergence of the Extreme Left in Lower Languedoc, 1848-1851: Social and Economic Factors in Politics," *American Historical Review*, LXXIII, 1968.

13. Pieyre, *Histoire de Nîmes*, II, 105.

14. *S.G.F.*, II, table 19, and Schram, *Protestantism and Politics*, p. 90, fig. 9.3.

15. Bouillon, "Les Démocrates socialistes," p. 85 and p. 82, map 1.

16. Pieyre, *Histoire de Nîmes*, I, 325-362.

17. Loubère notes that Favand's support reflected "roughly the percentage of Protestant voters in the department," Loubère, "Extreme Left in Lower Languedoc," p. 1042.
18. *D.P.F.*, II, 614. Favand won with 34,218 votes to 22,719 for the more moderate legitimist and 11,619 for the extremist.
19. A.N., C 953, "Enquête" for Gard.
20. Pieyre, *Histoire de Nîmes*, I, 359, and Lubère, "Extreme Left in Lower Languedoc," p. 1027.
21. Schram, *Protestantism and Politics*, pp. 83-85, and A.N., C 953 (Gard).
22. Loubère, "Extreme Left in Lower Languedoc," p. 1023. Nîmes possessed 157 mills employing more than twenty workers each.
23. *S.G.F.*, II, table 45, and A.N., C 953 (Gard).
24. Loubère, "Extreme Left in Lower Languedoc," pp. 1024 and 1040.
25. Ibid., p. 1035.
26. Bouillon, "Les Démocrates socialistes," pp. 89-95.
27. Ernest Labrouses, "Panoramas de la crise," and Rémi Gossez, "Carte des troubles en 1846-1847 (Cherté des grains)," in E. Labrousse, ed., *Aspects de la Crise et de la dépression de l'économie française au milieu du XIXᵉ siecle: 1846-1851*, Bibliothèque de la Révolution de 1848, vol. XIX (La Roche-sur-yon, 1956).
28. *S.G.F.*, II, table 19.
29. *D.B.F.*, IX, 632-633.
30. *D.P.F.*, III, 255.
31. Bouillon, "Les Démocrates socialistes," p. 73.
32. *D.P.F.*, V, 364 (François-Laurent Tamisier); and II, 344 (Derriey).
33. A.N., BB³⁰ 373, P.G. to M.J., 30 November 1849; A Désaunais, "Le commissariat de Jules Grévy," in *Volume du centenaire de la révolution de 1848 dans le Jura*, ed. Société d'émulation du Jura (Lons-le-Saunier, 1948), pp. 180-182.
34. *S.G.F.*, II, table 27.
35. A.N., C 955 (Jura).
36. Ibid.
37. Ibid.
38. *S.G.F.*, II, table 19.
39. Ibid.
40. Charlemagne-Emile de Maupas, *Mémoires sur le second empire* (Paris, 1884), I, 179.
41. Ténot, *La Province*, pp. 26-30.
42. Except when otherwise noted, the information used for the description of Allier is drawn from Rougeron, "De la révolution," and Leguai, "Félix Mathé."
43. Quoted by Rougeron, "De la révolution," p. 40.
44. Ibid., p. 11.
45. A.N., C 944 (Allier).

46. Ibid.
47. *S.G.F.*, ɪɪ, table 19, and A.N., C 944 (Allier).
48. *S.G.F.*, ɪɪ, table 27.
49. Gilbert Garrier, *Paysans du Beaujolais et du Lyonnais, 1800-1870* (Grenoble, 1973), pp. 156-157, 198-213.
50. Ibid., p. 208.
51. Ibid., p. 144.
52. Ibid., pp. 197 and 209.
53. Ibid., p. 327.
54. Dutacq and Latrielle, *Histoire de Lyon*, p. 137. The discussion of the city is based on the information provided in Book 3, chap. 1, of this volume.

Appendix 2
The Standard Interpretation: Social Fear after 1849 as a Hoax

1. Seignobos, *Révolution de 1848*; Duveau, *1848*; Tudesq, *Les Grands notables*; Girard, *Libéralisme*; Guillemin, *Le Coup de 2 décembre*; Price, "Introduction"; Merriman, "Radicalisation and Repression"; Machin, "The Prefects and Political Repression"; and Merriman, *The Agony of the Republic*.
2. Tudesq, *Les Grands notables*, ɪɪ, 992-1072.
3. Ibid., ɪɪ, 1028.
4. Seignobos, *Révolution de 1848*, p. 157.
5. Dutacq, "Notes et documents," 345-357, and Emile Dagnan, "La Réaction conservatrice dans l'ouest, le centre et le sud-ouest de la France en 1848, 1849 et 1850," *La Révolution de 1848*, xɪ (1925), 309.
6. Dansette, *Louis-Napoléon*, pp. 309-341; Vigier, *Seconde république*, p. 87; and Howard C. Payne, "Preparation of a Coup d'Etat: Administrative Centralization and Police Powers in France, 1849-1851," in *Studies in Modern European History in Honor of Franklin Charles Palm*, ed. Frederick J. Cox et al. (New York, 1956).
7. Vigier, *Seconde république*, p. 87.
8. Ibid., p. 88, and Dansette, *Louis-Napoléon*, pp. 309-341.
9. Payne, "Preparation of a Coup d'Etat," passim. While necessarily sketchy, Payne's article points out that the frustrations and fears of the police bureaucrats were *real*, as opposed to "neurotic" or self-serving.
10. Price, "Introduction"; Merriman, "Radicalisation and Repression"; Ted Margadant, "Modernisation and Insurgency in December 1851: A Case Study of the Drôme," in *Revolution and Reaction*, ed. Roger Price (New York, 1975); Machin, "The Prefects and Political Repression"; Vincent Wright, "The *Coup d'état*"; and Merriman, *The Agony of the Republic*.

11. Charles Tilly, "How Protest Modernized in France," in *The Dimensions of Quantitative Research in History*, ed. W. Aydelotte et al. (Princeton, 1972), pp. 192-255; Charles Tilly, "The Changing Pace of Collective Violence," in *Essays in Theory and History: An Approach to the Social Sciences*, ed. Melvin Richter (Cambridge, 1970), pp. 139-164; and Charles Tilly and Lynn H. Lees, "The People of June 1848," in *Revolution and Reaction*, ed. Roger Price (New York, 1975).

12. Tilly and Lees, "The People of June," p. 174.

13. Price, "Introduction," p. 55.

14. Machin, "The Prefects and Political Repression," p. 286; Vincent Wright, *"The Coup d'état,"* p. 305.

15. Merriman, The *Agony of the Republic*, p. xxv.

16. Ibid., pp. 97, 111, 164-169, 184, 210-215.

Sources and Bibliography

The lists that follow are selective. I have omitted certain manuscript sources, articles, and books that were consulted but had only a general or indirect bearing on this particular research project.

I. Manuscript Sources—Archives Nationales

A. Justice Ministry Sources

BB[6] II. Personnel dossiers of the attorneys general.

BB[18] (*Correspondance générale de la Division criminelle*) 1449, 1460, 1461, 1462, 1465[2], 1466, 1467[1], 1467[2], 1468, 1469, 1470[2], 1470[3], 1471, 1472, 1473, 1474[1], 1474[2], 1476, 1477, 1478, 1479, 1480, 1481, 1482, 1483, 1484, 1485[1], 1485[2], 1486, 1487, 1488, 1489, 1490, 1491, 1493, 1494, 1496, 1501, 1502. Correspondence between the attorneys general and the Justice Ministry on criminal investigations and prosecutions undertaken throughout the period of the Second Republic.

BB[30] (*Affaires politiques*), 333, 334, 335, 359, 361, 363, 364, 365, 366, 369, 373, 374, 379, 382, 385, 386, 390, 391, 392[1], 392[2], 393, 395, 1161, 1162. Attorneys' general reports on the political situation in their *ressorts* and ministerial circulars on political matters for the period of the Second Republic.

BB[30] (*Affairs politiques*) 396, 397. Attorneys' general reports on events following the coup and on the operations of the Mixed Commissions. Ministerial directives and circulars on Mixed Commissions.

BB[30]* 402, 424. Registers, by department, of those arrested after the coup and usually tried by the Mixed Commissions. Initialed by the *procureur-général* responsible for the given department and usually cosigned by the prefect and military officer serving on the Mixed Commission.

B. Enquête sur le travail (*Constituent Assembly*)

C 944 (Allier), 948 (Charente-Inférieure), 953 (Gard and Gironde), 955 (Jura), 963 (Rhône), 967 (Vendée).

C. Interior Ministry Sources

F[1a] 598. Correspondence of the prefects with the Conseil d'état on the question of the appointment or election of mayors.

F[1b1]. Personnel dossiers of the prefects.

F[7] 2588, 2589, 2590, 2591, 2592, 2593, 2594, 2595. Alphabetical listing, person by person for all of France, of those arrested after the coup and usually tried before the Mixed Commissions. Signed by the minister of interior and officials of the Interior Ministry's Division of General Police. Initialed (or marked *vu*) by the minister of police.

II. Manuscript Sources—Archives Départementales

A. Allier

M 643³. Prefectoral correspondence on the insurrection of 3-4 December 1851 and ministerial instructions and pamphlets on administrative reform.

B. Charente-Maritime

11 K 2. Circulars and directives to the prefect and subprefects from the Interior Ministry.

27 K 1. Circulars to the subprefects and mayors from the prefect.

2 J 205. Letters and private papers of Antoine Tortat, a political ally of the Elysée, on the petition campaign for the revision of the constitution to allow Louis Napoleon to run for reelection.

4 M 2/15, 4 M 2/20, 4 M 4/3, 4 M 10/4. Correspondence of the prefect with the subprefects, the local military command and the Interior Ministry.

5 U 6, 5 U 7. Correspondence between the *procureurs de la république* at Marennes and Rochefort with the attorney general in Poitiers.

9 U 4, 9 U 17, 10 U 5, 10 U 7, 10 U 9. Correspondence between the *procureur de la république* at Rochefort with the attorney general in Poitiers.

C. Gard

2 M 51. Correspondence and circulars exchanged between the prefect and the Interior Ministry on electoral matters under the Second Republic.

4 M 1/8, 4 M 1/9. Prefectoral correspondence with the subprefects and Paris on the occasion of the elections for Gard's *Conseil Général* in 1848 and the special elections for the same body held in 1850.

6 M 376. Telegraph dispatches addressed to the prefect by the Interior Ministry during the days immediately following the coup.

6 M 376 bis. Reports on the local political situation and on incidents which troubled public order in Gard submitted by the prefects during the years 1848 through 1850.

6 M 438. *Colportage* in Gard under the Second Republic as reported in prefectoral correspondence with the Interior Ministry.

6 M 613. Reports to the prefect submitted by the police *commissaires* and

the subprefects on the subject of political banquets during 1850 and 1851.

6 M 615. Political events—elections, "troubles," seditious literature—reported to the prefect by the subprefects and prefectoral reports to Paris based on this information.

6 M 694. Prefectoral reports on the political press submitted from 1830 through 1862.

6 M 1096. Prefectoral correspondence on the carrying out of sentences levied by the Mixed Commission.

14 M 107. Prefectoral reports on the economic condition of the department submitted each year on the occasion of the trade and agricultural fair at Beaucaire: 1846 through 1849.

3 U 5/1, 3 U 5/2, 3 U 5/3. Transcripts of Mixed Commission hearings (fragmentary).

4 U 5/25. Correspondence between the department's *procureurs de la république* and the attorney general in Nîmes on political matters.

4 U 5/102. Correspondence among the *procureurs de la république* in Gard. Vaucluse and Ardeche on the subversive movement in their *arrondissements* during 1850, 1851, and 1852.

D. Gironde

1 M 330. Correspondence between the prefect and sub-prefects on the department's political situation under the Second Republic.

3 M 4. Prefectoral correspondence with the Interior Ministry and with the subprefects and mayors during the presidential campaign of December 1848.

3 M 5. Prefectoral correspondence during the preparations for the plebiscite of 20 and 21 December 1851.

3 M 89/2. Prefectoral circulars and directives to the subprefects, mayors, and justices of the peace during the revision of the electoral lists in accordance with the law of 31 May 1850.

4 M 184. Regular reports of the commandant of the gendarmerie to the prefect during the Second Republic.

4 M 841. Circulars and directives sent by the prefect to the subprefects during the Second Republic.

E. Jura

M 34, 35, 37, 38, 39, 40, 41, 43, 67, 68, 69, and documents in unclassified boxes and dossiers in the M series. Prefectoral correspondence with the subprefects, with the local military command, and with the Interior Ministry on the state of public order in the department from 1849 through 1851 (*Police générale et administrative*).

F. Rhône

No manuscript sources were found in this departmental archive.

G. Vendée

2 M 28. Prefectoral correspondence on the subject of the presidential elections of December 1848.

2 M 69. Correspondence between the prefect and Paris on the occasion of the elections for the department's *Conseil Général* in 1848.

4 M 25. Ministerial circulars and telegraphic dispatches addressed to the prefect during the June Days of 1848 and during the period immediately following the coup.

4 M 26. Correspondence of the prefect with the Interior Ministry during the period just after the coup.

11 M 9. Prefectoral circulars and directives sent to the subprefect at Les Sables d'Olonne during the Second Republic.

11 M 11. Correspondence between the prefect and the subprefects and mayors during the legislative elections of 1849. Instructions from Paris and prefectoral directives to the subprefects, mayors and justices of the peace after the restriction of universal manhood suffrage in May 1850.

4 U 1/165, 4 U 2/212, 4 U 2/213. Correspondence between the *procureur de la république* at Fontenay and the attorney general in Poitiers: 1848 through 1850.

III. Printed Primary Sources—Newspapers and Candidates' *Professions de Foi*

A. Newspapers and periodicals published in Paris which circulated nationally (consulted at Bibliothèque Nationale)

Le Constitutionnel, La Gazette des Tribunaux, Journal des Débats, Le National, La Réforme, Revue des Deux-Mondes.

B. Departmental newspapers and periodicals consulted at the Bibliothèque Nationale (issues missing in this collection were often found enclosed with reports of the attorneys general)

Allier: *Le Mémorial de l'Allier, Le Républicain de l'Allier, Le Républicain Démocrate de l'Allier, Le Travailleur de l'Allier et de la Creuse.*
Charente-Inférieure: *Le Phare de La Rochelle, Le Travailleur.*
Gard: *La Gazette de Bas-Languedoc, Le Républicain du Gard.* Gironde: *Le Cour-*

rier de la Gironde, La Guienne, Le Mémorial Bordelais, Le Peuple Souverain, La Tribune de la Gironde.

Jura: *La Démocratie Jurassienne, Le Patriote Jurassien, La Tribune de l'Est, La Tribune du Jura.*

Rhône: *Le Courrier de Lyon, Le Peuple Souverain, La Revue Démocratique* (single issue for August 1849).

Vendée: *Le Démocrate Vendéen, L'Indicateur.*

C. *The electoral programs of the candidates for the Legislative Assembly in each department of our sample were consulted (when available) in the Bibliothèque Nationale's collection of these pamphlets and broadsides: 8° Le70.*

IV. General Reference Sources

Almanach National annuaire de la République Française 1848-1849-1850. Paris, 1850.

Almanach National 1851. Paris, 1851.

Almanach National 1852. Paris, 1852.

Almanach Royal et National 1846. Paris, 1846.

Almanach Royal et National 1847. Paris, 1847.

Dictionnaire biographique du mouvement ouvrier français. Edited by J. Dautry, R. Dufraisse, G. Duveau, R. Gossez, J. Maitron (general editor), and J. Vidalenc. Paris, 1966.

Dictionnaire de biographie française. Edited by Marcel Prévost, Jean-Charles Roman d'Amat, et al. Paris, 1933—in progress.

Dictionnaire des parlementaires français. Edited by Adolphe Robert, Edgar Bourloton, and Gaston Cougny. Paris, 1891.

Moniteur Universel, 1848 through 1852.

Statistique Générale de la France, 2nd series, "Territoire et Population," II. Paris, 1855.

V. Books and Articles

Agulhon, Maurice. *1848 ou l'apprentissage de la République.* Paris, 1973.

———. *La République au village: les populations du Var de la Révolution à la Seconde République.* Paris, 1970.

Amann, Peter. *Revolution and Mass Democracy: The Paris Club Movement of 1848.* Princeton, 1975.

Artz, Frederick B. *Reaction and Revolution: 1814-1832.* New York, 1934.

Bagge, Dominique. Selection from *Les Idées politiques en France sous la restauration. French Liberalism 1789-1848.* Edited by W.M. Simon. New York, 1972.

Barrot, Odilon. *Mémoires Posthumes.* Paris, 1875.

Bastid, Paul. *Doctrines et institutions politiques de la seconde république*. 2 vols. Paris, 1945.

Bergier, Joseph. *Le Journal d'un bourgeois de Lyon en 1848*. Published and annotated by Justin Godart. Paris, 1924.

Bouillon, Jacques. "Les Démocrates socialistes aux élections de 1849." *Revue française de science politique*, VI (1956), 70-95.

Calman, Alvin R. *Ledru-Rollin and the Second French Republic*. New York, 1922.

Castellane, Maréchal de. *Journal*. 5 vols. Paris, 1895-1897.

Charles, Albert. "Un exemple de carrière administrative dans la première moitié du siècle dernier: Le Baron Neveux." *Revue historique de Bordeaux*, XLIII (1954), 229-240.

———. *La Révolution de 1848 et la seconde république à Bordeaux et dans le département de la Gironde*. Bordeaux, 1945.

Charlton, D. C. *Secular Religions in France, 1815-1870*. New York, 1963.

Chevalier, Louis. *Laboring Classes, Dangerous Classes in Paris During the First Half of the Nineteenth Century*. Translated by Frank Jellinek. New York, 1973.

Chevènement, Jean-Pierre. *Les Socialistes, les communistes et les autres*. Paris, 1977.

Clough, Shepard Bancroft. *France, A History of National Economics*. New York, 1964.

Collins, Irene. *The Government and the Newspaper Press in France: 1814-1881*. Oxford, 1959.

Constant, Benjamin. "On Popular Sovereignty and Its Limits." In *French Liberalism 1789-1848*, edited by W.M. Simon. New York, 1972.

Crozier, Michel. *The Bureaucratic Phenomenon*. Chicago, 1964.

Dagnan, Emile. "La Réaction conservatrice dans l'ouest, le centre et le sud-ouest de la France en 1848, 1849 et 1850." *La Révolution de 1848*, XI (1925), 213-223, 290-313.

Dansette, Adrien. *Louis-Napoléon à la conquête du pouvoir*. Paris, 1961.

De Luna, Frederick A. *The French Republic Under Cavaignac: 1848*. Princeton, 1969.

Désaunais, A. "Le commissariat de Jules Grévy." In *Volume du centenaire de la révolution de 1848 dans le Jura*, edited by Société d'émulation du Jura. Lons-le-Saunier, 1948.

Dutacq, F. "Notes et documents sur le complot du sud-est (1850-1851)." *Révolution de 1848*, XI (1925), 345-359.

Dutacq, F., and Latrielle, A. *Histoire de Lyon de 1814 à 1940*. Lyon, 1952.

Duveau, Georges. *1848: The Making of a Revolution*. Translated by Ann Carter. New York, 1968.

Eisenstein, Elizabeth. *The First Professional Revolutionary: Filippo Buonarotti*. Cambridge, 1959.

Elwitt, Sanford. *The Making of the Third Republic: Class and Politics in France, 1868-1884*. Baton Rouge, 1975.

Epszstein, Léon. *L'Economie et la morale aux débuts du capitalisme industriel en France et en Grande Bretagne.* Paris, 1966.

Fabre, Jean; Hincker, François; and Sève, Lucien. *Les Communistes et l'état.* Paris, 1977.

Fasel, George. "The French Moderate Republicans." Doctoral dissertation, Stanford University, 1965.

Faucher, Léon. *Correspondance.* Paris, 1968.

Flaubert, Gustave. *Sentimental Education.* Translated by Robert Baldick. London, 1969.

Garrier, Gilbert. *Paysans du Beaujolais et du Lyonnais, 1800-1870.* Grenoble, 1973.

Gaussens, J.-G. "Essai sur le comportement politique charentais 1848-1870." D.E.S. Paris, 1951.

Génique, Gaston. *L'Election de l'assemblée législative en 1849.* Paris, 1921.

Girard, Louis. *Le Libéralisme en France de 1814 à 1848: doctrine et mouvement.* Paris, 1967.

Godart, Justin. *A Lyon en 1848: Les Voraces.* Paris, 1948.

Godechot, Jacques. *La Contre-révolution: doctrine et action (1789-1804).* Paris, 1961.

Goguel, François. *L'Influence des systèmes électoraux sur la vie politique.* Paris, n.d.

———. *La Politique des partis sous la IIIe république.* 3rd ed. Paris, 1957.

Gouldner, Alvin W. *The Coming Crisis of Western Sociology.* New York, 1971.

Gramsci, Antonio. *Selections from the Prison Notebooks.* Edited and translated by Quintin Hoare and Geoffrey Nowell Smith. New York, 1975.

Guillemin, Henri. *Le Coupe de 2 décembre.* Paris, 1951.

Guizot, François-Pierre-Guillaume. *Memoirs to Illustrate the History of My Time.* 8 vols. London, n.d.

Haussmann, Baron. *Memoires.* 3 vols. Paris, 1890-1893.

Henry, Pierre. *Histoire des préfets—cent cinquante ans d'administration provinciale: 1800-1950.* Paris. 1950.

Hoffmann, Stanley. "Confrontation in May 1968." In *Decline or Renewal: France Since the 1930s,* edited by Stanley Hoffmann. New York, 1974.

———. "Paradoxes of the French Political Community." In *In Search of France,* edited by Stanley Hoffmann et al. Cambridge, 1965.

Jardin, A., and Tudesq, A. J. *La France des Notables.* Vol. 1. Paris, 1973.

Johnson, Douglas. *Guizot: Aspects of French History, 1787-1874.* Toronto and London, 1963.

Kent, Sherman. *Electoral Procedure Under Louis Philippe.* New Haven, 1937.

Langer, William L. *Political and Social Upheaval: 1832-1852.* New York, 1969.

Le Clère, Bernard, and Wright, Vincent. *Les Préfets du Second Empire.* Paris, 1973.

Le Clère, Marcel. *Histoire de la police.* Paris, 1971.

Lefebvre, Henri. *L'Explosion.* Paris, 1970.

Legendre, Pierre. *Histoire de l'administration de 1750 à nos jours.* Paris, 1968.

Leguai, A. "Félix Mathé." In *La Révolution de 1848 à Moulins et dans le département de l'Allier*, edited by Comité départementale du centenaire de la révolution de 1848. Moulins, 1950.

Levasseur, Emile. "Un épisode du second ministère de Léon Faucher." *La Révolution de 1848*, III (1906), 3-13.

Loomis, Stanley. *A Crime of Passion*. New York, 1967.

Loubère, Leo. "The Emergence of the Extreme Left in Lower Languedoc, 1848-1851: Social and Economic Factors in Politics." *American Historical Review*, LXXXIII (1968), 1019-1051.

Lukács, Georg. *History and Class Consciousness: Studies in Marxist Dialectics*. Translated by Rodney Livingstone. Cambridge, 1971.

Machin, Howard. "The Prefects and Political Repression: February 1848 to December 1851." In *Revolution and Reaction*, edited by Roger Price. New York, 1975.

Mangolte, Charles. "La Presse en 1848 dans le Jura." In *Volume du centenaire de la révolution de 1848 dans le Jura*, edited by Société d'émulation du Jura. Lons-le-Saunier, 1948.

Manuel, Frank E. *The Prophets of Paris*. Cambridge, 1962.

Margadant, Ted. "Modernisation and Insurgency in December 1851: a Case Study of the Drome." In *Revolution and Reaction*, edited by Roger Price. New York, 1975.

Marx, Karl. *Class Struggles in France*. New York, 1964.

———. *The Eighteenth Brumaire of Louis Bonaparte*. New York, 1969.

Maupas, Charlemagne-Emile de. *Mémoires sur le second empire*. 2 vols. Paris, 1884.

———. *Memoirs of the Coup d'Etat*. Translated by Lord Kerry. London, n.d.

Maurain, Jean. *Baroche, ministre de Napoleon III: un bourgeois français au XIXᵉ siecle, d'après ses papiers inédits*. Paris, 1936.

Mayer, Arno J. *Dynamics of Counterrevolution in Europe, 1870-1956*. New York, 1971.

Mérimée, Prosper. *Correspondance générale*. Edited by Maurice Parturier, Pierre Josserand, and Jean Mallion. 1st series, 6 vols. Paris, 1941-1947.

Merriman, John M. *The Agony of the Republic: The Repression of the Left in Revolutionary France, 1848-1851*. New Haven, 1978.

———. "Radicalisation and Repression: A Study of the Demobilisation of the '*Démoc-Socs*' during the Second French Republic." In *Revolution and Reaction*, edited by Roger Price. New York, 1975.

Michels, Robert. *Political Parties: A Sociological Study of the Oligarchic Tendencies of Modern Democracy*. Translated by Eden Paul and Cedar Paul. Glencoe, 1962.

Mills, C. Wright. *The Power Elite*. New York, 1959.

Moore, Barrington, Jr., *Social Origins of Totalitarianism and Democracy: Lord and Peasant in the Making of the Modern World*. Boston, 1966.

Morauzeau, L. "Aspects vendéens de la Seconde République." In *Revue d'études historiques et archéologiques*, edited by Société d'émulation de la Vendée. Luçon, 1960.

Mosca, Gaetano. *The Ruling Class, Elementi di scienza politica*. Edited by A. Livingston. Translated by Hannah D. Kahn. New York, 1939.

Neumann, Franz. *Behemoth*. New York, 1942.

Normanby, Lord. *Year of Revolution: From a Journal Kept in Paris in 1848*. London, 1857.

Payne, Howard C. *The Police State of Louis Napoleon Bonaparte*. Seattle, 1966.

———. "Preparation of a Coup d'Etat: Administrative Centralization and Police Powers in France, 1849-1851." In *Studies in Modern European History in Honor of Franklin Charles Palm*, edited by Frederick J. Cox et al. New York, 1956.

Perreux, Gabriel. *Arbois: première cité républicaine de la France*. Paris, 1932.

Pieyre, Adolphe. *Histoire de la ville de Nîmes depuis 1830 jusqu'à nos jours*. 2 vols. Nîmes, 1886.

Pinkney, David H. *The French Revolution of 1830*. Princeton, 1972.

Pont, Marie-Hélène. "La Seconde république en Charente-Inférieure." D.E.S. Bordeaux, 1960.

Ponteil, Félix, *Les Classes Bourgeoises et l'avènement de la démocratie 1815-1914*. Paris, 1968.

———. *La Monarchie parlementaire: 1815-1848*. Paris, 1949.

Pouthas, Charles H. "Une enquête sur la réforme administrative sous la seconde république." *Revue historique*, CXCIII (1943), 1-11.

Price, Roger. *The French Second Republic: A Social History*. London, 1972.

———. "Introduction." In *Revolution and Reaction: 1848 and the Second French Republic*, edited by Roger Price. New York, 1975.

Raginel, Charles. *Histoire des votes des représentants du peuple dans nos assemblées nationales depuis la révolution de 1848*. 2 vols. Paris, 1851.

Rémond, René. *The Right Wing in France from 1815 to de Gaulle*. Translated by James M. Laux. Philadelphia, 1968.

Rémusat, Charles de. *Mémoires de ma vie*. Introduced and annotated by Charles H. Pouthas. 4 vols. Paris, 1962.

Ridley, Frederick F., and Blondel, Jean. *French Administration*. London, 1969.

Romieu, M. A. *Le Spectre rouge de 1852*. Paris, 1851.

Rosenberg, Arthur. *Democracy and Socialism*. Boston, 1965.

Rossi, A. (Angelo Tasca). *The Rise of Italian Fascism*. London, 1939.

Rougeron, Georges. *Les Administrateurs du département de l'Allier*. Montluçon, 1956.

———. "De la révolution de février au 2 décembre." In *La Révolution de 1848 à Moulins et dans le département de l'Allier*, edited by Comité départementale du centenaire de la révolution de 1848. Moulins, 1950.

Schmidt, Charles. *Des Ateliers Nationaux aux Barricades de Juin*. Paris, 1948.

Schram, Stuart R. *Protestantism and Politics in France*. Alencon, 1954.

Seignobos, Charles. *La Révolution de 1848—le second empire* Paris, 1921.

Smelser, Neil J. *Theory of Collective Behavior*. London, 1962.

Spitzer, Alan B. *The Revolutionary Theories of Louis Auguste Blanqui*. New York, 1957.

Starzinger, Vincent E. *Juste-Milieu Political Theory in France and England*. Charlottesville, 1965.

Ténot, Eugène. *La Province en décembre 1851*. Paris, 1865.

Tilly, Charles. "The Changing Pace of Collective Violence." In *Essays in Theory and History*, edited by Melvin Richter. Cambridge, 1970.

———. "How Protest Modernized in France." In *The Dimensions of Quantitative Research in History*, edited by W. Aydelotte et al. Princeton, 1972.

———. *The Vendée*. Cambridge, 1964.

Tilly, Charles, and Lees, Lynn H. "The People of June 1848." In *Revolution and Reaction*, edited by Roger Price. New York, 1975.

Tilly, Charles; Tilly, Louise; and Tilly, Richard. *The Rebellious Century: 1830-1930*. Cambridge, 1975.

Tocqueville, Alexis de. "Letter of December 11, 1851, to the London *Times*." In *December 2, 1851*, edited by John B. Halsted. Garden City, 1971.

———. *The Old Regime and the French Revolution*. Translated by Stuart Gilbert. Garden City, 1955.

———. *Recollections*.Edited by J. P. Mayer and A. P. Kerr. Translated by George Lawrence. Garden City, 1971.

Tudesq, Andre-Jean. *L'Election présidentielle de Louis-Napoléon Bonaparte: 10 décembre 1848*. Paris, 1965.

———. *Les Grands notables en France (1840-1849): étude historique d'une psychologie sociale*. 2 vols. Paris, 1964.

Véron, Docteur. *Mémoires d'un bourgeois de Paris*. 6 vols. Paris, 1896.

Vigier, Philippe. *La Seconde république*. Paris, 1967.

———. *La Seconde république dans la région alpine: étude politique et sociale*. 2 vols. Paris, 1963.

Vivien, Alexandre-François. *Rapport sur le projet de loi relatif à l'administration intérieure*. Paris, n.d.

Weber, Max. *The Theory of Social and Economic Organization*. Edited by Talcott Parsons. Translated by A. M. Henderson and Talcott Parsons. New York, 1969.

Weill, Georges. *Histoire du parti républicain en France 1814-1870*. Paris, 1928.

Williner, Alfred. *The Action Image of Society*. Translated by A. M. Sheridan Smith. New York, 1970.

Wright, Gordon, *France in Modern Times*. New York, 1968.

Wright, Vincent. "The *Coup d'état* of December 1851: Repression and the Limits to Repression." In *Revolution and Reaction*, edited by Roger Price. New York, 1975.

Zeldin, Theodore. *France: 1848-1945*. 2 vols. Oxford, 1973-1977.

———. *The Political System of Napoleon III*. London, 1958.

Index

administrative centralization, xii-xiv, 6-12, 55-57, 61, 138
Aide-toi le ciel t'aidera, 65
Alcock, 93, 95-97. *See also* Loyson
Ambert, Colonel, 65, 66, 71, 256-257
army: and elections, 214, 218; in Gironde, 116-117; and radicalism, 105; in Rhône, 128, 276-277; and risings, post-coup, 229
association: in electoral periods, 52, 209, 210; law on (1849), 105; law on, and clubs (1848), 51-52, 104, 208, 211; laws on, 29, 200, 208-209
attorneys general: power and responsibilities, xvi, 58-60, 101; recruitment and promotion under Second Republic, 92-101; and *ressort*, 55, 59
attroupements, law on, 48

Banquet Campaign (1847-1848), 44-45, 95-96
Baraguey d'Hilliers, General, 78-79
Barbès, Armand, 38, 49, 218
Bareste, Eugène, 180
Baroche, Jules, 45, 80, 93-95, 168, 261; circulars of, 109, 171, 173, 175
Barrot, Ferdinand, 72, 80, 84; circulars of, 109-110, 157
Barrot, Odilon, 52, 94-95, 112; career before January 1849, 44, 46, 49, 51; circulars of, 109-110, 157-158, 192, 200; and *colportage*, 193-194; and coup, 111; and election of May 1849, 209, 210, 213, 215; and schoolteachers, 164
Basset, 162-163
Becquey, Charles, 77-78, 83, 254-255
Besson, Charles-Jean: career of, 74-75, 85, 86, 254-255; and republican mayors, 154-155
Blanc, Louis, 36-39, 41, 46, 64
Blanqui, Louis Auguste, 38, 39, 49
Boby de la Chapelle, Alphonse-

Charles: career of, 79-80, 85, 86, 258-259; and Mixed Commission, 230; and schoolteachers, 164
Bonaparte, Louis Napoleon, xv, 100, 104, 125, 260-261; and attorneys general, 93-94; and prefects, 67, 70-71, 76, 79-82, 87-90
Bonapartism, xiv, 41-42, 92, 226, 247; in Charente-Inférieure, 114-116, 260-261
Bonnin, Casimir: career of, 73, 82, 256-257, on *colportage*, 198
Bouillon, Jacques, xx, 266-267
Brian, Charles-Jean: career of, 71, 85-86, 250-251; and mayors, 155, 165; and minor officials, 167; and press, 171; reports on Charente-Inférieure, 115-116
Bugeaud, Marshal, 183, 185, 261
bureaucratic structure and discipline, xviii-xix, 101
by-elections, 106-107, 122, 138, 210; of *1848* (Charente-Inférieure), 260; of *1849* (Allier), 156; (Gironde), 116, 165, 262; (Jura), 143; (Rhône), 128; of *1850* (Allier), 137, 214; (Gard), 120-121, 165. *See also* electoral manipulation; electoral law of 31 May 1850

cabaret, 117, 168, 169, 195
Cabet, Etienne, 37, 42
Carnot, Hippolyte, 51, 107
Carrel, Armand, 34-35, 65
Castellane, General de, 73, 82, 100, 227
Catholic Church, 27, 39, 40, 41, 106; law of 22 March 1822, 178. *See also* legitimists; Falloux law
Caussidière, Marc, 51
cautionnement, 30, 53, 106, 177, 189
Cavaignac, General: and prefects, 65, 69, 74, 76, 80; and repression after June Days, xx, 51-53, 77, 271, 276
Cavaignac, Godefroy, 35, 36, 65

Cazavan, 64
censitary electoral system, 27-29, 32,
43-44, 66, 99, 263
Chambrun, Aldebert, vicomte de: career of, 90-91, 254-255; and post-
coup rising, 230
Chanal, François-Victor-Adolphe: career of, 66-67, 69, 84-85, 250-251; and
election of May 1849, 213; on election of mayors, 157; reports on
Gard, 120-121
Changarnier, General, 79, 83, 148
Charnailles, Gabriel-Léonce, Cortois,
vicomte de, 71; career of, 78-79, 85-
87, 250-251; and events at Commentry, 218; and press, 187
Chevalier, Louis, 33
civil servants: Marx on role of, 16; and
petition campaign, 217; and repression, 114-116, 152, 158-162, 166-168
Clemenceau, Dr., 176, 230
Collins, Irene, 170, 190
colportage, 106, 161, 170-171, 178, 188;
repression of, 191-200. See also electoral law of 31 May 1850, petition
campaign against
Comité de la rue de Poitiers, xx, 51,
71, 78. See also Party of Order
commissioners and commissioners
general, 61-63, 66, 74, 99, 134, 267
complot of Lyon and Midi, 108, 209,
219-223, 279; and Gard, 122, 123,
125, 126, 158; and Jura, 145; and
Rhône, 206; trial by court-martial,
151. See also Young Mountain
Conseil d'état, 152-153, 156
Considérant, Victor, 37, 268
Constant, Benjamin, 31
Constituent Assembly, 45, 48, 51-53,
63, 96, 121, 260
constitutional prohibition of
president's reelection (Article 45),
xv, 78-79, 80-82, 85, 91, 101-102, 108,
124-126, 131-132, 138-139, 144-147;
petition campaign against, 114, 132,
140, 145. See also legitimists
Coquet, Armand Alexis: attack on
Ledru-Rollin, 215; career of, 65, 66,
71, 250-251; and mayor, 155-156,

185, 186; and minor officials, 167;
and press, 155-156
counterrevolution: as police activity, xi;
descriptive language of, used by historians, xi; theories of, 3-23, 149,
280-281
coup d'état of 2 December 1851, xv,
10, 12, 67, 81, 82-84, 101, 109, 110-
112, 226. See also Mixed Commissions; Morny
Cour de cassation, 59, 96, 99, 193, 198
courts-martial, in Lyon after June 1849,
128, 129, 151, 184, 209, 219, 222, 223;
after coup, 226, 231-232. See also
state of siege
Crémieux, Adolphe, 100
Crozier, Michel, xviii

Dagnan, Emile, 112
Damay: career of, 93; and colportage,
170, 192-193, 194; and justices of the
peace, 160-161; and petition campaign against limitation of suffrage,
217; and press, 171-176; reports on
Charente-Inférieure, 114-116; reports
on Vendée, 113-114; and schoolteachers, 164; and secret societies,
203-204, 207
Dansette, Adrien, 109-110, 117
Darcy, Hugues-Iéna: career of, 72, 77,
83-84, 256-257; and Devienne, 99
Deflotte, Paul, 107
Demians, 159
department, as administrative unit, 55-
56
Derriey, Louis-Adolphe, 268
Desages, Luc, 187
De Sèze: attack on Ledru-Rollin, 215;
career of, 94; and colportage, 196; and
elections, 210-211, 212; and mayors,
155; and petition campaign against
law of March 1850, 217; on press,
168, 186-187; and schoolteachers,
164; on secret societies, 217-218
Devienne, Adrienne-Marie: and Besson, 75; career of, 93, 98-99; and
press, 170, 177-181; reports on Gironde, 118; and schoolteachers, 165;
and secret societies, 206

Dufaure, Jules, 44, 45, 72, 105, 109, 111, 193
Dunoyer, Charles, 34, 37
Dupont, Pierre, 108
Durand, Claude, 173-174, 175-176
Dutacq, F., 219, 221, 223, 279
dynastic opposition, 42-45, 61, 95, 99

échéance of 1852, 107-108, 124, 131-133, 146, 181, 199, 200, 216, 221, 227, 242, 246
Ecole d'administration, 60-61
elections of April 1848, xix, 47, 61, 96, 99, 143, 267, 271, 276
elections of 10 December 1848, xix, 160
elections of May 1849, xix-xxi, 104, 160, 209-211; in Allier, 214-215, 272; in Charente-Inférieure, 261; in Gard, 120, 264; in Gironde, 262; in Jura, 143, 188, 267; in Rhône, 276-277; in Vendée, 272
electoral law of 31 May 1850, 106-107, 123, 138-139, 145-146, 159, 161, 179, 209; petition campaign against, 175-177, 209, 216-217; press protests against, 179-180
electoral manipulation: under censitary regime, 43-44, 69, 74; under Second Republic, 160-161, 209-216
Engels, Friedrich, 14

Falloux, vicomte de, 40, 49, 52, 106
Falloux law on education, 106, 135, 162-165
Fargin-Fayolle, 137, 215
Faucher, Léon: and choice of prefect and attorney general of Lyon, 72, 98; circulars of, 109-110, 157, 192, 200; and coup, 111-112; and elections of May 1849, 209-210, 212-213; and Maupas, 87-88. *See also* prefectoral corps, recruitment and promotion
Favand, Etienne, 121-122, 165, 211
Favre, Jules, 128
Flocon, Ferdinand, 36, 66
Fourier, Charles, 37, 268
French Revolution, 4, 5, 8-9, 25-26, 36, 39, 40-41, 44, 50, 63, 109, 112, 134-135, 207

Gallay, Georges, 155-156, 185-186, 214
Gallois, Napoléon, 175, 230
Garnier-Pagès brothers, 35, 65
Gasparin, Comte de, 72
Gauja, Prosper, 74
Gendarmerie Nationale, 117, 161, 163, 195, 218, 229
Genoude, Abbé de, 40, 120, 213
Gent, Alphonse, 220, 221, 222
Gilardin, Alphonse: career of, 93, 97-98; and civil servants, 158, 161; and *colportage*, 195-196; and mayors, 154; on press, 168, 169, 183-185; reports on Rhône, 128-133; and secret societies, 201-202, 204, 208, 219-223, 231
Girardin, Emile de, 65, 172
Goguel, François, xx, 4-5, 8-9
Gramsci, Antonio, 21, 246
Grévy, Jules, 105, 143, 146, 187, 205, 267, 268
Guizot, François, 26, 31-32, 42-44, 72, 74-75, 247

Haussmann, Georges, 83, 89, 230, 252-253
Hautpoul ministry, 109-110, 117, 157, 164
Henry, Charles, 208
Hoffmann, Stanley, 4, 5-9
holding of bureaucratic and elective office, 43, 96-97
house searches, 206-207
Huber, Aloysius, 48, 63

Jacqueau, 145
Joigneux, Pierre, 191-192, 198
judicial independence, 8, 58-59, 151-153, 197, 199, 208, 209, 218, 223, 224
juge d'instruction, 59, 117, 152, 204, 208
June Days of 1848, xx, 45, 49-51, 69, 76, 104, 188, 212, 227, 246, 276-278
jury, 8, 30, 151, 190, 199, 223; in Allier, 134-135, 153, 190; in Charente-Inférieure, 173, 193; in Gard, 124, 181, 182, 207; in Jura, 190, 211, 212, 219; in Rhône, 130, 183, 184, 221-222; in Vendée, 193
justices of the peace, 159-161, 212, 229

La Coste du Vivier, Charles-Aristide
de, 77; career of, 72-73, 82-83, 256-
257; and press, 185; reports on
Rhône, 128
Lagarde, Barthélemy, 116, 165, 262
Lagarde, Eugène, 125, 153; career of,
77-78, 83-84, 252-253; reports on
Gard, 120-121, 123, 124; and schoolteachers, 162
Lamartine, Alphonse de, 36, 39, 48,
62-63
Lamennais, Abbé de, 37, 53
Ledru-Rollin, Alexandre Auguste, xxi,
128, 175, 182; assaulted at Moulins,
135, 215; career before 1848 revolution, 35-37, 45; and commissioners
and commissioners general, 62, 134,
271; and journée of 15 May 1848; 48;
and June Days, 49-51; and May 1849
election, 120, 153, 156, 272; and prefects, 64, 66, 68, 71, 80
legitimists, xx-xxi, 34, 39-41, 46, 50, 86,
119; in Allier, 187, 272; in Charente-
Inférieure, 176; in Gard, 120-121,
123-124, 181-182, 213, 264-266; in Gironde, 118, 262; in Jura, 145; in
Vendée, 74, 113-114, 176, 260. See
also "white" Mountain; constitutional prohibition of president's reelection; Party of Order
Leroux, Pierre, 36, 187
Loiseau: career of, 93-94; on colportage,
196-198; and elections, 211; on
judges, 224; on mayors, 155; and
Mixed Commissions, 230-231; and
petition campaign against March
1850, 217; on police, 161-162; on
press, 168, 169, 187-190; reports on
Jura, 141-147; and secret societies,
202, 205, 208, 209, 218-219
Loyson, Henri-Antoine: career of, 97-
98; on press, 183; reports on Rhône,
127-128; on secret societies, 203

Machin, Howard, 280
Margadant, Ted W., 280
Marie, Alexandre, 35, 65

Marrast, Armand, 35, 36, 51, 65
Martin (de Strasbourg), 66
Marx, Karl, xvii, 8-10, 12-17, 149, 246,
280
Mathé, Félix, 134, 136, 186, 215, 271-
272
Mayer, Arno J., xviii, 3, 149
mayors: in Allier, 135, 153, 229; in
Jura, 146; and petition campaign
against restriction of suffrage, 217;
and police bureaucrats, 55, 58, 152-
157. See also Roman expedition, protests of; schoolteachers
Mérimée, Prosper, 46
Merriman, John M., 280-281
Michelet, Jules, 37, 39
Michels, Robert, 19-21, 44, 246
Ministry of National Police, 232
Mixed Commissions, 149, 226-247
moderate republicans: in Allier, 136,
270-271; in Charente-Inférieure, 260-
261; and Falloux law, 165; in Gironde, 262; in Jura, 143, 267-268; and
the prefectoral corps, 62, 64-67, 69-
70, 84-85, 91. See also unity of "advanced" and moderate republicans;
Cavaignac, Godefroy; Favand; Grévy
Montalembert, Charles de, 106-107
Morny, comte de, 81, 83-85, 89, 91
municipal elections, 123, 137, 155, 166

Naquet, Gustave, 183-184, 185, 211
National Guard, 48, 74, 101, 117, 136,
154, 213, 229, 276
National Workshops, 48-49, 276
Neveux, Baron: career, 67-69, 71, 76,
82-83, 252-253; circulars, 117; and
elections, 214; and press, 177-178;
and Solidarité Républicaine, 95
Noir, Dr. Jean-Baptiste, 230-231

Ode, Albert, 158, 213, 220-221
Orleanism, 19-20, 24-32, 34-35, 110-
112, 151-153. See also Faucher; Guizot; Michels; Tocqueville
Orleanists, xx-xxi, 46, 50; in Allier, 272;
in Gard, 213, 264; in Gironde, 83,
118, 181, 262-263; in Vendée, 74, 260;

as veteran police bureaucrats of July Monarchy, 70-86, 93-101. *See also* Party of Order

Pagès, Bonaventure, 67-69, 74, 83, 252-253
Paget, Lupicin, 189-190, 197-198, 206-207, 241
Parieu law of January 1850, 163, 165
Paris Commune, 4, 15, 103
Party of Order, 10-11, 45, 95-96, 278; in Allier, 137, 187, 272; in Charente-Inférieure, 114; in Gard, 123, 213; in Gironde, 118-119, 262; in Jura, 139, 143-144; and police repression, 51-52, 85, 88, 91, 104-105, 217; struggle among components of, 70, 80-81, 109, 111-112, 214
Payne, Howard C., 279-280
Périer, Casimir, 68, 77
Persigny, duc de, 81, 84, 91
police courts, 151, 174, 178, 188, 189, 194-195, 208
police force, complaints about: in Allier, 196-197; in Charente-Inférieure, 193; in Gard, 122, 202-203; in Jura, 144, 161-162, 195, 202, 205; in Rhône, 154, 161, 201; in Vendée, 193
police judiciaire, 59, 152
Pougeard du Limbert, Henri-François, 89, 90, 252-253
prefectoral corps: powers and responsibilities, xvi-xvii, 53, 55-58, 97, 101, 193-194, 200-201; recruitment and promotion, 57, 60-91, 157
press: in Allier, 134-135, 155-156, 159, 180, 214-215; in Charente-Inférieure, 116, 166, 180, 204, 216; in Gard, 121, 124-125, 159; in Gironde, 118, 156, 159, 163, 166, 216; in Jura, 142, 145, 156, 163, 166; repression of, 168-191; in Rhône, 130-131; in Vendée, 114
press laws: 21 October *1814*, 175-176, 178, 193; September laws of *1835*, 30; closings by decree (*June 1848*), 52; laws of 9 and 11 *August 1848*, 53, 104-105; law of *1849*, 105-106; law of *1850*, 106

Price, Roger, 280-281
Protestants, 120-121, 123, 181, 213, 219, 261, 263-266
Proudhon, Pierre-Joseph, 37, 268

Raspail, Benjamin, 221-222
Raspail, François-Vincent, 38, 45
Récurt, Adrien, 64
red scare as hoax, 12, 113, 117-119, 223, 242
Rémond, René, 4, 25
Rémusat, Charles de, 20, 34, 44, 49
reporting procedures, xvii, 57, 60
republicanism under July Monarchy, 29, 34-36, 38-39, 150
revolution of 1830, 26-27, 36, 42-43, 66, 72, 75
Richardet, Victor, 145, 188, 205
risings after the coup (3-4 December 1851), 83, 119, 133, 147, 227, 228, 229, 230, 233-243, 265, 268, 272, 277, 279
Roederer, Pierre-Louis, 56
Roman expedition, 10, 66, 79, 96, 212; protests of (June 1849), xv, 10, 66, 104-106, 119, 172, 188, 209, 212-213, 215; (in Allier), 134-135, 137, 166, 217-218, 229, 272; (in Gard, press), 159, 181-182; (in Gironde, press), 176-177; (in Jura), 141, 218, 268; (in Rhône), 72, 128, 185, 203, 219. *See also* secret societies; state of siege
Romieu, M. A., 107-108, 247
Rouher, Eugène, 80-81, 95, 208; circulars of, 109-110, 111, 112, 131, 157, 159, 160, 168, 173, 180, 182; on jury and judges, 223-224

Sand, George, 37, 49, 195
Sartin, 218
schoolteachers, 16, 106, 116, 158, 162-166, 182, 217
secret agents, requests for, 115, 129, 140
secret societies, 38-39; in Allier, 134, 137, 140, 217; in Charente-Inférieure, 115, 203-204; in Gard, 121, 123, 202-203, 207, 231, 265; and ignorance of

secret societies (*cont.*)
   police bureaucrats, 149-150, 198-201,
   223, 228, 280; in Jura, 141-143, 145-
   146, 161, 197, 202-203, 218-219, 268,
   270; repression of, 200-209; in
   Rhône, 127-132, 196, 208, 227, 231.
   See also Solidarité Républicaine; association, laws on
seditious songs, 108, 173-175
Seignobos, Charles, 52, 109-110, 117,
   278-279
Sénard, Antoine, 52, 64
Sentenac affair, 205-206
Smelser, Neil J., 21-23
social question, 5, 6, 18, 29, 32-34, 36-
   37, 41, 103
Société des droits de l'homme et du
   citoyen, 29, 65, 128
Solidarité Républicaine: in Charente-
   Inférieure, 115, 207; in Gard, 120-
   121; in Gironde, 95, 118, 208; in
   Rhône, 127; in Vendée, 161
Sommier, Antoine, 188, 205
state of siege, 105, 140; after coup, 147,
   149, 228, 230-231; in Rhône after
   June 1849, 72-73, 126, 128, 129-131,
   168, 170, 183-185, 195, 202, 209, 277
Sue, Eugène, 34, 37, 107, 122, 170, 195

Tandonnet, Eugène, 116, 177, 178, 179,
   180, 237, 241
Thiers, Adolphe, 29, 44, 46, 106-107
Thomas, Emile, 49
Thourel, André, 100
Thourel, Léon: by-election of 1850,
   212; career of, 93, 99-100; and civil
   servants, 158-160; and elections of
   May 1849, 211; and press, 170, 181-
   183; reports on Gard, 120-126; and
   secret societies, 202-205, 207, 231

Tilly, Charles, 3, 280-281
Tocqueville, Alexis de, xvii, 8-12, 17-
   18, 33, 43-47, 110, 111, 280
Tourangin, Denis-Victor, 71-72, 77, 98,
   256-257
Trélat, Dr., 49
Troplong: career of, 93-95, 97; on *colportage*, 170; on press, 176-177; reports on Gironde, 116-118; and secret societies, 207-208
Tudesq, A. J., 33, 278

unity of "advanced" and moderate republicans, xx, 107, 120-122, 130, 137,
   143, 147, 165, 173, 268

Véron, Dr., 46
Versini, 145
Vidal, François, 107
Vincent, Baron Louis-Charles de: career of, 75-77, 83-86, 254-256; and
   mayors, 153, 155; and minor officials, 166-167; and press, 169; reports
   from Jura, 144-145; and secret societies, 204; and schoolteachers, 162
Vivien, Alexandre-François, xiii, 156

Weber, Max, xviii, 21
"white" Mountain, 120-121, 161, 181,
   211, 264
Wissocq, Paul-Emile: career of, 65, 66,
   71, 250-251; and civil servants, 167;
   and mayors, 157; and press, 171-172

Young Mountain, 100, 122, 123, 131,
   158, 220, 221. *See also complot* of
   Lyon and Midi

Library of Congress Cataloging in Publication Data

Forstenzer, Thomas R
  French provincial police and the fall of the Second
Republic.

  Bibliography: p.
  Includes index.
  1. France—Politics and government—1848-1852.
2. Prefects (French government) 3. Attorneys general—
France.   I. Title.
DC272.5.F67   944.07   80-8549
ISBN 0-691-05318-9

*Thomas R. Forstenzer received his Ph.D. in history from Stanford
University and taught at Rutgers, The State University of New
Jersey, from 1973 to 1980. He is currently a consultant to the
United Nations Educational, Scientific, and Cultural Organiza-
tion (UNESCO) and is living in Paris.*